Literature-Based History Activities for Children, Grades 1-3

Literature-Based History Activities for Children, Grades 1-3

Patricia L. Roberts

California State University–Sacramento

Allyn and Bacon

Boston ■ London ■ Toronto ■ Sydney ■ Tokyo ■ Singapore

Copyright © 1998 by Allyn & Bacon
A Viacom Company
Needham Heights, MA 02194

Internet: www.abacon.com
America Online: keyword: College Online

Library of Congress Cataloging-in-Publication Data

Roberts, Patricia.
    Literature-based history activities for children, grades 1–3 /
Patricia L. Roberts.
        p.   cm.
    Includes bibliographical references and index.
    ISBN 0–205–27090–5
    1. History—Study and teaching (Primary)—United States.
    2. Education, Primary—Activity programs—United States.   I. Title.
LB1530.R63   1998
372.89—dc21   96-53228
                                                                        CIP

Printed in the United States of America
10   9   8   7   6   5   4   3   2   1   01   00   99   98   97

*Dedicated to James E. Roberts,
who has a wonderful memory
and a keen sense of history*

Contents

List of History Masters

Preface

America, remember . . .
We are the ones fighting for freedom;
We are your daughters and sons;
We stand together tall and proud,
Not afraid to say out loud,
We love you . . . the red, white, and blue . . .
America. America, remember . . . .
　　　　　—*America's Army National Guard*

Gather the children together for a time of history storytelling and studying in which the children hear, read, and dramatize stories; interpret poetry selections about historical figures through choral reading; and present brief reports with their ideas in written compositions about their reflections of places and faces from prehistory to the present.

To assist you as you present history's ideas and usefulness and add new and different dimensions to your students' lives, *Literature-Based History Activities for Children, Grades 1–3* is a guide that offers historical views through quality children's books with various perspectives. Using this guide will enable pre-service and in-service teachers, classroom aides, resource teachers, principals, curriculum directors, parents, and others to locate children's books that will enrich students' knowledge of the people, places, and events in the past.

How to Use This Book

This book provides you with some background and practical ideas for a history program related to children's literature in which children actively think and communicate. The emphasis is on teaching views of history through carefully selected children's books for grades 1 through 3. A strong focus is placed on children's books, related activities, and charts of multicultural perspectives for each time period as well as ways to extend children's experiences with the books that reflect topics in history. Though group size is suggested for the activities, you will decide when the activities are best suited for the whole group, small group, partnerships, and individual inquiry according to your teaching needs.

Generally, with the book's chronological arrangement and multicultural perspectives charts,

you will have flexibility in organizing focused lessons. For example, you can select not only a topic in history by using the books and activities for a certain time period but you may also select additional literature from other time periods that reflect on the topic. This feature provides you with sources to give children a horizontal look at a selected time period as well as a chronological sequence. Specifically, the features in this book include the following:

• *Multicultural Charts.* This book begins each time period with a multicultural chart that focuses on perspectives that are interpreted by children's books that reflect people and their actions in the time period. The books are views of different people related to African American, Asian American, Latino and Hispanic American, original Native American, and European American heritages as well as women and girls, religious groups, and those who are developmentally different. The perspectives are included so children can listen to the heritage of each other's voices and recognize that as society becomes larger, individuals seem to require not only the larger identity of being Americans but also the smaller identities of their heritages. The books are suggested so children can share their heritages with one another and foster an understanding of a healthy diversity that acknowledges the varied sources of the American people.

Each multicultural chart can be used as a reference to views about a particular period and to related children's books. With the chart, an interested child can focus on an overall view of the heritage of different people in the time period. Also, a child can follow a selected perspective from a chart in one time period to a chart in another to gain information about the similarities, differences, conflicts, or changes related to a perspective over time. Tracking a perspective through time periods can develop children's insights into the feelings, emotions, and problems that are universal even though the specifics of a time period are different.

• *Topics, Themes, Units.* Topics and themes related to history are identified for teachers by state and district curriculum materials. The children's books in this resource can support a school's history curriculum recommendations. For example, the documents in one western state indicate the following topics to guide teachers:

Grade 1:   Learning to Work Together; Exploring, Creating, and Communicating; Reaching Out to Times Past; Developing Social Skills and Responsibilities; Expanding Children's Geographic and Economic Worlds; and Developing Awareness of Cultural Diversity, Now and Long Ago

Grade 2:   People Who Supply Our Needs; Our Parents, Grandparents, and Ancestors of Long Ago; and People from Many Cultures, Now and Long Ago

Grade 3:   Continuity and Change; Our Local History; Discovering Our Past and Our Traditions; Our Nation's History; and Meeting People, Ordinary and Extraordinary, through Biography, Story, Folktale and Legend

• *Thematic Book Lists, Topics, and Activities.* Beginning with a chapter entitled 2.0 Million–1.0 Million B.C., this book suggests children's informational books, folk literature, historical fiction, and realistic stories with settings in sequential centuries. The activities are described as an integral part of a chapter covering a given time period but many can be adapted to almost any period of study. Some of the activities will be most useful for the whole class, whereas others are more appropriate for small groups, partnerships, or individualized inquiry.

• *History Master Reproducibles.* Many of the reproducibles in the book have thematic book lists and support the book-related activities for classroom use that are easily adapted for a selected grade level.

• *Differing Points of View.* Whenever possible, differing points of view about the exciting people and meaningful events as seen by parallel cultures are included to reflect America's rich diversity. Children can hear or read about the ways different books express the values of specific time periods and diverse cultures and reflect about how the views in some stories present views different from their own. Children can explore stories written in different periods and realize that any "ism" (i.e., racism, sexism, ageism, etc.) of the period does not have to be supported or shared by the reader.

With these features, this book will assist you as you get firsthand experience with children's literature related to history—an opportunity that will be both a reading adventure and a creative project you will long remember. This is an opportunity that, as you suspect, will have no end.

CHAPTER ONE

2.0 Million–1.0 Million B.C.

What was going on in prehistory?

Multicultural Perspectives

Our history class goes back in time,
back in time, back in time, back in time;
Our history class goes back in time,
so we can learn what happened.

Sing these words to the tune of "This Is the Way We Wash Our Clothes" and have the children clap their hands with the beat. The musical coaxing will help the children focus on history at a certain time during the school day. Of course, different words can be suggested by the children (e.g., "This is the day we study our state, study our state, study our state," etc.) to initiate various topics of history, culture, and heritage during the academic year.

Related to a study of prehistory, a study can be concerned not only with the children's state of long ago but also with the singing poems of Arctic-dwelling Eskimos, the stories of creation told by Africa's early people, America's Native People, the resilient inhabitants in Europe and Asia, and young people's lives of the differently abled, women and girls, and others who were the ancestors of many of us in the United States today. The children can prepare colorful bulletin boards and feature sketches of people and their first encounters with others, as well as family scenes, artifacts, and titles of stories they have read or heard about early people and their beliefs about the origins of the earth, skies, living things, and the seasons. Regardless of the topic of study, the class environment and lessons can be carefully planned to help the children develop concepts and generalizations as they learn about others through the vehicle of thought-provoking children's books related to prehistory. Some of the perspectives of people living in parallel cultures and recorded in stories suitable for this time period are shown in Figure 1–1.

First Encounter of People

"I wonder/ If on some far hillside/ There is a boy who sits alone," are the thoughts of a boy in prehistory who keeps his responsibilities in Byrd Baylor's *One Small Blue Bead* (Scribner's, 1992, Grades 1–3). Read aloud to the children some excerpts from the story about the people who think *they* are the only humans and discuss the boy's first encounter with another boy, a stranger from another group who offers a turquoise bead, a sign of friendship and material exchanges. Encourage the children to team up in pairs and play the roles of the young boy and the stranger who gives him the blue bead. Ask them to answer the question, "What would happen or change in your way of life after you met the stranger-boy for the first time?" Ask the children what questions could be asked by the two boys and what each boy would feel, say, and do in the situation when the bead is offered and accepted. Have children reverse their roles and then replay the situation. Ask them to transform the role-playing into an artwork and draw, paint, or sketch how the encounter might have happened. Make transparencies of some of the sketches and encourage children to use them for background scenery during additional role-playing.

FIGURE 1–1   **Children's Books about 2 Million–1 Million B.C.**

PERSPECTIVES

African Heritage

Anderson, D. A. *The Origin of Life on Earth: An African Creation Myth*. Sights Productions, 1993. This myth emphasizes humankind's respect for determination, effort, generosity, and the sacredness of life. Folk literature. Grade 3 up.

Greger, C. S. *Cry of the Benu Bird: An Egyptian Creation Story*. Ill. by adapter/author. Houghton Mifflin, 1996. The Benu bird, the eternal protector of light, rises from an ocean surrounded by chaos and starts time on earth while Atum, another being, breathes and creates life and order. Folk literature. Grades 3–5.

Maddern, E. *The Fire Children: A West African Creation Tale*. Ill. by F. Lessac. Dial, 1993. This is a "Why" tale that explains the origin of people in many different skin tones. Folk literature. Grades 1–3.

Nevin, T. *Zamani: African Tales from Long Ago*. Jacaranda, 1996. These 10 folktales from Kenya and other African countries are set in the long-ago time when humans talked with the animals. Folk literature. Grades 3–6.

Asian Heritage

Carpenter, F. *Tales of a Korean Grandmother*. C. E. Tuttle, 1972. These Korean paintings illustrate this collection of folktales. Folk literature. Grades 1–3.

Young, E. *Cat and Rat: The Legend of the Chinese Zodiac*. Ill. by the author. Holt, Rinehart and Winston, 1995. The Emperor announces a race through the forest and says he will name each of the 12 years in the zodiac after the winners. Folk literature. Grades K–3.

Zhang, S. N. *Five Heavenly Emperors*. Tundra Books, 1994. Chinese myths of creation are depicted. Folk literature. Grade 3 up.

European Heritage

Bilenko, A. *Ukranian Folk Tales*. Ill. by R. Adamovich. Dnipro Pub. of Kiev, 1974. This is a collection of 20 stories about good deeds and punishment for the wicked. Grade 3 up.

Osborne, M. P. *Favorite Norse Myths*. Ill by T. Howell. Scholastic, 1996. These 14 stories include "How Thor Got His Hammer" and "The Golden Apples." Folk literature. Grade 3 up.

Turner, A. *Time of the Bison*. Ill. by B. Peck. Macmillan, 1987. This story portrays family life in prehistoric times. Scar Boy wants to earn a new "true" name and is surprised when he is honored for sculpting a horse's image from clay. Historical fiction. Grades 2–3.

Latino/Hispanic Heritage

Gershator, P. *Tukama Tootles the Flute: A Tale from the Antilles*. Ill. by S. Saint James. Orchard, 1994. A two-headed giant captures Tukama, but the music of his flute helps him escape. Folk literature. Grades 1–3.

Greger, C. S. *The Fifth and Final Sun: An Ancient Aztec Myth of the Sun's Origin*. Houghton Mifflin, 1994. This folktale tells of when the first four suns are destroyed by jealous gods; humans live in the Age of the Fifth Sun. Folk literature. Grades 1–4.

Rohmer, H. *The Legend of Food Mountain/La Montana del Alimento*. Ill. by G. Carillo. Children's Book Press, 1982. This tale, written in both English and Spanish, tells how the earth was created by the god Quetzalcoatl. Folk literature. Grades 2–3.

FIGURE 1–1   **Continued**

Middle Eastern/Mediterranean Heritage

Al-Saleh, K. *Fabled Cities, Princes and Jinn from Arabic Myths and Legends*. Schocken Press, 1985. This is a collection of stories with Arabian and Persian heritage. Selected stories can be read aloud to primary-grade children. Folk literature. Grades 1–3.

Asimov, I., & F. Reddy. *Astronomy in Ancient Times*. Gareth Stevens, 1995. This book discusses some prehistoric evidence of celestial observations related to the ancient Greeks. Nonfiction. Grades 3–4.

Native American Heritage

Gates, F., reteller. *Owl Eyes*. Ill. by Y. Miyake. Lothrop, 1994. This is a Mohawk legend about how Raweno, the creator, gives each animal its traits while Owl pesters everyone. As a consequence, Raweno gives the owl a body with no neck and big eyes to see only what is in front of him, big ears to hear what he is told, and a lifestyle at night to keep him out of the way of others. Folk literature. Grades 1–4.

Hausman, G., reteller. *Eagle Boy: A Traditional Navajo Legend*. Ill. by C. and B. Moser. HarperCollins, 1996. The learning of the Eagle Way is culturally significant to the Navajo and is told in this legend about a boy who dreams of eagles and is taken up to the clouds to meet Eagle Chief. When he disobeys Eagle Chief, the boy is returned to human form with a name of power, Eagle Boy, and sent back to his family's hogan. Folk literature. Grades K–3.

Hodges, M. *The Firebringer: A Paiute Indian Legend*. Little, Brown, 1972. This is a "Why" tale about how fire first came to the Native People. Folk literature. Grade 3 up.

Larry, C. *Peboan and Seegwun*. Ill. by the author. Farrar, 1993. This Ojibwa tale is about the seasons and Seegwun (the Spirit of Spring) and old Peboan (Old Man Winter). Folk literature. Grades 2–3.

Philip, N. *Songs Are Thoughts: Poems of the Inuit*. Ill. by M. Foa. Orchard, 1995. This book has 10 free-verse selections that were originally intended to be sung. The poems reflect the happiness and wisdom of the Eskimo people. Folk literature. Grades 2–5.

Young, E. *Moon Mother: A Native American Creation Tale*. Ill. by the author. HarperCollins, 1993. This "Why" tale tells how people and tribes came to be, why the moon waxes and wanes, and why newborn babies cry. Folk literature. Grades Pre–3.

Differently Abled Heritage

De Armond, D. *The Seal Oil Lamp*. Sierra/Little, 1988. The sensitivity of some early people to the differently abled is shown in this ancient Eskimo tale about Allugua, a longed-for child who is born blind and allowed to live until he is age 7. At that time, his community determines that he should be abandoned and left behind. Mouse Woman, however, intervenes to save him. Folk literature. Grades 1–3.

Female Image Heritage

Gerson, M. *How Night Came from the Sea: A Story from Brazil*. Ill. by C. Golembe. Little, Brown, 1994. Jemanja, an African sea goddess, brings the gift of night to the land of hot light and allows the people to rest from the burning sun. Folk literature. Grades 2–3.

Religious Heritage

Baylor, B. *The Way to Start a Day*. Ill. by P. Parnall. Macmillan, 1986. The text details ways different people—cave people, Peruvian Indians, Egyptians, and others—have celebrated the sunrise and the dawn in different ways with beating drums, ringing bells, and gifts of gold and flowers. Nonfiction. Grades 1–3.

Fahs, S., & Spoerl, D. *Earth Sky Life Death*. Starr King Press, 1988. This collection includes some creation stories including Adam and Eve, the creation of humans by Prometheus, and Odin's ancestors. Grade 3 up.

Activity #1: "Friends"

Relate encounters of early people in parallel cultures (as in *One Small Blue Bead*) to the children's experiences by engaging children in a monthly Friendship Day where they become a Friend-for-a-Day in a partnership with a child usually not included in their friendship group. The two Friends-for-a-Day can eat unfamiliar foods together at a Friendship breakfast at school, assist one another in lessons, and interview each other about their family life. Additionally, Friends-for-a-Day can make one another a gift that reflects something from their cultures. Perhaps they would rather perform dances, learn new games together, or engage in singing songs from their heritages.

History and Artifacts

Explain the meaning of *archaeology* to children and discuss ways that historians use artifacts (such as one small blue bead) to piece together the past (i.e.,

What does a historian do when he or she finds an artifact from the past?) To emphasize the concept of archaeology, read aloud J. P. Walsh's *Lost and Found* (Andre Deutsch, 1985, Grades 1–3). The book has four short stories about children losing an object that is found by another child in the same place hundreds of years later, who makes a connection between the object from the Stone Age and the present. If appropriate, discuss the meaning of archaeology further by reading aloud any of the books in Figure 1–2.

Activity #2: "Somebody Lost Something"

Engage children in an activity called "Somebody Lost It, I Found It," where they imagine that they are digging with partners and find an artifact—perhaps another small blue bead—from earlier times. Have them decide on the artifact. Ask them to turn to their partner and tell one another about the artifact with some predictions about *who, what, where, when,* and *why*. They can respond to such questions as:

FIGURE 1–2   Children's Books about Artifacts

Dragonwagon, Crescent. *Home Place*. Macmillan, 1990. This is a story of change over time. The modern family in the story imagines what an early family is like so strongly that their thoughts bring the earlier family into the modern time period for a while. Grades 1–3.

Fradin, D. B. *Archaeology*. Children's Press, 1983. This book suggests ways children can use artifacts as clues to the past. Grades 1–3.

Hooper, M. *The Pebble in My Hand: A History of Our Earth*. Viking, 1996. A child reflects on a pebble's history from its beginnings in a volcano up through each passing era to the day she finds it on the ground. Timeline included. Grades 2–4.

Hoopes, L. L. *Half a Button*. Harper & Row, 1989. Suggestions are given for helping children to discover artifacts as clues to the past. Grades 1–3.

Pickering, R. B. *I Can Be an Archaeologist*. Children's Press, 1987. This book suggests ways children can use artifacts as clues to the past. Grades 1–3.

Pryor, B. *The House on Maple Street*. Mulberry, 1992. This is a story of an arrowhead that is lost in the original landscape and found many times by humans as hundreds of years go by, and a house, village, and city are built over it. The arrowhead finally shows up as an artifact of the past in some contemporary children's present lives. Grades 1–3.

Sheldon, D. *Under the Moon*. Ill. by G. Blythe. Dial, 1994. Jenny imagines a long-ago world and the people who made the flint arrowhead she recently found. She imagines their tepees and fire at night. Grades 1–5.

Wheatley, N., & Rawlins, D. *My Place*. Australia in Print, Inc., 1988. This story starts in 1988 with 10-year-old Laura, who lives on a crowded street in Australia and goes back in time. The pages of the book turn back the years to the original landscape. Grades 1–3.

"*Who* do you think made it, used it, and lost it? *What* artifact did you find? *Where* and *when* do you think it was made? *Why* do you think it was buried in the ground?" To transform what children talked about to partners into an art expression, ask them to sketch the artifact and their ideas of who made it, used it, and lost it. For a second transformation, ask children to change their sketches into word pictures and then to write or dictate a description of what they drew on the back of their artwork. Ask them to show their sketches to the whole group and read aloud what they wrote. As an option, ask children to dictate their ideas about their sketches for a language experience story on a chart to read aloud individually or as a group.

Activity #3: "I Lost Something"

Emphasize the idea of losing an item that becomes an artifact with an activity entitled "I Lost Something, But Somebody *Will* Find It." In the activity, ask the children to pretend that *they* have lost something and someone in the future will discover it years from now. Engage them in writing about what they lost, and what the lost item will tell someone in the future about their lives now. Ask them to transform their words into a drawing of the scene they envision, where someone in the future discovers the lost item. Invite volunteers to show their drawings to the whole group and discuss their sketches and writing with others (i.e., What will happen when somebody finds the artifact you lost?)

Activity #4: "Artifact Almanac"

With the whole group, ask the children to think about the idea of a small blue bead from the story *One Small Blue Bead* as being one of the oldest human-shaped objects found by archaeologists today. Invite the children to tell as much as they can imagine about the object—who owned it, the bead's use, and what it tells about its time period. Then ask the children to think of something they own today that they think they will keep all their lives. Have them draw the object. Tell the children to talk with partners and predict (give guesses and hunches) what would happen in the future if an archaeologist—a person who studies the life and customs of people of ancient times—found their object(s). Ask them to respond to "What might the archeologist say about you—the object's owner?" and then have them dictate or write their thoughts on the back of their drawings before placing their works in a class almanac entitled *Artifact Almanac*.

Activity #5: "Role of Archaeologists"

On a subsequent day, show children objects (or place sketches of several artifacts on an overhead transparency) and ask the children to take the role of archaeologists who have discovered the artifacts. Ask the children to make their observations and conclusions about each of the artifacts (i.e., who might have owned it, its use, and what it tells them about its time period). Engage them in making drawings of the artifacts to add to the *Artifact Almanac*.

Activity #6: "Oldest Objects"

Ask the children to play the role of an archeologist and look for the oldest human-made objects in their homes. The object can be anything—clothing, furniture, a letter, a photograph, a tool or utensil, and so on. Tell them to discuss the object with an adult in the home and find out any or all of the following:

- Who owned it first?
- How was it used?
- What does the object say about the object's owner and the time period in which the object was used?

Tell the children to sketch the object and, if appropriate, label its parts. When the children bring their sketches to school, let them discuss their drawings in small groups and determine which object is the most unusual (category 1), the oldest (category 2), and the most useful (category 3) in their lives today. The small groups may then report back to the whole group and tell which object was determined for each category. Follow up by asking the children to invite an antique collector or the owner of an antique store to visit the class and talk about the history of some of the oldest objects he or she brings to class.

Activity #7: "Visit of Early Family"

Artifacts from a family who lived centuries ago are found by a contemporary family in *Home Place* (Macmillan, 1990, Grades 1–3) by Crescent Dragonwagon, a story of change over time. The modern family in the story imagines what the early family is like so intensely that their thoughts bring the earlier family into the modern time period for a while. When this happens, a child begins to understand the big picture about the life of early families and the changes that have taken place over time. Mention to the children that it is possible to study what changes happen over time in order to have a better perspective on one's own life as well as to realize what happened in the lives of others in the past and—and perhaps predict what might happen in the future.

After listening to *Home Place*, have the children pretend that an earlier family visits them in contemporary times for a while, and that they have to explain some of the objects or changes in their lives the earlier family finds unusual. Ask the children to meet with partners and have one of them role-play a member of the earlier family, and the other a contemporary child. Have the member of the earlier family ask questions about modern objects or changes and the contemporary child explain the use of the objects in today's world. Back in the whole group, ask children what they learned from this activity and what message the story has for their own experiences. What predictions about objects and changes do they want to make related to the future?

Ideas of How the World Began

One of the ways Native Americans believed their world began is explained in John Bierhorst's retelling of *The Woman Who Fell from the Sky: The Iroquois Story of Creation* (Morrow, 1993, all grades). This is a story of Sky Woman, who creates the earth, stars, and sun while her twin sons make the animal and plant life and create snow, monsters, and river water. Invite the children to take the role of "history mirrors" of the early people who told the tale and have them retell the story to one another. Additionally, invite children to listen to other stories about how the world began from a favorite source or from *Earth Sky Life Death* (Starr King Press, 1988, Grade 3 up) by Sophia Fahs and Dorothy Spoerl. This collection includes stories about Adam and Eve, the way Prometheus created man, and the early ancestor of Odin. Clarify any unfamiliar words used in the tales. Invite the children to recall and repeat some of the terms in order to introduce the words into their language repertoires related to different cultures.

Activity #8: "How People Thought They Came to Be"

The beginning of the human family, with its diversities and commonalities, is explained in an African creation tale in *The Fire Children: A West African Creation Tale* (Dial, 1993, Grades 1–3), a story retold by Eric Maddern. Nyame, the sky god, sneezes and sends two spirit people down to earth. They are lonely and so they shape children from clay that can be baked. When Nyame visits them each afternoon,

the spirit people are not able to take the clay figures from the fire at the proper moment and so some of the children are white, some are shell pink, and others are honey yellow and cinnamon red. Still others are beautifully browned. To relate the diversity in this tale to contemporary times, ask the children to look through magazines, newspapers, catalogs, and other materials to find illustrations of diversities in the human family around the world. Have the children cut out the illustrations and make collages titled Fire Children of Today. Display the artwork in the room.

Activity #9: "Stories Came to People"

How stories were given to the people of Africa is told in Gail E. Haley's book *A Story, A Story* (Atheneum, 1970, all grades), a tale of how Anansi, the Spider man/trickster of Africa, receives the world's stories from Nyame, the Sky god, and brings them down to earth. Further, the Spider man's character portrays the idea that a small person's wit can overcome strength and verbal ability of others. After hearing *A Story, A Story*, ask children to listen to some different types of traditional folktales that Anansi allegedly brought down to earth. The stories can be examples of talking animal tales, cumulative tales, "Why and How" tales, noodlehead tales, realistic fanciful tales, and fairy tales. Ask children why they think different people living in various regions enjoyed these similar types of stories in their parallel cultures.

Activity #10: "Pretend You Were There"

Read aloud one of the folktales from the different heritages of people from Figure 1–1 and engage the children in a "You Were There" activity. The children are to imagine the lives and time periods of the people who told the folktales. After hearing the selected folktale, encourage the children to tell what information they gained from the tale about the early people who were in the story and to use the information to suggest different words for the rhyme of "One, Two, Buckle My Shoe." Write the children's suggestions on an overhead transparency for choral reading by the whole group. (*Example:* One, two, people hunted and moved./ Three, four, they searched land and shore./ Five, six, they learned hunting tricks./ Seven, eight, they'd move fast, then wait./ Nine, ten, they hunted again and again.) Add different words to the rhyme as often as needed to record all of the information the children suggest.

"How and Why" Tales of Early People

Early people of the area now called Mexico tell a "How and Why" tale to explain why there is music in the world. It is retold in H. Ober's *How Music Came to the World: An Ancient Mexican Myth* (Macmillan, 1995, Grades 1–4). In the sky, Quetzalcoatl, the wind god, goes to the House of the Sun to bring back music to the earth. He becomes angry when the Sun and his musicians ignore him and so he creates a violent storm that carries the musicians back to earth. On earth, the musicians wander from place to place and spread their music. After hearing the story, divide the children into groups to represent the continents and tell them to imagine they are musicians living on different continents in the world. Have all the groups listen to recorded music representative of the people of the continents and ask the children to tell if the music is fast or slow, happy or sad, and so on. Ask them to take the role of wandering musicians, who will spread their music and songs on their continent, and to write words for a song related to the continent they represent (i.e., a happiness song, a harvest song, a weaving song, a warrior song, a wisdom song, a respectful song for the sun, moon, and stars, etc.). Have volunteers read the words aloud to the whole group, and if appropriate, have the children suggest a melody.

Activity #11: "What 'How and Why' Tales Tell Us"

After reading aloud "How and Why" tales from different cultures about how early people explained the world's beginnings (see Figure 1–3 for suggestions), discuss early people's ideas about how they thought the world got going. Ask the children, "Which of the following sentences might be true?" Write the sentences on the board:

1. "How and Why" tales help tell us the ways early people believed the world began.
2. "How and Why" tales do *not* tell us the ways early people believed the world began.

Have the children discuss which statement might be true and guide them to collecting additional evidence for their points of view by reading other "How and Why" tales and reporting their findings back to the group. Continue reading several "How and Why" tales aloud to the children and point out that people in different countries/cultures are similar—they all have enjoyed this type of

story. Additional tales given in Figure 1–3 can help the children locate various tales to read for a discussion of the similarities among the characters in the stories.

Activity #12: "A 'Why Tale' in My State"

Some Native Americans' early beliefs about why birds are banished to the south—their migration journeys—are explained in a Native American tale, *The Great Ball Game: A Muskogee Story* (Dial, 1994, Grades K–3) by Joseph Bruchac. In the "Why" tale, the animals and birds argue over which of them is better, and decide to settle the argument with a ball game. Bat, small and weak, is not chosen for either team, but it is Bat who eventually wins the match for the animals, who then banish the birds. Mention to the children that this is a type of tale that early people told to help explain what was happening around them. Have the children imagine that this tale was told long ago in their state because early people noticed the migration journeys of birds and wanted to explain why this happened. Ask them to reflect on what the land must have looked like for the migrating birds as they traveled:

- For water birds (cranes, ducks, geese, herons)
- For mountain birds (buzzards, eagles, grouse, owls, partridges, pigeons, quail, roadrunners, vultures, woodpeckers)
- For songbirds (meadowlarks, mocking birds, thrushes, finches, sparrows, wrens, blackbirds, bluebirds, orioles)

Invite a wildlife representative to visit the class to identify the route that ducks and other migrating birds follow to fly across the state. Have each child cut out a small silhouette of a flying bird and affix the shape to a state map in a migratory line to mark the pathway the birds follow when they migrate.

As an option, repeat the activity and ask the children to imagine what their state looked like long ago for the fish and animals (coyotes, deer, foxes, wolves, mountain lions, rabbits, squirrels, wildcats, porcupines, badgers, raccoons). If appropriate, have the children acknowledge the study of their state by suggesting different words for the tune of "This Is the Way We Wash Our Clothes:"

This is the day we study our state,
study our state, study our state.
This is the day we study our state
to see how birds once traveled.

FIGURE 1-3   **Children's Multicultural "How and Why" Tales**

PERSPECTIVES

Origins of Animal Characteristics

Africa

Bryan A. "How the Animals Got Their Tails" in *Beat the Story Drum, Pum-Pum*. Atheneum, 1980. The creator realizes his mistake in creating skin-biting flies and gives animals their tails so they can swish the pests away. Grades 3–5.

Daly, N., reteller. *Why the Sun & Moon Live in the Sky*. Ill. by N. Daly. Lothrop, Lee & Shepard. 1995. This is a "Why" tale from the Inibio people about what happens when the Sea and her children visit the abode of the Sun and Moon. Grades 2–4.

Knutson, B. *Why the Crab Has No Head*. Carolrhoda, 1987. This is a Zaire tale about how the Creator was offended by Crab's pride and why the embarrassed Crab now walks sideways. Grades 3–5.

Lester, J. *How Many Spots Does a Leopard Have?* Ill. by D. Shannon. Scholastic, 1989. This is a collection of tales to explain animal characteristics. Grades 1–4.

Asia

Hong, L. T., reteller. *How the Ox Star Fell from Heaven*. Albert Whitman, 1991. The ox, in disfavor, is sent to earth to be a beast of burden. All grades.

Australia

Maraingura, N., et al. *Tales from the Spirit Time*. Indiana University Press, 1976. This is a revised edition of several "Why" tales about animals that were collected from Aborigine student teachers in Australia. Grades 3–5.

Mexico

Kurtycz, M., & Kobeh, A. G. *Tigers and Opossums*. Little, Brown, 1984. This collection has tales from Mexico that explain ways animals received their characteristics (e.g., why the hummingbird is brightly dressed, how the opossum got his tail, the way the tiger got his stripes, etc.). Grade 3 up.

North America

Hausman, G., reteller. *How Chipmunk Got Tiny Feet: Native American Animal Origin Stories*. Ill. by A. Wolff. HarperCollins, 1995. This is a collection of "How and Why" tales from the Navajo, Koasati Creek, and Tsimshian people. Grades K–4.

Keams, G. *Grandmother Spider Brings the Sun*. Ill. by J. Bernardin. Northland, 1995. In this Cherokee tale, animals want to take the sun to the dark half of the world, but Possum gets burned and suffers a hairless tail and Buzzard burns off his head of feathers. Grandmother Spider delivers the sun in a pot, and to this day, one can see the sun in the center of her web. Grades K–4.

Ross, C. *How Turtle's Back Was Cracked: A Traditional Cherokee Tale*. Ill. by M. Jacob. Dial, 1995. Thrown in the river by wolves because of the death of one of their pack, Turtle hits a rock and his shell is cracked. He sews his shell together but the joints can be seen to this day. Grades K–3.

Origins of Natural Events

Asia

Melmed, L. K. *The First Song Ever Sung*. Ill. by E. Young. Lothrop, Lee & Shepard, 1993. In Ancient Japan, a young boy of the mountain people asks those around him, "What was the first song?" The boy's question about the beginning of song causes others to consider its genesis (i.e., a game song, a harvest song, a moon song, a warrior's song, and a weaver's song). Grades 1–3.

FIGURE 1–3   **Continued**

North America

de Paola, T. *The Legend of the Bluebonnet*. Ill. by the author. Putnam, 1983. An unselfish child gives up her special possession and is rewarded in this Comanche tale. Grades 1–4.

Dixon, A. *How Raven Brought Light to People*. Ill. by J. Watts. McElderry, 1992. Trickster Raven tricks a powerful Tinglit Indian leader and releases the sun, moon, and stars. Escaping through a smoke-hole in the lodge, Raven is covered with soot and has remained black forever. Grades K–4.

Esbensen, B. J. *The Star Maiden*. Ill. by H. K. Davie. Little, Brown, 1988. In this Ojibway tale, a star maiden makes her home on the surface of a lake as a water lily. Grades K–3.

Origins of Seasons
Africa

Anderson, J. S. *The Key into Winter*. Ill. by D. Soman. Whitman, 1994. This is a tale of a family who has four keys that open the doors to the seasons. Grades K–3.

Greece

Geringer, L. *The Pomegranate Seeds: A Classic Greek Myth*. Ill. by L. Gore. Houghton Mifflin, 1995. When Persephone eats three pomegranate seeds, she must spend three months of the year in her uncle's kingdom of the underworld. Grades 3–5.

Hodges, M. *Persephone and the Springtime, A Greek Myth*. Ill. by A. Stewart. Little, Brown, 1973. This is a myth about Persephone. who is released from Hades to bring spring. Grade 3 up.

Italy

McDermott, G. *Daughter of Earth: A Roman Myth*. Delacorte, 1984. This is a myth from Italy of how spring came to earth. Grade 3 up.

Origins of Skies
Africa

Dayrell, E. *Why the Sun and the Moon Live in the Sky*. Ill. by B. Lent. Houghton Mifflin, 1968. This book is an explanation of how water caused the sun and moon to live above earth. Grade 2 up.

Asia

Hillman, E. *Min-Yo and the Moon Dragon*. Harcourt Brace Jovanovich, 1992. To keep the moon from falling, Min-Yo and the Moon Dragon throw diamonds into the sky. Grades 1–2.

North America

Goble, P. *The Lost Children*. Ill. by author. Bradbury, 1993. This is a sacred Blackfoot myth that tells the origin of the Pleiades, and yet gives some contemporary message with a final illustration of modern cars and telephone poles. All grades.

McDermott, G. *Raven: A Trickster Tale from the Pacific Northwest*. Harcourt Brace, 1994. Raven confronts a nest of boxes that holds the sun. Grades K–3.

Shetterly, S. H. *Raven's Light: A Myth from the People of the Northwest*. Atheneum, 1992. This is a traditional story of the Northwest that is used as the basis of a creation myth. Grades 2–5.

or

This is our state from long ago,
long ago, long ago.
This is our state from long ago.
We'll draw what wildlife saw.

Use the overhead to enlarge the state map onto mural paper on the wall. Have the children use the image of the state to make decisions about which illustrations of mountains, valleys, waterways, fish, and animals they will draw. Tell the children to make their drawings and affix them to the large map.

CHAPTER TWO

1.0 Million–20,000 B.C.

What was going on in ancient times?

Multicultural Perspectives

Children can draw scenes to show energetic early people cultivating corn in areas such as New Mexico and the Ohio River Valley, the environment they traveled, the caves they explored and painted, and the hunting, trapping, gathering, and other work they did. Children's colorful drawings also can re-create the pictographs early artists left. Additionally, sketches of the people's animal traps, baskets, clothing, implements, pottery, tools, weapons, and other possessions, along with some captions, can lead the children to a better understanding of ways people adjusted to their environment and to other humans in this period.

Children can build replicas of early communities with blocks, invent some of the tools they need, measure a planting area, and plant, grow, and harvest corn on the playground. They can decide what to do with corn (purchased locally) and implement different ways to use it, store it, and cook it. They can design and make baskets in which to store different types of corn. They can draw sketches to show their decisions. They can write their own recipes for a group book entitled *Everybody Likes Corn*. In a sand area outside, or on a sand table inside, they can form a terrain with different types of rocks and soil and show ways to get water from higher elevations to lower farming lands to simulate the irrigation needed to water a corn crop. They can listen to information such as *Corn Is Maize: The Gift of the Indians* (Crowell, 1976, Grades 1–3) by Aliki, a book that discusses the ways ancient people used corn and how it was planted, cultivated, and harvested. As a culminating activity to the study of corn, children can prepare and perform a play or skit to show others how corn was grown and used by the

early people. Perhaps the final scene can show how corn is processed and used today. A contemporary corn exhibit can feature displays of cans of corn, boxes of cornbread and muffin mixes, corn tortillas, jars of corn relish, and so on.

Reading historical fiction related to this time period, the children can discuss some of the problems of the main characters in folk literature from parallel cultures and relate the problems of the characters to problems the children find in their own experiences. To assist in this comparison, read aloud some of the books in Figure 2–1 that have perspectives of people for this time period.

Problems of People

Mention to children that a trait, such as selfishness, that they notice in others today is not too different from a trait held by a character in a folktale from centuries ago. For example, Iwariwa, a selfish cayman, hoards fire in a small basket that he keeps in his mouth in *How Iwariwa the Cayman Learned to Share: A Yanomami Myth* (Clarion, 1995, Grades 2–4). This is a story from the Yanomami people of the South American Amazon rain forest as retold by George Crespo. The other animals need the strange orange heat that "dances" to cook their food and they devise a plan to trick the cayman into sharing. They invite Iwariwa to a celebration and a feast (so the cayman will have to open his mouth to eat). After reading this story to children about the animals' conflict, help children see that the problem of selfishness and other problems they find today are not too different from problems faced by main characters in folktales from early times. This similarity can be a way for the

FIGURE 2–1   **Children's Books about 1 Million–20,000 B.C.**

PERSPECTIVES

African Heritage

Kimmel, E. A. *Anansi and the Talking Melon*. Ill. by J. Stevens. Holiday, 1994. Anansi eats Elephant's melon and is too full to crawl away. So, he decides to play a trick and convinces Elephant that the melon is a talking melon. Elephant tells this wonderful news to others, but King Monkey is insulted by the melon, and disorder prevails to Anansi's amusement. Folk literature. Grades K–2.

McDermott, G. *Anansi the Spider: A Tale from the Ashanti*. Holt, Rinehart and Winston, 1972. Nyame, the sky god, helps Anansi and puts the moon in the sky. Folk literature. Grades 2–3.

Asian Heritage

Yep, L. *The Man Who Tricked a Ghost*. Bridgewater Books, 1993. Traveling with a fierce warrior ghost as a companion, Sung learns the warrior's secret, which Sung uses to defeat him, and in doing so, makes himself rich. Folk literature. Grades 1–4.

European Heritage

Chandler, R. *Russian Folktales*. Ill. by I. I. Bilibin. Random House, 1980. This is a collection of folk literature from Eastern Europe. Folk literature. Grade 3 up.

Latino/Hispanic Heritage

Aardema, V. *The Riddle of the Drum: A Tale from Tizapin, Mexico*. Ill. by T. Chen. Four Winds, 1979. To marry the king's daughter, a man guesses the kind of leather in a drum. Folk literature. Grades 2–3.

Belpre, P. *The Dance of the Animals: A Puerto Rican Folk Tale*. Ill. by P. Galdone. Warne, 1972. This is a talking animal tale. Folk literature. Grades 2–3.

Blackmore, V. *Why Corn Is Golden: Stories about Plants*. Ill. by S. Martinez-Ostos. Little, Brown, 1984. This book has a collection of folk stories about corn and other plants. Folk literature. Grades 2–4.

Heuer, M. *El Zapato y el Pez*. Mexico City: Trillas, 1983. This is the story of a shoe and a fish, a Spanish language story. Folk literature. Grades 1–3.

Middle East/Mediterranean Heritage

Kimmel, E. A. *The Three Princes: A Tale from the Middle East*. Ill. by L. E. Fisher. Holiday, 1994. A wise, beautiful princess sends her suitors on a quest and says she will marry the one who returns with the greatest wonder. She marries the one who sacrifices his treasure for her. Folk literature. Grades 2–4.

Native American Heritage

Ehlers, S. *The Bossy Hawaiian Moon*. Ill. by W. H. Kiyabu. Edward Enterprises of Honolulu, 1979. This is a tale of how the stars and clouds show a bossy moon that they are supposed to live in the sky. Grade 3 up.

Greene, E. *The Legend of the Cranberry: A Paleo-Indian Legend*. Simon & Schuster, 1993. This is a Delaware legend about the friendship between Native People and the mastodons that died out about 25,000 years ago. At the mastodons' demise, cranberries, a gift from the Great Sprit that symbolizes peace, appear wherever the giant animals fall. Folk literature. Grades 2–3.

FIGURE 2–1   Continued

Female Image Heritage

Bernhard, E., reteller. *The Girl Who Wanted to Hunt: A Siberian Tale*. Holiday House, 1994. Anga, a young girl who wants to be a hunter like her father, uses magical carvings to escape a demanding stepmother. Folk literature. Grades 1–4.

Gerspem, M. *People of the Corn: A Mayan Story*. Ill. by Carla Golembe. Little, Brown, 1995. This is a creation myth about the role of corn in the Mayan civilization. When corn is planted by the Grandmother of Light, the gods—Plumed Serpent and Heart of Sky—create the Mayan people who can remember their origins and honor the gods in celebration. Folk literature. Grades K–3.

Religious Heritage

McDermott, G. *Arrow to the Sun*. Viking, 1974. This is a Pueblo Indian tale about the people's reverence for the sun and about the Lord of the Sun who sends a spark to Earth. The spark becomes a boy who searches for his father. Folk literature. Grades K–3.

---

children to connect the present *back* to a past historical period. Ask, "Would the trick the animals played on the selfish cayman work today on a selfish person? Why or why not?" Help children see that some problems, such as dealing with a selfish person, are universal and are always with people despite the differences in their cultures or time periods.

Invite children to study a problem such as selfishness or greed across cultures and time periods so that they can begin to understand some problems are universal and have been faced by people in history. To do this, have children read folktales (or stories set in different time periods) about greed or selfishness, discuss the problem in the story, and point out the way the problem was resolved. Have the children mention any similar or different ways people in various cultures reacted to the problem. Have each child report his or her independent findings about the problem(s) back to the whole group.

Activity #13: "Unselfishness"

In *The Story of Jumping Mouse: A Native American Legend* (Lothrop, 1984, Grades 1–3), John Steptoe says that his storytelling style is one where he tells it from memory—most of it in his own words. Jumping Mouse is assured by Magic Frog that he will reach his destination if he keeps his hopes alive. The mouse is given powerful legs to help him on his journey, and along the way he is generous to others. As a reward for his unselfishness, Magic Frog turns Jumping Mouse into an eagle so he can live in the far-off land

forever. Have the children listen to Steptoe's storytelling style and take the role of listeners who have a responsibility. Just as Native American children were asked to do, have the children put the information together to arrive at a conclusion about the story's worth to them and tell how it applies to *their* lives.

Activity #14: "Conflict with Others"

Family relationships among people who value marriage as well as the beauty and attractiveness of nature are described in *The First Strawberries: A Cherokee Story* (Dial, 1993, all grades) by Joseph Bruchac. In the story, a woman is scolded by her husband and she leaves in anger. When her husband is saddened, the sun helps him by causing berries to grow in the woman's path, thereby slowing her down so the husband can catch up and apologize. Neither raspberries, blackberries, nor blueberries catch her attention. But when strawberries, glowing like the sun, appear in front of the woman's feet, she stops to taste one. The sweetness of the berries reminds her of the sweetness of her marriage and the story ends when the two reconcile.

After reading the story aloud, mention to children that both a Native American storyteller and the audience have always had special roles. The teller's purpose is to share as much knowledge as he or she can about the subject in the story; the teller wants the audience to be responsible for making connections between the topics themselves. Thus, it is the responsibility of a listener in the audience to put the information together and to arrive at a conclusion about its worth and how it applies to the listener's life. Discuss with the children the importance of each listener's responsibility when he or she hears a story such as *The First Strawberries* and encourage them to listen to the story again to make connections between the topic and themselves. Have them tell the ways the story applies to *them*—just as Native American storytellers would expect them to do. For example, they might be asked, "What sweetness in your life reminds you of a strawberry's sweetness?"

Activity #15: "Conflict with Climate"

The way some early people faced a conflict with the environment and how they coped by sharing is portrayed in *The Dragon's Pearl* (Clarion, 1993, Grades 2–5) by J. Lawson. Xiao Sheng and others in his village suffer when their land is ruined by a drought. Xiao discovers a magic pearl that keeps his mother's food jars full, which she shares with others during this difficult time to repay the people's kindness to her. After hearing the story, ask the children

to reflect on the following: "Would the solution that Xiao Sheng's mother used—sharing with others—work today? Why or why not? How is sharing water (food, money) during a drought implemented today? How are such items shared in today's world?" Have the children tell what they know about the hardships of drought (and some of the other conflicts they believe ancient families faced) and then identify the hardships that they think people endure in today's time period. Which hardships of today are similar to the hardships of people in ancient times? Write the children's ideas in two lists on the board, using the headings of Hardships in Ancient Times and Hardships Today.

Have the children illustrate on a sheet of paper their ideas of ways people share during a hardship (one idea per sheet), and place the illustrations on a bulletin board. Point out that children and adults in prehistory faced problems similar to those faced by people today and suggest additional stories that can develop the children's awareness about the universality of conflicts from Figure 2–2.

FIGURE 2–2   Children's Books about Conflicts of Early People

PERSPECTIVES

Conflict with Basic Needs: Food, Clothing, and Shelter

Gerspem, M. *People of the Corn: A Mayan Story.* Ill. by Carla Golembe. Little, Brown, 1995. Corn is planted by the Grandmother of Light, which leads to the creation of the Mayan people. Folk literature. Grades K–3.

Goble, P. *Crow Chief.* Orchard, 1992. When Crow Chief warns the buffalo of the Native American hunters, Falling Star, one of the hunters, captures Crow Chief and ties him where the tipi poles cross until Crow's feathers turn black from the tipi's fire. When Crow Chief learns that everyone must share, he is released. Folk literature. Grade 3 up.

Goble, P. *The Return of the Buffaloes: A Plains Indian Story about Famine and Renewal of the Earth.* Nation Geographic, 1996. In this Lakota myth, two men are sent out to find the buffalo herd in a time of famine. They encounter Buffalo Woman, who takes them to Wind Cave and assures them that she will send her Buffalo People to rescue the tribe. That night, the Buffalo Nation arrives and food becomes plentiful and the dried rawhides used for storage are filled. Included are the author's note about Buffalo Woman and Wind Cave and instructions for making a dried rawhide for storage purposes. Folk literature. Grade 3 up.

Rappaport, D. *The Long-Haired Girl: A Chinese Legend.* Ill. by Yang Ming-Yi. Dial, 1995. Searching for water during a drought, Ah-mei makes the Thunder God angry when she discovers his secret spring. He threatens her life if she reveals the spring, but as she watches her family and other villagers suffer from the drought, she is compelled to reveal the water's location in the nearby mountain. Folk literature. Grades K–3.

FIGURE 2–2   Continued

Conflict with Clan Taboos and Customs

Troughton, J., reteller. *Whale's Canoe: A Folk Tale from Australia.* Bedrick/Blackie, 1993. The value that is placed on sharing in a clan is emphasized with this story of the animals who are eager to cross the ocean to settle in a beautiful new land mentioned by the birds. Whale has a canoe large enough to carry them, but he is mean and bad tempered, and the conflict comes when he will not share. Starfish thinks of a plan to outwit Whale, and the animals use his canoe to reach the shores of the new land—Australia. Folk literature. Grades K–2.

Conflict with Climate, Natural Forces, and Elements

Aardema, V. *Bringing the Rain to Kapiti Plain.* Dial, 1981. This is a Kenyan tale with an accumulating style about animals during a long drought. Folk literature. Grades 1–3.

Alexander, E. *Llama and the Great Flood: A Folktale of Peru.* Crowell, 1989. This is a tale from the Andes about how a llama leads people to safety and saves them from a flood. Folk literature. Grades 1–3.

Anderson, M. *Light in the Mountain.* Knopf, 1982. Early Maori people overcome a cold and harsh climate. Folk literature. Grades 2–4.

Bernhard, E. reteller. *The Tree That Rains: The Flood Myth of the Huicholy Indians of Mexico.* Ill. by D. Bernhard. Holiday, 1994. This story tells how the world is repopulated after a flood punished the people. Folk literature. Grades K–3.

Lawson, J. *The Dragon's Pearl.* Clarion, 1993. During a drought, Xiao Sheng's mother shares food acquired with a magic pearl with others to repay their kindness to her. Folk literature. Grades 2–5.

Mollel, Tolowa M., reteller. *The Princess Who Lost Her Hair: An Akamba Legend.* Ill. by C. Reasoner. Troll, 1992. When a vain princess refuses to give a bird a strand of her hair she loses her hair, and causes a famine to come upon the land. Folk literature. Grades 1–3.

Conflict with Others

Bruchac, J. *The First Strawberries: A Cherokee Story.* Dial, 1993. A woman leaves her husband in anger, but a strawberry's sweetness reminds her of the sweetness of her marriage and the two reconcile. All grades.

Beliefs and Feelings of People

The belief that a person's character is a person's destiny is reflected in the Korean tale *Older Brother, Younger Brother: A Korean Folktale* (Viking, 1995, Grades K–3) retold by Nina Jaffe. At their father's death, a greedy elder brother turns Hungbu, his younger brother, and his family out of the family home. Hungbu finds an injured baby sparrow, mends its broken wing, and cares for it until it can fly. In the spring, the sparrow returns with a gift of great wealth for Hungbu. Wanting wealth too, the elder brother captures a sparrow, breaks its wing, and complains about caring for it. When the bird flies away, the elder brother waits for his wealth to return but receives a disastrous consequence instead. Emphasize to the children the beliefs of early people related to this folktale, their feelings, and what might have motivated them to tell this tale.

Activity #16: "Feelings Matter"

Engage children in listening to (or reading independently) different types of folktales that come from different countries—cumulative tales, talking animal tales, noddle tales, "Why" tales, realistic fanciful, and fairytales with elements of magic. To focus on the feelings of the characters in one type of tales, have the children read selected stories and name feelings of the characters to foster an awareness that emotions and feelings are universal, special, and matter to people. Ask children to share this awareness of human nature by expressing words that reflect feelings. Write the words in groups on a diagram on the board or overhead transparency (see Figure 2–3).

On subsequent days, read aloud (or ask the children to read independently) examples of other types of tales found in various cultures and ask children to talk further about the similar feelings of humans—joy, fear, grief, awe—expressed in the tales. Add the feelings words to the diagram and group the words into categories of Brave Words, Curiosity Words, and so on. If the study of feelings of people in folktales from different cultures is to be an extended one, have the children read cumulative tales from different heritages during one week and other types of tales during the following weeks. To assist in this, suggestions of children's books are given in Figure 2–4. Where titles are not given, the stories can be selected by the children.

At the end of the first week, ask the children to talk about the inner feelings of humans—joy, fear,

grief, awe—expressed in the cumulative tales. Have the children tell about the tales they heard (or read) and record the tale's country of origin on a chart to determine the extent to which cumulative tales from *different* heritages are read. Record the children's ideas about feelings on a data sheet on an overhead transparency (see Figure 2–5). Repeat the activity during other weeks for other types of tales.

Myths and Legends of People

Help the children expand their view of the lives of early people by reading different versions of myths and legends. Examples include R. Lewis's *All of You Was Singing* (Atheneum, 1991, all grades), an Aztec myth, and Nancy Van Laan's *Buffalo Dance: A Blackfoot Legend* (Little, Brown, 1993, Grades 1–4), a story of the interdependence of humans and animals. After reading different myths and legends aloud, discuss with the children some of the differing attitudes and behaviors in the stories that are held by people in different geographical locations. Mention the distinction between a *myth* and a *legend*:

- A myth is a story from early times that tries to explain why things happen as they do. Ask, "In the myth, *All of You Was Singing*, what event seems to be explained?"
- A legend is a story based some way on ancient *facts* that have been passed down by people over many years. Ask, "What information from the story *Buffalo Dance* would you consider to be facts that might have been passed down by early people?"
- Both legends and myths offer a way to discover some of the ideas early people valued. Ask, "What do you think the people valued by telling these two stories?"

Activity #17: "What Myths and Legends Tell Us"

With the whole group, discuss the children's ideas (guesses, hunches, predictions) about what the people of a selected heritage valued after reading a selected myth or a legend related to a history study. Ask the children, "What can we learn about people from a myth or legend?" If appropriate, elicit the children's comments related to Figure 2–6 and write their responses under the appropriate heading. Ask, "What does this information tell you about this character's culture?" and "How can you use the information in acting out some of your favorite scenes

---

FIGURE 2–3 Words That Reflect Feelings

Happy Words
Giggly
Helpful
Joyful
Kissable
Loving
OK
Proud
Relaxed
Silly
Ticklish

Unhappy Words
Disappointed
Embarrassed
Frustrated
Miserable
Crying
Grief

Curiosity Words
Curious
Involved

WORDS ABOUT FEELINGS

Afraid Words
Afraid
Fear
Nervous

Brave Words
Brave
Courageous

Other Words
Awe
Excited
Yucky
Zonked

FIGURE 2–4   Children's Books about Types of Tales

PERSPECTIVES

Cumulative Tales

African Asian

Alexander, L. *The Fortune-Tellers*. Ill. by T. S. Hyman. Dutton, 1993. This is a rags-to-riches tale from Cameroon about a trickster. Grades 1–3.

Asian

Lichtveld, N., reteller. *I Lost My Arrow in a Kankan Tree*. Ill. by N. Lichtveld. Lothrop, 1994. To feed his large family, a boy shoots a pigeon with his arrow and gives the bird to a woman. She gives him a pumpkin in exchange, and he keeps trading with each person he meets. Grades 1–3.

Hispanic

Native American

Baker, B. *Rat Is Dead and Ant Is Sad*. Ill. by M. Funai. Harper & Row, 1981. This tale is from the Pueblo Indians. Grades 2–3.

European

Kellogg, S. *Chicken Little*. Morrow, 1985. This British tale has a contemporary twist. Grades 1–3.

Other

How and Why Tales

Asian

African

Grafalconi, A. *The Village of Round and Square Houses*. Little, Brown, 1986. This story tells the origin of the custom of men living in square houses, and women and children in round houses. Grade 3 up.

Hispanic

Bernhard, E. reteller. *The Tree That Rains: The Flood Myth of the Huicholy Indians of Mexico*. Ill. by D. Bernhard. Holiday, 1994. This myth tells of how the world is repopulated after a flood punishes the people. Grades K–3.

Native American

Duncan, L. *The Magic of Spider Woman*. Ill. by S. Begay. Scholastic, 1996. When Weaving Woman is obsessed with making the most beautiful blanket in the world, her life loses its balance and her spirit becomes trapped in the blanket. Spider Woman saves her when she pulls a strand from the border to free the woman's spirit. To this day, every Navajo blanket is woven with a pathway strand so the weaver's spirit will not be trapped by its beauty. Grades 3–6.

European

Other

continued

FIGURE 2–4   Continued

Noodlehead Stories

Asian

Hispanic

Pitre, F. *Juan Bobo and the Pig*. Lodestar, 1993. This tale is about Juan's silly behavior and what happens when he dresses up the family pig and takes him to church. Grades 1–4.

European

Rockwell, A. *The Three Sillies and Ten Other Stories to Read Aloud*. Harper, 1986. A collection. Grade 3 up.

Realistic Fanciful Fiction

Asian

Levine, A. A. reteller. *The Boy Who Drew Cats: A Japanese Folktale*. Ill. by F. Clement. Dial, 1994. A boy, skilled at drawing cats, seeks shelter in a deserted temple, where he paints cats on the screens and panels. They come to life and destroy a rat goblin that haunts the temple. Grades 2–6

Hispanic

European

Araujo, F. P. *Nekane, the Lamina & the Bear: A Tale of the Basque Pyrenees*. Ill. by Xiao Jun Li. Rayve Prod., 1993. Nekane takes a basket of fish and olive oil to her Uncle Kepa. She is warned about the lamina, a shape-changing being, who loves olive oil and tries to take it. Nekane outwits the lamina and a real bear and arrives at her uncle's place safely. Grades K–3.

African

Native American

Goble, P. *Iktomi and the Buzzard*. Orchard, 1994. Dressed to show off as an Eagle Dancer, Iktomi talks Buzzard into flying him across a wide river. When Iktomi makes fun of Buzzard's appearance, Buzzard gets even. Grades K–3.

Other

Yolen, J. *Little Mouse & Elephant: A Tale From Turkey*. Ill. by J. Segal. Simon & Schuster, 1996. A silly mouse convinces himself that he has defeated an elephant. Grades K–3.

African

Day, N. R. *The Lion's Whiskers: An Ethiopian Tale*. Ill. by A. Grifalconi. Scholastic, 1995. In this Amhara tale, a woman earns a lion's trust and wins the love of her stepson. Grade 3 up.

Native American

Baker, O. *Where the Buffaloes Began*. Ill. by S. Gammell, Warne, 1981. Buffaloes magically originate in a lake. Grade 3 up.

Other

FIGURE 2–4 **Continued**

Fairy Tales
Asian

Heyer, M. *The Weaving of a Dream: A Chinese Folktale*. Viking, 1986. Fairies steal a poor widow's brocade woven with her dreams, and her three sons attempt to recover it. Grades 3–5.

African

Hispanic

Native American

European

Hastings, S. reteller. *The Firebird*. Ill. by R. Cartwright. Candlewick, 1993. A huntsman, with the help of his horse, captures the magical Firebird and marries beautiful Princess Vasilisa. Grades 1–4.

Other

Talking Animal Tales
Asian

Schroeder, A. reteller. *The Stone Lion*. Ill. by T. L. W. Doney. Scribner's, 1994. In Tibet, an honest boy meets a magic stone lion who rewards him with gold coins and punishes the greedy brother. Grades 1–4.

African

Aardema, Verna. *Who's in Rabbit's House?* Ill. by L. & D. Dillon. Dial, 1977. This is a Masai folktale with talking animals. Grades 1–3.

Hispanic

Dupré, J. *The Mouse Bride: A Mayan Folk Tale*. Knopf/Umbrella Books, 1993. This is based on a fable told by the Choi Indians who are descendents from the Mayans. It is about a pair of mice who want their daughter to marry the most powerful force in the universe, and finally select a mouse for her husband. Grades 1–3.

Native American

Stevens, J. *Coyote Steals the Blanket: A Ute Tale*. Holiday House, 1993. Coyote takes and wears a beautiful blanket that isn't his, and Hummingbird warns him of the consequences to come. Coyote says, "I go where I want. I do what I want, and I take what I want." Coyote's consequences comes in the shape of a magic boulder that pursues him. Grades 1–3.

European

Other

FIGURE 2–5   Data Sheet for Group Report

Groups of Folktales	Examples of Feelings	Heritage
Cumulative tales		
Talking animal tales		
Noddlehead tales		
"How and Why" tales		
Realistic fanciful tales		
Fairytales		

---

from the myth or legend?" Have the children dramatize a scene from the myth or legend and then describe their favorite scene—perhaps not the one they dramatized. Scenes suitable for dramatization are in the stories listed on History Master 1 (at the end of this book).

Stories of African People

Encourage the children to learn more about the people of Africa by using a drama activity and researching elaborate features for the drama. For example, in a study about Africa's cultures in this period, have the children comprehend that a play or skit can be a brief "story" of this time period and recreate a performance from a resource such as *Plays from African Tales: One-Act, Royalty-Free Dramatizations for Young People, from the Stories and*

FIGURE 2–6   What Myths and Legends Tell Us

Who — What
Where — When
Why
INFORMATION FROM MYTHS AND LEGENDS

Legends of Africa (Plays, Inc., 1992, all grades) by Barbara Winther. The book has plays related to the stories of nations and cultures of Africa. Winther gives a brief history of each tale and a description of the tale's cultural beginnings that can initiate the cross-checking of facts by the children.

Engage the children in gathering information about Africa from various sources for the purpose of inserting some of the information into their play or skit. Tell them that the information should be cross-checked before they use it in the drama. Demonstrate one way to cross-check information by making transparencies of pages from an encyclopedia, a dictionary, and an informational book. Put the transparencies on the overhead and show children how you read each source to cross-check a fact you want to insert into a drama about Africa.

Activity #18: "Stage a Play about Africa"

With a selected play from Winther's book (*Plays from African Tales: One-Act, Royalty-Free Dramatizations for Young People, from the Stories and Legends of Africa*) or another source, talk with the children about the author's included notes, the production possibilities of the play, the main characters, and ways to insert the information they have researched into the play. Encourage the children to suggest dance movements or music to add to the performance and to portray themselves as "history kids in motion." Have them select a musical background and choreograph some simple dance moves when they "stage" the production. Suggest they write invitations to ask another class to be the audience.

CHAPTER THREE

20,000–1200 B.C.

What was going on in 20,000–1200 B.C.?

Multicultural Perspectives

Studying about this time period requires that children travel vicariously back to a different time and place through books—perhaps by listening or reading *Beginnings: How Families Came to Be* (Albert Whitman, 1994, Grades 1–3) by Virginia Kroll. Journeying back in historical time through books will put the children close to strange places and different faces such as ancient Egyptian pharaohs with their headdresses, priests and priestesses at the pyramids near the Nile, and busy workers grinding corn, making spears, and writing documents. Children can get acquainted with talented stone carvers and other craftspeople; with people living in the Maya, Greek, and other grand civilizations; with the inhabitants of larger-than-life fabled cities of Persia and Arabia; and with rugged Asian individualists in the Stone Age who crossed the Bering Land bridge over 20,000 years ago to an area now known as North America. Reading about Stone Age people can help children learn about early families and what they did—fishing, gathering berries, hunting, making clothes, trading, fashioning weapons, and fighting their enemies in the early villages and regions of this period.

Like being a newcomer in an unfamiliar land, the historical study of this period requires the children's adjustment to reading about the beliefs of others, such as the Native American people's reverence for the sun. Like becoming a friend of a newcomer, a study of this period also can lead to new understandings about the similarities of people. Indeed, the class environment and lessons can

be carefully planned to help the children develop concepts and generalizations as they read about what was going on in all parts of the world. Some books tell children about specific individuals and their special skills—drum makers of Africa, silk cloth makers of China, pyramid builders and sculptors of Egypt, and the traders in an area now called South America. Other books inform them about rulers and slaves, philosophers and soldiers as well as what went on in the ancient Hindu and Sikh world—all of which can be a part of a history study. To assist children, Figure 3–1 lists books giving perspectives of people related to the period of 20,000–1200 B.C.

Native People Long Ago

Read aloud A. A. Flor's *Feathers Like a Rainbow: An Amazon Indian Tale* (Harper, 1989, Grade 3 up), a tale from the Yanomami people, an ancient society (15,000 B.C.) of the Stone Age, whose descendents live in Brazil's Amazon jungle. Discuss the idea that ancient societies of people in North and South America, including the ancestors of the Pueblo people, were in existence before Columbus and other explorers came to the Americas. For examples, mention that early people had societies in the Ohio River area 19,000 years ago, in early western Pennsylvania 14,000 years ago, in northern Alaska 11,000 years ago, and in northeastern Colorado in the Arikaree River Valley 10,000 years ago. All of these places have been documented by archaeological findings and can be located on a map by the children. If appropriate, use the overhead to repre-

FIGURE 3–1   **Children's Books for 20,000–1200 B.C.**

PERSPECTIVES

African Heritage

Courtalon, C. *On the Banks of the Pharaoh's Nile*. Young Discovery Library, 1988. This text introduces children to the culture through illustrations and a text that should be read aloud by an adult. Nonfiction. Grades 1–3.

Giblin, J. C. *The Riddle of the Rosetta Stone: Key to Ancient Egypt*. Crowell, 1990. This is the story of the discovery of the stone, how its message was deciphered, and ways the message affected our knowledge of Egyptian people and their civilization. Grade 3 up.

Mike, J. M. *Gift of the Nile: An ancient Egyptian Legend*. Ill. by C. Reasoner. Troll, 1992. This is the story of wise and talented Mutem Wia, who is given by her father to Pharaoh Senefru as a gift. When she becomes homesick, Senefru imprisons her but finally gives her freedom. Folk literature. Grade 3 up.

Souhami, J. *The Leopard's Drum: An Ashante Tale from West Africa*. Ill. by author. Little, Brown, 1996. Osebo the leopard has a drum that is envied by Nyame, the Sky-God. When Osebo refuses to give up the instrument, Nyame offers a reward to the animal that can bring it to him. All of the animals try and fail, except for one small clever creature—Achi-cheri, the tortoise. Folk literature. Grades Pre–3.

Walsh, J. P. *Pepi and the Secret Names*. Ill. by F. French. Lothrop, Lee & Shepard, 1995. To assist his artist-father in decorating a royal tomb, Pepi makes friends with real animals, guesses their secret names, and gets them to pose for his father. Hieroglyphics and key included. Fiction. Grades 2–5.

Asian Heritage

Hong, L. T. *The Empress and the Silkworm*. Ill. by the author. Albert Whitman, 1995. Set in China nearly 5,000 years ago, Si Ling-chi, the empress, unwinds the thread of a cocoon that falls from a mulberry tree. She dreams that the thread can become yellow cloth to make a robe for her husband, Huang-Ti, the emperor, and follows her dream to create the first silk material. Folk literature. Grades K–4.

McDermott, G. *The Stone-Cutter: A Japanese Folk Tale*. Ill. by the author. Puffin Books, 1981. This is a retold tale from Japan about foolish Tasaku, who longed to be more powerful than a prince, stronger than the sun, and mightier than a cloud. Folk literature. Grades 1–5.

Maestro, B. *The Discovery of the Americas*. Lothrop, 1991. This text supports the view that people crossed the Bering Land bridge over 20,000 years ago to North America. It details travels of Stone Age people and visits by others from Japan and other areas. Maps included. Nonfiction. Grades 2–3.

European Heritage

Smirnova, G. *Fairy-Tales of Siberian Folks*. Trans. from Russian by O. Myazina and G. Shchitnikova. Vital, 1993. This book includes over 60 animal fables with animals dressed in clothing that represent 15 ethnic groups in Siberia. Glossary. Folk literature. Grade 3 up.

Latino/Hispanic Heritage

Baquedano, E. *Aztec, Inca & Maya*. Knopf, 1993. This text introduces three major civilizations of the Americas in a compare/contrast approach through photographs of the Mexican National Archeological Museum's recreations of ancient activities such as trading, paying tribute, and healing. Nonfiction. Grade 3 up.

FIGURE 3–1 **Continued**

Latino/Hispanic Heritage

Flor, A. A. *Feathers Like a Rainbow: An Amazon Indian Tale*. Harper, 1989. This is a tale from the Yanomami people, an ancient society (15,000 B.C.) of the Stone Age, who lived in Brazil's Amazon jungle. Set in the Amazon rain forest, the tale explains how birds got their colors. Grade 3 up.

Pitre, F. *Paco and the Witch*. Ill. by C. Hale. Lodestar, 1995. A Puerto Rican boy is trapped by a *bruja* who casts a spell on him that can only be broken when he guesses her name. A crab at the river teaches Paco a song to remember the name and the boy is saved. The witch still looks for the animal that betrayed her and so the crab hides when he sees humans. Folk literature. Grades 1–3.

Middle Eastern/Mediterranean Heritage

Al-Saleh, K. *Fabled Cities, Princes and Jinn from Arabic Myths and Legends*. Schocken Press, 1985. This is a collection of stories from Arabian and Persian heritage that can be read aloud to primary-grade children. Grades 1–3.

Climo, S. *Atalanta's Race: A Greek Myth*. Ill. by A. Koshkin. Clarion, 1995. After Atalanta races her lover, Melanion, they face Aphrodite's revenge. Folk literature. Grades 3–7.

Coolidge, O. *Greek Myths*. Ill. by E. Sandoz. Houghton Mifflin, 1949. Stories about Jason and others are retold in this excellent collection. Folk literature. Grades 3–7.

Rockwell, A. *The One-Eyed Giant and Other Monsters from the Greek Myths*. Ill. by the author. Greenwillow, 1996. Presented here are 10 myths about such monsters as Typhon, Echidna, Hydra, Cyclopes, Medusa, and the Minotaur. Folk literature. Grades 1–3.

Native American Heritage

Orie, S. D. C. *Did You Hear Wind Sing Your Name? An Oneida Song of Spring*. Ill. by C. Canyon. Walker, 1995. This is a poem with questions that explores the sensations, feelings, and interactions related to spring, including seeing snails, dewdrops, new green leaves, and spider webs. Folk literature. Grades K–4.

Female Image Heritage

Kimmel, E. *Rimonah of the Flashing Sword: A North African Tale*. Ill. by O. Rayan. Holiday, 1995. Princess Rimonah escapes her jealous stepmother and queen and joins a band of 40 thieves. She rides with them against the jealous queen. Folk literature. Grades K–4.

Maddern, E. *Rainbow Bird: An Aboriginal Folktale from Northern Australia*. Ill. by A. Kennaway. Little, Brown, 1993. Bird Woman snatches fire from the open jaws of tough Crocodile Man and flies around putting fire into the heart of every tree. From that time, people can make flames from dry wood. To celebrate, Bird Woman puts the firesticks into her tail as feathers and turns into the beautiful Rainbow bird. Folk literature. Grades K–3.

Religious Heritage

Aroner, M. *The Kingdom of Singing Birds*. Kar-Ben, 1993. This is a classic Hasidic tale about making one's own choices. Rabbi Zusya is called by the king to make his silent birds sing. Zusya tells the king that if he truly wants to hear the songs of the birds, he must set them free. Folk literature. Grades 1–3.

Sasso, S. E. *But God Remembered: Stories of Women from Creation to the Promised Land*. Ill. by B. Anderson. Jewish Lights, 1995. This collection has stories about women of the Old Testament: Lilith, Serach, Meroe, Zephaniah's daughter. Folk literature. Grades 2–5.

sent the sun and use a globe to demonstrate day and night and seasonal change that early people experienced in these places.

Activity #19: "Native Americans Long Ago"

On a large outline map of the children's state, write the names of Indian tribes who lived long ago in the area and locate where they lived. With the children's help in cutting out symbols from art paper, show places where snow falls each year (snowflakes), where the most rain falls (raindrops), and where trees and plants grow well. Divide the children into groups and assign a tribe to each group. Ask the children to read the weather symbols and determine possible weather conditions for their assigned tribe and write the conditions on a group chart. Have the children identify trees of their state and determine what food and shelter, if any, the trees provided for the tribe. Tell the children to use the map and symbols to decide on the best places for villages (near water and food supply) and to offer suggestions about how the Native People got food, clothing, and shelter. Write their decisions and suggestions on the board.

Activity #20: "Food of Native Americans"

Have the children sketch examples of the important foods of the Native People who lived in their region long ago and discuss what they know or want to know about the cooking procedures of the people. Invite them to mime some of the cooking procedures as a whole group. As an example, California Indians gathered acorns and the seeds of wild oats and other grains for food. The children can mime the actions of gathering grain as you read aloud the procedures:

1. Each person took a beater (paddle) and a carrying basket to beat the heads of grain over the basket.
2. The seeds were put into a wide flat basket.
3. Hot coals were dropped in the basket.
4. The basket was shaken hard so that the grain was toasted, not burned.
5. Then the seeds were put in stone bowls (mortars) and pounded with another stone (pestle).
6. The grain was ground until it became meal.
7. The meal was put into a tight cooking basket and water was poured over it.
8. Hot stones (lifted with two long sticks used like tongs) were dropped into the basket. The hot

stones made the water boil and cooked the meal into mush. The mush was stirred and cooled.

As an option, divide the children into small groups and give each group a basket, a stone, and two long sticks (branches). Encourage the children to take turns and practice a skill used in cooking by early Native Americans—using two long sticks (branches) like tongs to drop a stone into a basket (see item 8 in the preceding list).

Activity #21: "Tools and Utensils of Native Americans"

From an informational source, photocopy drawings of cooking baskets and other cooking utensils and tools related to the Native People in the children's state, and identify them for the children. Have the children cut out the drawings and paste small pieces of flannel or felt on the back of each cut-out drawing and place the drawings on a flannel or felt board. Ask a child to take the role of a member of the Indian tribe whose utensils are shown. The child says, "I belong to the _____ tribe. Bring me my _____ (wedge made from elk horn) and my _____ (adz made from shell)," and then names two things on the felt board. The child calls another child to bring the items from the board. After the child called selects the two items mentioned, that child becomes the one to ask that other items be brought. Children role-playing members of California tribes can name such objects as a carrying basket, beater, mortar, pestle, cooking basket, wooden paddle, acorn storehouse, hot stone, trap, net, spear, raft made of tules, bow, and arrow. Other Indian tools can include a thong, a digging stick, a hatchet and knife of stone, a wedge for splitting wood made from elk horn, an adz made from a shell fastened to a handle of bone or wood, a carrying bag, a net made of cord formed from fibers, as well as choppers and spear points made of black, glassy obsidian rock.

Activity #22: "Clothing of Native Americans"

Repeat Activity #21 on subsequent days with drawings of clothing of early people who lived in the children's state. For example, children role-playing members of California tribes can name articles of clothing such as a skirt made of soft deerskin (Hupa tribe), a bark skirt (Yokut tribe), and a cape of wildcat skins (Yana tribe).

Activity #23: "Water as a Resource of Native Americans"

The importance of water to Native People who live in a dry, arid region is explained in the myth *The Precious Gift: A Navaho Creation Myth* (Simon & Schuster, Grades 1–3) that is retold by Ellen Jackson. In the story, First Man sends out groups of animals to search for more water to drink. Beaver and Otter forget to search, and play instead, so First Man sends them to live in swampy lakes away from fresh, clear water. Frog finds a spring that is dirty and unfit for drinking and is sent to live where water is muddy and unclear. Snail is the creature who finds the fresh water—it leaks out of her flask as she crawls along—and First Man saves the last drop. He sings a water chant, creates a river, and rewards Snail a shell home to carry proudly. First Woman also gives Snail a silvery, wet trail that serves as a reminder of the precious value of water to all who see Snail.

After hearing this Native American story about the value of water, ask children to take the role of early Native water-searchers and divide into groups. Give them colored water (food dye) in paper cups. Group 1 receives green water, Group 2 red water, and so on. Ask each group to simulate being searchers who have found but never seen this type of water before and are concerned about drinking it. Would it be safe for other tribal members to drink? How would they know about its safety? Ask each group to make some decisions about drinking/not drinking the water, and to talk about what they would do—if anything—to determine the safety of the water. Back in the whole group, have a volunteer from each group report on the group's decisions (decision 1: don't drink it; decision 2: take a risk and drink it; decision 3: test it in some way; and so on.) Write each group's decision on the board and discuss each one and what consequences, if any, could happen if the water searchers acted on the decision.

Activity #24: "Salt as a Resource of Native Americans"

The Native American Tewa People tell a "How and Why" tale that mentions the early people's need for salt for cooking. The tale, which explains why butterflies flutter in zig-zag lines is retold in H. P. Taylor's *Coyote and the Laughing Butterflies* (Macmillan, 1995, Grades K–3). This is a legend about Coyote, who is sent several times to bring back salt for cooking. Instead, Coyote naps by the shore and the butterflies play a joke on him—they carry him home without the salt. To this day, but-

terflies cannot fly in a straight line because they are still laughing at the joke they played on Coyote.

After hearing the story, engage children in collecting salt, one of the resources of Native Americans, in a manner to simulate the way Native People who lived near sea water might have collected salt. Distribute one toothpick and one small paper cup to each child. Have the children, in turn, dip the toothpick in a shallow bowl of water (just as Native People drove willow sticks into a shallow sea pool on shore) and then into a bowl of salt (to see how salt collected on the sticks when the sea water slowly dried up). At the end of the school day when the salt is dry, have the children knock off the salt into the cups (just as Native People knocked off the salt into their baskets). Invite the children to take the paper cups and salt home with them to show a family member or friend and to tell them about the way some early people collected salt from sea water.

Activity #25: "Art of Native Americans"

Rock art of early Native Americans often emphasize hunting scenes. With an opaque projector, show the children some hunting scenes from *Stories on Stone: Rock Art: Images from the Ancient Ones* (Little, Brown, 1996, Grades 1–4) by Jennifer Owings Dewey. In the book, Dewey discusses her trips to see rock art and the meanings that some of the images have for her. Have the children divide into four groups to decide what could be said about the hunting scenes and to role-play being tribal members discussing the scenes. Have each group role play one of the following situations:

Group 1: *Point of view:* The rock art scenes are a *summary* of a hunt by tribal members. Tribal members are talking about the results of a recent hunt that they drew on the rocks.

Group 2: *Point of view:* The rock art scenes are a hunting *story* that is being told by older members to younger ones. Before they go on their first hunt, younger tribal members listen to older, wiser tribal members, who tell them the hunting tips that they sketched on the rocks.

Group 3: *Point of view:* The rock art scenes are a hunting *plan* that is being discussed by the tribal hunters before a real hunt. The tribal scouts have returned with information about what nearby wildlife can be hunted, and all of the hunters are talking about the best plan that they draw on the rocks.

Group 4: *Point of view:* The rock art scenes are the center of discussion among the hunters about an *untried hunting strategy.* On the rocks, they draw what they think they need to do to have a successful hunt.

Have the groups trade situations and repeat the activity so all of the children can have an opportunity to discuss the rock art from the four different points of view. Ask the children to show what their group did in sketches or drawings to represent rock art. As an option, have a recorder from each group write a description of what the group did. Have volunteers read the descriptions aloud to the whole group. Display the simulations of rock art drawing and the descriptions in the room.

Activity #26: "Lifestyles of Native Americans"

Provide information to assist children, in grade 3 and older, in becoming more knowledgeable about original Native Americans with an information video. Carefully select videos that can supplement the information in history texts and books, and allow the children to make additional inferences about Native People and their early way of life. The videos listed in Figure 3–2 are available and can provide views of early people and their daily activities, as well as become a forum for children to tell in what ways their ideas about Native Americans *changed* after viewing the material.

Activity #27: "What I Know/Learned"

Assess the current knowledge that children have about the Native Americans *before* they see a selected video, and have them write what they know on a Word Map similar to Word Map 1 shown in Figure 3–3.

Before showing the video, ask the children to take notes about any new information they learn from the video and to prepare for a postvideo discussion about any changes that occurred in their thoughts about the Native Americans as a result of seeing the video. Mention that they will hear new information and ask them to listen for facts about the Native Americans of prehistory who lived in the area thousands of years ago. Ask the children to watch the video. *After* the video, determine the following:

1. The number of items the children wrote on Word Map #1 that *were included* in the video
2. Other items in the video; items they wrote that were *not* in the video
3. Any questions the children *now have* after seeing the video
4. Any ideas in the video that *conflicted* with the ideas the children had about early Native Americans

After viewing the informational video, ask the children to use Word Map 2 and write additional facts they learned about early Native Americans living in their state from the video they saw. Have them record what they know/learned about the culture. Word Map 2 about the early people might look like Figure 3–4.

Native American Children

As one of their lessons, Native American children learned ways to find food from the teachings of the older members of the tribe. For instance, they were taught to recognize the plants that had roots or seeds good to eat. Have the children relate this to their own experiences, and suggest names of plants they know about that have roots and seeds that are good for food. Ask the children to tell how they learned about the benefits of roots and seeds. Write their remarks on the board.

Roots of Plants We Eat   *Seeds of Plants We Eat*
1.   1.

After the children suggest roots and seeds of plants they use for food today, ask them to tell ways that they think they are similar or different from early Native American children who searched for plants for food.

Activity #28: "Activities of Native American Children"

In addition to learning to find plants for food, early Native American children learned other lessons, some of which are shown in the following list. Have the children pantomime actions related to what Native children learned and have them tell how these lessons might have helped Native children in their lives. What purpose did these activities serve? Then, have the children pantomime actions to show what they do today to accomplish the same activity that Native American children did in the past.

FIGURE 3–2   **Videos of Early Native American Life**

PERSPECTIVES

View: 40,000 Years Ago in California   Archaeological findings put humans on Santa Rosa Island and in Calico Hills near Barstow, California, as far back as 40,000 years ago.

Video   Though no video is available yet, information is available in "The Search for the First Americans" in *National Geographic Magazine* (September 1979, p. 330).

View: 19,000 Years Ago in Ohio   Found in Meadowcroft in a rock shelter above Cross Creek, a tributary of the Ohio River, several archeological findings showed the Native People's hearths, stone tools, blades, and fire pits that are perhaps as old as 19,000 years. From the findings, it appeared the people hunted elk and caribou and collected nuts and berries.

Video   *American Indians: A Brief History* (National Geographic, 1985) emphasizes the cultural traditions of the ancestors of the Adena people and other Native Americans in Ohio. Grades 3–6.

View: 14,000 Years Ago in Western Pennsylvania and Colorado   About 14,000 years ago, people had an ancient society in the area now western Pennsylvania, and about 10,000 years ago, Paleo People lived in shelters made of poles and bison hides in northeastern Colorado in the Arikaree River valley. Archeological findings indicate that the people wore clothes made from hide stitched with sinew, with the fur turned inside; they made fires in the 40-below-zero cold and ate bison meat jerky or pemmican made with powdered jerky; using hammerstones, they broke up lumps of chert; with antler hammers, they made spearpoints from chert and wore deer-hide pads to protect their hands from sharp stone slivers; and they honed their spearpoints to the desired sharpness with antler flakers.

Video   *Mesa Verde* (Finley-Holiday, 1989) portrays the ancient and early history of Mesa Verde, Colorado, and shows the cliff dwellings, ancient pottery, and other artifacts of the people who lived there. Grades 3–6.

View: 13,000 Years Ago in Nevada   Some Paleo People, perhaps predecessors of the Shoshone, lived in a rock shelter in Monitor Valley in Nevada, now called Gatecliff. At Gatecliff, the people lived on pinon nuts, rice grass seeds, fish, birds, rabbits, and other small game. Findings from the site indicated they used flint, made tools, fashioned rabbit nets from plant fibers, and roasted pinon nuts over fires. Their rock art emphasizes hunting scenes.

Video   *Ancient Indian Cultures of Northern Arizona* (Finley-Holiday, 1985) portrays ancient civilizations of the Sinugua and the Anasazi as well as the national monuments of Montezuma Castle, Wupatki, Tuzigoot, Walnut Canyon, and Sunset Crater. Grades 3–6.

View: 12,000 Years Ago in Pacific Northwest   Native People held similar beliefs about the connectedness of living things.

Videos   *Landmarks of Westward Expansion: First Peoples* (AIT, 1987) shows that Native People of the Pacific Northwest had different lifestyles but held similar beliefs about the value of living things. Grades 3–6. *Starlore: Ancient American Sky Myths* (Pyramid Films/Museum of the American Indian, 1983) has legends of the Eskimos and others. Grades 3–6.

FIGURE 3–3   **Before the Video: Word Map I**

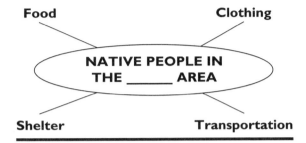

Word Map I

What I Know about the
Native People in the _____ Area

Food   Clothing

NATIVE PEOPLE IN
THE _____ AREA

Shelter   Transportation

FIGURE 3-4   **After the Video: Word Map 2**

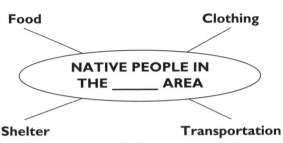

Word Map 2

What I Learned about the
Native People in the _____ Area

Food   Clothing

NATIVE PEOPLE IN
THE _____ AREA

Shelter   Transportation

Native American Children in Past

1. Gather wood (to keep the fire burning).
2. Grind acorns and seeds.
3. Recognize signs of animals in the woods.
4. Cut a tree (for canoes and shelter).
5. Practice shooting with a small bow and arrow.
6. Practice running.
7. Weave different types of basket shapes (acorn flour receiving basket, cooking basket, gift basket decorated with feathers, herb baskets, storage basket, and huge baskets for packing salmon and other fish).
8. Weave patterns of nature (i.e., bear claw, frog hand, morning star, rattle snake nose, swallow tail, etc.).

Today's Children

1. Turn up thermostat.

Activity #29: "Boundaries of Native American Children"

In Paul Goble's *The Friendly Wolf* (Bradbury, 1974, Grades 1–4), two small Native children wander about during a berry-picking expedition, become lost in the hills, and are protected by a wolf who leads them back to the tribe. The story focuses on what might happen to children who did not know the boundaries of their tribal land—the trees, rocks, and tops of hills were the landmarks. The older members of the tribe knew the boundaries and they took the children out and showed them the landmarks. The children had to say the landmarks over and over until they knew them. Sometimes, the children composed a song to help them remember the boundaries so that they would always hunt and gather food on land that belonged to them. Tell the children that they are going on a walking trip near the school to learn the boundaries of their school land, just as Native American children learned the boundaries of their tribal land. Lead the children outside and around the perimeter of the school land and have them suggest landmarks. Back in the classroom, have the children suggest new words for a familiar song that would help them remember the boundaries. (*Example:* A boundary song can be sung to the tune of "The Farmer in the Dell": *First verse:* "The boundaries of our land/ The boundaries of our land/ Hi, Ho, the derry-o/ The boundaries of our land. *Second verse:* One boundary is that tree/ One boundary is that tree/ Hi, Ho, the derry-o/ One boundary is that tree.")

As an option, encourage children to suggest different words for an accumulating verse about four boundaries—north, east, south, and west—to be said aloud, just as young children long ago might have done to recall their people's territory. (*Example: First verse:* Once a Native girl and boy/ Forgot how far to go/ So they said a boundary verse/ When walking fast and slow/ And the boundary mark—pine tree! pine tree!/ stayed right in their heads. [Add boundary marks to the last line in an accumulating manner.])

Activity #30: "Games of Native American Children"

Read excerpts about the recreational activities of the Wampanoag people from M. Sewall's *People of the Breaking Day* (Atheneum, 1990, Grades 2–4). The text portrays the Wampanoag people as proud industrious individuals in southeastern Massachusetts before the settlers arrived. After listening to the excerpts, invite children to take the role of Native American children playing one of the following games:

A Game of Dropping Sticks   Have the children divide into two teams to play a stick game similar to a Native American children's game of dropping sticks. Just as Native children did, have the children use a handful of flat sticks (substitute tongue depressors) that are white on one side and red on the other (affix sticker dots). The players sit on the ground facing each other. A hide (cloth) is between the two lines of players. Each side takes turns holding the bundle of sticks and then dropping them on the ground. White side up counts more points than red side up. The players keep the score with a row of 10 short sticks (use toothpicks) that are stuck in the ground for 10 markers. The side that gets the most points on each throw gets one of the markers. The object of the game is to get all the markers.

A Game of Guessing   Divide the children into two teams. Have the children use four pieces of white, smooth bone (use large buttons). Two of the bones are wrapped with grass (use string). Have 10 short sticks (toothpicks) available for 10 markers. The object is to win all 10 markers. One team selects two players who take the four bones and hold one in each hand. They sit beside a large hide on the ground. The other team selects one player who sits on the other side of the hide. The two players who have bones put their hands behind their backs. They pass the bones back and forth from one hand to another. Then they shut their hands and put them out in front. Now the player facing them has to guess, with one guess, which two hands hold the white bones tied with string. The players on the team who hold the bones sing to bring good luck. What good luck song do the children want to compose to sing along in the game? For example, different words can be written to the tune of "Row, Row, Row Your Boat": "Luck, luck, luck to you,/ As you look for bones/ Passing, passing, passing, passing,/ Whose hand still hides the bones?"

Native People's Government

Mention to the children that three ideas are basic to the understanding of the central organization—the government—of human societies. Write the ideas on an overhead transparency and project them on a screen and use a slide projector to show slides of your choice on a second screen that are scenes/examples of each idea. With each idea, point out to children the slides that show the related examples:

- The first idea is that all groups have ways of developing and keeping social order of some kind.
- The second idea is that the central order-maintaining organization—whether a king or a council—has great power over the lives of individuals subjected to it.
- The third idea is that all governments demand and expect a loyalty to them when they are threatened by hostile and opposing forces.

These three basic ideas about societies can be found in children's literature, and are often discovered in the talking animal tales where animals act like humans. With the children, point out the three basic ideas related to the government of societies after reading aloud any one of the following stories, and, if appropriate, show slides of scenes from the books that relate to the three ideas. Scenes for slides include the following:

1. The first idea that all societies have developed ways of establishing and maintaining social order is shown in *Why Mosquitoes Buzz in People's Ears* (Dial, 1775, all ages) retold by Verna Aardema. A sequence of events prevents the owl from waking the sun and bringing in a new day, and the social order of the animals is revealed with the way the people value a council when King Lion calls a meeting of the animal council to uncover the reason for the long night. After hearing of all the events, the king discovers the culprit—the mosquito.

2. In the same story, the second idea that the central order-maintaining organization in a society has great power over the lives of individuals subjected to it is shown when the mosquito attempts to hide from the King and the other animals by taking cover. To this day, the insect is aware of the power of the group and buzzes in the ears of those around it to say "Zeee! Is everyone still angry at me?"

3. The third idea that all systems demand and expect a loyalty whenever threatened by hostile oppos-

ing forces is shown in Verna Aardema's *Who's in Rabbit's House?* (Dial, 1987, Grades 1–3), a repetitive story that shows compassion for small creatures. When the animals suspect a hostile and threatening animal in rabbit's house, they join together and support one another in a system of interaction that demonstrates loyalty to one another as they group together for protection.

Activity #31: "Village Council"

Have the children role-play the government found in some Native American villages by asking them to divide into three groups called villages. Ask them to select a chief or leader in each group/village. Have them all play the role of members of the council of the village who talk things over with the chief and make the laws of the village. Ask each of the "village governments" to role-play one of the following situation(s), announce their decisions back to the whole group, and tell what they learned about government from the activity:

1. *Situation 1:* A member of the tribe has behaved badly and broken a village law. Have the council make a list of three laws for their village and identify which law the member has broken. Have the council decide what should be done to the lawbreaker after having a talk with the chief. Have the chief talk to the offender and tell what he or she ought to do to get along with others. Have the council members decide what the chief should say and what the consequence for breaking the law will be.

2. *Situation 2:* The chief and council are planning excursions to get food. The chief needs to know the best places to find food for the village. He wants to plan a rabbit drive, a grasshopper drive, and a hunting trip. Have the council members decide what needs to be done to prepare for this.

3. *Situation 3:* The chief and council have to make plans for a big celebration and dance. How many messengers should be sent to invite neighboring tribes and how far will they have to travel? What supplies should they take with them? What should they say to the invited tribes? In what ways can the chief and the council determine that there will be plenty of food for the visitors? Have the council members decide what needs to be done to prepare for the celebration.

Activity #32: "Government in Free Verse"

Write the word *government* on the board and ask the children what meaning(s) the word has for them.

Record their ideas on the board and discuss them. Show the children how they can transform information about the word *government* into poetry—they can write or paraphrase a line or two from an informational book, an encyclopedic definition, or a dictionary definition into an example of free verse for the classroom:

> In a democratic county
> like the United States,
> government is the means
> the people use
> to promote the welfare
> of the nation.

Ask the children to look for information about a government of a society of their choice, and transform their ideas about government into free verse so that their words look like a poem. Ask for volunteers to read their verses aloud to the group and to display the verses in a unique way. Ask for the children's suggestions. If appropriate, invite the children to write their verse in a poetry maze shaped after the meanderings of a nearby river, to disguise their free verse in their own original rock art sketches, to include their verse in their own original drawings of a Native American tale, or to write their free verse on tongue depressors or large button-shaped paper to represent game pieces used by Native American children when they played their games.

Early People of Orkney Islands, 4,000 B.C.

The Neolithic world of the Orkney Islands around 4,000 B.C. with all its customs and traditions is the background for O. Dunrea's informational book, *Skara Brae: The Story of a Prehistoric Village* (Holiday House, 1986, Grades 3–6.) These people were social and political; they developed a cultural life and followed religion practices in their village of hilly dunes. The excavation of a 4,000-year-old archaeological site documents these findings and others. Read aloud some excerpts from the book and have the children use their "minds' eyes" to imagine a happening in the village to create their own pictures after hearing Dunrea's historical evidence. Encourage the children to visualize the past in this prehistoric village by drawing a family event. Display the drawings and ask volunteers to tell about the family's activities to the whole group.

Activity #33: "Services"

With illustrations (such as those in Dunrea's *Skara Brae: The Story of a Prehistoric Village*), ask the children to look at the drawings of an early community and to tell what they can discover about it from the illustrations. To relate what they have discerned about the early communities, ask children, " What's wrong with this early community from your point of view?" "What services are missing that you think the people need?" and "How could the people have made their community a better place to live?" After discussion, engage the children in drawing pictures to show what a community service in an early community could have been like if people had acted differently and provided improved services. For further extension of this topic:

1. Engage the children in drawing a double-collage that contrasts an early community (collage #1) with the children's ideas of an ideal community (collage #2). Demonstrate how to make a simple double-collage by folding a large sheet of paper in half so the two collages are placed side by side.

2. Invite the children to write words about their artwork on the back of the collages.

3. Later, with the whole group, ask the children to display their double-collages and discuss the ideas for community improvement that are shown in their drawings and written on the back.

Early People of Near East, 4,000 B.C.

Introduce a hero of the people in the early civilizations in the Near East and India with the story of *Gilgamesh* (Knopf, 1984, Grade 3 up) by John Gardener and John Maier. This is a story of Gilgamesh, who is close to the gods—indeed, sometimes the gods intervene on his behalf. If needed as background for the children, mention that the legend was written 3,000 years before the birth of Christ. Ask the children who know the Greek myths about Hercules, Jason, and Theseus to listen to see if they can recognize any similarities in their stories and this one.

Activity #34: "Gilgamesh in Mesopotamia"

Gilgamesh rules over the city of Uruk in *Gilgamesh the King* (Tundra, 1993, Grades 3–6), a story retold by Ludmila Zeman that shows children the features of the artwork from the Sumerian, Assyrian, and Babylonian people in the illustrations. Discuss the scene where the people ask for relief from their oppression and the relief appears in the figure of Enkidu, a man from the wilderness. To divert Enkidu, Gilgamesh sends a temple woman, Shambat, to lure the man to the city. Enkidu returns with her and engages Gilgamesh in combat. It is after Enkidu saves the king's life that the two become best friends. Discuss with the children the rivalry between the two that turns into friendship in the story, and have them relate the action to experiences in their own lives or to the rivalries and friendships of book characters they know. Ask, "In what way(s) can you turn a rival into a friend? In your experience, when have you seen a rivalry become a friendship? What made it happen? What advice do you have for others who are interested in developing friendships?"

Activity #35: "Possessions in Mesopotamia"

Show illustrations of some of the possessions owned by children and adults in the two stories about Gilgamesh. Discuss what the objects could be used for by the people in that time period. Ask the children to dictate their ideas about why each child would or would not enjoy living in this community and owning some of the possessions. Write their dictation on charts as a language experience story to read back and then to read together. Ask the children to draw an illustration of the object they would have liked to have if they had lived during this period of time, and to tell others what it is, what it is used for, and *why* they selected it.

Early People of Ancient Egypt, 4,000 B.C.

Possessions valued by children and adults in ancient Egypt are seen on the pages of *ABC Egyptian Art from the Brooklyn Museum* (Abrams, 1988, all grades) by Florence Cassen Mayers—amulets, rings, necklaces, statues in the form of animals, paddle dolls—are seen in full-color illustrations. Ask the children, "What would you enjoy about playing with some of the items in ancient Egypt?" and have them dictate their thoughts explaining why each would or would not enjoy living in Ancient Egypt and playing with some of the items of the time period. Write their dictations on charts to read back and then to read together.

Activity #36: "Possessions in Egypt"

Ask the children to draw and cut out an illustration of the Ancient Egyptian possession they would like to have, and have them tell how they would have used it if they had lived during this time. Paste the illustrations on the chart and display them in the room. Show interested children how to use some of the designs from the eighteenth to the twentieth Egyptian dynasties to frame their drawings with *Egyptian Design Coloring Book* (Dover, 1980, all grades) by Ed Sibbett, Jr.

Activity #37: "Egypt in the Library"

Before a trip to the library, suggest to the children that they look for books about Egypt (or any topic in history) on *any* shelf in the library's collection. Encourage the children to search for books about Egypt *everywhere* in the library book collection. For example, using a chart of the Dewey decimal numbers on a transparency to discuss the system of classification, guide the children to poetry related to Egypt in Dewey's 800 classification; to books about art, music, and architecture of the times in the 700s; and to related technology in the 600s. To foster library research during a study about ancient Egypt, also show the children the 300s section in the library and the books about mummies and burial customs in Egypt and other cultures.

Activity #38: "Writing in Ancient Egypt"

Peter Der Manuelian, recipient of a doctorate in Egyptology from the University of Chicago, introduces children to hieroglyphics—the way ancient Egyptians transformed their spoken language into writing—in *Hieroglyphs from A to Z: A Rhyming Book with Ancient Egyptian Stencils for Kids* (Museum of Fine Arts, Boston, 1991, all grades). He shows children some of the signs from the Nile region by introducing single letters of the English alphabet from *A* to *Z* along with a colored hieroglyph that shows a picture of a word that begins with the letter—cat is on the *C* page, pyramid is on the *P* page, and so on. With the book, explain the idea of hieroglyphics (picture writing) by writing some on a transparency for the children to decipher, and ask volunteers to write words for others to read. Engage the children in additional activities such as the following:

- Show the children how to combine one hieroglyph with another to create new words. (Der Manuelian discusses this topic.)
- Encourage the children to use a stencil of hieroglyphs in *Hieroglyphs from A to Z: A Rhyming Book with Ancient Egyptian Stencils for Kids*

so they can write their own messages and make their own new words.

- Encourage the children to write brief stories of Ancient Egypt and end them with a favorite Egyptian closing: "Its beginning has come to its end, as it was found in writing," a phrase that means "the end."
- Help the children use the included key to decode one of the 10 messages in the book *Croco'Nile* (Farrar, 1995, grades K–3) by Roy Gerrard. Demonstrate and show children a way to use the stencil that is inserted and place it at an activity table/center.
- Discuss Stephane Rossini's easy-to-follow instructions in *Egyptian Hieroglyphics: How to Read and Write Them* (Dover, 1989, all grades) and encourage children to write their choice of words.

Activity #39: "From Ideas to Topics"

To further focus a discussion on life in ancient Egypt, elicit facts about what the children know about Egypt and then record their ideas in a list on the board or on an overhead transparency. For instance, the children might offer their ideas about pharaohs, pyramids, and the arts. Some may mention facts about jewelry, mummies, and picture writing, while others might talk about scientific achievements or the gods mentioned in Egyptian myths. Write the children's ideas on the board and demonstrate to them the way you can identify a topic by grouping their written ideas. For example, the children's offerings about wall paintings and statues can be grouped together in a list as you point out the related topic—art. With the children's help, identify and list as many topics as their ideas will allow. Use the overhead to enlarge an outline map of Egypt onto butcher paper on the wall and put location points for the topics on the map. As the study of Egypt continues, ask the children to write any information they have gathered related to the topics on the outline at the location points.

Activity #40: "Differences and Similarities"

Introduce a compare/contrast situation for children in grade 3 and older with, "Looking at the topics we listed, what are the differences and similarities between the topics in our country *now* and in Ancient Egypt?" As the children to make their suggestions, write the similarities and differences in a Venn diagram on the board:

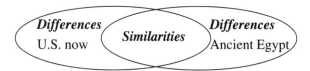

If appropriate, distribute History Master 2. It has a list of related topics and references and it can guide children in researching a topic of interest. Use it as a basis for a discussion about the differences and similarities between ancient Egypt and contemporary America and add to what children know about the topic.

CHAPTER FOUR

1200–500 B.C.

What was going on in 1200–500 B.C.?

Multicultural Perspectives

A perfect way for children to learn about the life of a particular citizen of this period is to walk, in appropriate clothing, as a citizen of Athens or castle times or China or Africa in the Kingdom of Kush. Invite the children to don appropriate clothing to participate in a living history banquet about the time period, 1200–500. This activity will be more enriching for children than looking in a history textbook, for it gives children an opportunity to do research, develop personal views, and see for themselves what life was like then. After all, very few children will remember the exact words in a text about the topic being studied. An activity such as preparing for a banquet sustains the children's interest in the topic and motivates them to read more and more about what went on in this time period. The children can learn what life was like in this period by preparing for banquets set in different locales:

• A banquet set in Africa can include kings, warriors, doctors, traders, and nomads, as well as citizens who lived in the port city of Carthage or in the ancient city of Meroe in the Kingdom of Kush. Have guests give themselves an African name related to an historical figure if they wish. Let verses and folktales from Africa be researched and read aloud to the audience. Listen to music performed by Africans. Have the children use patterns from clothing of different peoples to prepare banners and tissue-paper coverings for the room's windows. Additionally, invite the parents to come and join the children in the banquet. Encourage the parents to volunteer to bring food in keeping with the fes-

tivities. At the close of the activity, indicate that many of the children—both girls and boys—will be recognized by the African king they nominated for showing their outstanding participation in the study of Africa.

• A banquet set in China can begin as the children nominate an Empress and an Emperor of the Court, with all others serving as court members. Invite the children to be artisans, astronomers, generals, medicine people, and guards with swords. Have diners tell what they know about the "new" Chinese silk technology (c. 1000 B.C.) and the artisans who raise silk worms and weave beautiful silk fabrics. Encourage volunteers to talk about the law(s) against the export of silk, silkworms, and any knowledge about silk to other countries. Related to this, a Vienna University team of chemists recently found a few strands of silk in the hair of an Egyptian female mummy (1069–945 B.C.), which raised a question and a history mystery that the children can ponder: "If there was a prohibition on silk exports by China in this period, then how did silk threads reach Egypt in 945 B.C.?" Gifts from royalty to royalty? Smugglers? Ask the children to select folktales from China to read aloud to the audience. Also have them prepare banners, draw patterns from silk clothing, and design tissue-paper coverings for the room's windows. Additionally, invite the parents to come and join the children in the banquet. Encourage parents to volunteer to bring food in keeping with the festivities—tea, vegetables, rice. At the close of the activity, indicate that many of the children—both girls and boys—will be recognized by the Empress and Emperor for showing their outstanding participation in the study of China.

• A banquet for the Olmec people—ancestors of the Maya, Toltec, and Aztec—can serve appropriate food and be held in a room decorated as a beautiful plaza. It can begin as the children nominate a leader, with all others serving as political allies, writers of hieroglyphs, painters, and others. Invite the children to be craftspeople who make the cave paintings, mosaics, statues, jaguar masks, and special beads of ilmenite, a weighty lustrous ore. Some can be basalt and travertine workers, or makers of the latex rubber balls used in Olmec games. Encourage the children to read aloud nature poetry and folktales to the invited audience. Also have them sketch drawings of guests as Olmec ball players and design headdresses and chest ornaments for themselves and the guests. The children can make drawings of the jaguar, the tropical jungle's powerful predator revered by the Olmec; carvings of Olmec ball players on simulated stone slabs (gray art paper); and sketches on long sections of butcher paper of colossal carved heads of basalt. Additionally, invite the parents to join the children at the banquet. Encourage the parents to volunteer to bring food in keeping with the festivities—particularly shellfish and fish. Engage all in playing activities such as soccer and volley ball, and listen to flute music. At the close of the activity, indicate that the children will be recognized by the Olmec leader for showing their outstanding participation in the Olmec kingdom.

• A banquet set in the European Middle Ages can begin as the children nominate a Queen of the Court and her escort, with all others serving as lords, ladies, and other court members. Invite the children to be jesters, jugglers, sorcerers, and guards with swords. Let poetry and folktale readings and math problems of the time be read aloud to the audience. Have the children prepare banners, tapestries, and "stained glass" (tissue paper) scenes for the windows. If appropriate, invite the parents to come with period props (such as wearing a cloak) and have them join the children in a medieval banquet. Ask volunteer parents to bring straw to sprinkle on the floor and to bring food in keeping with the festivities—cakes, chicken, fruit, raw vegetables, and veal. Engage all in playing activities such as chess and spindle spinning, and listen to music reminiscent of the times. At the close of the activity, indicate that the children—both girls and boys—will be knighted by

the queen for showing their outstanding participation and academic achievement in the study of the kingdom. To guide interested children further, Figure 4–1 has additional books related to perspectives for this time period.

Ancient Greek Fables

Mention to the children that a fable is a special type of story—usually very brief—sometimes it has only a single episode and it teaches a lesson. Usually, the moral—a useful truth—is stated at the end of the story. The implication is that people can learn something helpful from a fable since people have these same characteristics and the ability to exercise control over them. Introduce some of the fables and the morals that have been told for centuries in *The Aesop for Children* (Checkerboard/Macmillan, 1984, Grades 2–3), a version illustrated by Milo Winter. Mention that some of the expressions that we use today, such as "Cry wolf," have their origin in the fables. Point out that sometimes Aesop said through the fables what could not be said directly in his time period, and read aloud some of the tales to listen for words that might be critical of the time period in *Aesop's Fables* (Viking, 1981, all grades), a version retold and illustrated by Heidi Holder. Another choice, *Aesop's Fables* (Holt, Rinehart and Winston, 1985, all grades) retold and illustrated by Michael Hague, has 13 fables with useful truths at the end of each.

Activity #41: "Good Choices"

Since a fable is designed to teach a lesson, ask the children to refer to the moral that is stated at the end of the tale and tell a partner what people can learn from the moral. Have them tell what they have learned from the fable about the ways that people control the choices/decisions they make in their daily lives.

After listening to a selected fable, ask the children to decide if the problem-solving method in the fable was an effective one from their point of view and if the fable character made the right choice. Suitable for younger children is the fable of "The Fox and the Crane" in *Show Animal Fables from Aesop* (Godine, 1991, Grades 2–3) by Barbara McClintock. This tale and others are illustrated in unusual scenes of an animal theater repertory company dressed in costumes. Other choices for this activity include the following:

FIGURE 4–1 **Children's Books for 1200–500 B.C.**

PERSPECTIVES

African Heritage

Araujo, F. P. *The Perfect Orange: A Tale from Ethiopia.* Ill. by Xiao Jun Li. Rayve, 1994. An orphan girl gives the King a perfect orange and accepts a donkey in return, not knowing its bags are full of jewels and gold. Folk literature. Grades K–3.

Bryan, A. *Turtle Knows Your Name.* Atheneum, 1989. This is a folktale from the West Indies about the importance of names to family members. Folk literature. Grades 1–4.

Cowen-Fletcher, J. *It Takes a Village.* Scholastic, 1994. This tale illustrates a West African proverb—"It takes a village to raise a child"—in a way similar to fables with morals. Yemi's mother asks her to care for her younger brother while they are at the market. When Yemi loses the toddler, she imagines terrible things happening to him. The boy is lovingly cared for by the villagers who see him—they give him food, drink, and play with him before he is put down to nap. Folk literature. Grades 1–2.

Jupo, F. *Atu, The Silent One.* Holiday House, 1967. This story depicts the life of Atu, an African boy, and the way his people might have lived years ago. Note that the term *bushmen* is used and should be discussed related to terms of respect today. Historical fiction. Grades 1–3.

Harris, N. *Everyday Life in Ancient Egypt.* Ill. by K. Maddison. Watts, 1995. This book provides an overview of the history of Egypt and topics such as clothing, food, education, shelter, and religion with full-color illustrations. Nonfiction. Grade 3 up.

Metropolitan Museum of Art. *The Giant Book of the Mummy.* New York, Metropolitan Museum, 1991. This 2-foot high book describes life in ancient Egypt circa 1,000 B.C. and the discovery of the tomb of Tutankhamen, the Boy King who ruled Egypt, and the treasure buried with him. Nonfiction. Grades 1–3.

Asian Heritage

Ishii, M. *The Tongue-Cut Sparrow.* Trans. by K. Paterson. Ill. by S. Akaba. Dutton, 1987. Different rewards are given to a kind husband and his selfish wife. Folk literature. Grades 2–4.

Jaffe, N. *Older Brother, Younger Brother: A Korean Folktale.* Ill. by W. Ma. Viking, 1995. A younger brother shows his character and cares for an injured baby sparrow who returns with a gift of wealth. Folk literature. Grades 1–3.

Mahy, M. *The Seven Chinese Brothers.* Scholastic, 1990. This folktale describes siblings with special abilities who outwit cruel authority. Folk literature. Grades K–3.

Mosel, A. *The Funny Little Woman.* Ill. by B. Lent. Dutton, 1972. A woman escapes from the wicked Oni and takes a magic cooking spoon. Folk literature. Grades 1–4.

Shute, L. *Momotaro, the Peach Boy: A Traditional Japanese Tale.* Lothrop, Lee & Shepard, 1986. Born in a peach, a small boy grows rapidly and challenges the evil *oni* who prey on his community. Folk literature. Grades K–3.

Wells, R. *The Farmer and the Poor God: A Folktale from Japan.* Ill. by Yoshi. Simon & Schuster, 1996. In old Japan, a farmer is impoverished by the Poor God who lives in his attic. When the farmer and his wife decide to run away to get rid of this unlucky curse, the god decides to follow and therefore weaves sandals for the journey. The couple stays and the sandals make the couple rich and happy. Folk literature. Grades K–6.

Yep. L. *Tiger Woman.* Ill. by R. Roth. BridgeWater, 1995. This is a picture book version of a folk song from Shantung about a greedy old woman who refuses to share her bean curd with a beggar who transforms her into a tiger and other animals each time she sees food. Folk literature. Grades K–4.

FIGURE 4–1   **Continued**

European Heritage

Crossley-Holland, K. *The Faber Book of Northern Legends*. Faber & Faber, 1983. This collection includes myths and legends from Germany, Iceland, and Norway. Folk literature. Grades 3–6.

Latino/Hispanic Heritage

Gaudiano, A. *Azteca: The Story of a Jaguar Warrior*. Roberts Rinehart/Denver Museum of Natural History, 1992. This is the story of an Aztec warrior and how his beliefs in the power of the jaguar influenced his life. Folk literature. Grade 3 up.

Kurtz, J. *Miro in the Kingdom of the Sun*. Ill. by D. Frampton. Houghton Mifflin, 1996. In this Incan folktale, Miro runs swiftly and understands the language of the birds. Her abilities help free her imprisoned brothers when she finds a magic lake and a cure for the ailing son of the Incan king. Folk literature. Grades K–4.

Mora, P. *The Race of Toad and Deer*. Ill. by M. Itzna Brooks. Orchard, 1995. In this Guatemalan tale, a deer (Venado) challenges a toad (Sapo) in a race similar to that of "The Tortoise and the Hare." Sapo gets help from his toad friends while jaguars, toucans, spider monkeys, and other animals watch. Spanish words are italicized. Folk literature. Grades Pre–1.

Middle East/Mediterranean Heritage

Aesop. *Aesop's Fables*. Ill. by M. Hague. Holt, Rinehart and Winston, 1985. This book includes 13 fables with useful truths. Folk literature. All grades.

Aesop. *Aesop's Fables*. Ill. by H. Holder. Viking, 1981. Aesop (620–560 B.C.) said through fables what could not be said directly, and some of the nine tales included here criticize the time period. Folk literature. All grades.

Bahous, S. *Sitti and the Cats*. Ill. by N. Malick. Roberts Rinehart, 1993. This is a Palestinian fairytale about the daily needs and harsh realities of village life that includes some magic. The tale tells how to behave to yourself, to others, to the village, and to the environment. Includes facts about language, culture, and geography of old Palestine. Folk literature. Grades 1–3.

Hort, L. *The Goatherd and the Shepherdess: A Tale from Ancient Greece*. Ill. by L. Bloom. Dial, 1995. In this Greek myth that portrays creatures existing in harmony, Chloe, the shepherdess, follows the cowherd Dorcon's dying advice to take his pipes and blow a cattle call to save her love, Daphnis, from kidnapping pirates. With the call, the cattle capsize the ship and bring Daphnis back to shore. Folk literature. Grades 2–4.

Hutton, W. *The Trojan Horse*. McElderry, 1991. Around 800 B.C., when Helen is abducted by Paris, the Greeks retaliate by fighting the Trojans for 10 years. Finally, Ulysses has a huge wooden horse built and hides soldiers inside it. He leaves the great animal outside the walls of Troy and the rest of the Greek navy and army pretend to sail away in their ships. The Trojans pull the horse inside the city walls, and in the night, Greek soldiers creep out of the horse, open the city gates, and let in the Greek forces, who burn the city. One of the several Trojans who escapes is Aeneas, the hero of Virgil's *Aenid*. Folk literature. Grades 2–5.

Pearson, A. *Everyday Life in Ancient Greece*. Ill. by E. Dovey. Watts, 1995. This book has an overview of clothing, food, housing, education, and religion of Greek citizens with full-color illustrations. Nonfiction. Grades 3–6.

Sutcliff, R. *Black Ships Before Troy: The Story of the Iliad*. Ill. by A. Lee. Delacorte, 1993. This is a retelling of the violent Trojan War from its origin, with drawings of authentic uniforms, weapons, and ships. Folk literature. Grade 3 up.

continued

FIGURE 4–1   **Continued**

Middle East/Mediterranean Heritage

Shepard, A. *The Gifts of Wali Dad: A Tale of India and Pakistan*. Ill. by D. San Souci. Atheneum, 1995. This is a retold tale of Wali Dad, a grass cutter who saves his money and buys a gold bracelet for the young queen of Khaistan. The queen sends him a gift in return, which he sends to the young king of Nekabad. The king sends a gift in return, which Wali sends to the queen. The extravagant gifts continue until Wali, with the help of peris (fairies), brings the two young rulers together. They marry and Wali returns to being a grass cutter. Folk literature. Grades 3–5.

Native American Heritage

Costable, E. D. *The Early People of Florida*. Ill. by author. Atheneum, 1992. This book details the life of the indigenous people of the area now Florida from prehistoric times to 1845. It discusses the arrival of the Spanish, French, and English, and the events that led to statehood. Nonfiction. Grade 2 up.

Stevens, J. *Old Bag of Bones: A Coyote Tale*. Holiday, 1996. This is a retelling of a Shoshoni tale about Old Coyote, aging and near death, who asks Buffalo for strength, youth, and power. Buffalo shares the first two qualities with Coyote in a unique way—they both hurl themselves off a butte. When they hit the ground, Buffalo gets up and Coyote, who has turned into a Buff-a-yote, gets up. Buff-a-yote pesters Old Rat, Lizard, and Rabbit until they hurl themselves off the butte, but when they hit the ground, everyone is the same except for Buff-a-yote, who did not get power from the Buffalo and has changed back into Old Coyote. Folk literature. Grades K–3.

Differently Abled Heritage

de Paola, T. *The Legend of the Indian Paintbrush*. Putnam's, 1988. Little Gopher cannot be like other children and so he records the people's achievements in his paintings. He is rewarded with magical paintbrushes that hold color, take root on a hillside, and bloom in bright colors. Folk literature. Grades K–2.

Female Image Heritage

Yep, Lawrence. *The Shell Woman and the King*. Dial, 1990. In China, a young girl outsmarts a selfish king. Folk literature. Grades K–3.

Religious Heritage

Eisler, C. *David's Songs: His Psalms and Their Story*. Ill. by J. Pinkney. Dial, 1992. Forty-two Psalms that have endured for over 2,000 years are from David, the young shepherd who becomes King of Istael, and record his joys and sorrows. Folk literature. All grades.

Kuskin, K. *A Great Miracle Happened There: A Chanukah Story*. HarperCollins, 1993. A mother tells her son about the celebration of the miracle of the oil that kept the eternal flame burning for eight days after the Rededication of the Temple of Jerusalem. Historical fiction. Grades 1–3.

MacGill-Callahan, S. *When Solomon Was King*. Ill. by S. T. Johnson. Dial, 1995. King Solomon (922 B.C.) is attacked by a lion while hunting and is saved by an older lioness whom Solomon had once restored to health in his youth. Folk literature. Grades 1–4.

Paris, A. *Jerusalem 3000: Kids Discover the City of Gold*. Pitspopany Press, 1995. Archaeological research supports this history of the city, including the conquering and occupation of it from 1300–1004 B.C. through subsequent rulers up to present times. Nonfiction. Grade 3 up.

Yolen, J. *O Jerusalem*. Ill. by J. Thompson. Scholastic. 1996. Poetic words express the history of Jerusalem related to three religions. Nonfiction. Grade 2 up.

• *Birds of a Feather: And Other Aesop's Fables* by Paxton (Morrow, 1993, Grades 1–3) is a collection of fables and morals told in verse.

• Eva Rice's *Once in a Wood: Ten Tales from Aesop* (Greenwillow, 1979, Grades 2–3) is a poetic text. Rice sums up the moral of the fable about the fox with, "You know at least a hundred tricks, but now you've learned something new. Even the fox can be outfoxed!"

• Attractive single versions of fables include Paul Galdone's *The Hare and the Tortoise* (McGraw-Hill, 1962, Grades 1–3), Janet Stevens's *Androcles and the Lion* (Holiday, 1989, Grades 1–3), and Paul Galdone's *The Monkey and the Crocodile* (Clarion, 1969, Grade 2 up), a fable from East India. *La Cigarra y la Hormiga* (Mexico: Libros del Rincon, 1989, Grades 1–3) by Beatriz Barnes is a translation of the fable about the ant and the grasshopper and is suitable for Spanish-reading children.

Ancient Greek Myths

Mention to the children that myths are ways people tell about the cycle of life—creation, life and its natural phenomena, and death. Some myths tell about how the world began; others explain natural phenomena; and still others advocate how members of a particular society should behave, or describe death and an afterlife. For the children interested in Western cultures, the most familiar mythology outside the Judaic-Christian tradition are the myths of ancient Greece and Rome. Indeed, it seems that children's daily lives are filled with references to the ancient Greeks and the heroes of that civilization. To show this, invite the children to add to the following list with their own references to the ancient Greeks: Achilles, Aires, Atlas, Herculon, January, Mercury, and Olympics. Write their suggestions on the board.

Activity #42: "Pandora's Myth, Daedalus's Myth"

Introduce a modern version of "Pandora's Box" with Rosemary Wells's book, *Max and Ruby's First Greek Myth: Pandora's Box* (Dial, 1993, Grades 1–3), and ask the children to think about what the sister and brother do in the story and to listen to find out how they get along. In the story, Ruby is annoyed with her younger brother's snooping, and to teach him a lesson, she reads her own version of the Greek myth. In the illustrations, Pandora looks like

Max and promises not to open her mother's jewelry box. Pandora/Max breaks her promise and sees insects and one green spider emerge. When the spider takes care of the insects and returns to the box, Pandora promises not to snoop again. However, in real life, Max is firm about what he wants to do and Ruby cannot get him to make the same promise. Invite the children to offer their responses to the following situation: "When a Greek storyteller told the story of "Pandora's Box," what lesson do *you* think was being taught to the audience?"

Ask the children to describe Ruby and Max's behavior and discuss how Ruby and Max got along. Have the children give their own reasons for what Ruby and Max did and encourage them to compare the two story characters with members of their own families or families they know. Repeat the activity with *Max and Ruby's Midas: Another Greek Myth* (Dial, 1995, Grades Pre–1) by Rosemary Wells. Max tries to sneak off with a plate of cupcakes, and Ruby uses the incident to read him a story of the young prince Midas who likes sweets and turns food dishes into sweet del;;ights (as well as anyone he happens to touch.) Thus, his family members are turned into life-size samples of Midas's favorite desserts—one even looks something like green (lime) gelatin.

The punishment for murder and treason is emphasized in the Greek myth of Daedalus's exile from ancient Greece and his journey to Crete, where he builds the labyrinth of the Minotaur in *Greek Myths* (Macmillan, 1993, Grade 3 up) by Geraldine McCaughrean. Reread with the children one of the picture book versions about Daedalus and his son, Icarus, who were imprisoned by Minos. To escape, Daedalus made large wings of feathers and wax, and on their flight, Icarus fell into the sea, while Daedalus flew on to Sicily. Ask the children to imagine they are the main character facing the problem of being captured by Minos and to dictate a brief letter to a mythical hero or heroine, god or goddess, of the time period to explain their feelings about the problem. They can tell the recipient what they want the recipient to do and tell what they will do if they do not have help in this situation.

Activity #43: "Problems"

With *Greek Myths* (Macmillan, 1993, Grade 3 up) by Geraldine McCaughrean, reread aloud the myth about proud Daedalus, a brilliant engineer, and Icarus, his beloved son. With the children, discuss what happens when Daedalus begins to think of himself as equal to the Greek gods and his pride angers them. Ask the following questions:

1. "What were your feelings about the myth? What was the problem faced by the characters?"
2. "What would life be like in the times shown in the illustrations?"
3. "If you were a child in Greece in this time period and heard the story, what would you learn from the story about how to live, what to believe, and how to behave?"
4. "What is there about the United States today, if anything, that relates directly to the Greek myths?"

Activity #44: "Greek Literary Chorus"

Introduce the Greek literary chorus from Jane Yolen's *Wings* (Harcourt Brace Jovanovich, 1991, Grades 3–6) as a dimension of historical study of this period, and read the story aloud. Project the Greek chorus shown by italicized words in the book on an opaque projector or write it on the board/ overhead transparency and ask the children to read it together. Point out to the children that in *Wings*, the author includes a Greek chorus that is shown by a commentary in italics in the text. Ask a child to research the topic of Greek Chorus and report back to the class to tell what was learned about this. For instance, a child might report that his or her independent inquiry uncovered that the tradition goes back to the Greek tragedies of fifth century B.C., when the final speech of the chorus would reveal the play's moral. Ask the children to suggest their own reasons why the final speech of the chorus would have been used. Ask," Why do you think the Greek people would want an audience/chorus to say a literary chorus? What would repeating a chorus do for the members of the audience? The storytellers?

Activity #45: "Sioux Literary Chorus"

Ask the children to participate in another literary story-chorus, one enjoyed by the Sioux people and found in Paul Goble's trickster stories, *Iktomi and the Berries* (Orchard, 1989, Grades 1–3) and *Iktomi and the Boulder* (Orchard, 1988, Grades 1–3). Ask the children to suggest what the Greek chorus and the Sioux story-chorus have in common, and what a literary chorus could tell them about the similarities of the people who used the two choruses for audience or chorus participation.

Encourage children in grade 3 and older to write a group chorus script to extend a tale such as Goble's

Iktomi and the Ducks (Orchard, 1990, Grades 1–3). This is a script that the children can prepare in class to perform for younger children as part of a Native American story. Write their suggestions for the script on the board. After the children write a brief original script, have them rehearse it and perform it for younger children. Here is an example:

Narrator 1: Iktomi, the trickster, was walking along.

All: Every story about Iktomi starts this way.

Narrator 2: Iktomi was walking along. He was looking for his horse to ride in the parade.

All: Iktomi is always looking for something.

Iktomi: I have my best clothes on today. I'll look magnificent on my horse!

All: Iktomi always thinks he is so great.

Ancient Stories to Solve

Point out to the children that problems and puzzles of all kinds in folktales have intrigued people in all parts of the world for as long as anyone can remember and that this is a feature that people around the world have in common. To demonstrate, read aloud some of the puzzle stories in *Standing on One Foot: Puzzle Stories and Wisdom Tales from the Jewish Tradition* (Holt, 1993, Grade 3 up, no author cited).

Activity #46: "A Folktale Problem"

After reading aloud a puzzle tale from *Standing on One Foot: Puzzle Stories and Wisdom Tales from the Jewish Tradition* and before revealing the outcome of the tale, pause and review the dilemma aloud with the group. Ask the children what they would do if they were in the same situation. Use stick-picture diagrams drawn with chalk on the board to illustrate a solution to the story's problem suggested by the children. Encourage them to meet with partners for a given length of time to suggest more than one way to solve the problem. Have them report their suggestions back to the whole group. Reveal the outcome of the tale and have children determine which of their suggestions were similar to the tale's ending.

Ancient Bible Stories as Literature

The Bible has an important place in history study, for the Bible is a written record of people's continuing search to understand themselves, others, the world around them and their creator. Interested children should be given an opportunity to gain knowledge about the traditional literature of the Bible—it is logical for children to read/hear not only the story of small Momotaro and the large Wicked Oni but also about David and Goliath. In keeping with this point of view, versions of biblical stories can be made available to children, when approved by a school district and agreed to by the teacher and the child's parent or guardian. Further, interested educators and parents usually agree with the ruling of the U.S. Supreme Court (1963) and its support of the study of the Bible as literature: "It certainly may be said that the Bible is worthy of study for its literary and historic qualities."

Activity #47: "Bible Heroes and Heroines"

For the children in the primary grades interested in reading Bible stories, several available picture books can be grouped into a category titled "Stories of Biblical Heroes and Heroines." These books can be made available for independent reading. Consider some of the following:

• *Stories of Noah* Warwick Hutton's *Stories of Noah and the Great Flood* (Atheneum, 1983, Grades 2–3) is an adaptation of the story from the King James version and *Noah and the Rainbow* (Crowell, 1972, Grades 2–3) by Max Bollinger is an retelling of the old story translated from the German language. *Noah's Ark* (Candlewick, 1993, Grades 1–2) by Lucy Cousins highlights God's words to Noah in bold handscripted letters over backgrounds of colors. Another version, *Noah's Ark* (Doubleday, 1977, all grades), by Peter Spier is a wordless picture book with humorous insights, such as slow-moving snails and turtles. The illustrations show how Noah prepared the ark and collected the animals.

• *Stories of Esther and Others* Barbara Cohen's *The Binding of Isaac* (Lothrop, 1978, Grades 2–3) tells the story of Abraham and his dilemma; and *I Am Joseph* (Lothrop, 1980, Grades 2–3), also by Cohen, relates what happened to Joseph, the boy who wore the coat of many colors who was sold as a slave into Egypt. The story of Moses (1400?–1200? B.C.) is retold in *A Basket in the Reeds* (Lerner, 1965, Grades 1–3) by Raphael Saporta, and the flight of Joshua and the people of Israel for the Promised

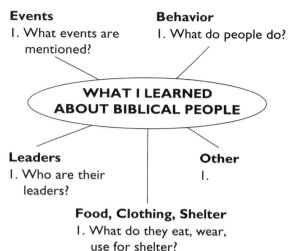

FIGURE 4–2 **What I Learned**

Events
1. What events are mentioned?

Behavior
1. What do people do?

WHAT I LEARNED ABOUT BIBLICAL PEOPLE

Leaders
1. Who are their leaders?

Other
1.

Food, Clothing, Shelter
1. What do they eat, wear, use for shelter?

Land (1400?–1200? B.C.) is presented in *Joshua and the Promised Land* (Clarion, 1982, Grades 2–3) by Miriam Chaikin. The confrontation between David and Goliath (c. 1000 B.C.) is told in *David He No Fear* (Crowell, 1971, Grades 2–3), and the story of the prodigal son is found in *Hongry Catch the Foolish Boy* (Crowell, 1973, Grades 2–3). Both are versions by Lorenz Graham who heard the stories in Liberia. *Esther* (Atheneum, 1980, Grades 2–3), by Lisl Weil, (c. 519–465 B.C.) tells the story of the beautiful heroine who tricks Haman and saves her people, an achievement honored in the feast of Purim.

• *Stories of Jonah* In *The Book of Jonah* (Doubleday, 1985, Grades 2–3), Peter Spier adapts the story of the Hebrew prophet (c. 700 B.C.) from a Dutch translation of the King James version, and in *Jonah and the Great Fish* (Atheneum, 1983, Grades 2–3), by Warwick Hutton, the familiar story is retold from Hebrew Scriptures.

If appropriate, ask independent readers to reflect about biblical heroes and heroines and to make a diagram titled What I Learned that is similar to Figure 4–2. Ask the reader to think of information he or she has learned about the biblical people and to write the facts under a related heading in the diagram.

CHAPTER FIVE

500–1 B.C.

What was going on in 500–1 B.C.?

Multicultural Perspectives

Studying this period, children can have the opportunity to move outside themselves through children's literature and to explore the lives and thoughts of different people. Such a study allows children to see faces and places they have never seen and to think about ideas they may not have reflected on before. Children can learn what life was like for people in Ancient Africa's civilizations, for the audience who listened to the messages in the *Jakata Tales* and the *Panchatrantra*, for artists in ancient Mexico, for citizens in ancient Rome, and for Native Americans who had a special relationship with living creatures. Colorful display boards in the class can feature the people's lifestyles on different continents and show the environments different families faced and the ways they traveled, as well as display colorful maps that identify the routes of trade merchants.

In this time period, there are opportunities to learn about the philosophers in Asia and the storytellers in Africa and Australia, as well as the building engineers in Asia, Central America, and Egypt. Related to the ancient people in the area now Mexico, scenes of Chichen Itza and Tulum with its temples, plazas, trades, and marketplaces can be displayed in the classroom from *Maya Dioramas to Cut and Assemble* (Dover, 1989) by M. Kalmenoff. Studying about Mexico's great City of the Gods can become a part of a larger thematic unit about Great Constructions through history.

Additionally, drawings of the people's possessions and related captions on the bulletin board can motivate children to inquire about what people needed to adjust to events in environment in this period. If children require recommendations for books to read, perspectives of the people for this time period, 500–1 B.C., are found in Figure 5–1.

Values, Circa 500 B.C.

To help make this time period come alive through books, guide the children, in small research groups, to different books to find and record quotes from their reading that support the acceptance of a selected value by people in different cultures and time periods. Have the children consider the question, "What did people in Africa (Asia, Europe, the Americas, Australia) say about unselfishness in their stories?" As an example, children can select unselfishness as a value to identify in stories from various people and read Marcia Brown's *The Blue Jackal* (Scribner, 1977, Grades 2–3). This is a fable from the *Jataka Tales* about unselfishness. The jackal, colored with indigo dye, is accepted as a ruler by the animals only until he reveals his true nature. Unselfishness is one of the values introduced to India around 500 B.C. by Siddhartha Guatama, the Buddha. Children will find that Guatama's life and teachings included other values that can also be identified in stories—compassion for the suffering of others, tolerance and nonviolence, as well as prohibition of lying, stealing, killing, finding fault with others, and gossiping. Later in India, Asoka, a great philosopher-king, unified almost all of the country and established Buddhism as the state religion. Doing this, Asoka renounced violence as a national policy. Engage the children in reading stories related to people of *this* time period and help them find similar values in stories told by people of vari-

FIGURE 5–1   Children's Books Related to 500–1 B.C.

PERSPECTIVES

African Heritage

Millard, A. *Ancient Egypt.* Ill. by A. McBridge and others. Warwick, 1979. This book gives an overview of Egyptian civilization from 3118 B.C. to 31 B.C. Nonfiction. Grades 3–6.

Stanley, D., & P. Vennema. *Cleopatra.* Ill. by D. Stanley. Morrow, 1994. This is a portrayal of Cleopatra (69–30 B.C.) as a brilliant and daring ruler. Includes notes, map, epilogue, pronunciation guide, and bibliography. Biography. Grades 3–6.

Stolz, M. *Zekmet, the Stone Carver: A Tale of Ancient Egypt.* Ill. by D. N. Lattimore. Harcourt Brace Jovanovich, 1988. Egyptian King Kharfe orders a monument and the vizier, Ho-tep, meets with Zekmet, a skilled stone carver, whose ideas result in the Great Sphinx. Contributions of the stone carver are portrayed. Historical fiction. Grade 3 up.

Asian Heritage

De Roin, N. *Jataka Tales: Fables from the Buddha.* Houghton Mifflin, 1975. Thirty fables from India teach moral lessons and include Buddha (563–483 B.C.) as a noble example. Folk literature. Grades 3–5.

Fisher, L. E. *The Great Wall of China.* Ill. by author. Macmillan, 1986. This history of the Great Wall gives facts about the political changes of the times and the magnitude of its construction. The Great Wall of China was built about 221–207 B.C. during the Ch'in Dynasty, from which the name China was taken. Nonfiction. All grades.

Tata, M. *Favorite Tales from the Panchatantra.* Ill. by H. Benton. Tata Pub., 1994. Here are three tales from the Eastern Indian *Panchatantra:* a rabbit who tricks a lion, a stork who tries to fool fish, and a blue jackal who tries to be king. Folk literature. Grades K–3.

European Heritage

Cohen, D. *Ancient Rome.* Ill. by H. Bond. Bantam, 1992. This book describes the Etruscans, the conflict with Carthage, and the famous general, Hannibal (247–183 B.C.). It recounts the emperors from Julius Caesar (100–44 B.C.) to Constantine the Great, the gladiator contests, the destruction of Pompeii, and the rise of the city-states and the arts. Nonfiction. Grades 3–5.

MacDonald, F. *A Roman Fort.* Peter Bedrick, 1993. This book shows the construction of a Roman fort and its use between 50 B.C.–A.D. 200. It includes drawings, diagrams, and cutaways of the inside and outside of the buildings as well as the living conditions of the soldiers and the weapons they used to defend the fort. Includes a glossary of English words derived from Latin. Nonfiction. Grades 3–6.

Latino/Hispanic Heritage

Glubok, S. *The Art of Ancient Mexico.* Harper, 1968. This book discusses achievements of the people prior to the arrival of the Spaniards in Mexico and includes photographs of jewelry, ornaments, religious objects, temples, and weapons of such pre-Columbian cultures as the Aztec, Mixtec, Toltec, Olmec, and Zapotec. Nonfiction. All grades.

Martinez, G., & J. Edwards. *The Mexican Americans.* Houghton Mifflin, 1973. This book discusses a history of pre-Columbian Mexico, those who explored the area, and what life was like in the Spanish Colonies as well as the mission period in California. It concludes with Mexico's independence, reform, and revolution. Nonfiction. Grades 3–6.

continued

FIGURE 5–1 **Continued**

Native American Heritage

Moroney, L. *The Boy Who Loved Bears: A Pawnee Tale*. Ill. by C. W. Chapmen. Children's Press, 1994. Set in the western Plains of the past, a man saves the life of a bear cub and names his son Little Bear because of the event. Little Bear develops a bond with the bears and when killed by tribal enemies, he is returned to life by the grizzlies and the sun and is given secrets of healing. Folk literature. Grades K–3.

Middle East/Mediterranean Heritage

Kuskin, K. *A Great Miracle Happened There: A Chanukah Story*. HarperCollins, 1993. A mother tells her son about the celebration of the miracle of the oil that kept the eternal flame burning for eight days after the Rededication of the Temple of Jerusalem (c. 165 B.C.). Historical fiction. Grades 1–3.

Lasky, K. *The Librarian Who Measured the Earth*. Ill. by K. Hawkes. Little, Brown, 1994. This is the life story of Eratosthenes of Cyrene, a librarian and geographer who estimated the circumference of the Earth around 200 B.C. He becomes famous for his scientific accomplishments, tutors the son of King Ptolemy III of Egypt, and was designated as the head of Alexandria's large library. Biography. Grades 2–5.

Female Image Heritage

Jiang, W. *La Heroina Hua Mulan/ The Legend of Mu Lan*. Ill. by author and Xing Gen. Monterey: Victory Press/ T. R. Books, 1992. Set in ancient China circa 400 B.C., Mu Lan disguises herself as a boy to fight for her country. Folk literature. Grades 2–3.

Lee, J. M. *The Song of Mu Lan*. Ill. by the author. Front Street, 1995. Set around 400 B.C., this Chinese poem is the story of courageous Mu Lan, who takes her ailing father's place in battle. She lives the life of a male soldier for 10 years and receives camels as final payment. When she returns home, she puts on women's clothing and convinces others that women can become skilled fighters. Folk literature. Grades K–5.

Religious Heritage

Hodges, M. *The Golden Deer*. Ill. by D. San Souci. Scribner's, 1992. This is one of the *Jataka Tales* that reflects Buddhist origins in which the king realizes that all living creatures should be protected. Folk literature. Grades 2–3.

Tata, M. *The Geese and the Tortoise and Other Stories*. Ill. by H. Benton. Tata, 1995. Here are three stories originally written in Sanskrit from the *Panchatantra:* "The Crows and the Snake" (theme of peace), "The Four Friends" (theme of friendship), and "The Geese and the Tortoise" (consequence of being vain). Folk literature. Grades 3–5.

Uchida, Y. *The Dancing Kettle*. Creative Arts Books, 1986. This is a collection of Japanese legends and myths that have stories related to Shinto principles. Folk literature. Grades 2–3.

Van de Wetering, J. *Little Owl: An Eightfold Buddhist Admonition*. Houghton Mifflin, 1978. Stories about animal characters introduce aspects of the Buddhist religion for children. Each of the eight chapters emphasizes one aspect, such as "Right Insight" or "Right Talking." Folk literature. Grades 2–3.

White, R. *A Precious Life*. Dharma Pub, 1989. These are versions of *Jataka Tales* that are similar to fables and reflect Buddhist teachings and beliefs. Folk literature. Grades 2–3.

ous cultures (see Figure 5–2), and if interested, in *other* time periods.

Activity #48: "Love and Self-Sacrifice"

The Buddhist culture and principles of love and self-sacrifice can be introduced with the story of *The Golden Goose King: A Tale Told by the Buddha* (Parvardigar Press, 1995, Grades 3–6) retold by Judith Ernst. Buddha tells the story of a queen who wants a pair of golden geese. When the Golden Goose King (the Buddha) is captured, his attendant stays with him, and the royal hunters realize they are in the presence of greatness. Both the queen and her king are impressed with Golden Goose King's wisdom to rule their kingdom righteously and win the hearts of their people. If appropriate, challenge the children to live one day at school according to the value of being unselfish (or one of the other values mentioned previously, such as showing compassion for the suffering of others; being tolerant and nonviolent; avoiding lying, stealing, finding fault with others, and gossiping.) At the end of the day, have the children meet in a group to self-evaluate and determine how they did when they behaved according to the value and to discuss what effect, if any, following the value had on their lives during the day. If other books that promote the values of early people are needed for read-alouds, consider the titles in Figure 5–2.

Activity #49: "Unselfishness, Compassion, and Nonviolence"

Since the time when Buddhism was established as the state religion in India, the values of unselfishness, compassion for suffering, and nonviolence have been accepted by various people in different cultures in different time periods, and several children's stories portray this. To broaden children' perspectives about these values, read aloud some of the tales from the Bhuddist monks in Cambodia that portray the teachings of Bhudda in *Cambodian Folk Tales from the Gatiloke* (Tuttle, 1987, Grades 3–7), a collection edited by Muriel Carrison, or read a companion book, *The Cat Who Went to Heaven* (Macmillan, 1930, Grades 3–6) by Elizabeth Coatsworth. It is a story that portrays the compassion for all creatures in the teachings of Buddhism. Have children browse in the library and select stories about compassion for others, unselfishness, and nonviolence (see Figure 5–2). Ask the children to report what they found after

---

FIGURE 5–2   **Children's Books about Values of Early People**

PERSPECTIVES

Brown, M. *Once a Mouse*. Ill. by author. Scribner's, 1961. A fable from India about pride and a mouse who wanted to be a larger animal. Folk literature. Grades 1–3.

Carew, J. *Children of the Sun*. Ill. by L. & D. Dillon. Little, Brown, 1980. To find the values they want to have in their lives, twin boys (called children of the sun) begin their quest. Folk literature. Grades 2–4.

Carew, J. *The Third Gift*. Ill. by L. & D. Dillon. Little, Brown, 1974. The Jubas value the gifts of beauty, imagination, and work. Folk literature. Grades 2–4.

De La Mare, Walter. *The Turnip*. Ill. by Kevin Hawkes. Godine, 1992. A generous man prospers and his greedy brother does not. Folk literature. Grades 1–3.

Guy, R. *Mother Crocodile*. Ill. by J. Steptoe. Delacorte, 1981. This is a West African folktale from Senegal that emphasizes the value of paying attention to the advice of your elders. Folk literature. Grades 2–4.

Meller, E. reteller. *The Value of Friends*. Ill. by the reteller. Dharma Pub., 1986. This is a Buddhist tale about friendship from the *Jataka Tales*. Folk literature. Grades 1–3.

Williams, J. *Everyone Knows What a Dragon Looks Like*. Macmillan, 1976. Some of the features of the story are similar to Taoist principles. Folk Literature. Grades 1–3.

reading the stories they selected, and invite them to tell *why* they think unselfishness and the other values have been respected by people in different cultures across time periods.

Ancient Greece, Circa 490 B.C.

Introduce the concept of panic by reading aloud two Greek myths—"Pan Shouts and Invents Panic" and "Pan at the Battle of Marathon" from Mordecai Gerstein's *Tales of Pan* (Harper & Row, 1986, all grades). This is a collection of tales about the Greek god Pan and his family and relatives. In the story about how Pan invented panic, Pan is napping one day when an ant sneezes. Pan jumps up and shouts the loudest most surprising shout ever heard in the land: "CAN'T YOU SEE I'M SLEEPING KEEP THE NOISE DOWN!" This shout startles every living thing: shepherds run in circles, and birds, butterflies, and bees bump into rabbits, foxes, and other animals, who get all tangled up in the vines, bushes, and trees. When the people and creatures all asked each other "What was that?" Pan said proudly, "I call it *panic*. I just invented it." Have the children imagine the scene of living things being startled by Pan's loud shout. What would be bad about it? What would be good about it?

Panic is also part of the myth about the Battle of Marathon circa 490 B.C. In Athens, Pan sees frightened people gathering and learns that they are at war with the Persians. The Persians have a bigger, stronger army and are ready to battle. To get help, the Greeks send their fastest runner, Phidippides, to Sparta to ask the Spartans for assistance, but they refuse to get involved. As Phidippides is returning to Athens, Pan tells the runner, "Build me a shrine in Athens and I'll help you beat the Persians." When Phidippides tells the Greek people what Pan wants, they build a shrine to Pan that morning and pile it high with honey, roast venison, and flowers. That afternoon, the battle begins in a field called Marathon but the sound of Persian swords beating back the shields of the Greeks is suddenly drowned out by a terrific shout that sounds like the beginning and the end of the world: GGGRRRRAAAOOOWWLLLRRROOOAAARRR! The Greeks know that it is Pan's loudest shout but the Persians turn pale and they turn and run away in every direction—they fall over each other in panic.

To connect the two stories about Pan to the children's experiences, ask the children to think of a time when they have helped others, as Pan did, and tell the group how they felt, or to think of a time when they thought they felt panicky. Further, ask them to mention times when people might feel panicky (i.e., firefighters might feel panicky when fighting an intense fire) and ways we use the word in our language today.

Activity #50: "I'm *Not* Panicky"

Show the children the following words on cards and ask them to tell which of the following feelings a person would experience if he or she were/were not panicky: afraid, brave, cheerful, disappointed, embarrassed, excited, frustrated, giggly, helpful, involved, joyful, kissable, loving, miserable, nervous, OK, proud, quiet, relaxed, silly, ticklish, unhappy, vain, worn-out, yucky, and zonked. Ask each child to transform one or more of the words into a dual-picture format and illustrate a figure showing his or her feelings in situations where the figure is panicky (picture 1) and is not panicky (picture 2).

Ancient Mexico

To direct the children's attention to an ancient culture of early Mexico in the 7,000-foot high plains of central Mexico, show the illustration of the Great Temple of Tenochtitlan in *The Aztecs* (Viking, 1993, Grades 3–6) by T. Woods. The name *Teotihunacan*, meaning City of the Gods, was given to the culture's pyramid and temple ruins by the Aztecs. Recent evidence indicates that the population was as large as Athens in this time period. The population covered an area as large as ancient Rome and developed from 100 B.C., thrived, and then suddenly died about 750 A.D. Reasons why a thriving culture might have suddenly died out are considered as mysteries by certain archaeologists. Elicit the children's ideas about why a civilization such as this might have died out (i.e., perhaps years of drought created lack of water for people and food crops).

Activity #51: "Sites in Early Mexico"

To locate the sites of these history mysteries, ask the children to locate the high plains in central Mexico on a map and to record what they can discover about the region of this early culture from the map's legends and symbols. Ask the children to search for reference material about early Mexico and then to browse, read, or scan pages before they make their predictions (hunches, guesses) about reasons why such a thriving culture might have suddenly died out. Have them report their predictions to the whole group and write their ideas on the board. Ask them to record the group's ideas to use as notes for further discussions.

Ancient Egypt

With the children, read aloud excerpts from *Cleopatra* (Morrow, 1994, Grades 3–6) by D. Stanley and P. Vennema. In this life story (69–30 B.C.), Cleopatra is shown as an astute and active ruler and politician. Mention that a biography of a person is more than simply the life story of that person. The author of the biography usually intends to say something else as he or she tells the life story, and thus, a biography can reflect different points of view for a reader. For example, a biography can do the following:

1. Give the story of a people and a social movement in history. (What was in Cleopatra's biography that told you something about the people in Egypt at this time?)
2. Reflect cultural evolution. (What did you hear in Cleopatra's biography that told you that the culture was/was not changing?)
3. Personalize a cause. (What was in Cleopatra's biography that told you she had/did not have a cause?)
4. Give meaning to faith. (What did you hear in Cleopatra's biography that told you something about her beliefs, her faith?)
5. Give body to an idea. (What was in Cleopatra's biography that told you something about a particular idea that she wanted/did not want to implement?)
6. Give motion to facts. (What did you hear in Cleopatra's biography that told you something *more* about facts you already knew?)
7. Mirror the personalities of great people in history. (In what ways could you call Cleopatra's biography a mirror? What did the mirror show you about Cleopatra?)
8. Reflect a way of life. (What was in Cleopatra's biography that told you something about the way of life in Cleopatra's time period?)

Activity #52: "Letter about Biographies"

With the children, carefully examine biographies about Cleopatra and other figures related to this time period and look for omissions, inaccuracies, or dialogue in a biography that is too "fictionalized." Instead of ignoring errors or inaccuracies or excusing too much "fiction" in the stories of people's lives, invite the children to write to publishers asking them to account for what is in the biographies—that seem to fail to measure up from the children's point of view.

CHAPTER SIX

A.D. 1–1399

What was going on from the first century through the fourteenth century?

Multicultural Perspectives

A study about this time period between the first and fourteenth centuries can offer possibilities of learning about different people from the Lion King of Mali in Africa, to Native Americans in their villages, to pirates to Saint Francis and Saint Valentine, from village families in Asia and castle families in Europe, to Latino/Hispanic heroes of legends and heroes and heroines of other cultures. For children interested in the perspectives in Figure 6–1, guide them to several of the books so they can read or listen and reflect on the way people in different cultures are portrayed for this time period.

Native American Families: A.D. 1–99

The early world of Native Americans provides a rich background for Stephen Trimble's *The Village of Blue Stone* (Macmillan, 1990, Grade 3 up). In Trimble's story, a fictionalized Anasazi village called the Village of Blue Stone is named after the turquoise stones found nearby. Trimble tells about the villagers, their clothing, and the customs and beliefs true to what could have happened based on the current research of artifacts and historical data. Further, the book details one year in the village and includes codes of behavior and the rituals of the people living there. The illustrations show the structure of the village, the work, and the way pottery is made. Additionally, the author's notes mention the scientific events that correlate with the fictional story and include a list of Native American ruins to visit in Arizona, Colorado, New Mexico, and Utah.

Charts, maps, a glossary, and index are included and are useful reference tools for the children's reflections as they think about the contributions made by the Blue Stone villagers long before contemporary times.

Activity #53: "Village Contributions"

Ask the children to imagine a family living in the Village of Blue Stone and to think of some contributions the family members could make that we might appreciate today. Have the children write their reflections:

1. The imagined family members are _____ .
2. One family member makes this contribution:

   _____ .
3. For this person, success is when _____ .
4. A time when the person is happiest is when

   _____ .
5. The person feels good when_____ .
6. This person reminds me of someone I know because_____ .

Inca Families: A.D. 100–199

Show the children two or three sketches or drawings of Pre-Inca or Inca families. See History Master 11 for suggested sources of illustrations. Have the children describe the pictures. Ask how they might know that the pictures are of families. Ask what families do. After each response, rephrase the answer in a sentence that begins with the word *families* and that generalizes the information. Have the children repeat the

FIGURE 6–1   **Children's Books about 1–1399 A.D.**

PERSPECTIVES

African Heritage

Aardema, V. *Anansi Finds a Fool: An Ashanti Tale*. Ill. by B. Waldman. Dial, 1993. Anansi, while trying to trick someone, is outtricked in this amusing tale. Folk literature. Grades K–3.

Wisniewski, D. *Sundiata: Lion King of Mali*. Clarion, 1992. This book relates the life of Sundiata (c. 1100), the founder of the Mali empire, as told by African storytellers. It begins when Sundiata overcomes being unable to speak or walk, describes his exile by a rival queen, and ends when he reclaims the throne of Mali as the Lion King, the rightful ruler. Biography. Grades 2–4.

Asian Heritage

Han, S. C. *The Rabbit's Escape*. Ill. by Y. Heo. Holt, 1995. The author states that this tale probably traveled to Korea from India along with Buddhism in the fourth century. It is a folktale about Rabbit's fast-talking escape from a turtle that intends to deliver him to the Dragon King of the East Sea. Folk literature. Grades K–3.

Ho, M., & S. Ros. *The Two Brothers*. Ill. by J. and Mou-Sen Tseng. Lothrop, Lee & Shepard, 1995. This is the story of Sem and Kem, two orphaned brothers from Cambodia. A wise abbot in a Cambodian monastery prophesies that Sem is destined for kingship and Kem for wealth. Folk literature. Grades K–4.

Leaf, M. *Eyes of the Dragon*. Ill. by E. Young. Lothrop, Lee & Shepard, 1987. A Chinese artist agrees to paint a dragon on the wall of a village, but the magistrate's insistence that he paint eyes on the dragon brings the dragon to life,, who then rises into the air in black clouds. Folk literature. Grades 1–5.

Uchida, Y. *The Wise Old Woman*. Ill. by M. Springett. McElderry, 1994. Set in medieval Japan, a cruel lord of a village decrees that the elderly at age 70 be abandoned in the mountains. A farmer hides his elderly mother to protect her. When the village is attacked by another invading lord, the farmer's mother gives her son the answers to defeat the invader. The cruel lord hears the man's confession about his mother, reverses his decree, and realizes that wisdom comes with age. Folk literature. Grades 2–4.

Latino/Hispanic Heritage

Joseph, L. *The Mermaid's Twin Sister: More Stories from Trinidad*. Ill. by D. Perrone. Clarion, 1994. Tantie, a storyteller, tells children magical stories of the island of Trinidad about people who became legends. Folk literature. Grades 2–3.

Native American Heritage

Arnold, C. *The Ancient Cliff Dwellers of Mesa Verde*. Ill. by R. Hewett. Clarion, 1992. This book describes the history of the Anasazi and their disappearance about 200 A.D. in area now southwestern Colorado, after they constructed dwellings and ceremonial chambers in the cliffs of Colorado's canyon walls. Nonfiction. Grades 3–6.

Baylor, B. *Moonsong*. Ill. by R. Himler. Scribner's, 1982. This is a tale from the Pima Indians of how coyote was born of the moon. Folk literature. All grades.

Bierhorst, J. *Doctor Coyote: Native American Aesop's Fables*. Ill. by W. Watson. Macmillan, 1987. This is a collection of brief fables that have traveled from Aesop to the Aztec people to New Mexico, a journey that has been researched. Grades 3–6.

FIGURE 6–1   Continued

Native American Heritage

Johnston, T. *The Tale of Rabbit and Coyote*. Ill. by T. de Paola. Putnam Group, 1994. This is a humorous "Why" tale from the Zapotec people where Rabbit outwits Coyote and explains why animals howl at the moon. Nonfiction. Grades 2–3.

Nashone. *Grandmother Stories of the Northwest*. Sierra Oaks Press, 1988. This collection includes stories showing ways Native Americans have left a mark of their heritage in the west. Folk literature. Grade 3 up.

Sage, J. *Coyote Makes Man*. Ill. by B. Techentrup. Simon & Schuster, 1995. This legend derives from the Crow people, one of the Great Plains nations. Coyote creates a creature that incorporates the best of all the animals' characteristics. Folk literature. Grades K–3.

Talashoema, H. *Coyote & Little Turtle: A Traditional Hopi Tale*. Trans. from Hopi by E. Sekaquaptewa & B. Pepper. When Little Turtle refuses to be bullied into singing for Coyote, he tricks Coyote into throwing him into the pond instead of other terrible fates. Folk literature. Grade K up.

Taylor, H. P. *Coyote Places the Stars*. Ill. by author. Bradbury Press, 1993. This is a Wasco Native American legend about how Coyote moved the stars around and formed the shapes of his animal friends. People see them today as the designs of the constellations. Folk literature. Grades 1–2.

Warren, S. *Cities in the Sand: The Ancient Cities of the Southwest*. Chronicle, 1992. This book presents life in the cliff dwellings of the Anasazi, the irrigation canals of the Hohokam, and the colorful pottery of the Mogollon. Includes index, glossary and maps. Nonfiction. Grades 3–7.

European Heritage

Carrick, C. *Whaling Days*. Ill. by D. Frampton. Clarion, 1993. This book depicts the development of whaling, beginning with twelfth-century Basque whalers through Native American hunters, and ending with modern whaling methods, as well as a plea for the preservation of whales. Nonfiction. Grades 3–6.

Gag, W. *Gone Is Gone*. Putnam, 1960. This is the story of Fritzl, who takes over Liesi's work. Folk literature. Grades 2–4.

Pushkin, A. *The Fisherman and the Goldfish*. Ill. by V. Konashevich. Trans. by P. Tempest. Moscow Progress Publishers, n.d. Children who are familiar with "The Fisherman and His Wife" can ascertain the similarities with this Russian version of the old man who asked a goldfish for favors. Folk literature. Grade 3 up.

Pushkin, A. *The Tale of the Dead Princess and the Seven Knights*. Ill. by V. Konashevich. Trans. by P. Tempest. Moscow Progress Publishers, n.d. Children who are familiar with "Snow White and the Seven Dwarfs" can ascertain the similarities with this Russian version of the Tsarita's jealousy over the Tsar's young, beautiful daughter. Folk literature. Grades 3 up.

Talbott, H. reteller. *King Arthur and the Round Table*. Ill. by the reteller. Morrow, 1995. During civil wars in Britain, Arthur asks Merlin to help unify the people. Later, he meets and marries Guinevere, and establishes the Round Table where he assembles the knights. Folk literature. Grades 2–4.

Differently Abled Heritage

de Angeli, M. *The Door in the Wall*. Ill. by author. Doubleday, 1949. In 13th-century England, with his parents away, Robin falls ill, is unable to move his legs, and is cared for by Brother Luke. With his strong spirit, Robin becomes a hero when he gets help for a castle under attack. Historical fiction. Grades 3–5.

FIGURE 6–1   Continued

Differently Abled Heritage

Hodges, M. *The Hero of Bremen*. Holiday, 1993. Hans, a cripple, sets out to acquire land needed by the town of Bremen because the town is growing. He is assisted by Roland, a legendary hero. Folk literature. Grades 1–5.

Female Image Heritage

San Souci, R. D. *Young Guinevere*. Ill. by J. Henterly. Doubleday, 1992. This is a life story account of Guinevere (c. 1100), a young girl who spends her days in the forest with her bow. When she wounds a shape-changing wolf-boy, she cares for him. In return, he helps her evade the siege of her father's castle, escape from a dragon-beast, and journey to King Arthur's court to request assistance. Arthur falls in love with her and the story ends with their marriage. Author's notes tell the rest of her story. Biography. Grades 3–5.

Religious Heritage

Davis, M. G. *The Truce of the Wolf: A Legend of St. Francis of Assisi*. In *Anthology of Children's Literature* by Edna Johnson et al. Houghton Mifflin, 1979. St. Francis of Assisi, Italy (c. 1100) makes peace between a hungry wolf and fearful villagers. Prayerful words attributed to the saint are included. Folk literature. All grades.

Fisher, L. E. *The Wailing Wall*. Ill. by the author. Macmillan, 1989. The author discusses the architectural features of the high wall in Jerusalem thought to contain stones from Solomon's temple, a site where Jews gathered before their Sabbath and Feast Days as early as the 700s. Nonfiction. Grade 3 up.

Fleetword, J. *While the Shepherds Watched*. Ill. by P. Melnucsuk. Lothrop, Lee & Shepard, 1992. Eight-year-old Matthias participates in a night filled with wonder as he sees the birth of a lamb, is visited by an angel, and visits a humble stable in Bethlehem. Nonfiction. Grades K–2.

Saabuda, R. *Saint Valentine*. Atheneum, 1992. Valentine, known as the priest of the Christians, becomes a legend after his service as a humble Roman physician whose patients include a jailer's blind daughter. Biography. Grades 1–4.

Topek, S. R. *Ten Good Rules*. Ill. by R. Schanzer. Kar-Ben, 1992. This book has tablet-shaped drawings that introduce the Ten Commandments and includes a miniature Moses, the shape of a child's hand to finger-count the rules, and colorful borders. Nonfiction. Grades Pre–1.

Wildsmith, B. *Saint Francis*. Eerdmans, 1996. The major events, including his love of birds and animals, in Saint Francis's life are told in a first-person text. Nonfiction. Grades Pre–3.

---

generalization aloud. (*Example:* "Families work (play, sing) together and _____ .") Write the generalizations on the board.

Activity #54: "Similarities to Inca Families"

Have the children discuss what they do in their families today (or what they know about) that is similar to what they can imagine families doing in the sketches. Write their responses on the board in two lists with the headings Families in the Past and Families Today. Ask the children to select one response about a family experience similar to one they saw in the illustrations of the Incas, and turn it into a Past/Present picture of families for a room display. Have the children tell the group about their pictures.

Asian Families: A.D. 200–299

Help young children recognize a theme in a folktale about siblings by stating the theme for them. Then ask them to find other stories that seem to have the same theme. For example, after you ask children to listen for ways that brothers help one another (to show the theme "You can win if you stick together"), read aloud the story of *The Five Chinese Brothers* (Coward-McCann, 1938, Grades 1–3) by Claire Huchet Bishop. To extend the story, ask the children to tell *why* they think the idea or theme of "sticking together to win" might have been an important idea for people in the culture in which the story originated. To relate this theme to their own experiences, have the children work with partners and look for a similar "brothers/sisters who stick together" theme in other stories. Read several of the stories aloud to the children. In a whole group arrangement, engage the children in brainstorming their responses to "What is there about the United States today that relates directly to this theme?" "Why would the idea of 'sticking together to win' be important to some people?"

Activity #55: "Sticking Together"

After listening to a story with a theme of "sticking together," engage the children in discussing the story further. For interested children, purchase two paperback copies of a favorite story with the theme and cut the pages apart. Paste the illustrations on construction paper and ask the children to review the theme by putting the pages in order on the chalk rail to show the sequence of the story. Encourage children to respond to, "What do we do (or have) today that shows this idea of sticking together?" Write their responses on the board.

Folk Hero of Early Irish Families: A.D. 300–399

Introduce the children to the idea that the children in Ireland probably were very aware of the life story and achievements of St. Patrick (A.D. 387–463). Help them understand the ways St. Patrick is recognized today by reading aloud *St. Patrick's Day* (Holiday, 1994, Grades K–2) by Gail Gibbons. Talk about the Celtic harps, leprechauns, shamrocks, and other symbols that are described in the book. Display illustrations of the symbols that help recognize St. Patrick today, and ask the children to dictate a description of how the shamrocks (leprechauns, harps) might *feel* (smooth, soft), and what the object reminds them of as they see it (shamrocks could be green stop signs for leprechauns). Write the children's descriptions on

the board. Engage the children in drawing pictures to illustrate any descriptions they want to select from the board. Display their work in different ways in the room—as mobiles, as a picture display made in a Rolodex™ style, as designs pasted on green balloons, and on boxes.

Activity #56: "Patrick, Patron Saint of Ireland"

At age 16, Patrick is kidnapped by pirates and spends years as a slave. After he escapes, he becomes a monk. A vision leads him to return to Ireland and become the country's first bishop. He establishes many churches and spreads Christianity during his work there. Read aloud these events and others in the Saint's story from Tomie de Paola's *Patrick: Patron Saint of Ireland* (Holiday, 1992, Grades Pre–3). As the children listen, ask them to sketch scenes that they imagine from hearing the text, and then have them arrange their scenes in chronological order on the chalkrail of the board to review Patrick's life story and his contributions to the people of Ireland. The children may respond to:

- "What is there about Ireland (United States) today, if anything, that relates directly to Saint Patrick?"
- "Saint Patrick of Ireland allegedly said, 'May the strength of God pilot me; the power of God preserve me today.' What meaning does this saying has for you? What examples of strength, power, and preserve do you know about from your experience?"
- "What is present today in the world that shows Saint Patrick's influence?"

Activity #57: "Special Symbols"

Suggest to the children that they can make and share certain symbols with one another to celebrate the day that recognizes St. Patrick. The symbol, cut from art paper, should be something that has a special meaning to the child. The symbol can be a cut-out of an object related to Ireland or to St. Patrick, or it can be a contemporary item—a child's favorite rock that reminds him or her of a rocky landscape, his or her favorite cookie in the shape of a shamrock, or his or her pet. Have the children place the cut-outs in a container such as a shoebox. Let them take turns with partners and describe their cut-outs of objects. The partner take three guesses as to what each symbol is that is special to the child who made them.

Families in Hamelin: A.D. 400–499

What family life in a European village was like for some people is depicted through Robert Browning's *The Pied Piper of Hamelin* (Derrydale Books, 1985, all grades). Show the illustrations on an opaque projector. With the children in a total group, ask them to identify the actions in the story and which value—generosity, independence, aggression, and so on—is shown by the action of the people from their points of view. The following are some examples of the values that are shown by the people's actions:

> *Generosity*   Hamelin town has a plague of rats, until a Pied Piper generously offers his music to rid the town of rats.
>
> *Aggression*   When the piper rids the town of rats and claims the offered reward of 1,000 gilders, the Mayor becomes verbally aggressive and offers him only 50.
>
> *Knowledge and Independence*   In return, the Piper knows he has the knowledge to play music no child can resist. He is independent and retributive in his thinking, so he plays his music and the children 'follow him to the open side of Koppelberg Hill, where they all disappear inside.

Activity #58: "Knowledge Helps Others"

Select *knowledge* as a value that people recognize, and ask the children to suggest a list of ways (situations) that tell how individuals can use knowledge to help other people. After the children develop the list, discuss each of the ways—and any consequences—that might happen if the ways were put into practice. What advice would the children give to someone in each situation? Engage the children in selecting three of the ways that they think are the most practical about using knowledge to help people, and ask them to tell their reasons for their choices. This activity can be repeated with the other values listed previously.

Activity #59: "Serfs, Nobles, and Strangers"

With the children, examine the role of the serfs and the noblemen in the feudal system of this period by reading Gloria Skurzynski's *What Happened in Hamelin* (Four Winds, 1979, Grade 3 up). In 1284, Geist, a baker's apprentice, is befriended by a flute-playing stranger, Gast. Gast convinces Geist to use tainted flour to bake treats for the town's children. Gast then eases their pain with his music and lures them away to be sold as serfs to a distant nobleman. After reading the story, engage the children in talking about the economy of the times, the need for labor, and this early version of today's contemporary warning often given to children by their parents and guardians—never talk to strangers.

Follow up the story with creative drama; decide who will play the part of the narrator, the baker's apprentice, the flute player, and so on. All of the children can engage in the drama and speak lines they select as a chorus. Choose simple props—perhaps a flute and a baker's apron—and have the other characters make face masks from paper plates. These can be held up as the character speaks. Paste the speaking parts on the back of the masks and have children read them aloud when it is their turn. Take the drama out of the classroom and down the hall by performing for other groups at school.

If appropriate, guide interested children to several examples of stories reflecting values of people in different time periods listed on History Master 3.

Other Families in Middle Ages: A.D. 500–599

For interested children, examine some people's beliefs about dragons and other enemies in this time period and read aloud *A Dragon in the Family* (Little, Brown, 1993, Grades 2–4), a time fantasy by Jackie French Koller. Darek, a young boy living in the Middle Ages, befriends a dragon, Zamor. Darek takes the creature to his village, knowing full well that the people have always fought fiercely against dragons. The people are suspicious of anyone who likes dragons, and thus, the presence of Zamor results in the arrest of Darek's father. He is blamed for allowing his son to keep the dragon—an enemy of the villagers. Darek and Zamor decide to rescue Darek's father. Have the children listen for words that show how suspicious the villagers were of Derek.

After hearing or reading the story, engage the children in writing a description of how the village people felt about their enemy—the dragon—and how Darek felt about his friend. Ask, "Would the actions of the villagers against Darek's father be allowed today? Why or why not? In what way would people in your neighborhood today be suspicious of you if you befriended an enemy? What could you do? Just as the villagers punished Darek's father, in what ways do people in the community today blame and punish parents for what their children do?"

Activity #60: "Feast"

With the children together as a group, show them details about the Middle Ages with Aliki's *A Medieval Feast* (Crowell, 1983, Grades 2–3). This is a book of illustrations that show the exotic foods that a medieval lord creates for the king and his company. Use the opaque projector to enlarge the pictures, and have the children imagine some of the simple things of life in this time period that they see in the illustrations. Ask the following:

1. "What will nighttime be like for you if there is no good artificial light in the lord's castle?"
2. "What will a winter day be like when there is no constant heat?"
3. "What will it be like to wear the clothes that people wore? What will the clothing feel like?"
4. "What will a wet and rainy day be like without the protection of rubber and vinyl rainwear?"
5. "What will you do to keep track of time without watches with minute hands?"

Have the children make a chart of the list of jobs people in this time period do in the illustrations. Have each child make a picture of a time when he or she did a job similar to a job listed on the chart.

Activity #61: "Combats"

While listening to *Life in the Middle Ages* (Nelson, 1967, Grades 2–3) by Jay Williams, ask the children to close their eyes and imagine some of the details of the scenes during the tournament combats in the Middle Ages. Have them elaborate on events such as:

1. In the Middle Ages, a fine lady is at the combats and she offers a prize of a swan-shaped diamond brooch to the man who is judged the most worthy of all.
2. At last, searchers locate the most worthy man at the combats—he is called William the Marshal and is found in a smithy.
3. William the Marshal kneels with his head on an anvil, and the smithy uses metal snips and pincers to cut William's combat helmet from his head.

4. William's helmet is so battered from the battles of the day that he cannot get it off without the smithy's help.

Have the children divide into small groups, and for each group, photocopy and cut out an illustration of a man in armor at a tournament combat in the Middle Ages (to represent William the Marshal). Cut the shape of the armored man apart. Give each child a piece of the illustration and ask the children to use rulers to enlarge the piece they have by drawing it on a larger sheet of paper. When the piece measures 1 inch, have the children enlarge it to 10 inches. Have the children cut out the enlarged pieces and then let each group assemble their pieces on the wall to make an enlarged picture of William ready for his next combat.

Cinderella in Many Families: A.D. 600–699

Have the children listen to several versions of *Cinderella* to determine which variation carries the most impact for them in the way the tale shows characters and events and information about the version's culture. For example, children can listen to a Chinese version of *Cinderella* entitled *Yeh-Shen: A Cinderella Story from China* (Philomel, 1982, all grades), a story translated by Ai-Ling Louie that dates back to the 600s and portrays China's culture around 618–907. The story describes the young girl, Yeh-shen, as a little orphan who grows to girlhood in her stepmother's home. She is bright and lovely with smooth ivory skin and dark eyes. She is treated badly by her stepmother, and when a festival approaches, she is left weeping at home while her stepmother and stepsister go off to the festival. The magical bones of a fish grant her wish for some beautiful clothes, and she receives a blue-feathered cape and golden slippers, one of which she loses at the festival. The lost slipper is presented to the king, who searches for the woman to whom the shoe belongs. He finally discovers Yeh-Shen as his true love. The stepmother and stepsister are sent to live in a cave home as punishment, but meet their fate in a shower of flying stones.

Activity #62: "Chinese Cinderella"

After *Yeh-Shen: A Cinderella Story from China* is read aloud, encourage the children to tell what they learned about the Chinese culture through this version. Write their suggestions on the board in a list. For example:

We Learned That:

People lived in families.	They celebrated with
People had clothiers and	festivals.
goldsmiths.	There were workers
Fish was valued by	who created capes
the people.	decorated with
Punishment was given	feathers and shoes
for evil deeds.	decorated with gold.

Reading aloud *Yeh Shen* or any of the other Cinderella variations, have the children listen for information about the places that are important to the cultural group in the story, for any special language or vocabulary they hear, and for the facts that tell details about the people in the tale—information about the people's belongings, family patterns, food, shelter, and tasks in the culture of the story. Elicit the information from the children and write their remarks on the board in three lists under the headings of Important Places, Special Language, and Details about People. Discuss what this information tells the children about the cultural group that told this story. To assist the children in locating additional versions of the Cinderella tale, distribute History Master 4 for the children's book search. The children can record the information they gain from a *Cinderella* story on a data sheet or chart entitled "Questions about Cinderella" (see Figure 6–2).

As an option to get information about the culture of the aboriginal tribes in the area of Younzhou, in what is now the Guangxi province, interested children can read *Wishbones* (Bradbury, 1993, Grades 1–3), a *Cinderella* story retold by Barbara Wilson, where the beautiful young Yeh Hsien has a pet fish as a counselor instead of a fairy godmother.

Activity #63: "Native American Cinderella"

Invite the children to get information about the Ojibwa culture through a version of *Cinderella* entitled *Sootface: An Ojibwa Cinderella Story* (Doubleday/Dell, 1994, Grades 1–3) by Robert D. San Souci. In this version, Sootface does not have a fairy godmother but relies on her own abilities to meet the challenge to see an invisible warrior. The warrior has said he will marry the woman who is kind enough of heart to see him. While others fail, Soot-

---

FIGURE 6–2 Questions about Cinderella

1. What are Yeh-Shen's (Turkey Girl) belongings?
2. What belongings did Yeh Shen use by herself? With others?
3. How are Yeh Shen's belongings used?
4. Which belongings do you think Yeh Shen will use most often? Least often?
5. What did you notice that was special about the belongings you wrote on this paper?
6. In what way did the sisters/stepsisters use their belongings alone or with others?
7. Are the sisters/stepsisters' belongings used to please themselves or others?
8. Which belongings helped Yeh Shen?
9. Which belongings in her shelter/ house do you think Yeh Shen could have done without?
10. Which belongings in her shelter/ house would have to be replaced often? Seldom?
11. What does this information tell you about this culture?

---

face's kindness is so great that it enables her to see the beauty of the rainbow the warrior carries, and the two are betrothed and married. After hearing the story, have the children get together in writing groups and write what they learned about the people who told this story. For example, the children can recognize that the Ojibwa people lived in families, had cookfires, honored mighty warriors, had skills to make bows and arrows, recognized beauty in rainbows, and valued kindness and coping with adversity. If the children prefer to sketch scenes of what they learned, have them form illustration groups and create pictures so they can "read" the illustrations aloud to others.

Repeat the activity with another version told by the Zuni people, *The Turkey Girl: A Zuni Cinderella Story* (Little, Brown, 1996, Grades K–3) retold by Penny Pollock and illustrated by Ed Young. In this story, a poor Zuni girl tends turkeys and wants to attend the Dance of the Sacred Bird. The turkeys outfit her in a white doeskin dress adorned with shells and give her a necklace and earrings of turquoise and bracelets of silver. She promises that she will return from the dance before the sun comes up, but is unable to keep her word. In a twist different from the *Cinderella* story most U.S. children know, the turkeys abandon her forever—an act that symbolizes the Zuni idea that when one breaks a trust with Mother Earth (and her creatures), one pays the price.

Activity #64: "French and Irish Cinderella"

Invite the children to read or browse through another version from another culture, perhaps Marcia Brown's *Cinderella* (Scribner's, 1954, Grades 1–3), the traditional story of Cinderella who goes to the ball to meet her prince, or *The Irish Cinderlad* (HarperCollins, 1996, Grades K–2), a tale retold by Shirley Climo and illustrated by Loretta Krupinski. The Irish cinderlad Becan, son of a traveling peddler, receives the tail of a magic bull hide that protects him from a giant and a dragon before he meets the one who loves him. After reading two versions of the tale, have the children tell the whole group which version satisfied them the most and *why* they selected the version they did. Ask the children to meet with partners and discuss some of the story events and tell what they learned about the people who told the stories in their cultures.

Activity #65: "Italian Cinderella"

Continue having the children compare different versions of *Cinderella* from many different heritages, and help them understand that all people have created such stories, that people's interest in telling such tales is universal, and that some details, characters, and events can vary in different societies and even in different time periods. To focus on a different time period, for example, introduce a Cinderella story with a modern setting, such as *Cinderella* (Green Tiger Press, 1993, Grade 3 up) by D. Delamare. Ask the children to listen for similarities between the Cinderella stories they know and Delamare's story set in a contemporary setting. Delamare's version is set in Venice, where Ella's father remarries and the traditional plot begins. Ella goes to the Grand Duke's Ball in a magnificent gondola, loses her slipper at the appropriate time, and is searched for by the Grand Duke. In the search, her glass slipper is shattered when a stepsister forces her oversize foot into it. To help the children compare this version with the traditional one, write on the board two headings: Sequence of Events for Traditional Cinderella and Sequence of Events for Modern Cinderella. Ask the children to dictate the events of the two stories. Record the events of the traditional story and the modern one and ask the children to compare the events in the two versions as being the same or different. Point

out any items that are the same, and guide the children to the idea that many people have had a need to create a Cinderella tale, even though some specific details vary according to the culture and the time period.

Possessions of Families: A.D. 700–799

Show the children some of the possessions owned and valued by the people in this period from *ABC: The Alef-Bet Book, The Israel Museum, Jerusalem* (Abrams, 1989, all grades) and *ABC Musical Instruments from the Metropolitan Museum of Art* (Abrams, 1988, all grades), both by Florence Cassen Mayers (or from other sources). For instance, select illustrations of a Peruvian flute (*quena*), an instrument used since pre-Columbian days, or some ancient beads of carnelian, glass, agate, and silver discovered in caves near Jerusalem.

Activity #66: "Suppose Statements"

Show children the illustrations and ask them to "suppose" something about the eighth-century item seen in the pictures that is related to their topic of study. For example, show the picture of the eighth-century Peruvian flute and ask children to make a "suppose" statement such as, "I suppose this flute is made out of wood." Have the children continue:

1. Ask the children to elaborate further on the first statement and make additional "suppose" statements such as, "Since the flute is made of wood, I suppose there were wood carvers" and "Since it is a musical flute, I suppose there were musicians who composed tunes for it and players who performed for others."
2. Ask the children to keep going and elaborate still further and make other "suppose" statements such as, "I suppose there were craftspeople who carved the flutes, and master carvers who taught carving, and teachers who taught people how to play the instrument."
3. List the children's "suppose" statements on the board to show them how many predictions they can make from observing a single item from this time period.
4. Repeat the activity with other items representative of this time period. Then ask the children to work with partners and look at additional illustrations as they make "suppose" statements to one another about the items they see.
5. Have each child select a favorite item, sketch it, and record all of the "suppose" statements

he or she can generate around the sketch. Have them share their work in small groups. Repeat the activity with other objects in *this* time period or with *other* time periods as the periods are studied.

Beliefs of Some Families:
A.D. 800–899

In this period, myth and symbolism were as real to the people as the happenings in their everyday lives. Some of the beliefs about creatures, flowers, herbs, knights, and maidens, are explained in *The Unicorn Alphabet* (Dial, 1989, all grades) by Marianna Mayer, who was motivated to write the book by the medieval Unicorn Tapestries. Ask the children to listen to some of the people's beliefs from this earlier time as you read parts of the book aloud. For example, this was a time when ground ivy was believed to ward off the plague, when elderberry root was used to cure the bite of a poisonous snake, and when hawthorn flowers were believed to ease a person's pain. Ask the children, "Would the solutions for plague, snake bite, and pain that the people used in this time period work today? Why or why not? What are your reasons for thinking this way?"

Activity #67: "Plants Used Long Ago"

Ways that flowers were used years ago are discussed in *A Wildflower Alphabet* (Morrow, 1984, all grades) by Elizabeth Cameron. As examples, elderberry was made into skin lotions; the heather plant in Scotland was used to build and thatch houses and to make beds and brooms; and yellow-flowered bedstraw was the added ingredient that curdled milk to make cheese. Have the children place adhesive-backed stickers on a large map of Great Britain and Scotland to represent some of the native flowers. Encourage the children to respond to, "What flowers or plants in the children's neighborhood are used by people today? In what way?" Write the children's ideas on the board in two lists with the headings Plants Used Today and How Plants Are Used. Ask the children to compare people's beliefs about flowers today with the beliefs of medieval times, and if appropriate, sketch a plant they would have used if they had lived in this time period:

Plants Used Today	*How Plants Are Used*
1.	1.

Riddles of Early Families:
A.D. 800–899

Mention to the children that some early families enjoyed riddles not only for the humor but also to show their inventiveness. Riddles from the people in Africa are in Aardema's *Ji-Nongo-Nongo Means Riddles* (Four Winds, 1978, Grade 2 up) and riddles in 20 different languages from Original Native Americans—including Aztec, Comanche, and Pawnee—are found in *Lightning Inside You: And Other Native American Riddles* (Lothrop, Lee & Shepard, 1992, all grades) by John Bierhorst. In keeping with the Native American tradition, Bierhorst's collection of riddles offers humor for interested readers. Project a riddle on an overhead transparency and divide the class into cooperative groups to talk together to solve the riddle. Additionally, invite each child to read and browse through these riddle books to select a riddle to ask others in the class. When someone answers the riddle, have the child state what the riddle tells him or her about the people who created the riddle.

Activity #68: "What Am I?"

Several riddles from the Aztecs and other early people are not as humorous as those of Native Americans. The riddles usually ask, "What am I?" and are found in *A Basket Full of White Eggs: Riddle-Poems* (Orchard, 1988, all grades) by Brian Swann. Ask some riddles from Swann's book and elicit answers from the children before you show the illustrations and give the answers in the book. When the riddle is answered, have the children tell what they think the people who invented the riddle had to be able to do to create the riddle. Here are some examples:

> *Aztec* "We enter by three doors. We exit by one." What is it? (a shirt). "I go through the valley slapping my palms together like the women in town who are making tortillas." What am I? (butterfly). Ask, "What do you think the people who invented these riddles did (or had to do) to create the two riddles?" (Have an ability to use similes such as referring to the openings of a shirt as doors; observing the similarities between the flapping wings of a butterfly and the slapping palms of women making tortillas.)

> *Maya* "Over a flat rock, a tomato's redness slowly spreads out." What am I? (rays of morning sun). Ask, "What do you think the people who invented this riddle had to know or do, to

create the riddle?" (Get up at sunrise and observe the spreading red rays of the morning sun.)

Ten'a of Alaska   "We are riding upstream in our red canoes. What are we?" (salmon swimming upstream). "Far off in the distance, something white is chasing a flash of red fire. What am I?" (fox's tail). Ask, "What do you think the people who invented these riddles did (or had to do) to create these two riddles?" (Have an interest in using similes such as calling the bodies of red salmon red canoes; observing fish and animals carefully.)

Tell the children that they will have an opportunity to invent a riddle, just as early people did, and ask them what they have observed in nature that would help them create a riddle. Have the children work with partners to create a riddle based on their observations. Have them write their riddles and make drawings that show the answers. Ask volunteers to tell their riddles aloud to the whole group and to show their drawings.

Trickster Stories of Early Families: A.D. 900–999

Raven: A Trickster Tale from the Pacific Northwest (Harcourt, 1993, all grades) by Gerald McDermott, is the story of Raven, the shape-shifter, who flies to the house of the Sky Chief to get light and warmth for people living in the gloomy cold. Mention to the children that every culture's collection of folktales has various adventures of trickster figures who are go-betweens for the sky-world and earth-world and represent the "You can win if you go it alone" theme. This is in contrast to the "You can win if you stick together" theme that is mentioned in a previous section. With the children, read aloud a tale about Raven or another solitary trickster and then select the tale's culture of origin to have children study in small groups as they read more stories about the culture's trickster who "did it alone." Ask the children to collect information from the story about a particular trickster that is from a culture other than their own. Ask them to give reasons why they think a particular culture developed tales about a particular "trickster" who "had to go it alone." Have the children discuss, "What do we have in the United States today that shows the influence of this ancient trickster idea?" (jokes, comedy, April Fool's Day).

Activity #69: "Native American Trickster"

Coyote: A Trickster Tale from the American Southwest (Harcourt Brace Jovanovich, 1994, Grades K–2), by Gerald McDermott, tells about the time when Coyote wants to fly like the crows. The crows give him feathers and tolerate him as he dances out of step and sings off key. He struggles in midair on a flight and because he has boasted and ordered the crows about, they remove his feathers one by one and he falls toward earth. Have the children discuss the following questions to introduce issues about when it is appropriate to trick and *not* trick others:

- "Suppose you were a trickster who _____ . What happens next?"
- "In this situation, do you think it was right to trick or not trick the others?"
- "What does the trickster story tell you about the people in the culture where the story originated?"

For more examples of events for role-play, invite the children to listen to or read some of the trickster tales in Figure 6–3. Encourage them to add to the list the titles of other books they find about tricksters.

Activity #70: "African Trickster"

Ask the children to gather together to hear several Anansi stories—the Spider man stories—just as some of the people in Africa might have done at the end of the day. Develop a mood for the story and set the background for storytelling by reading the preface from *A Story, A Story* by Gail E. Haley. Invite the children to read or hear other legends about Anansi and then discuss what the stories tell them about the people who told these stories.

After reading an Anansi story aloud, ask the children, "What stories do we tell that are similar to the Anansi stories? What other people do you know who tell stories like this, too?" List the children's suggestions on the board. To emphasize that people have things in common—including their stories—read aloud other stories from other cultures that have tricksters who are similar to the trickster Anansi. Discuss with the children their reasons why they think stories about a trickster would be favored by different groups of people. Ask them to decide if the trickster made the right choices in the stories they read. Take a class survey of their decisions and

FIGURE 6–3   Children's Books about Tricksters

PERSPECTIVES

Culture/Country	Trickster	Books
Africa	Hare	"The Two Swindlers" in *Bury My Bones But Keep My Words: African Tales for Retelling* (Holt, 1993, Grades 13) by T. Fairman
	Rabbit	*Zomo the Rabbit: A Trickster Tale from West Africa* (Harcourt, 1992, Grades 1–3) by G. McDermott
Burma	Animals	*Make Believe Tales: A Folk Tale from Burma* (Bedrick/Blackie, 1991, Grades 1–3) by J. Troughton
China	Monkey	*Stealing the Magic Fruit* (Beijing: Foreign Languages Press, all grades) adapted by L. Shufen
France	Animals	*Balarin's Goat* (Crown, 1972, Grades 1–3) by H. Berson
		Puss in Boots (Seabury, 1976, Grades 1–3) by P. Galdone
Hawaii	Human	*Mauai and the Sun: A Maori Tale.* (North-South, 1966, Grades 1–5) by G. Bishop
Jamaica	Spiderman	*Anansi the Spider Man, Jamaican Folk Tales* (Crowell, 1954, Grades 1–3) by P. M. Sherlock
Korea	Human	*Sir Whong and the Golden Pig* (Dial 1993, Grades 1–3) by O. S. Han and S. H. Plunkett
Original Native America	Coyote	*Coyote Stories for Children* (Beyond Words, 1991, Grades 2–3) by S. Straus
		Ma'ii and Cousin Horned Toad: A Traditional Navajo Story (Scholastic, 1992, 1–2) by S. Begay
	Raven	*Trickster Tales from Prairie Lodgefires* (Abingdon, 1979, Grades 2–3) by B. G. Anderson
Other Cultures/ Countries		Other titles to be added by children.

write the results on the board. Have the children give their reasons why they think the trickster made the right (wrong) choice.

Viking Families: A.D. 1000–1099

The voyage of Leif Ericson can be made meaningful to children through the story of a young Viking girl,

Sigrid, in *Leif's Saga: A Viking Tale* (Simon & Schuster, 1996, Grades 3–5) by Jonathan Hunt. Sigrid's father tells her the long-ago story of Leif Erikkson/Ericsson, his childhood in Greenland, and his voyages around 1000 A.D. to Vinland (thought to be early America.) After hearing the story, have the children locate an early Viking settlement called Jorvik, near the area now York, England, an area they can find on a world map. Ask them to get information from the map's legend and symbols and determine the geographical features of Jorvik and the nearby area. Discuss, "What features would be reasons why the Vikings would settle there?" If the uses of symbols and meanings of map legends need to be reviewed with the children, read aloud *The Whole World in Your Hands: Looking at Maps* (Ideals, 1992, Grades 1–3) by M. and G. Berger, and with the children, develop an understanding of the different types of maps and how maps help people.

Activity #71: "Viking Information Lost and Found"

Show the children what life was like for Viking adventurers as they traded and raided. Project overhead transparencies of more than 30 scenes of Viking explorations, raids, ship construction, art, literature, and weapons from *Story of the Vikings Coloring Book* (Dover, 1989) by A. G. Smith. Show how the Vikings farmed, fished, and prepared meals with *Food & Feasts with the Vikings* (Silver Burdett, 1995, Grade 3 up) by Hazel Mary Martell. Have the children collect information about the Vikings with a Viking Information Lost and Found display board, where they can post requests for the information they need about Vikings as a topic of study or post notices about any information they have found that could help others. To keep the information flowing to and from the board, ask different children to be responsible for the board on different days. Each day, it can be a child's responsibility to add at least one unanswered question to the board.

Africa's Lion King: A.D. 1100–1299

Set against a background of twelfth-century Africa, *Sundiata: Lion King of Mali* (Clarion, 1992, Grades 2–4) by David Wisniewski, describes in words and pictures the dramatic life story of Sundiata (c. 1100), a boy who overcomes his early inability to speak or walk. Heir to the Mali throne, he is exiled by a rival queen, but he perseveres and returns to Mali to claim his heritage as the rightful Lion King.

Have the children respond to, "What characteristics does the lion have that would make an African king, such as Sundiata, choose to be known as the Lion King of Mali?" Engage the children in further research to find similarities and differences between Sundiata and the Mali people and other groups and their kings in the early African kingdoms. Have the children report back and write their findings on the board in two lists:

The Lion King	*Other African Kings*
1.	1.

Activity #72: "Animal Symbol for a King"

Write the word *lion* on a large piece of butcher paper taped to the chalkboard. Ask the children what they know about lions or what comes to mind when they see or hear the word. Write their contributions on the paper. Then have the children search for facts about the lion, its characteristics, and its habitat. Invite them to add their information to the paper.

Ask interested children to conduct inquiries about the animals chosen by other kings of Africa to represent them, and the animals's characteristics and habitats. Write their findings on another paper. Help children understand that diversity among people is natural—such as choosing different animals to represent one's role as a king—yet they still will have many things in common with others.

Heroes and Heroines: A.D. 1200–1299

Mention to children that young people in the Middle Ages found their favorite stories in the available adult literature, oral and written. Thus, some children in the British Isles may have listened to the stories of Robin Hood and other local legends about real or mythical heroes. To revisit this time period for the children, introduce them to the legend of Robin Hood (c. late 1300s) with *The Adventures of Robin Hood* (Candlewick, 1995, Grades 3–5) retold by Marcia Williams. This edition has Robin's adventures, cartoon-style illustrations, plenty of dialogue and humorous asides. In contrast to this humor, point out to the children that the Middle Ages in Europe was a very religious period, and that children probably heard many biblical tales as well as the stories of the lives of saints (see Activity #47).

Activity #73: "Hero of Bremen"

Heroes and heroines come in all shapes, sizes, and abilities. Hans Cobbler, the crippled hero in *The Hero of Bremen* (Holiday, 1993, Grades 1–5) written by Margaret Hodges, represents the differently abled. In the story, the citizens of Bremen need the land owned by a countess living nearby because their town is growing. Her hard-hearted nephew agrees that the citizens can have all the land a man can walk around in one day from town gate to town gate, and the man he chooses to do this is Hans, a cripple. Hans sets out bravely to journey through the forest and when he believes he has failed the town, Roland, a legendary hero, appears and stops the sun until Hans has traveled the distance and obtained the property for the town.

Encourage the children to talk about what the words *hero* and *heroine* mean to them, and what they think it takes for a person like Hans to be known as "heroic." Invite them to suggest some of their heroines and heroes and what makes them "heroic" to the children. Write the suggested names on the board. Additionally, have the children discuss any accents in dialects they hear in this story (and others) about heroes and heroines that are read aloud. Then locate on a world map the countries from which the stories come. Around the edge of the map, have the children place index cards with the titles of the stories, and with yarn and pins, connect the index cards to the appropriate geographical origins on the map. Some of the stories that the children might be interested in reading are listed on History Master 5.

Activity #74: "Ali Baba and Aladdin"

Ask the children to discuss the pros and cons of accepting someone else's treasure as their own and tell what message *they* think is being sent through the stories of *Ali Baba and the Forty Thieves* (Abrams, 1989, Grades 2–3) by Margaret Early and *Aladdin and the Enchanted Lamp* (Macmillan, 1985, Grades 2–3) by Marianna Mayer. Ali gets into the treasure cave of the thieves by using their magic password, "Open Sesame." His life is saved by Morgianna, a slave who pours boiling oil into the jars where the thieves have hidden. Aladdin, the son of a poor tailor, is hired by a wicked magician to go into an underground cave to get a magic ring and lamp. Aladdin rubs the lamp and discovers a powerful spirit, a genie, who appears and does what he is ordered to do. These are stories whose origins relate to the Mediterranean area, a region that can be emphasized with a display on the bulletin board. Have the children begin a bulletin board for news events from the Middle East and connect the discussion of any news events by finding the locations of the events on a world map. Invite the children to decorate the board with a boarder of titles of stories whose origins are from the Middle East and to add to it as they find and read additional stories.

Castle Families and Travelers: A.D. 1300–1399

Select several illustrations from the books on History Master 6 that show activities in a castle and ask the children to suggest the different members of a family that might live there. Ask the children to think about what a family might do in the illustrations and to imagine how the family members got along living together in a castle. Encourage the children to describe how different family members might act in the different pictures they see. Ask the children to create a group story about a family living in a castle and record it on chart paper. Invite the children to respond to the following:

- Who should we include in this castle story?
- What might happen?
- Where in the castle will the story take place?
- When should the story happen and to whom?
- Why do you think these things happen?
- How should the castle story end?

Activity #75: "Eleanor and Thomas: 1300s"

In *The Ramsay Scallop* (Orchard, 1994, Grade 3 up), Frances Temple tells the story of Eleanor of Ramsay, a girl reluctant to wed her fiance. It is the 1300s and her betrothed, Thomas of Thornham, has returned from the Crusades. The two take the advice of Father Gregory and journey on a pilgrimage to Spain to get better acquainted. They get involved in several medieval era adventures, and at the story's closing, they accept one another.

Put the words *The Ramsay Scallop* on a large piece of mural paper taped to the chalkboard and ask the children what comes to mind about daily life in this time period after reading or hearing the story. Write the children's contributions on the paper. Elicit information about daily life in the 1300s, any mention of folklore, the type of music people heard, architecture, glassblowing and other crafts, as well as the beliefs of Moslems and other religious groups of the times. Leave the paper up so the children can add information as they study the 1300s.

Activity #76: "What Travelers Saw"

Select Mitusmasa Anno's *Anno's Medieval World* (Philomel, 1980, all grades) to present scenes of this period to children. Use an opaque projector to show the blue clad traveler as the main character in

FIGURE 6–4   **Children's Wordless Books**

PERSPECTIVES

Anno, M. *Anno's Britain*. Ill. by author. Philomel, 1982. A traveler, clothed in blue, tours the British Isles in detailed scenes that show period costumes, anachronistic objects, and fictional characters. There are scenes from *Romeo and Juliet* and from paintings by John Constable and Jean Millet. Historical monuments, thatched roof cottages, St. Paul's, Stonehenge, Big Ben, and other historical moments are seen.

Anno, M. *Anno's Flea Market*. Ill. by author. Philomel, 1984. This book shows an early way of living that begins on a Saturday morning in the town square, where an elderly couple with a filled cart arrive at the massive city walls to go inside to the outdoor market to set up their wares. As more and more tradespeople arrive, the market becomes more and more crowded. Gradually, the spaces on the page and inside the town fill up with a collection of objects from around the world and from different periods of history.

Anno, M. *Anno's Italy*. Ill. by author. Collins, 1980. This wordless book starts with scenes of Adam and Eve cast from Eden, the travels of Mary and Joseph, the birth and death of Christ, and then shows later time periods and the cities of Rome, Florence, and Venice as they become more populated.

Anno, M. *Anno's Journey*. Ill. by author. Philomel, 1978. This book has detailed scenes with hidden pictures that show folktales and stories (plots) during a journeyman's travels through northern Europe and that give rich impressions of the land, the people, and their heritage.

Goodall, J. S. *The Story of a Farm*. Ill. by author. Macmillan, 1989. This book shows an English farm from its beginnings in the Middle Ages to the present.

Goodall, J. S. *The Story of a Castle*. Ill. by author. McEldererry/Macmillan, 1986. The illustrations in this book begin in 1170 A.D. when Normans built a castle for protection and end in the 1970s when the castle is opened as a public attraction.

Goodall, J. S. *The Story of a Main Street*. Ill. by author. Macmillan, 1987. This story moves through several time periods—from Elizabethan, Restoration, and Georgian, to Regency, Victorian, and Edwardian—and shows the changes caused by commerce and trade that begins with some local trading at a stone market cross in a path (a "main street" in the Middle Ages) and ends with bustling shops on an Edwardian main street at Christmas time.

Goodall, J. S. *The Story of an English Village*. Ill. by author. Atheneum, 1979. This story shows six centuries of history, in changing landscape scenes, from pastoral settings in the fourteenth century to urban congestion in the twentieth.

the book. Mention to the children that the traveler represents "every person" and he challenges them to think about ways that ideas in society can grow and change. Discuss the scenes and ask the children to think about the people they see in the illustrations and about any hardships the people might have endured as they lived their daily lives. Following are some topics to generate class discussions:

- How many examples of new ideas can the children find as you project the illustrations?

- What examples are happening in the United States today that illustrate these same ideas?
- What is seen in the United States today that shows Americans value certain ideas and beliefs?

Activity #77: "History through Wordless Books"

Select a wordless book (see Figure 6–4) and, using an opaque projector, project the illustrations that focus on this time period. Engage the children in doing one or more of the following:

1. Use the book's illustrations to prepare a word web about this time period of history that is shown in the pictures.
2. Use the book's illustrations to write brief summary paragraphs about this time period.
3. Use the book's illustrations to make several conclusions about this time period.
4. Use the book's illustrations to write descriptive words (phrases or brief paragraphs) about this time period.
5. Use the book's illustrations to name characters, develop conversations, and describe actions related to this time period.
6. Use the book's illustrations to write a short story about this time period. Transform the story into a free-verse poem.

Activity #78: "The Knockabout Middle Ages"

Have the children select books to research a topic related to People and Castles in the Knockabout Middle Ages. For interested children, refer them to History Master 7 and ask them to discuss the book selection criteria before choosing books on the topic. In small groups, have them recommend the books they found to others.

Ask the children to participate in various individual and whole-class activities based on the books. For example, after listening to a book about castle life, have the children meet in small groups to brainstorm everything they know about castles. Back in a whole-group situation, ask the children to dictate or write their information and record their ideas on the board. Let them "reserve" topics that they want to study. Take the children to the library to collect sources related to the topics they have chosen and encourage them read, browse, and inquire into the topics. Tell them to record any interesting facts they find and to share the information with the total group when they return to the classroom. On the board, elicit the facts from the children and write down the information under headings. Transform the children's information into a data diagram similar to Figure 6–5.

Encourage the children to continue inquiring into the topic of their choice—let them work individually and in small groups. Have them each write a brief paper about their inquiries and prepare a final project related to their findings. Examples of the final projects can include singing a song from the time period, drawing a map, writing a book, creating a visual display, designing a costume, drawing a floor plan of a castle, or teaching a game from the period.

If appropriate, schedule whole-group activities that relate to various areas of the curriculum in preparation for a culminating day about the study of castle times. Engage the children in designing banners, shields, and bulletin board displays (art); designing a replica of a tapestry (art); role-playing a person from the time period (drama); estimating foods needed for a feast for group members (math); designing and building a model of a castle (math and science); listening to music of the era (music); practicing stories related to the period to read aloud (reading); creating a time line of this period (social studies); and participating in a final "Knockabout Days" finale with the whole group.

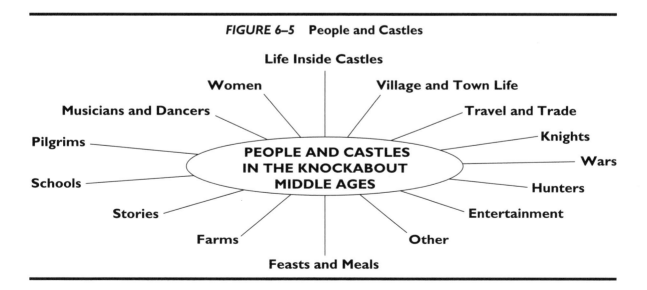

FIGURE 6–5 **People and Castles**

Life Inside Castles

Women — Village and Town Life — Musicians and Dancers — Travel and Trade — Pilgrims — Knights — Wars — Schools — Hunters — Stories — Entertainment — Farms — Other — Feasts and Meals

PEOPLE AND CASTLES IN THE KNOCKABOUT MIDDLE AGES

CHAPTER SEVEN

A.D. 1400–1499

What was going on in the fifteenth century?

Multicultural Perspectives

Africa's diverse people; Asia's Emperors, settlers, and explorers; peaceful Native People and their leaders in Australia and the Americas; as well as Europe's rulers and explorers can all be a part of a study of the 1400s. Children can inquire about early peacekeeping ways of Native People, the invading European explorers who went into unexplored lands, and the effect they had on Native People in the Americas. Thought-provoking questions can be asked about such figures as Hiawatha, St. Francis, Michelangelo, and others. Ask the children to contribute "sight bytes" (i.e., informational lines from children's books about history that can be displayed on a bulletin board in the room). Here is an example:

Sight Byte of the Week

> In 1492, When King Ferdinand and Queen Isabella gave Jews four months to get out of Spain, Jewish property and wealth were confiscated to help finance Columbus's voyages to the New World (from The Jews of New Amsterdam [Atheneum, 1988, Grade 3 up]) by E. Deutsch.

For children interested in the perspectives in Figure 7–1, suggest some of the examples of children's literature for independent reading.

Michelangelo: A.D. 1400

Help the children see that world cultures vary in certain ways—not only do people have different clothing, houses, and rituals but people also see reality in different ways. Related to seeing things in an imaginative way, introduce the life story of Michelangelo Buonarroti by reading aloud *Intro-*

ducing Michelangelo (Little, Brown, 1992, Grades 1–3) by R. Richmond and *Michael the Angel* (Doubleday, 1993, Grades K–2) by Laura Fischetto. Show the children the illustrations of the Sistine Chapel and its recent restoration, as well as some of the reproductions of Michelangelo's art in Richmond's book. Ask the children, "Do any of these art works seem to belong together as a group?" Help them find similarities as a basis for grouping the artworks of Michelangelo and ask them to suggest a label or title for each of the groupings. If appropriate, photocopy the artworks so the children can group them on the chalk rail of the board. What would the children call each group of artworks that they have put together? Invite volunteers to say in one sentence something about each one of the groups, and then say something for *all* of the groups the children have made. After reading excerpts from the two books, discuss the contrasts in the artist's name and in his personality. Discuss the idea that Michelangelo's imaginative interests in heavenly things added emphasis to his works of art. In what ways do the children think the artist was/was not really angelic, as mentioned in the book *Michael the Angel*?

Activity #79: "Artists and Their Art"

Using an opaque projector, show Michelangelo's works of art with the illustrations in *Michelangelo* (Harper & Row, 1975, all grades) by Howard Hibbard. Discuss some of the artworks and ask the children what they noticed and *why* they think Michelangelo's art reflects the subjects it does. Ask them to think about the art and what it tells them about the things people valued in this time period. Ask them to look at the art again and to

FIGURE 7–1   Children's Books for 1400–1499 A.D.

PERSPECTIVES

African Heritage

Bryan, A. *Lion and the Ostrich Chicks and Other African Folk Tales*. Atheneum, 1986. These are Hausa tales that include Ananse stories such as "The Foolish Boy." Folk literature. Grades 2–3.

Asian Heritage

Lauber, P. *Who Discovered America? Settlers and Explorers of the New World Before the Times of Columbus*. Random House, 1970. This text is an overview of pre-Columbian explorers. Nonfiction. Grade 3 up.

European Heritage

Asimov, I. *Ferdinand Magellan: Opening the Door to World Exploration*. Ill. by J. R. Karpinski. Gareth Stevens, 1991. This life story has details about Magellan's (1480?–1521) early childhood, his life at court as a page, and his life as the navigator to lead the first expedition to sail around the world. Biography. Grades 2–5.

Fisher, L. E. *Gutenberg*. Ill. by the author. Macmillan, 1993. This life story mentions Gutenberg's setbacks in establishing his business as well as his impact on changes in history. Biography. Grades 3–5.

Fisher, L. E. *Kinderdike*. Ill. by the author. Macmillan, 1994. This is a poem that pays tribute to the inhabitants of a small Dutch town who rebuilt after a devastating flood in 1421. Nonfiction. Grades K–3.

Latino/Hispanic Heritage

de Trevino, E. B. *Here Is Mexico*. Farrar, Straus & Giroux, 1980. This book begins with pre-Columbian history and traces the later colonial period, revolution, geography, arts, and economics. Nonfiction. Grades 3–6.

Jacobs, F. *The Tainos: The People Who Welcomed Columbus*. Putnam, 1992. This book portrays the life of Native People on a Bahamian island in the late 1400s. Nonfiction. Grades 2–3.

Native American Heritage

Fradin, D. *Hiawatha: Messenger of Peace*. Margaret K. McElderry/Macmillan, 1992. Hiawatha, an Iroquois Indian, preaches peace and helps unite Iroquois tribes—Seneca, Onondaga, Oneida, Mohawk, Tuscarora, and Cayuga—into the Iroquois Confederacy. Biography. Grades 2–3.

Hausman, G. *Turtle Island ABC*. Ill. by C. and B. Moser. HarperCollins, 1994. This is a collection of Native American symbols in alphabetical order. Nonfiction. Grades 1–3.

European Heritage

Adler, D. *A Picture Book of Christopher Columbus*. Ill. by J. Wallner & A. Wallner. Holiday House, 1991. This book focuses on the contributions of Columbus. Biography. Grades 2–3.

Conrad, P. *Pedro's Journal*. Ill. by P. Koeppen. Caroline House, 1991. This story is the fictionalized diary of 12-year-old Pedro, a ship's boy, on the first voyage when he is at the helm of the *Santa Maria*. Pedro sails into a coral reef and sinks the ship. Historical fiction. Grades 2–5.

Marzollo, J. *In 1492*. Ill. by S. Bjorkman. Scholastic, 1991. This book has a rhyming text about Columbus and his arrival in the world of present-day Latin America from Spain. Historical fiction. Grades 1–3.

continued

FIGURE 7–1 **Continued**

European Heritage

Schlein, M. *I Sailed with Columbus*. Ill. by T. Newsom. HarperCollins, 1991. Julio, a skilled ship's boy, befriends a native boy, Tonoro, who keeps a diary of the voyage and sings verses to calm the superstitious crew. He studies navigation through astronomy and learns the measurement of knots and distance. Fiction. Grades 3–6.

Differently Abled Heritage

Foreman, M., & R. Seaver. *The Boy Who Sailed with Columbus*. Arcade, 1992. Leif, an orphan, is left behind as punishment after he runs the *Santa Maria* aground. He is captured by Native People, renamed Morning Star, and trained to help a blind wise man who teaches him to be a medicine man. Historical fiction. Grades 3–5.

Female Image Heritage

Fisher, A. *Jeanne d'Arc*. Ill. by A. Fortenberg. Crowell, 1970. This life story depicts the achievements of the 19-year-old girl (1412–1431) who dressed in white armor and led the French army. She became a French saint and is considered the national heroine of France. Biography to be read aloud to young children. Biography. Grade 5 up.

Garden, N. *Dove and Sword: A Novel of Joan of Arc*. Ill. by the author. Farrar, Straus & Giroux, 1995. This is the story of Gabrielle, a plucky young girl, who joins the Maid's call to the battlefield and to war. Excerpts from this story can be read aloud to young children. Historical fiction. Grade 5 up.

Religious Heritage

Swamp, C. J. *Giving Thanks: A Native American Good Morning Message*. Ill. by E. Printup, Jr. Lee & Low, 1995. This text gives thanks to Mother Earth and living things—weather, elements, and the sky. The Great Spirit and Spirit Protectors are thanked for showing the people how to live in peace and harmony. The words are taken from the ceremonial traditions of the Iroquois, and a final page shows the message reprinted in Mohawk. Folk literature. Grades K–3.

---

think of a title for the collection of art works. For the children interested further in this topic, mention that they can explore the topic of artists and their art going forward into other time periods with additional reading found in History Master 8.

Da Vinci: A.D. 1452–1519

"1492 was a very good year," write Alice and Martin Provensen to begin their paper-engineered biography entitled *Leonardo da Vinci* (Viking, 1984, Grades 3–6). Things were happening all over the European world: In Spain, Christopher Columbus was about to be famous. In Italy, Leonardo da Vinci was teaching his apprentices to play the lute, sing sweetly, do their arithmetic, mix paint and plaster, and create masterpieces. The pop-up pages of da Vinci's inventions will keep the children's attention on the subject of ways inventions affected people's lives and the changes that some of the inventions influenced in later periods of history. Have the children vote for the invention they deem most important, and tally the results on the board. Encourage interested children to present arguments for and against the winning invention.

Activity #80: "Inventors Touch Lives"

Observe the illustrations in *Leonardo da Vinci* (Viking, 1984, Grades 3–6) again and discuss other features—the birds that flutter across the page when

Leonardo experiments with flight, the sight of the heavens and his discoveries of the stars and planets, and his drawings of anatomy and his painting of the famous *Mona Lisa*. Ask the children, "What effect do *you* think da Vinci's contributions had on people's lives in this time period?

If appropriate, write on the board the inventions by other inventors that the children know about. Help the children connect the "cause" of the inventions in the period to some "effects" in later periods and have them look for information from additional sources on History Master 9. Ask them to report their findings back to the whole group.

Flat Earth, Round Earth

"He was a strong and tall boy with fiery blue eyes and reddish-blond hair. His name was Christopher Columbus." This description of Columbus as a young boy is found in *Columbus* (Doubleday, 1955, Grades 1–3) by Ingri and Edgar Parin D'Aulaire. In this biography, Christopher, the son of a Genoese weaver, wants to prove that the world is round. Christopher studies map making in Portugal and waits many years for financial support before he makes four voyages to the world that is different and new to him. To elaborate on his journeys in search of the treasures of the east at a time when most "civilized" people believed the world was flat, show the children the large full-colored illustrations in *Columbus*.

Activity #81: "An Orange and Butterfly"

Distribute oranges to the children and have them cut out shapes of butterflies to reenact the observations of Columbus as described in *Columbus* by the D'Aulaires. Have the children hold the orange in one hand at eye level, just as Christopher held an orange in his hand. With the other hand, have the children move the butterfly behind the orange so that the wings come up slowly from behind the orange and up over the top. Encourage children to look closely at the tips of the wings peeping up behind the orange. This is what Columbus saw and he remembered that the sails of a ship, far away, rise slowly over the horizon and looked just like the wingtips of the butterfly. With this observation, he concluded that it must be true that the world was round. Have the children repeat the activity with an orange and a cut-out shape of a ship's sails to help them see similarities between the butterfly's wings and the sails.

Activity #82: "Contradictory Words"

Read aloud two apparently contradictory paragraphs from the same book and ask the children to explain from their points of view why they think the two paragraphs were included in the same book (see Figure 7–2 for sources). As examples, the two following excerpts were written by the D'Aulaires in *Columbus:*

> *Excerpt 1:* The King [of Portugal] called in his advisers. For long years they kept Columbus waiting while they quibbled and argued. Some of them said the ocean was too vast to be crossed. Some said it might perhaps be possible to sail down the sea toward the setting sun, but how could a ship climb up the watery hill and get home again? At last they agreed it could not be done, since it had never been done before. They [the people] laughed at the learned men who said that the world was not small and flat but a huge ball that spun around in space.

> *Excerpt 2:* Once, when Christopher held an orange in his hand, he saw the tips of a butterfly's wings peeping up behind it. He thought that just like this did the sails of a ship, far away, rise slowly over the horizon. It must be true that the world was round!

Earth's World: A.D. 1492

Discuss with the children a limited number of events about the world in 1492 from the book *The World in 1492* (Holt, 1992) with contributions from writers such as Fritz, Highwater, the McKissacks, Mahy, and others. Help the children increase their understanding of many different events going on at the same time. The book shows the first voyage of Columbus in a world perspective, and from the information in this book, children can discover that some of the world's ancient civilizations were more advanced than those in Europe during the Renaissance, and in some ways, more tolerant of others. For instance, mention to the children that by 1492, China's Ming fleet had already explored faraway seaports, medical doctors in Africa's kingdom of Songhai (now Western Sudan) were removing cataracts from the human eye, Indonesians had trade routes all over Asia and Arabia, and Mehmet II, a scholarly conqueror of Constaninople, allowed Christians and Jews to worship freely in his Muslim empire. As you discuss these events and others in this period, ask the children to locate the geographical places on a large map or globe. They can also sketch selected scenes on a mural to show a horizontal "slice" of history rather than a vertical one as a backdrop for

FIGURE 7–2   Children's Books about Columbus

PERSPECTIVES

D'Aulaire, I., & P. D'Aulaire. *Columbus*. Ill. by the authors. G. P. Putnam's, 1980. This book details Columbus's childhood and the voyages to the new lands. Biography. Grades 3–6.

Anderson, J. *Christopher Columbus: From Vision to Voyage*. Ill. by G. Ancona. Dial, 1991. The text goes back to 1459, Columbus's childhood in Genoa and his early life as agent in his father's weaving business. He learns navigation and languages and dreams of sailing to India. The chapters have fictionalized conversations and include his 1492 voyage. Members of Spanish National Opera are dressed in period clothing for the illustrations. A map of four voyages and a list of important people and places are included. Biography. Grades 3–5.

Ceserani, G. P. *Christopher Columbus*. Ill. by P. Ventura. Random House, 1979. This book focuses on the first voyage of Columbus to the Americas. Biography. Grades 1–3.

Levinson, N. S. *Christopher Columbus: Voyage to the Unknown*. Lodestar, 1991. The text discusses where Columbus really landed and where he thought he was. It details the four voyages (1493, 1498, 1502–1504) as well as his relationship with his men and with the Original Native Americans. Includes bibliography, chronology, list of crew members, letters authorizing his voyages, early maps, and index. Biography. Grades 3–5.

Los Casos, B. *The Log of Christopher Columbus' First Voyage to America in the Year 1492*. Repr. 1938/84. Linnet Press, 1989. This book tells how Columbus falsified daily distance records so the men would not be terrified about how far they had gone. False hope, daily tedium, and the twigs and birds that signaled landfall before landing at Guanahani where Native People were met are mentioned. Nonfiction. Grade 3 up.

Roop, P., & C. Roop. *I, Columbus: My Journal*. Walker, 1991. This text has excerpts from the journal of Columbus about his first voyage to the New World. Primary source material is given about his navigational choices, the politics, the mood aboard ship, and some of the encounters with the Original Native Americans. Endpapers show maps of voyage to the New World and his return home. Nonfiction. Grades 3–5.

Sis, P. *Follow the Dream: The Story of Christopher Columbus*. Ill. by author. Knopf, 1991. This book gives details of the life of Columbus in Genoa, his early childhood, and includes maps of the times. Biography. Grades 2–4.

Weil, L. *Christopher Columbus*. Atheneum, 1981. The text discusses the idea that Columbus thought the Americas were actually the Far East, and the ways he exploited friendly Native People. Biography. Grades 1–3.

---

a display of books about the fifteenth-century world and its architecture, climate, cuisine, folklore, geography, legends, and myths.

Activity #83: "Walk a Time Line"

The children can get an idea of just how many years have gone by (through the 1990s) since Columbus landed in the Americas in 1492 by measuring a time line outside on the school grounds. A time line offers the children an opportunity to develop their un-

derstanding(s) of chronology and a structure for reading aloud excerpts from tradebooks that match events on the line. Additionally, the children can develop their skills in asking questions about people and their difficult decisions, places, and events on the line. Begin the line by asking a child to stand at one end of the "time line" you and the others will be measuring. If needed, ask the child to label a sign that reads, "Columbus–1492." That end of the time line will represent 1492, the year Columbus sailed to the Americas. Now walking one step for each year, you and the children can walk abreast and go ahead in time 128 steps to reach the time of the pilgrims. Ask a child to stand there to mark the spot and hold a sign about the Pilgrims. Then walk ahead 156 steps to reach the time of America's Revolution; again, have a child stand there with a sign. Walk ahead 80 more steps to mark America's Civil War days. Finally, walk ahead enough steps to take the children up to the current year.

Back in the classroom, ask the children to focus on people and events in the fifteenth-century, use references to collect information about it, and illustrate a scene about it to put on a time line in the room. Remind the children that the classroom time line can show how related events happen in chronological order and show the relative amount of time that separates them. A time line will help them place the happenings in proper sequence. Encourage the children to select only a limited number of events that are clearly a part of a study of the fifteenth-century to enhance their understanding of this period.

Activity #84: "Voyages and Spices"

Display a map that shows the Americas and San Salvador, the first land that Columbus saw, and Cuba, from which Cortes sailed later. With chalk, trace the voyages of Columbus, and later, the route of the ship of Cortes sailing from Cuba to Mexico and other explorers. Point out that spices were part of the cargo of the Spanish ships and give the children an opportunity to smell the spices of cinnamon, cloves, pepper, ginger, and nutmeg in a Name the Mystery Spice activity. Have them relate their own experiences about ways the spices are used and valued today.

Earth's People: Natives Meet Europeans

To focus the children's attention on the Native People's point of view before Columbus landed in San Salvador, invite the children to listen to a Taino creation myth and read aloud *The Golden Flower: A Taino myth from Puerto Rico* (Simon & Schuster, 1996, Grades 2–5) retold by N. Jaffe and illustrated by E. O. Sanchez. A Taino Indian is the storyteller who tells of a boy who looks for food on Earth at a time when Earth is a waterless desert at the foot of a tall mountain. The boy finds a seed and puts it in his pouch. When he finds more seeds, he plants

them on the mountain top. A forest grows, and at the base of one tree, a vine produces a beautiful garden flower that turns into a pumpkin. The pumpkin makes strange noises that frighten everyone except for two men who fight over the fruit until the vine breaks. The pumpkin breaks open, releases a torrent of sea water and all the sea creatures, and the people rush to the mountain top to escape the flood. The mountain top becomes their island home.

To focus the children's attention on the Tainos' point of view when Columbus landed on their island, read aloud *Encounter* (Harcourt, 1992, Grades 2–6) by Jane Yolen. It is a story about a Taino boy who retells the story of the arrival of Columbus's ships and the way he tried to warn his people not to accept the strange, white visitors.

After hearing the two stories, ask the children to tell their ideas of what they have learned about the Taino people on San Salvador and what they think the Native People were like in this time period.

Activity #85: "Problems of Native People"

Ask, "What problems do you think the Native People of San Salvador had once the Europeans arrived?" Record the children's responses on the board, chart, or overhead transparency. Ask them to select one or more of the problems listed on the board and transform the words into a sketch to illustrate what they think went on. Display the sketches and select a few problems that are shown and have the children suggest some alternatives that might have resolved the problems. For additional resources on this topic that will guide interested children to further reading, distribute History Master 10.

Columbus: A.D. 1492

"There are lots of queer things that discoverers do,/ But his was the queerest, I swear," begins the poem, "Christopher Columbus," in *A Book of Americans* (Holt, 1986, all grades) by Rosemary and Stephen Benet. Engage the children in dramatizing actions related to one of Columbus's voyages—playing on the ship, spreading the sails, studying maps—and in drawing sketches of scenes that they can imagine from the verses. As an example, discuss the meanings of unfamiliar words in verses about the sailors' beliefs that there were monsters in the watery miles that looked like "great krakens with blubery lips" and "sea-serpents with a crocodile-smile" who waited for sailors on ships.

Have the children look in other poetry books and record their favorite poems about Columbus on student-made poetry "ships" made from discarded cardboard boxes, or on paper cut like a ship's sail, or on narrow paper strips that can become banners.

Activity #86: "My Perceptions of Columbus"

Leaving off the title of the poem "Columbus" that is found in *The Arbuthnot Anthology of Children's Literature* (1971, all grades) by Annette Wynne, write the rest of the poem on a chart, the board, or an overhead transparency. Mask the lines of the poem and reveal only one line at a time. Each time you reveal a line, ask the children if they can identify the explorer being described. Use each line as a clue for the children to guess the explorer (e.g., "an Italian boy that liked to play"). As each line is revealed, the children receive more and more data about the unknown explorer—Columbus. As children guess, ask them to tell what they were thinking with each line, and invite them to give reasons for choosing the explorer they identified. Reveal the title after the last line of the poem. If appropriate, repeat this activity with other poems about other famous people in this time period or in other time periods being studied.

History Is Made with Writing

Discuss with the children the idea that a historian is often a writer who thinks of words that make pictures about the past, and that a historian's writing is not only influenced by artifacts that are found but also by the time period in which he or she lives and by his or her culture. Because of this, a writer thinks of words that make pictures about the past and can find several points of view (POV) about a particular event in history. To further strengthen the POV idea for the children, read aloud *Jamaica's Find* (Houghton Mifflin, 1987, Grades 1–3) by Juanita Havill, a picture book about a young girl in contemporary times who wants to keep a toy dog she finds on the playground (Ramsay, 1992). Her mother says that the toy "probably" belonged to another child who misses it and wonders what happened to it. When Jamaica hears the other child's point of view, she takes the toy back to the lost-and-found department on the playground. Have children suggest some similarities and differences in this story and the story of Columbus and what he "found." Write their suggestions on the board.

Jamaica's Find	*Columbus's Find*
1. Wants to keep something that is found	1.
2. Is advised that it belongs to someone else	2.
3. Returns it	3.

Activity #87: "POV Story"

Introduce another POV story and read aloud *Let's Be Enemies* (Harper, 1961, Grades 1–3) by Janice May Udry, a tale of fighting between contemporary two boys, John and James. After reading the story, mention to the children that they might not see the event in the same way that the main character does. Engage them in exploring their own points of view by imagining what their version of the story could be. Ask them to draw or write their point of view about the story. Connect the idea of different points of view in this story to Columbus by asking the children to draw or write what they imagine the point of view of Columbus to be when he found something he wanted in the new world.

History Is Made with Events

Have children imagine being historians as they listen to excerpts read aloud from *I Columbus* (Walker, 1990, Grade 3 up), a translation of the sailor's first voyage by Peter and Connie Roop. Discuss the value of keeping a journal—a type of primary source material that a historian can read before writing about a selected topic. Just as Columbus wrote in a journal, engage the children in writing a page in a daily journal that tells about their activities and lifestyles during a selected school day for the year _____. Tell them they will have the opportunity to take the role of historians and trade their pages with other. As historians, they can use this information just as an historian would to find out about life in the year _____. Ask them to imagine finding this information in the future. Have them read the information and make inferences (guesses, hunches, predictions) about what life was like for the year _____ .

Activity #88: "Columbus's Journal— My Journal"

Discuss with the children that History is not only studying artifacts—such as objects from an ancient ship—it is also an accounting of events that happened in the past. Invite the children to create, as

Connie and Peter Roop did in their story about Columbus's journal, an event from their own personal histories by writing a brief description of themselves as babies or young children. Distribute construction paper (12×18 inch sheets) and ask the children to fold a sheet in half to make an individual one-page personal history. Ask them to think of titles for their histories and to write their names as the authors. Have each of them write his or her "history" on the inside right-hand page and to illustrate the events on the left-hand page. Ask each child to select a part where he or she learned something important in his or her childhood, and read it aloud to a partner. Encourage the children to add more pages to continue a more detailed history of their lives.

Activity #89: "Diary and Journal Writing"

Invite the children to listen or read stories about book characters who wrote diaries and journals and then introduce to the children the idea of writing in their own journals as a way of doing what Mark Twain said he did—"wandering when you please and coming back when you are ready." Encourage the children to write what they think on a page in their journals and to add quotes and facts from what they have heard or read during each day. Daily, elicit the children's own experiences to relate to what you read aloud about this historical period and to emphasize ways the children can compose their thoughts orally before writing. Encourage the children to write about ways their own experiences connected to the story they heard. To keep interest and motivation high, vary the ways that the children can respond in their journals on subsequent days, and if needed, introduce different ways of writing in the journals without using a pencil. For example, demonstrate ways to write in the journals with crayons, tube glue, glitter glue, markers, paint and brushes, chalk, collage figures and arrangements, letters assembled from macaroni and spaghetti, pictures from magazines, headlines from newspapers, words cut from news articles, and so on.

History Is Made When Figures Become Symbols

Point out to the children that history is (1) studying artifacts and documents, (2) reading about events that happened in the past, (3) discovering the different points of view of the many writer(s) who write about the same event and (4) understanding the ways that historical figures become historical symbols that evoke feelings in the people of the time period and their descendants. Discuss the idea that, to some people, Columbus became the historical symbol of the period—a symbol of "conquering the unknown" and "a discoverer" and "a voyager." Because of this acceptance, some people today feel Columbus has been idealized too much and made larger than life through the years. Elicit the children's points of view about these feelings.

Activity #90: "Real Person and Symbol of History"

Ask the children to make a portrait poster of Columbus and to write sentences underneath that tell about Columbus. In the whole group, ask the children to show their portraits and read their sentences aloud. On the board, write the headings for two groups: Description as a Real Person and Description as a Symbol in History. To place the posters in one of the two groups, discuss each poster and sentences with the children to determine which sentences describe Columbus as a real historical figure (Group 1) and which describe Columbus as a symbol of what people in the United States *thought* he should be (Group 2). Display the posters on different sides of the room to visually show the division of the two groups and the two points of view.

CHAPTER EIGHT

A.D. 1500–1599

What was going on in the sixteenth century?

Multicultural Perspectives

Encourage the children to read about the thriving civilizations of the Native People and the European explorers in the area now the Americas, as well as the explorers' effects on the Native People. Some of the children may be interested in the rivalry between Queen Elizabeth and Queen Mary and other historical events in Europe, while others may want to read the folk literature from parallel cultural groups in areas now Africa, Australia, Asia, Israel, and South America. With the children who are interested in selected perspectives of this period, suggest some books from Figure 8–1. If appropriate, discuss the way the perspectives portray what was going on in this time period through brief book talks.

Civilizations: A.D. 1502

Challenge the children to see how many countries they can list that they think are important in this time period. Write their suggestions on the board. Have them find the countries on a world map or globe and identify the countries with adhesive-backed colored dots. Invite the children to talk with others about what they think was going on in these countries. Further, the locales of the ancient Maya, Aztec, and Inca civilizations can be included as children read about their cultures (i.e., Montezuma II ascends the Aztec throne in 1502 in the ancient capital, Tenochtitlan [now Mexico City]).

If appropriate, have the children keep track of all the places they read about in the books related to a history study through the year. Encourage them to look for books about different places and

to add more colored dots on the map or globe as they read.

Activity #91: "Differences"

To Introduce the idea of differences in civilizations in different parts of the world, read aloud *Let's Go Traveling* (Lothrop, 1992, Grade 2 up) by Robin Rector Krupp. Show the children the illustrations to give them a view of the Maya ruins and other sights constructed by people in other locales. Some of the scenes include the cave paintings of France, the Great Wall of China, the pyramids, and Stonehenge. Engage the children in a discussion: "Why do you think a civilization would want to have (cave paintings, a Great Wall, pyramids, Stonehenge)?" and "What does the idea of civilization mean to you?" Record the children's ideas in a word association web on an overhead transparency or a class chart so they can see the way their related ideas can be grouped into categories.

Activity #92: "Features and Concepts"

Ask the children to brainstorm some of the features they know about related to people in the Maya (Aztec, or Inca) civilization for the purpose of identifying some of the concepts that are common to almost all civilizations. For example, if the children mention the pyramids in the Yucatan as a feature of civilization, suggest to them that architecture is a concept common to that civilization. If the children mention the bright ornaments of a ruler, suggest to them that another concept to study is jewelry and body ornaments. Record on the board or a chart all

FIGURE 8–1 **Children's Books for the 1500s**

PERSPECTIVES

African Heritage

Musgrove, M. *Ashanti to Zulu: African Traditions*. Ill. by L. & D. Dillon. Dial, 1976. This book introduces customs from 26 different cultures in Africa, with representations of food, clothing, and shelter. Nonfiction. Grade 3 up.

Asian Heritage

Li Shufen. *Stealing the Magic Fruit*. Ill. by Zhang Jianping and Qi Jun. Beijing Foreign languages Press, 1985. This is the seventh of a 34-part series of books telling the story of resourceful, brave, and humorous Monkey. Monkey is the irrepressible disciple of a Tang Priest, Xuanzang, and found in the ancient Chinese fantasy novel *Journey to the West* over 400 years old. This adventure tells what happens when Monkey and Pig steal and eat some magic fruit of immortality. Monkey's ingenuity saves the day. Folk literature. Grade 3 up.

Latino/Hispanic Heritage

Fisher, L. E. *Pyramid of the Sun, Pyramid of the Moon*. Ill. by author. Macmillan, 1988. A time line shows a history of Mexico with each period identified by a symbol. Symbols show the periods on subsequent pages, and the text describes ways Toltecs used pyramids and how the Aztecs build the Great Temple Pyramid. Illustrations (including one of human sacrifice) are in black and white. Nonfiction. Grade 3 up.

Mathews, Sally S. *The Story of an Aztec Victory and a Spanish Loss*. Clarion, 1994. This is a story that remembers the courage and steadfastness of the Aztec people led by Montezuma during the conflict with Cortes and the Spaniards in an area now Mexico. Nonfiction. Grade 3 up.

European Heritage

Burdett, L. *Twelfth Night for Kids*. Firefly Books/Black Moss Press, 1995. This play is presented in rhyming couplets and is illustrated by the reteller's second-grade students. Fiction. Grade 2 up.

Gibbons, G. *Pirates: Robbers of the High Seas*. Little, Brown, 1993. This book reviews the history of ship piracy on the seas from ancient times, through the Barbary Coast in the 1300s, to the buccaneers of the 1600s. Nonfiction. Grades 1–2.

Native American Heritage

Bendick J. *Tombs of the Ancient Americas*. Watts, 1993. This is a factual text supported by photographs showing people's ornaments, the city of Cuzco of the Incas, and the fortress of Sacsaythyuaman. Nonfiction. Grades 3–6.

Goble, P. *The Gift of the Sacred Dog*. Bradbury, 1980. Coronado's men on horseback introduce the horse to the Plains people, an event told in other ancient tales. Folk literature. Grades 2–3.

Yolen, J. *Sky Dogs*. Harcourt Brace Jovanovich, 1990. A Blackfoot Indian tells how he, a young motherless boy, saw a horse for the first time and was called He-Who-Loves-Horses, back in the time when the Plains Indians were given horses. Folk literature. Grades 3–7.

continued

FIGURE 8–1 Continued

Female Image Heritage

Brighton, C. *Five Secrets in a Box.* Dutton, 1987. This is a story of Virginia, the daughter of Galileo (1564–1642), who opens a gold box and sees her famous father's instruments. She uses them to look at the world in a new way she has never experienced before. Historical fiction. Grade 2 up.

McCully, E. A. *The Pirate Queen.* Ill. by the author. Putnam, 1995. This is the story of Grania O' Malley, who could outdo most of the sailors in dancing, gambling, speaking Latin, and performing courageous acts in raids in the Mediterranean. Historical fiction. Grades 2–5.

Stanley, D., & Vennema, P. *Good Queen Bess: The Story of Elizabeth I of England.* Ill. by D. Stanley. Four Winds, 1991. This life story portrays the queen's (1533–1603) influence on religion, politics, the exploration of the New World, growth of English power, and her support for Shakespeare as well as other sixteenth-century people and events. Biography. Grades 3–5.

Religious Heritage

Cooney, B., reteller. *Chanticleer and the Fox.* Illustrated by the reteller. Crowell, 1958. This is a retelling of "The Nun Priest's Tale" from *The Canterbury Tales* by Geoffrey Chaucer, as is *Chanticleer and the Fox* (Disney, 1992) by Fulton Roberts. Folk literature. Grade 3 up.

---

the features the children suggest and the concepts that relate to the features, as in the following:

Feature	*Concept*
Pyramids _____	Architecture
Ornaments _____	Jewelry

To assist children further in identifying features, show illustrations of the Maya, Aztec, and Inca civilizations from *Aztec, Inca, and Maya* (Knopf, 1993, Grades 3–5) by E. Baquedano and L. E. Fisher's *Pyramid of the Sun, Pyramid of the Moon* (Macmillan, 1988, Grade 3 up). In Fisher's pictures, the children can see one method the Aztecs might have used to build the Great Temple Pyramid and can compare their methods with the Egyptian methods that are shown in *Pyramid* (Houghton Mifflin, 1975, all grades) by D. Macauley.

Activity #93: "Concept of Civilization"

Guide the children to data from other materials about the Maya, Aztec, and Inca people—a children's book, a brief essay, a journal—and then have them add the features referred to in the material to their collection of facts on the chart about the concept of civilization (see Activity #92). For example, supplement what the children know about the Aztec civilization with the arts and crafts projects in *Aztecs* (Watts, 1993, Grades 3–8) by Ruth Thomson. The directions for the projects are clear and accompanied by photographs. Additional data are found in the books about the Maya, Aztec, and Inca civilizations on History Master 11. To assist the children in further identifying features of civilizations, see History Master 12.

Activity #94: "Early Cities: What's Wrong?"

Introduce a problem-solving situation to the children and ask them to take the role of eyewitnesses from a past civilization they are studying. Ask them to respond to, "From your point of view, what's *wrong* with this civilization?" Let the children talk about their ideas and write their ideas on the board. Use their ideas to have them infer what services in a particular city/civilization were helpful to the people, as well as what services were "missing" from the city/civilization. Ask the children to suggest ways the people could have made their cities better places to live in this city/civilization. Record the suggestions:

What's Wrong?	*Suggestions*
1.	1.

Ask the children to illustrate their suggestions for making the cities in the particular civilization better places to live. Invite volunteers to show their illustrations and to tell the whole group about the suggestions they have for making an early city a better place. As a follow-up to this activity, connect the past with the children's present and ask the children to be eyewitnesses of the present civilization. Have them respond to, "From your point of view, what's wrong with our city?" and "In what ways can we make our city a better place to live?" Ask them to suggest city officials to write to about their suggestions.

Coronado's Expedition: A.D. 1541

In 1541, Coronado and his men journeyed on an expedition into the area now Texas. A legend from the Sioux Indians in Paul Goble's *The Gift of the Sacred Dog* (Bradbury, 1980, Grades 2–5) tells how the horse was given to the people by Coronado's men. In another book, *Sky Dogs* (Harcourt Brace Jovanovich, 1990, Grade 3 up) by Jane Yolen, a man in the Blackfoot tribe tells how he, a young motherless boy, saw a horse for the first time. After reading the two stories aloud, ask the children to divide into four teams to represent groups of Coronado's men and to participate in a simulation activity about how the horse was given to Native Americans. Start the activity with the idea that Coronado's men are facing a number of conflicts such as sudden storms, dangerous snakes and other animals, sickness, and hostile Native Americans as they travel the last five miles of their expedition. Continue:

1. Have the children on each team write five conflicts—one each on index cards. As a member of each team in turn draws a conflict, team members make a decision about what to do—knowing that a bad choice can have negative effects on the entire team's progress to travel one mile forward and deliver the horse to the Native People. Have each team announce their decision to the other teams.

2. Invite members of other teams to give their opinions about each decision that is made. A good choice allows the team to move one mile forward on their journey (on the chalkboard) and a bad choice means the team stays in place. For each conflict, keep track of the miles traveled by each team by placing a √ in the appropriate place and erasing any previous √.

Miles to Go	Team 1	Team 2	Team 3	Team 4
5 Begin				
4				
3				
2				
1				
Arrival				

3. If a team member thinks that the decision is a bad choice, encourage the child to tell any negative effects that he or she predicts might happen. The object for each team is to journey five miles and get the horse to the Sioux people, as told in Goble's story, or to the Blackfoot people, as told in Yolen's story.

Activity #95: "Value of Horses"

Ask the children to tell about their experiences riding a horse, or seeing one on TV or in the movies, and tell what they know about horses. Invite them to listen to Goble's book, *The Gift of the Sacred Dog*, to find out some of the reason(s) Native People had in accepting the horse. After the story is read, write the reasons the children give on the board and use them as study questions for self-selected independent inquiry in additional resources. Have the children search to see if there is evidence in books to support their "reasons." Have them report to the whole group on what they found and tell others if the reasons that they gave were (or were not) verified in other books and reference materials, and if there are any additional reasons they want to add.

Shakespeare: A.D. 1564–1616

Discuss the days of Elizabethan London, when some of the first modern theaters were built and the contributions of William Shakespeare. Acquaint the children with some of the people, places, and events in Shakespeare's life by reading aloud *Bard of Avon: The Story of William Shakespeare* (Morrow, 1992, Grade 2 up) by Diane Stanley and Peter Vennema. Ask the children to listen for some of Shakespeare's famous quotations, for details about his suspected involvement in a treasonous plot against the queen, and to find out what happened during his last play that "brought down the house." Discuss the fire that destroyed the theater and ask the children, "What fire safety precautions could have been introduced after the fire in the Globe Theater? What fire safety procedures are used in today's theaters? What information could a local firefighter give us about fire regulations in theaters today, when he or she visits our class?"

Activity #96: "Quotes"

Ask the children to listen carefully to one of Shakespeare's quotations that you read to them, and have them tell what scene or picture they can imagine about the words. For example, ask the children to tell what picture they could create in their minds after hearing the words, "Bubble, bubble, toil and trouble." Write their descriptive words on the board, along with the quotation. Choose other quotes such as "This above all: To thine own self be true" or "Neither a lender nor a borrower be" or "Though this be madness, yet there is method in it" from *Hamlet;* "All the world's a stage/ And all the men and women merely players" from *As You Like It;* "and "This was the noblest Roman of them all" from *Julius Caesar.*

As an option, ask the children to consider Shakespeare's quotes in terms of what was going on in the New World in this period, and sketch a scene or picture about one of the quotations as the quotation might relate to Native People, explorers, Coronado's expedition and other happenings outside of Europe. For instance, what picture in the New World could be sketched to illustrate Shakespeare's caption, "Bubble, bubble, toil and trouble?" Help the children understand that parallel events were going on in the New World and in Shakespeare's world at the same time. Display the artwork in the classroom with the quotations as captions.

CHAPTER NINE

A.D. 1600–1699

What was going on in the seventeenth century?

Multicultural Perspectives

A study about this period can offer children possibilities to learn about their ancestors through a study of Africa's people, Asia's peace keepers, Australia's Native People and settlers, Europe's immigrants, and the encounters of the Native People of the Americas with Europeans.

If the focus is about what is going on in Japan, there are opportunities for learning about the Japanese samurai, the soldiers skilled with their swords, the shoguns who led the armies, the fishermen, and the storytellers. Bulletin boards can display scenes of people visiting shrines, pavilions, and castles; growing rice; living in the countryside; attending a festival; buying from vendors; walking in gardens; and appreciating the beauty of blossoms on cherry trees—and all will add to a thought-provoking history unit.

If the focus is about what is going on in Europe, a study of this period can offer opportunities to learn about European noble families, the law keepers, the peasants and their families, as well as what lives were like for the ship builders, the canvas sailmakers, and the crews living on ships. Nobles with daggers, Chief Magistrates, peasants with calloused hands, stooped crewmen on ships, and brilliant scholars can all be a part of children's inquiries about this period and will make research activities exciting ones. Colorful posters, similar to movie theater posters, can be designed by children to illustrate places and faces. The display boards can feature merchants' homes, flowing water fountains, a manor house on an estate, craftspeople making their wares, lantern makers, or workers thatching a roof on a Tudor Inn. Through children's books, they can see muscular silversmiths and iron workers, as well as cabins and forts in dark forests. There can be related maps that show the sea routes to the people's destinations.

Additionally, drawings of the people in areas other than Europe and some thought-provoking questions and word collages can lead the children to a better understanding of ways people adjusted to their environment in this period. For instance, children can review clothing of the times in early America, when a display board shows people dressed in busks, jerkins, shifts, and capes from *American Family of the Pilgrim Period Paper Dolls in Full Color* (Dover, 1988) by Tom Tierney. With children's books as resources, the class environment and lessons can be carefully planned to help the children develop concepts and generalizations as they learn about what was going on in other parts of the world. To assist in this, guide children to the books in the perspectives on Figure 9–1.

Galileo: Circa A.D. 1610

For children interested in the history of astronomy, introduce them to a series of events happening in Europe in the 1600s with the life story of the great scientist, Galileo (c. 1610), who saw thousands and thousands of stars that no one on Earth had ever seen. Use his life story as a springboard into a study of what was going on in this time period. Invite children to watch filmstrips of their choice about early astronomy and to take notes about what is presented

FIGURE 9–1   **Children's Books for the 1600s**

PERSPECTIVES

African Heritage

Bryan, A. *The Ox of the Wonderful Horns and Other African Folktales*. Atheneum, 1993. This book is a group of five stories retold in a lively manner. Folk literature. Grades K–3.

Mollel, T. M. *The Princess Who Lost Her Hair: An Akamba Legend*. Ill. by C. Reasoner. Troll, 1992. From East Africa, this is a tale of humble Muoma who shares the last of his food and water with living creatures and marries a humbled princess who refused to give a hair of her head to a bird for its nest. Folk literature. Grades 1–3.

Asian Heritage

Uchida, Y. *The Magic Purse*. Ill. by K. Narahashi. McElderry, 1993. A poor man on a pilgrimage crosses a swamp and meets a beautiful woman who asks him to do an errand for her. When he accepts, she gives him a magic purse of gold coins that support him through his life. Each year, the man honors the woman and follows her instruction to always leave one coin in the purse. Folk literature. Grades K–3.

European Heritage

Anderson, J. *The First Thanksgiving Feast*. Ill. by G. Ancona. Clarion, 1984. This book gives a first-person account of life at Plymouth in 1620s. The photographs are taken at Plimouth Plantation, a Living History Museum. Nonfiction. Grades 3–6.

Asimov, I., & E. Kaplan. *Henry Hudson: Artic Explorer and North American Adventurer*. Gareth Stevens, 1991. Henry Hudson (?–1611), a British sea captain, is sent to search for a northwest passage (1607, 1609, 1611). In 1611, the crew mutinies and places Hudson, his son, and loyal sailors adrift in a small boat and they are never heard from again. Labeled drawings of Hudson's ships and glossary included. Biography. Grades 2–5.

Bulla, C. *A Lion to Guard Us*. Crowell, 1981. Three motherless London children sail to Jamestown to find their father in the new colony. They keep their lion's head door knocker safe during a shipwreck, while surviving on an island, and during a voyage on to Virginia. There, they find their father, one of the few who survives the Starving Time in 1609. Young Jenny hangs the lion's head on a peg above the door latch, a symbol of their former home. Historical fiction. Grades 2–3.

Bulla, C. R. *John Billington, Friend of Squanto*. Ill. by P. Burchard. Crowell, 1956. This life story presents a brief picture of Billington and the Pilgrims at Plymouth Colony. Biography. Grades 2–4.

De Angeli, *M. Elin's Amerika*. Doubleday, 1941. This book tells a story of newcomers who journey from Sweden to the New Land in the 1600s. Historical Fiction. Grades 3–5.

Fritz, J. *Who's That Stepping on Plymouth Rock?* Putnam, 1980. This book portrays the history of early settlers landing on Plymouth Rock. It seems that in moving the rock in 1740, the townspeople split the rock in half but left part of it on the beach. Historical fiction. Grades 3–5.

Kagan, M. *Vision in the Sky: New Haven's Early Years 1638–1783*. Linnet Press, 1989. This story portrays the early Colonists with a focus on the strict Puritan values they live by and their relations with original Native Americans. The book ends with the defeat of the British Redcoats in the Revolutionary War. Historical fiction. Grade 3 up.

FIGURE 9–1 Continued

European Heritage

Lobel, A. *On the Day Peter Stuyvesant Sailed into Town*. Ill. by author. Harper & Row, 1971. When Stuyvesant arrives on the shores of present-day new York in 1647, he finds a town with streets of weeds and garbage, houses in disrepair, and the fort walls crumbling. He quickly tells the settlers to improve their town. In the next 10 years, the town doubles in size and becomes as neat as other Dutch communities in Europe. Historical fiction. Grades 2–4.

Monjo, F. *The Secret of Sachem's Tree*. Ill. by M. Tomes. Coward, McCann & Geoghan, 1972. This is the story of the people who hide the Connecticut charter in an oak tree in 1667 to keep the charter from being sent back to England. Based on historical facts. Historical Fiction. Grades 2–4.

Quackenbush, R. *Old Silver Legs Takes Over: A Story of Peter Stuyvesant*. Prentice Hall, 1986. This portrays the life of Stuyvesant, a colorful leader of New Amsterdam. Biography. Grade 3 up.

Sewall, M. *The Pilgrims of Plimoth*. Atheneum, 1986. This book is based on the writings of Governor William Bradford of the Plymouth Colony in 1620. It describes the lives and responsibilities of the children, women, and men who lived there. Nonfiction. Grade 3 up.

Spier, P. *Father, May I Come?* Bantam, 1993. Two young Dutch boys, both named Sietze Hemmes, participate in sea rescues, the first in 1687 and the other 300 years later in a similar parallel story. Cutaway diagrams included. Historical fiction. Grades 1–3.

Spier, P. *The Legend of New Amsterdam*. Doubleday, 1979. The text portrays Stuyvesant's dream that the colony will become a huge metropolis. "Crasy Annie" sees a vision in the distance and predicts the colony will have "people" and "stone." Historical fiction. Grades 2–4.

Stone, M. *Rebellion's Song*. Steck-Vaughn, 1989. This collection has six life stories about people of colonial times. Multiple biography. Grade 3 up.

Van Leeuwen, J. *Across the Wide Dark Sea: The Mayflower Journey*. Ill. by T. B. Allen. Dial, 1996. A 9-year-old boy journeys with others as newcomers. Historical fiction. Grades 1–5.

Walters, K. *Samuel Eaton's Day: A Day in the Life of a Pilgrim Boy*. Scholastic, 1993. Set in 1627 at Plimouth Plantation, the book shows the details in a day in the life of 7-year-old Samuel as he gets dressed, checks his animal snare, and gathers wood before he eats his breakfast of curds, mussels, and parsley. Doing his chores, he helps the men harvest rye, despite the pain of his blisters. Historical fiction. Grades 1–3.

Latino/Hispanic Heritage

Rohmer, H., O. Chow, & M. Vidauke. *The Invisible Hunters*. Children's, 1987. The text tells of the impact of the first European traders on the life of the Miskiot Indians in seventeenth-century Nicaragua. Historical fiction. Grades 3–6.

Native American Heritage

Brebeuf, Father Jean de. *The Huron Carol*. Dutton, 1993. This is the story of the birth of Christ, as set in the Huron world that was written by a missionary, Father Jean de Brebeuf in the 1600s. Folk literature. Grades 1–4.

Bulla, C. R. *Squanto, Friend of the Pilgrims*. Scholastic, 1988. This is the story of the life of Squanto (Tisqugntum, ?–1662), the Native American who befriends the European Pilgrims in the New World. It portrays the assistance he gave to the Pilgrims at Plymouth Colony (i.e., taught the Pilgrims the Indian way of planting corn which helped them survive their first winter in Plymouth). Biography. Grades 2–4.

continued

FIGURE 9–1   **Continued**

Native American Heritage

Kessel, J. K. *Squanto and the First Thanksgiving*. Ill. by L. Donze. Carolrhoda, 1983. Squanto, the last of the Paatuxet Indians, teaches the Pilgrims ways to survive the harsh winter in Massachusetts. Biography. Grades 1–3.

Sewall, M. *King Philip's War*. Atheneum, 1995. The fictionalized story is told in two voices: Wampanoag and Pilgrim. The two points of view explain the adverse relations between the English settlers in Plymouth and the Native People that grows into King Philip's War and eventually leads to the destruction of the Wampanoags and their allies. Map included. Historical fiction. Grades 2–4.

Sewall, M. *People of the Breaking Day*. Atheneum, 1990. The book portrays the Wampanoag people as a proud industrious nation in southeastern Massachusetts before the settlers arrived. Life in the tribe and the place of each member in the society is given along with gives details about hunting, farming, survival skills, and the value of a harmonious relationship with nature. Includes recreational and spiritual activities. Nonfiction. Grades 2–4.

Water, K. *Tapenum's Day: A Wampanoag Boy in Pilgrim Times*. Ill. by R. Kendall. Scholastic, 1996. Tapenum, a fictionalized figure, describes each family member's duties as they relate to food, clothing, shelter, and weapons, and shares his interest in becoming a respected member of his community. Photographs are taken at the recreated Indian homesite at Plimouth Plantation in Massachusetts. Author's notes provide background information. Glossary of definitions and pronunciation of Wampanoag words included. Nonfiction. Grades 2–4.

Differently Abled Heritage

De Trevino, E. B. *Nacar, The White Deer*. Farrar, Straus & Giroux, 1963. A mute Mexican shepherd boy protects a white deer and presents it to the King of Spain in 1630. Historical fiction. Grades 3–6.

Female Image Heritage

Accorsi, W. *My Name Is Pocahontas*. Ill. by author. Holiday House, 1992. This life story is about the Indian princess (1595–1617) who was the daughter of Indian leader, Powhatan. It includes her early childhood, her friendship with John Smith, a leader of the settlers, and her journey to England as the wife of John Rolfe (1614) and the mother of Thomas Rolfe (1616). As she travels back to Virginia, she becomes sick and dies in Gravesend, where she is buried (1617). Biography. Grades K–2.

Christian, M. B. *Goody Sherman's Pig*. Macmillan, 1990. Based on historical facts, this is the account of Goody Sherman who, in 1636, took up a legal battle over her runaway pig with church elders and the courts. It was said that her battle caused the colony to create two legislative branches of government. Historical fiction. Grade 3 up.

Fradin, D. B. *Anne Hutchinson*. Enslow, 1990. This is the life story of Hutchinson (1591–1643), who preaches that true religion is the following of God's guidance through an "Inner Light." In Massachusetts in 1638, Anne is found guilty of "traducing" the ministers and ordered to leave the colony. She moves and starts a settlement at Portsmouth that offers complete religious freedom for all, where she lives until a move to Pelham Bay, New York, where she is killed by Indians in 1643. Biography. Grades 3–5.

Fritz, E. I. *Anne Hutchinson*. Chelsea, 1991. The text describes Anne's early life and education and presents an historical context for her banishment from the colony in seventeenth-century New England. Biography. Grades 3–5.

FIGURE 9–1   **Continued**

Female Image Heritage

Moskin, M. *Lysbet and the Fire Kittens*. Coward, 1974. In 1662, with her parents away on a cold December night, 8-year-old Lysbet stays awake all night to keep the precious fire in their home going and accidentally builds the fire too high. In the morning, when she returns after trying her new ice skates, she finds that the heat has started a fire on their thatched roof. She tries to rescue her beloved (and pregnant) cat. Historical fiction. Grades 2–4.

Raphael, E., & D. Bolognese. *Pocahontas: Princess of the River Tribes*. Ill. by the authors. Scholastic, 1993. This brief life story is a narrative that lists facts about selected events in the life of Pocahontas, who died in England in 1617. Biography. Grades 1–3.

Van Woerkom, D. *Becky and the Bear*. Ill. by M. Tomes. Putnam's, 1975. Becky, a young girl who lives in Maine, wants to go hunting with her father and brother, but is left at home. When a bear confronts Becky, she feeds it molasses and rum to make it fall asleep. Becky and her grandmother tie the bear to a tree and wait for Becky's father to get home. Historical fiction. Grades 1–3.

Religious Heritage

Aliki. *The Story of William Penn*. Prentice Hall, 1984. William Penn (1644–1718), a Quaker, establishes the colony of Pennsylvania as a refuge for religious nonconformers and he treats fairly the Indians who call him *Onas*, which meant quill or pen. Biography. Grades 3–6.

Ammon, R. *Growing Up Amish*. Atheneum, 1989. The text details the history of the Amish movement and the Amish lifestyle in a Pennsylvania Dutch area. Nonfiction. Grades 3–6.

Costabel, E. D. *The Jews of New Amsterdam*. Atheneum, 1988. This story is an account of the struggles of the Jews who journeyed to America from Brazil during the colonial period. They discovered that the United States did not hold equality for all its people. Nonfiction. Grades 2–3.

Fisher, L. E. *Galileo*. Macmillan, 1992. This life story discusses the views of Galileo (d. 1645), who believed that ideas should be proven by tests, as well as the views of others in the Catholic church who attacked his astronomical observations. Centuries later, the church relented its view against him. Many of his achievements are discussed—building a microscope and recording his observations about astronomy, gravity, magnetism, and motion. Biography. Grades 3–5.

Good, M. *Reuben and the Fire*. Ill. by P. B. Moss. Good Books, 1993. The text portrays the life in an Amish family through the activities of Reuben, an active boy, and his five sisters. He is creative, wants to drive the buggy, and gives all of his animals names that end in *shine*. When he sees his neighbor's barn burn, his family and the rest of the community gather for a barn raising. Historical fiction. Grades 1–3.

on the topic. Additionally, ask each child to write original questions and answers from the films *and* a basic science book on the topic. Have them divide into astronomy study groups and ask their questions of the members in the groups.

Activity #97: "Galileo Fair"

To prepare for a Galileo Fair, have each child make a model of something related to an astronomy topic

he or she selects. Ask each child to write 10 to 15 sentences about the topic. Have them revise their sentences with a partner's help. After revisions, let them write final copies of their sentences and give it to the partner to read. Continue:

1. Ask the children to write descriptive paragraphs from their notes taken while viewing any related filmstrips and then give the writing to a partner to

read. Have them get into astronomy study groups and check on the information in their paragraphs with others in the group.

2. Have each child write a question related to something he or she saw in the educational films and search for the answer in different data sources. Ask the children to use the information to write a paragraph to answer the question as fully as they can.

3. Have a partner proofread each paragraph and help with capitalization, punctuation, and spelling.

4. For a culminating activity, plan a classroom Galileo Fair. Invite a local astronomer to visit the class and talk about the work that he or she does. Have the children display their writing, projects, and any accompanying diagrams or illustrations.

Mayflower: A.D. 1620

Show children an illustration of the *Mayflower* and ask them what they wonder about when they hear the name of the ship *Mayflower*. Write their questions on the board. Read aloud excerpts from *If You Sailed on the Mayflower in 1620* (Scholastic, 1991, Grade 3 up) by Ann McGovern. Discuss the children's questions in the whole group to see how many of their questions were answered by the reading. Review several of the book's questions with the children. Ask them to search for other books that could answer any of their questions unanswered by the book.

Activity #98: "Newcomers on the Mayflower"

Ask the children to imagine they were with the Pilgrims and lived in the conditions on the *Mayflower*. Place full-color cardboard ship parts on a flannel board—the fo'c'sle, main deck, half deck, rudder, masts, sails, and more—from A. G. Smith's *Cut and Assemble the Mayflower: A Full-Color Model of the Reconstruction at Plymouth Plantation* (Dover, 1981). Elicit the children's comments about what life on the ship would have been like.

Show two or three illustrations of the Pilgrims on the *Mayflower* from McGovern's book, and have the children describe the Pilgrims in the pictures. Ask, "How do you know that the pictures are of Pilgrims? What did the Pilgrims do on the *Mayflower*?" After each of the children's responses, rephrase it in a sentence that begins, *Pilgrims are people who . . .* Have the children repeat the response to make a generalization. As additional ideas about Pilgrims are

introduced, have the group repeat the generalizations. Reread McGovern's story aloud and ask the children to listen to find out what the Pilgrims do in the story and to pay attention to ways they got along together. After the story, encourage the children to compare the Pilgrims' *Mayflower* voyage with any voyages, summer rafting, and boating experiences they have had.

Immigrant Pilgrims

"It is grateful we were to reach any land safely" is the way Marcia Sewall portrays the feelings of the Pilgrims in her book *The Pilgrims of Plimouth* (Atheneum, 1986, all grades). Sewall mentions that on board ship, the Pilgrims agreed on laws of behavior before they came ashore. The very spot on which the Pilgrims came ashore in 1620 has withstood the erosion of centuries and is a symbol of the beginning of European civilization in the land now the United States. Today, children visiting Plymouth, Massachusetts, can see Plymouth Rock on Water Street along with *Mayflower II*, a replica of the original ship, before they visit Plimoth Plantation, a recreation of the Pilgrims' seventeenth-century village. They will see that Plymouth Rock is about six feet across and rests under a protective canopy. The rock is surrounded on three sides by granite and on a fourth side by an iron grill facing the waves of the Atlantic Ocean.

Using *The Pilgrims of Plimoth*, show the illustrations on an opaque projector so the children can write down facts they observe from the pictures. Ask them to meet in small groups and tell others what they have learned by referring to their notes.

Activity #99: "Writing Back to England"

Ask the children to listen to or read several stories about the voyage aboard the *Mayflower*. Then, playing the role of a Pilgrim, suggest news items to write for a newspaper (and suggest a name such as the *Colony Herald*) to be sent back to relatives and friends of Pilgrims in England. Discuss writing news items about the voyage itself, what condition the ship is in, birth and death notices, what is going on at the settlement, social news about the families, and ads asking for needed supplies. Engage the children in writing the news items and in assembling them together on a large chart. If appropriate, duplicate the newspaper and have children take copies to an adult in the home to tell what they learned from this activity.

Pilgrim Family Life: A.D. 1620

Three Young Pilgrims (Bradbury Press, 1992, Grades 1–3) by C. Harness details the family life of three young children, including their difficult voyage on the *Mayflower*. The Allerton children—8-year-old Bartholomew, 6-year-old Remember, and 4-year-old Mary—sail with other Pilgrims and land in 1620 in the area now United States. Give the children an opportunity to retell the story and engage them in making character cut-outs to use with a flannel board. Have the children give additional retellings and use the flannel board figures to help illustrate their stories.

Activity #100: "If I . . ."

Read aloud the poem "Pilgrims and Puritans" from *A Book of Americans* (Holt, 1986, all grades) by Rosemary and Stephen Benet. Ask the children to listen to details about the lives of the Pilgrims and Puritans who "were English to the bone" and settled in New England. Further, initiate a discussion about the settlers in the area now New York with the poem, "Peter Stuyvesant," who was a "sturdy" governor with a famous "timber toe." Ask the children to imagine the ships in which southern settlers journeyed while listening to the verse "Southern Ships and Settlers." Ask children to complete the phrases related to the Pilgrims, " If I attended the First Thanksgiving . . ." or "If I were English to the bone in New England . . ." or "If I sailed on a southern ship . . . ."

Pilgrim's Thanksgiving: A.D. 1621

In the fall of 1621, the Pilgrims, newly arrived, celebrated their first harvest with a bountiful feast. They invited the Indians who lived nearby to share the turkey, deer, roast corn, Indian pudding, and fresh fruit. Thus, the Thanksgiving holiday, as today's children know it, was brought to this country by the Pilgrims. This feasting was in keeping with the celebration of harvest festivals that go back to ancient times when most countries of the world celebrated a bountiful harvest or gave thanks for something. To enrich children's further understanding of the background of Thanksgiving Day, read aloud responses to the children's commonly asked questions about the lives of those attending the first Thanksgiving from *The Plymouth Thanksgiving* (Doubleday, 1967, Grade 3 up) by Leonard Weisgard, from a poem based on Governor William Bradford's diary,

The Thanksgiving Primer (Plimoth Plantation, Inc., 1987, all grades), or from excerpts from *Thanksgiving* (Garrard, n.d., all grades) by Lee Wyndham. This historical account shows how harvest festivals go back to ancient times and how the festivals are now celebrated in different ways throughout the world. Mention to the children that some historians believe that the Thanksgiving celebration descended from the British custom called Harvest Home. In the celebration, villages joined together to bring in the grain from the fields and share a feast when the work was completed. This custom may have been continued by the English Pilgrims with Massasoit, the leader of the Wampanoag tribe, and his people, who joined with the Pilgrims for what is called the first "thanksfiving."

Activity #101: "A Geographer's Circle"

Draw a circle on the board with the words *A Geographer's Circle* in the center. Tell the children that they will have an opportunity to work as geographers and use a procedure developed by geographers (Committee on Geographic Education, 1983) that allows them to inquire about a location on earth, and to analyze the relationships of the places to the people who live or lived there. With children, discuss the headings of location, place, relationships within the place, movement and regions and list them on the circle related to the topic of the first Thanksgiving. Write the children's contributions under the appropriate heading (see Figure 9–2).

Ask the children to transform the information on A Geographer's Circle into another format, such as Before Pilgrims and After Pilgrims drawings to show what changes took place in the geographic area after the arrival of the Pilgrims. Related to these changes were the harvesting and fowling the Pilgrims did. Edward Winslow, Pilgrim father, wrote an entry in his journal and his words can be reproduced on a chart for the children: "Our harvest being gotten in, our Governor sent four men on fowling, so that we might after a special manner rejoice together after we had gathered the fruit of our labor" (Edward Winslow, Pilgrim father [Morissey, 1991]). Read aloud Winslow's words, and ask children, "What is Edward Winslow, a Pilgrim father, saying to you? Will you tell us more about the words 'four men on fowling' and the 'fruit of our labor' and what the words mean to you? What does Winslow say to you personally?" After a discussion, have the children plan and create a mural that shows the information they gathered about the origin of

FIGURE 9–2   **A Geographer's Circle**

Location
Area now Massachusetts in 1620.

Place
Physical features, climate, seasons, wildlife (suggested by children).

Relationships within the Place
Massasoit, Wampanoag leader, and his people joined with the Pilgrims for the first Thanksgiving.

A GEOGRAPHER'S CIRCLE FOR FIRST THANKSGIVING

Regions
The region was changed because of the Pilgrims' acquisition of and effect on the resources, including the Native People themselves.

Movement
Sharing of food, fowling, recreations, sports, dancing, songs, and an exercise of arms.

Thanksgiving. Encourage them to make scenes on a mural to reflect the information they have discovered about the first Thanksgiving. For example, some children can draw scenes to show that the celebration closely resembled a traditional Harvest Home festival of English farmers (not a Thanksgiving as most children now know it) and that it was held in October 1621, with recreations, sports, dancing, songs, and an exercise of arms—all topics that can be documented. Other children can contribute when the first National Thanksgiving Day was officially proclaimed—in 1789 by Abraham Lincoln.

Activity #102: "Pilgrims' Houses"

Alice Dalgliesh's *The Thanksgiving Story* (Scribner's, 1954, Grades 2–3) provides details about the Hopkins family and their hardships during their first winter at Plymouth. Ask the children to look at illustrations about the colonists and identify items they see in the homes of the colonists during this time period. Record their suggestions on the board in a list with the heading In Colonists' Houses. Ask the children to meet with partners and identify the objects on the list that the children *do not* have in their houses today and to make a list of the items. Then have the children return as a whole group and report on the objects they identified. Add the names of the objects to a list on the board with the heading Not in My House.

Ask the children to tell the objects that they have now that the colonists *did not have* in their houses. Add the names of these objects to a third list with the heading In My House But Not the Colonists'. As a whole group, have children suggest items that they could do without if they had to do so today.

In Colonists' Houses	*Not in My House*	*In My House but Not the Colonists'*
1.	1.	1.

Families at Plimouth Plantation

Introduce children to a colonial child's activities by reading aloud K. Walters's *Sarah Morton's Day: A Day in the Life of a Pilgrim Girl* (Scholastic, 1989, all grades). Sarah Morton, a 10-year-old, describes her chores, her family and friends, and her hopes and dreams in Plimouth Plantation, Massachusetts. In the morning, Sarah dresses in stockings, shoes, petticoats, waistcoat, and apron. She makes hasty pudding for breakfast and eats standing up (there's no stool for her to sit on). She tends the fire, feeds the chickens, and milks the goats. Sarah draws water and pounds spices while her mother churns cream into butter. She does her school work, learns her letters so she'll be able to read, and looks forward to watching the unloading of a newly arrived boat of goods from England. After reading the story, ask the children to cite some of Sarah's responsibilities and actions and what she does for play. Group the comments on the board and have children compare their work, actions, and recreation today with Sarah's:

Sarah's Work	*Sarah's Actions*	*Sarah's Play*
1.	1.	1.

My Work	*My Actions*	*My Play*
1.	1.	1.

Activity #103: "Your Day or Sarah's?"

After the children hear brief excerpts about the activities in Sarah's life, ask them to suggest the activities of a one-day account of what yesterday was like in their lives, and then compare their daily activities and routine with a one-day account of what Sarah did.

Activity	What a Colonial Child Did	What I Did Yesterday
Get water		
Make breakfast		
Get milk		
Prepare food		
Get eggs		
Get butter		
Get spices		
Have heat		
Have clean clothes, etc.		
Be entertained		
Travel		

Invite the children to meet with their partners, read aloud their lists to one another, and respond to the question, "in which time period would you rather live—yours or Sarah's? Why?"

For adept readers in grade 3 and older who are interested further in this topic, introduce the series about *The Wild Rose Inn* (Bantam/Doubleday/Dell, 1994, Grade 3 up) by Jennifer Armstrong. The series takes readers from the late seventeenth century up through the late nineteenth century, and begins with *Bride of the Wild Rose Inn, 1695, Ann of the Wild Rose Inn, 1774, Emily of the Wild Rose Inn, 1858*, and is followed by *Laura of the Wild Rose Inn, 1898*, which concludes the series.

Reenacting the 1600s

Replicate the times of the 1600s in the classroom by having the children prepare and eat lunch and then move from activity table to activity table in the classroom for different crafts related to this period. For lunch, have the children mix and fry oatcakes to eat along with cheese, broth, and jam. Use brown paper plates to simulate eating lunch on wooden boards or plates. At various activity tables and assisted by a parent or older student-volunteers, the children can do the following:

Assemble brooms needed for housekeeping.

Dip candles.

Dye cloth strips for headbands.

Play a game popular in the seventeenth century.

Identify plants popular with the colonists by making an inventory of some plants shown in selected illustrations at a display.

Make corn dolls for good luck.

Mix lotions to make hand creams, pomanders, and sachets popular in the time period.

Practice writing with quill pens.

Try their skills at quilting.

Activity #104: "Painting with Vinegar"

Introduce a painting technique popular in colonial days—vinegar painting (Barfield, 1993). The children can make vinegar paint by mixing 1 cup of vinegar, 1 teaspoon of sugar, and powdered poster paint. They add the vinegar mixture to the powdered paint *very slowly* to make a liquid. Then they apply the vinegar liquid with a brush to paper, and while it is wet, use objects—such as sponge pieces, fabric remnants, fingers, even marshmallows and fruit and vegetable slices—to texture the paint into designs.

Activity #105: "Importance of Gardening"

The colonists got most of their food, many flavorings, some medicines, and color dyes from plants in their flower and vegetable gardens. Ask the children to design a garden they would have liked to plant if they had lived in colonial times, and engage them in study-inquiries to find the names of plants (flowers, herbs, and vegetables) that were grown hundreds of years ago. For example, the book *Housekeeping in Old Virginia* (Morton & Co., 1879, reissue) explains many herbs, vegetables, and plants and their uses. Have the children record what they find from their research on a class chart, and use the information to design a colonial garden they would have planted.

Herbs	Flowers	Vegetables
Basil		
Catnip		
Chives		
Cress		
Dill		
Lavender		

Activity #106: "Meeting More Newcomers"

Elin's Amerika (Doubleday, 1941, Grade 3 up) by Marguerite De Angeli details the story of a newcomer family that journeys from Sweden to the New Land in the 1600s. Discuss the idea that the family members might want to send a collection of items—a heritage box—from their New Land back to friends and relatives in Sweden. A heritage box is a collection of items and drawings that shows characteristics of a culture and a particular time period—in this case, the colonists' culture of the 1600s. Have the children suggest items to include in a colonial heritage box that might have been sent from the New Land back to Europe. To help the children brainstorm items, write the letters in the word *brainstorm* on the board as guides to the types of items that can be considered (see Figure 9–3).

Activity #107: "Heritage Box"

Elicit the children's ideas for creating objects for a heritage box. Then write the children's ideas on the board to help them organize their thoughts. Suggestions from the children can include a guessing game about the period, with the answers given somewhere on a paper in the box, along with a bibliography for further reading and a song sheet. The children can include their own original books or a page of recipes. Further, the children can put a list of the contents inside the lid of the box for a checklist to account for the items they make (see Figure 9–4).

Have the children meet in small groups with two children in each group taking a turn in the center of the group. Have the children in the center trade their boxes, open them, and show the contents to others in the group to ask for feedback and suggestions for additions, revisions, deletions, and so on. Schedule time for the children to add to the contents as they wish.

As an option, encourage the children to suggest places to deliver the heritage boxes—perhaps to the school library, a classroom book corner, the children's wing of a local hospital, or a nearby children's home—to give other children an introduction to the colonists time period.

FIGURE 9–4   Contents for Heritage Box

1. A bibliography for further reading
2. A corncob, dried apple, acorn, or crab claw
3. Drawings of articles of clothing (i.e., stockings, shoes, petticoats, waistcoat, and apron worn by girls and women)
4. Drawings of daily activities
5. A doll and instructions for making it from an apple, acorn, crab claw, or corn cob and husks (for corn cob doll, use corn silk or braid husks for hair; braid husks for arms; make skirt and kerchief from cornhusks; draw facial features)
6. Instructions for playing a game
7. Sketch of a hornbook
8. Sketch of a favorite toy
9. An original book about daily activities (making curds or hasty pudding for breakfast, tending the fire, feeding chickens, milking the goats, drawing water, pounding spices, churning butter, learning letters to read, checking an animal snare, gathering wood, harvesting rye, going to a barn raising, meeting a boat of supplies from England)
10. Paper replicas of items such as an animal snare
11. A recipe for hasty pudding or other dish
12. Seeds of rye or sprigs of dried parsley or other plants
13. Music/ a song sheet

FIGURE 9–3   Brainstorm

BRAINSTORM

B is for <u>books</u> related to the topic—in this case, the colonial time period.
R is for the child-created <u>replicas</u> related to the time period.
A is for <u>articles</u> of clothing.
I is for <u>instructions</u> for playing a game, performing a dance, completing crafts.
N is for <u>new</u> illustrations of the period the children want to create.
S is for <u>seeds</u> of plants related to the times.
T is for <u>toys</u> of the times.
O is for <u>an original book</u> the children want to develop related to the topic.
R is for <u>recipes</u> related to the time period.
M is for <u>music</u> (songs) enjoyed in this period.

Native Americans and Europeans

One of the most informative books about the Wampanoag people who lived in the area now southeastern Massachusetts before the English settlers arrived is Marcia Sewall's book *People of the Breaking Day* (Atheneum, 1990, Grades 2–5). Have the children look at the illustrations as you show them on an opaque projector and identify the items they see in the lives of the Wampanoag people as they hunted, farmed, and played. Write the items on the board in a list with the heading Items Wampanoag People Had. Ask the children to meet with partners and identify the objects on the list that the children *do not* have in their lives today and to draw sketches of the items.

Items Wampanoag People Had	*Items We Do Not Have Today*
1.	1.

Activity #108: "Belongings of the Wampanoag"

Ask the children to meet with partners and show one another the sketches of the items they identified that the Wampanoag people had but that the children do *not* have. Ask the children to read the names of the items on the original list on the board, and then have them identify the objects that they *have now* that the Native People *did not have* in their lives. Ask them to make two lists for the items:

Items We Have Today	*Items Wampanoag People Did Not Have*
1.	1.

Finally, ask the children to suggest items in their own lives today that they could do without if they had to do so. Have the children write the items in a list and then transform the items into sketches to show what they could do without. Collect the sketches and put them in a class book.

Activity #109: "Viewpoints"

Mention to the children that there may be viewpoints in history that are counter to their own and point out there are several books that show the bravery of Pilgrims who wanted religious freedom as well as the friendliness of the Native Americans who greeted them and taught the Pilgrims how to fish, hunt, and plant crops. As a contrast, also point out that there is a lack of stories that describe other events—such as how some hungry Pilgrims had to take food from Indian storehouses during the winter after the first Thanksgiving (Caldwell-Wood, 1992). Some questions to launch a discussion about the people and their times of hunger can include the following:

• "If you were one of the hungry Pilgrims, under what circumstances would you and would you not take food from another's storehouse? Do you think the behavior of the hungry Pilgrims was or was not a serious act? Why?"

• "Do you think that the Pilgrims who took food from another's storehouse were or were not likely to be dishonest in other ways? In what way does this information about the Pilgrims differ from the information you know? How would you explain the difference? What is the truth and how would you know it?"

• "What serious situation were early Virginia colonists in when they referred to a time without food as the Starving Time? What meaning does the word *starving* have for you? What questions do you have about the hardships of the people during these months? You can read about a colonist who lived through this life-threatening situation in Clyde Bulla's *A Lion to Guard Us* (Crowell, 1981 Grades 2–3). In the story, three motherless London children sail to Jamestown to find their father in the new colony. When they find him, they discover he is one of the few who survives the Starving Time in Virginia in 1609."

Activity #110: "Princess Pocahontas"

"Princess Pocahontas/ Powhatan's daughter,/ Stared at the white men/come across the water" are the words that begin the biographical story poem about Pocohantas in *A Book of Americans* (Holt, 1986, all grades) by Rosemary and Stephen Benet. After reading the poem and one or two biographies about Pocahontas aloud, ask the children, as a group, to dictate or write what they know about Pocahontas. Write their ideas on the board. With the children's help, arrange their ideas into a free-verse poem about the princess. Ask the children to draw illustrations to accompany their free-verse poem when it is transferred to a chart. Affix the illustrations as a border and display the chart for the children's oral rereading. Attach a tablet of writing paper at the foot of the chart so interested children can write additional verses about the princess.

Activity #111: "Princess Peacekeeper"

Discuss what the words *princess* and *peace keeper* means to the children and read aloud actions and dialogue that show Pocahontas was a peace keeper from *My Name Is Pocahontas* (Holiday House, 1992, Grades K–2) by William Accorsi or another source such as *Pocahontas* (Doubleday, 1949, Grades 2–4) by Ingri and Edgar Parin D'Aulaire or *Pocahontas* (Putnam, 1964, Grades 2–4) by Patricia Miles Martin. Discuss the princess's peace-keeping actions and ask, "Has something like this ever happened to you (where you were a peace keeper)? What did you do? As you think about that now, do you think that was a good thing to do? Why or why not? Is there anything you would have done differently? Why or why not? What can you do today at school to show you are a peace keeper?" Encourage children to do something to help keep peace during the school day. At the end of the day, have a class meeting and ask volunteers to tell what they did to keep the peace during the day, and invite others to tell something positive they noticed where someone was helping keep the peace at school.

Activity #112: "Hiawatha"

"By the shores of Gitchie Gumee,/ By the shining Big-Sea-Water,/ Stood the wigwam of Nakomis,/ Daughter of the Moon, Nokomis." These words begin the verses in "Hiawatha's Childhood" by Henry Wadsworth Longfellow from *The Arbuthnot Anthology of Children's Literature* (1971, all grades). Read the words aloud and ask the children to close their eyes to imagine the scenes of the shining Big-Sea-Water, the wigwam, the pine trees, old Nokomis, and little Hiawatha. Reread the verses and have the children sketch the scenes they think of while they are listening.

Show the children the way the artist, Susan Jeffers, has interpreted the classic poem *Hiawatha* (Dial, 1983, Grades 2–3), and have them look at the illustrations she drew to interpret Hiawatha's childhood. Write the words *Hiawatha's Brothers* on the board and ask the children what meaning the words have for them. Discuss Hiawatha's relationship with nature, and ask the children what Hiawatha did that showed his love and care for animals.

Activity #113: "Hiawatha's Picture Folder"

Discuss any words from Longfellow's poem suggested by the children. Write the words in lists in categories such as Name Words (nouns) and Descriptive Words (adjectives). Engage the children in making Hiawatha picture folders using art paper with Name Words on a page and Descriptive Words on another. Ask them to interpret the words in their own ways as Jeffers, the illustrator, did for Longfellow's poem.

Name Words	Descriptive Words
Shores	
Big-Sea-Water	
Wigwam	
Nakomis	
Moon	
Daughter	

If appropriate, mention that the Iroquois Confederacy (the League of Six Nations) was a league first founded by the Native American Deganawida; his work was continued by his disciple, Hiawatha. Ask the children how Hiawatha's love for animals might have affected his love for peace later in life when he helped perpetuate the Indian League of Six Nations and ask them to write their thoughts in the folder.

Activity #114: "Native American Families"

Details about the family life Native People are given in the book *People of the Breaking Day* (Atheneum, 1990, Grades 2–5) by Marcia Sewall. Read related excerpts aloud and ask the children to suggest other stories that reflect Native American families that they know and about whom they want to hear. After hearing each story, ask the children to suggest information from the story that is like or *not* like their family life and record the information on a chart similar to the following:

Name of Story	Like My Family	Not Like My Family
1. *People of the Breaking Day*	1.	1.

Activity #115: "Friends"

Initiate further discussion by asking the children to think of questions they would ask a Native American boy or girl their own age about their family life and activities. Write the questions on the board. Ask the children to suggest something friendly and neighborly they would do for the boy or girl; again, write their suggestions on the board. Ask each child to sketch a scene or object representing the suggestion on tag board cut to resemble the shape of something in the scene. Affix the shapes on a classroom bulletin board under the heading I Can Be a Friend. Encourage the children to do something friendly and neighborly during the day at school for a child who is not a close friend. At the end of the day, schedule a brief class meeting and invite the children to give their reports about what they did that was friendly and neighborly for someone they didn't know very well.

Activity #116: "Territory Treasure Hunt"

"The Abenaki lived along rivers and streams that stretched toward the rocky coast of the Atlantic Ocean," states Evelyn Wolfson in *From Abenaki to Zuni: A Dictionary of Native American Tribes* (Walker, 1988, Grade 3 up). It seems that the Abenaki built small villages high above the water on bluffs that offered them protection against attack. Wolfson mentions that her dictionary of Native American communities is intended to inspire children to fill in some gaps in information about Native American history. With information from Wolfson's book and a large map of America, engage children in a Native American Territory Treasure Hunt and have them locate several areas in their state where Native People lived. Ask the children to record the names of the Native American groups who lived in their region and schedule a time for them to read their word lists aloud. Ask the children to transform their lists of Native Americans in a unique way: They can make a poster or collage of the words, write sentences in color on art paper, draw pictures to represent the groups, or create a two-page picture dictionary of the Native American groups. Display these projects.

Activity #117: "Native Americans of My Area"

Schedule an interview with a representative from a local historical group. Some topics to pursue are the interviewee's knowledge about which Native Americans first settled in their area, what groups of people came later, and what parts of the culture of Native Americans and other groups are recognized in the children's community today. Have the children develop their own questions for the interviewee. Additionally, encourage the children to do the following:

1. *Relate to the home* and invite the parents, friends, or relatives of children to class to talk about their language, customs, and traditional ways they maintain their heritage and communicate with their ancestors' original home country.
2. *Relate to the school* and survey their classmates to find out the different languages spoken and prepare a list that identifies the languages.
3. *Relate to the neighborhood and community* and make a historical scrapbook of Native American groups and other ethnic groups in the community and note what they have contributed to the area.
4. *Relate to a larger geographic region* and survey the white pages in the local telephone directory to take notes for a multicultural report about names that appear to identify particular groups of people now living in the community.
5. *Relate to services available to people in a larger geographic area* and survey the yellow pages in the local telephone directory to take notes for a report about business or services that appear to be serving particular groups of people.

CHAPTER TEN

A.D. 1700–1799

What was going on in the eighteenth century?

Multicultural Perspectives

As part of an introduction to the 1700s, some children may want to inquire about the ordinary and extraordinary people in this time period through biographies, historical stories, folktales, and legends. Stories of Africa's kings, Asian travelers, Spanish settlers, and Native People in the Americas, as well as historical story songs—one of the cornerstones of America's common heritage—can lead the children to a better understanding of parallel cultures in this period. Bulletin boards can make a study of this period an exciting one when they feature the handmade crafts, the different geographical locations where they lived, and the ways they traveled. Colorful related maps can show the population centers of their parallel cultures. Captions can ask "What Were African People (Asian, European, Native People in the Americas, Latino/Hispanic) Doing during This Time Period?" "What Were Women (Differently Abled, Religious Groups) Doing?"

The exciting story of the American Revolution can be displayed on bulletin boards designed by the children and backed up with black-and-white sketches of Paul Revere's ride, Nathan Hale's actions, the Boston Massacre, and scenes made for the overhead projector (with the publisher's permission) from several books:

- *Story of the American Revolution Coloring Book* (Dover, 1988, Grades 3–6) by Peter Copeland.
- *Early American Trades Coloring Book* (Dover, 1988, Grades 3–6) by Peter Copeland has scenes of wigmakers, glassblowers, hatters, and other colonial craftspeople.

- *Everyday Dresses of the American Colonial Period Coloring Book* (Dover, 1987, Grades 3–6) by Peter Copeland includes portrayals of such people as a broom seller, a wagoner, and George Washington and his family.
- *American Family of the Colonial Era Paper Dolls in Full Color* (Dover, 1985, Grades 1–4) and *George Washington and His Family Paper Dolls in Full Color* (Dover, 1985, Grades 1–4) both by Tom Tierney have scenes of family life.
- *Colonial Williamsburg* (Macmillan, 1993, Grades 3–6) by S. Steen and S. Steen portrays the city from its early beginning around 1750 to its restoration, and gives details about everyday life of craftspeople and shopkeepers.
- *18th Century Clothing* (Crabtree, 1993, Grades 3–6) by B. Kalman has directions for making clothing of the time period after showing various fashions, footwear, wigs, and other accessories for children, women, and men.

For children who are interested in the heritages of this period, suggest some of the additional books in Figure 10–1.

Colonists' Almanac: A.D. 1732

In the settlements of the middle colonies, most families that could afford an almanac bought one. Show the children an example of an almanac—an all-purpose book that has a calendar, dates of historical events, and information about the predicted weather, the tides, and moon changes. Sometimes, an almanac also includes health hints, proverbs,

FIGURE 10–1   **Children's Books about the 1700s**

PERSPECTIVES

African Heritage

Bryan, A. *Beat the Story Drum, Pum-Pum*. Atheneum, 1980. This is a collection of tales related to African heritage. Folk literature. Grades 1–3.

Stanley, D., & P. Vennema. *Shaka: King of the Zulus*. Ill. by D. Stanley. Morrow, 1988. Exiled from his father's clan, Shaka (b. 1787) develops his skills as a leader and warrior, and returns to be the ruler of his clan and eventually the king of the Zulus. Biography. Grades 3–5.

Asian Heritage

Conger, D. *Many Lands, Many Stories: Asian Folktales for Children*. Ill. by R. Ra. Tuttle, 1987. This book has 15 folktales from different countries in Asia. Folk literature. Grades 1–3.

Latino/Hispanic Heritage

Anderson J. *Spanish Pioneers of the Southwest*. Ill. by G. Ancona. Dutton, 1989. This book portrays the life of a pioneer family in a Spanish community in New Mexico in the eighteenth century, and focuses on the family's hard work, harsh living conditions, and their traditions. Nonfiction. Grades 3–6.

Gray, G. *How Far, Felipe?* Harper, 1978. This story is about Felipe and his family as they move from Mexico to California in conjunction with the 1775 expedition of Colonel Juan de Anza. It seems that Felipe's burro is to be left behind but Felipe hides her among some other animals that are going on the journey. Historical fiction. Grade 2 up.

Native American Heritage

Young, R., & J. Dockery, editors. *Race with Buffalo: And Other Native American Stories for Young Readers*. Ill. by W. E. Hall. August House, 1994. Over 30 tales are arranged by subjects of ancient times, young heroes, "Why" tales, trickster tales, and beliefs in the spirit world. Author's notes included. Folk literature. Grade 3 up.

European Heritage

Adler, D. A. *Thomas Jefferson: Father of Our Democracy*. Holiday, 1987. This life story includes Jefferson's positions on issues of the times and his interactions with other important people of the period. Biography. Grade 3 up.

Giblin, J. C. *George Washington: A Picture Book Biography*. Ill. by M. Dooling. Scholastic, 1992. This life story focuses on Washington's days as a boy and as an adult. Biography. Grades K–3.

Giblin, J. C. *Thomas Jefferson: A Picture Book Biography*. Ill. by M. Dooling. Scholastic, 1995. This life story highlights Jefferson's childhood days and important events in his life as an adult. Biography. K–3.

Martin, P. M. *Daniel Boone*. Ill. by G. Dines. Putnam, 1965. This life story focuses on events in the frontier for this Kentucky trailblazer. Biography. Grade 2 up.

Monjo, F. N. *Grand Papa and Ellen Aroon*. Dell, 1974. In 1805, Jefferson's 9-year-old granddaughter tells about her family's life and about Jefferson, her Grand Papa. It mentions the children that Jefferson had through his legal marriage. Historical fiction. Grades 3–4.

Siegel, B. *Sam Ellis's Island*. Four Winds, 1985. A Tory named Sam Ellis acquires a small island one year before the Declaration of Independence is signed in the colonies. The island plays an important part in America's history. Historical fiction. Grade 3 up.

continued

FIGURE 10-1   Continued

European Heritage

Vance, M. *Martha, Daughter of Virginia: The Story of Martha Washington*. Ill. by N. Walker. Dutton, 1947. Martha cares for Mount Vernon during the Revolutionary War and spends winters at camp with General Washington. She does not recover from the shock of George's death in 1799 and dies in 1802. Both Martha and George are buried at Mount Vernon. Biography. Grades 3–6.

Wade, M. D. *Benedict Arnold*. Watts, 1995. This life story details Arnold's boyhood up through his service as a general in America's Revolutionary War, his heroic deeds (including his leadership at the battle of Saratoga), his later traitorous actions, and his death in London. There is some information about his wife, Peggy Shippen. Biography. Grade 3 up.

Walter, R. *The Story of Daniel Boone*. Dell, 1992. This is the life story of Boone, who explores the Kentucky frontier, is captured by the Indians and escapes, and becomes a soldier in America's Revolutionary War. Biography. Grades 2–3.

Female Image Heritage

Dalgliesh, A. *The Courage of Sarah Noble*. Macmillan, 1987. In 1707, 8-year-old Sarah goes with her father to the wilderness to cook and care for him. Sarah keeps up her courage as she confronts threatening animals and unfriendly strangers. This is a true story based on an actual incident. Historical fiction. Grades 3–4.

Griffin, J. D. *Phoebe the Spy*. Scholastic, 1977. This is the story of a tavern keeper's daughter, Phoebe Frances. She spies for General Washington and the colonists. Historical fiction. Grades 3–4.

McGovern, A. *Secret Soldier: The Story of Deborah Sampson*. Scholastic, 1975. This is the story of a young woman who disguises herself as a boy and joins the army to serve in America's War of Independence. Biography. Grades 3–4.

San Souci, R. *Cut from the Same Cloth: American Women of Myth, Legend and Tall Tale*. Philomel, 1993. This book has stories of women from different cultures who were "larger than life" and did extraordinary deeds to save themselves, their friends, and families, and to "pay back" deserving victims. Includes map with the characters sketched in locales. Folk literature. All grades.

Stevens, B. *Deborah Sampson Goes to War*. Ill. by F. Hill. Carolrhoda, 1984. This life story describes Sampson's early life and her experiences, including injuries and illnesses as a soldier in America's Revolutionary War. Her true identity is discovered near the end of the war. Biography. Grades 2–6.

Religious Heritage

Handel, G. F. *Messiah: The Wordbook for the Oratorio*. Ill. by B. Moser. HarperCollins, 1992. The text is by C. Jemmens,, who relies on the words in the Bible to tell the story of the Resurrection. The illustrations show the symbols of Christ, the Trinity, and the Resurrection to complement the words. The music by Handel (1685–1759) is included. Nonfiction. Grade 1 up.

Meyer, K. A. *Father Serra: Traveler on the Golden Chain*. Our Sunday Visitor Publishers, 1987. This book discusses Father Serra's personality as well as the dangerous and challenging time period in which Serra lived. The text provides facts about the phases of Serra's life as well as the founding of the California Missions from 1769–1798. Biography. Grades 2–5.

popular sayings, recipes, and humorous notes. Mention that in 1732, Benjamin Franklin published *Poor Richard's Almanac* (Peter Pauper Pr., n.d., all grades) and included some of his brief sayings such as "Waste not, want not" and "A stitch in time saves nine." Ask the children to suggest contemporary sayings of today that they can contrast to Franklin's:

What Franklin Said	*What We Say Today*
1. "Love your enemies for they tell you your faults."	1.
2. "A small leak will sink a great ship."`	2.

Invite the children to illustrate pairs of comic strip-style pictures with a word bubble to show Franklin's saying on the left side of the paper and a word bubble to show contemporary words on the right side.

Activity #118: "Original Almanac"

Invite the children to write pages for an original almanac for their families and engage them in collecting sayings, proverbs, and quotes from family members. Of course, they can make up their own sayings. Ask them to include the important dates in the lives of their family members; to make some weather predictions; to write their favorite recipes; to illustrate the pages and sayings with small illustrations; and to add anything else they think should be in their almanacs for their families.

Benjamin Franklin: A.D. 1706–1790

"And all our humming dynamos and our electric light/ Go back to what Ben Franklin found, the day he flew his kite/" are words that remind us of "Benjamin Franklin" from *A Book of Americans* (Holt, 1986) by Rosemary and Stephan Vincent Benet. Ask the children to suggest motions for the actions in the verses. Write their suggestions on the board and then ask them to perform the actions as the poem is reread:

Words in the Poem	*Suggested Actions*
Munched a loaf	
Walking down the street	
Wrote an almanac	
A smile on his lip	
Made a pretty kite	
Flew it in the air	
Was very clever	

Activity #119: "Franklin's Biography"

After reading the poem to the children, read aloud from a fictionalized biography of Benjamin Franklin, such as *Benjamin Franklin: The New American* (Watts, 1988, Grade 3 up) by Milton Meltzer, every day for one or two weeks. Ask the children to listen for their favorite quotes, such as "Early to bed, early to rise, makes a man healthy, wealthy, and wise" and record their favorites on banners to display in the classroom. Then, for a selected time period of your choice, engage children in studying Franklin's life as a topic and in independently reading several biographies about him. Ask them to write their reactions in Franklin journals (writing paper stapled together with an art paper cover). After children have listened to biographies (or excerpts) over several days, ask them to write their own original fictionalized biographies about this interesting figure. See Figure 10–2 for a list of biographies about this talented man who was an author, diplomat, inventor, philosopher, printer, publisher, scientist, and statesman.

War for America's Independence

Introduce the children to the subject of America's Revolutionary War by reading aloud *Yankee Doodle: A Revolutionary War Tail* (Dorling Kindersley, 1992, Grades 1–2) by Gary Chalk, who portrays the action with mice and other animals dressed in authentic clothing. Read aloud the overview of the song and talk about the colonists' actions toward independence. Leave the book at an activity center so children can look closely at the cartoon-style illustrations and informative side notes. Additionally, the children can read the verses of the popular Revolutionary War ballad in *Yankee Doodle* (Simon & Schuster, 1996, Grades 1–4) by Steven Kellogg. Further, the children can select clay or play-dough to make Liberty Bell replicas or other related items. They can locate materials for assembling individual books about this period, and they can select art supplies to make figures of Great Britain's King George II and other historical personages and objects for a display.

George II is king of Great Britain as America's colonies become an independent country, and Jean Fritz tells his biographical story in *Can't You Make Them Behave, King George?* (Coward, 1977, Grades 2–5), a book illustrated by Tomie de Paola. During these days, independence is urged by some colonists because of the English laws that the colonists considered restrictive, and the people rallied behind the words that "taxation without rep-

---

FIGURE 10–2   **Children's Books about Benjamin Franklin**

PERSPECTIVES

Adler, D. A. *Benjamin Franklin: Printer, Inventor, Statesman*. Holiday, 1992. This book is the life story of Franklin, portraying his childhood and his early work experiences along with his inventions, writings, and scientific experiments. Grades 2–4.

Daughtery, C. M. *Benjamin Franklin: Scientist-Diplomat*. Macmillan, 1965. This book points out that Franklin was able to make friends wherever he went. It also relates his experiences at the age of 70 in Paris. Grades 2–5.

Green, Carole. *Benjamin Franklin: A Man with Many Jobs*. Children's, 1988. Greene authentically portrays Franklin's contributions. Grades 1–4.

Meltzer, Marvin. *Benjamin Franklin: The New American*. Watts, 1988. This book shows Franklin as a strong problem solver. It also discusses several inventions such as bifocals, lightning rod, stove, and others. Grade 3 up.

Quackenbush, Robert. *Benjamin Franklin and His Friends*. Pippin Press, 1991. This book focuses on the friendships that Franklin kept during his life and on the ways his friends influenced his decisions. Grades 2–4.

---

resentation is tyranny." Additionally, there are restrictive navigation laws that are protested by colonial merchants who want easier trade laws, and the ill will between the colonists and the British soldiers lead to the Boston Massacre, an early skirmish that started when a colonial boy threw a snowball.

Activity #120: "Making Decisions"

Engage the children in examining choices and alternatives in problem situations related to the Revolutionary War. Ask them to make decisions for the following situations and to discuss possible consequences of the decisions that are made:

1. "A man in the street in Boston makes unpleasant remarks about the local colonists who want to break away from England. A crowd of colonists, calling themselves patriots, gathers and some begin to threaten the man. A nearby colonist militiaman approaches the group. The first man continues to make his remarks about being loyal to the King of England and the crowd becomes angrier. Someone shouts a threat of violence. The militiaman decides to take the first man to a nearby military barracks. Do you agree with what the militiaman did? Why or why not?"

2. "You see a colonist militiaman being pelted with stones and sticks by a small group of young people whose families are loyal to the King of England. The militiaman is trying to arrest one of the young men. What would you do if you were there? Give your reason(s)."

3. "Your English government is trying to pass a law in your colony that would allow the British soldiers to enter your home without a search warrant if they believed that there might be weapons in the home. You have to decide what you think about this law. What would you decide? Why?"

4. "You join the other revolutionaries in the 13 colonies of England and support the idea of breaking "ties" with England, the mother country. You support writing an open letter to the King, called the Declaration of Independence, and know that you are considered by some to be a rebel and a traitor to King George's English government for doing this. Knowing this, you don't know if you *should* sign your name to the declaration because you hear that you could lose your property, and possibly your life, if you do so. Would you risk being a revolutionary in this situation? Why or why not?"

5. "You are with Paul Revere and other patriots near Boston and all of you have been given the task of warning the colonists if the British soldiers decide to attack. What would you suggest as a plan? Draw a sketch of your ideas. Then read a biogra-

phy/informational reference about Paul Revere to discover the plan that was eventually adopted. What was this plan?"

Activity #121: "Paul Revere's Midnight Ride"

"Listen my children, and you shall hear/ of the midnight ride of Paul Revere" is the line that introduces Longfellow's poem, *Paul Revere's Ride* (Houghton Mifflin, 1971, all grades), from the version illustrated by Adrian J. Lorio and Frederick J. Alford. Give a chalkboard talk and mention what is going on in this event as you sketch a map of where the action takes place. As an example, sketch the outline of Boston Harbor, the shapes of the British Man-o-War ships, and the North Church Tower as you talk about Revere watching the North Church Tower in the night to look for his friend's coded signal—one light if the British (led by General Gage) left their ships and marched by land, and two lights if they left to arrive by sea. The endpapers of *Paul Revere's Ride* (Dutton, 1991, Grades 3–5), illustrated by Ted Rand, have a map of the routes taken by Revere and his colleagues, Dawes and Prescott, and these routes can be added to the chalk map. Enlarge the map in chalk on the board and mark in one color of chalk the route that Revere, Dawes, and Prescott took to warn the colonists, and with another color, mark the route that the British soldiers were traveling. Mention to the children that Revere did *not* make it to Concord to warn the colonists that the British were coming. He was arrested by the British. Show the children the clothing styles of British soldiers and colonists, methods of communication, and transportation of the times with another version, Agusta Stevenson's *Paul Revere: Boston Patriot* (Scholastic, 1986, Grade 3 up).

Activity #122: "General Gage's Drummer Boy"

At the same time Revere rides to warn the Minutemen that the British are coming, George, a young British drummer boy, marches with General Gage. His point of view is told in *George, the Drummer Boy* (Harper & Row, 1977, Grade 3 up) by Nathaniel Benchley. The British soldiers are sent to capture any hidden cannons and gunpowder belonging to the Minutemen in Concord in the colony of Massachusetts. Have the children meet with partners to play the role of young George and the role of a colonial child to tell the two points of view of this event. What would each child feel and say as they explained their

points of view? Have the children trade roles to play the other's point of view.

Activity #123: " 'The First Shot,' Cries a Town Crier"

At Concord, the first shot in America's first revolutionary battle is fired, and decades later, Ralph Waldo Emerson writes "Concord Hymn" (in *Story and Verse for Children* [Macmillan, 1966] by Marian Blanton Huber), which commemorates the event. Discuss the meaning of the first verse that ends, "The embattled farmers stood/And fired the shot heard round the world." Write the words on the board and invite the children to orally interpret the words in different ways for meaning—loud, soft, fast, slow—before they repeat them aloud as a choral reading.

The story of a small boy who defended himself in the Lexington battle is told in Nathaniel Benchley's *Sam the Minuteman* (Harper & Row, 1969, Grades 1–3). In 1775, in Lexington, Massachusetts, Sam and his father respond to Revere's message and they both fight against the British. In this battle, 80 Minutemen defended themselves and other colonists against approximately 1,000 British soldiers who considered the colonists to be traitors.

Mention to the children that in the colonies, a town crier walked the town and rang a bell to get the attention of the people before the crier announced the breaking news. (There were very few newspapers.) Tell the children they will have an opportunity to take the role of town criers to announce the news of the firing of the first shot in America's Revolutionary battle or of Sam's efforts at the battle of Lexington (or of another revent in this period). In small groups, have the children take turns as town criers who announce the news about what went on at Concord and Lexington.

Tories and Whigs

"Why this will never, never do!/ . . . , / And we are loyal subjects, who/ Will fight for good King Georgie!" are words that portray the views of a Tory in the poem "Oliver De Lancey" in *A Book of Americans* (Holt, 1986, all grades) by Rosemary and Stephen Vincent Benet. Discuss these times when some people, such as the British General Oliver De Lancey and his landowner family, were loyal subjects of the British King George and were called Tories along with other British supporters of the time. Discuss the poets' view in the poem about what would have happened if the Tories and British *had won* the war and why the Benets wrote in the previously mentioned poem that America would then have "rulers regal, No Stars and Stripes! No July Fourth! No bold American eagle!" Ask the children to meet in small groups to make their own speculations about what would have happened and how their lives would have been changed if the Tories and British had won the war. Have them report their speculations back to the whole group. List their speculations on the board and ask the children to select one to illustrate for a class book entitled If the Tories Had Won the War.

Activity #124: "Tory and Whig Are Friends"

Elaborate on the concepts of Tories and Whigs by reading aloud Alice Dalgliesh's book, *Adam and the Golden Cock* (Scribner's, 1959, Grades 1–3), a revolutionary war story about the friendship of two boys—one from a Tory family and the other with Whig loyalty—and about the conflict in which one boy is caught as he tries to maintain his friendship as well as his loyalty to the colonists' bid for independence. Ask the children to meet with partners to discuss the boy's dilemma—a problem with no easy solution—and his feelings, and to offer dilemmas from their own experience in situations where either of two choices is just as bad as the other.

Activity #125: "Tory or Whig?"

Ask the children to meet with partners and discuss which view—Tory or Whig—they would have supported if they had lived in this time period. Invite them to think carefully about writing a message on a lapel button as a personal way to show their views to others in the class. Children can make their own buttons by using a piece of adhesive-backed white shelf paper and crayons or felt marking pens. They can add sketches if they wish, pull off the adhesive backing, and wear their lapel buttons to show their views for this time in history—Tory or Whig.

Activity #126: "Struggling Revolutionists"

Tell the children that they are going to hear a story of an unusual girl named Tempe Wicke, who lived in Morristown. Have them listen to *This Time, Tempe Wicke* (Putnam's Sons, 1992, Grades 2–3) by Patricia Gauche to find out what made Tempe such a strong individual. (She could outrace her father on Bonny, her horse, and she could outwrestle the boys her own age.) During America's Revolu-

tion, she fed and clothed Revolutionary soldiers who were camped near her family's farm in 1780 and 1781. These two years were months of hard times for everyone—the soldiers lacked money, food, and blankets, and Tempe's family suffered greatly when Tempe's father died and her mother became ill. Later, mutinous soldiers try to steal Bonny, and Tempe shows her courage and cleverness when she protects her horse and the family farm. After hearing the story, ask the children to suggest behaviors that reflect Tempe's individuality and to write their suggestions on a character web about Tempe Wicke on the board (see Figure 10–3). Guide the children to other references that are suitable for an inquiry about the role of women and girls with History Master 13.

People Risk Their Lives

To emphasize the idea that people have risked their lives for others, acquaint the children with Deborah Sampson's early life and experiences, including her injuries and illnesses as a soldier in America's Revolutionary War. Have the children take turns reading excerpts to one another from B. Stevens's biography, *Deborah Sampson Goes to War* (Carolrhoda, 1984, Grade 2 up), a book illustrated by F. Hill. Ask them to suggest some of the problems that they think Sampson faced in her role of soldier and to write their suggestions on the board in a list entitled Problems. What would they suggest as ways to help overcome or resolve these problems? Write their answers on the board in a second list entitled Solutions. Other books suitable for this activity are found in History Master 14.

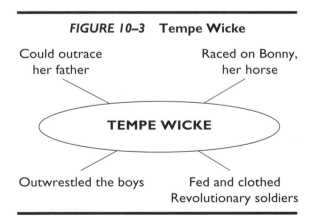

FIGURE 10–3 Tempe Wicke

Could outrace her father

Raced on Bonny, her horse

TEMPE WICKE

Outwrestled the boys

Fed and clothed Revolutionary soldiers

Activity #127: "Taking a Risk"

Elicit times from the children's experiences when someone has risked his or her safety to help another living thing. Bring this topic up to date by asking the children to identify news articles from the daily newspaper where an ordinary person risked his or her safety to help someone else. Have the children cut out the articles and display them in the classroom. Discuss what advice, if any, the children would give the people in the illustrations.

Activity #128: "Common People, Uncommon Contributions"

Children of all ages may hear or read current material and data sources to find the latest information about some of the legends related to America's Revolutionary War and report back to the whole group what they found. For example, some children may report about the following:

1. *The Legend of Betsy Ross: The American Flag* (Simon & Schuster, 1973, all grades), by Thomas Parrish, discounts the idea that Ross made America's first flag; another source, *A Flag for Our Country* (Steck-Vaughn, 1993, Grades 1–3), by Eve Spencer, mentions that the story comes from the oral tradition handed down from one generation to another, and there is no supporting factual data that Ross, a young war widow, designed the first flag of the United States. Additional facts are found in Peter Spier's *The Star Spangled Banner* (Doubleday, 1966, Grade 3 up).

2. *The Legend of George Washington and the Cherry Tree: Washington's America* (Grosset & Dunlap, 1961, all grades) by Robin McKown, mentions that the cherry tree tale is fanciful. *If You Grew Up with George Washington* (Scholastic, 1985, Grade 3 up), by Ruth Belov Gross, has a question-and-answer format that helps a child review this time period from Washington's point of view.

3. *The Legend of Paul Revere: Paul Revere's Ride* (Houghton Mifflin, 1988, all grades), by Henry Wadsworth Longfellow and illustrated by Nancy Winslow Parker, points out that Paul Revere was captured and never reached Concord, but two other men, William Dawes and Samuel Prescott, warned the colonists that the British were coming.

4. *The Legend of Washington Crossing the Delaware:* Children in Grade 3 and older can look carefully at the painting *Washington Crossing the Delaware*, painted by Emanuel Leutze. Have them look carefully at the way that Leutze visualized the scene, and then tell them to locate references to find information about the following to crosscheck the "historical mistakes" shown in the painting: "How can you tell when this event takes place (time of year)? How can you tell if this event happens during the day or at night? How difficult would it be for Washington to stand up in the front of a boat of this type? Do you think that America's famous flag, the 'Stars and Stripes,' had been designed and was flying with Washington's troops at this time? Why do you think this way?"

From Colonists to Americans

Discuss the idea that people in the colonies not only had identities as former British citizens and colonists but also as new citizens of the United States of America. Today, it seems some people need an identity other than just being an American. The desire of wanting an identity other than being known as an American is the same desire people have when they want to become members of a church or want to join certain groups. It seems that some people desire additional identities as U.S. society gets larger. Help children understand what it means to be an American, as well as what it means to have an additional identity by having them write their names on adhesive-backed colored dots to place on a map of the state in which they live. If appropriate, have them write their U.S. identity and additional identities as well—each child can be a daughter or son, cousin, student, friend, church member, scout member, and so on, and can indicate this on the dot.

Activity #129: "Fourth of July Story"

Review the theme of the colonists' independence and ways they restored relationships with England with Alice Dalgliesh's *The Fourth of July Story* (Scribner's, 1956, Grades 1–3). Dalgliesh's text tells about the leading figures, other people, and events that played an important part in America's history. Bring the celebration of the Fourth of July into contemporary times for the children with Wendy Watson's *Hooray for the Fourth of July* (Clarion, 1992, Grades Pre–K). The book shows pleasant rural-town festivities of fireworks and picnics with people eating fried chicken and potato salad. There are also excerpts from patriotic songs, rhymes, and chants. Have children compare the scenes in Watson's book with the experience they have when they celebrate the Fourth of July.

Activity #130: "Revolutionary War Activity Center"

Make a variety of activities available to the children and create a center where the children can discover some special items related to America's Independence by working with partners or individually. Make poems, prose, and audio tape recorders available so the children can record and listen to their own voices. For example, a child can record facts about America's Liberty Bell for others to hear and show his or her painted interpretation of the bell:

> *Kept in Philadelphia, the Liberty Bell was so big that it had cracked and been repaired for years before it rang on July 9, 1776. It rang for the first public reading of the Declaration of Independence. The next year, it was hidden because people were afraid the British would melt it down for ammunition. The bell was taken back to Independence Hall and it rang its last time in 1846, when the Abolitionists adopted it as a symbol and called it the Liberty Bell. Today, it is in its own glass pavilion across from Independence Hall.*

Other activities suitable for a center are the following:

1. *The Meaning of the Stars and Stripes:* Ask children to suggest meanings for the symbols in America's flag and then guide them to reference books with information about the history of the U.S. flag, and when it was designed and officially adopted (June 14, 1777).

2. *The Meaning of the Flag's Symbols:* Invite the children to inquire into the meaning of the symbols in the flag given by others—the stars (heaven), the color red (from flag of England), the color white (liberty), and the stripes (showing separation from England). Using what they know about U.S. history today, invite the children to design a new flag for the United States using new symbols that have meanings related to historical events that they select.

3. *The Seal of America:* Have the children imagine they are with Benjamin Franklin, John Adams, and Thomas Jefferson, and all of them have been given the task of designing a seal for the united colonies. The seal will be stamped on important papers. What could be shown on this historic seal? What do the children suggest? Have them draw a sketch of their ideas for a seal. Then show the children the back of

a dollar bill to see the seal that is eventually adopted. What is on this historic seal that the children suggested (stars, eagle)? Write the similarities as the children dictate them, and ask the children to give their reasons why they selected what they did for their interpretation of the seal.

America's Constitution

Read selections from Peter Spier's book *We, the People: The Constitution of the U.S.* (Doubleday, 1987, Grade 3 up) and discuss the line-by-line pictorial presentation of the preamble to the constitution that begins, "We, the people . . ." Show children the illustrations in the book and the contrasting aspects of life in the 1700s and life as it is now. Review the events that led up to the writing of the Constitution by reading aloud excerpts from H. S. Peterson's *Give Us Liberty: The Story of the Declaration of Independence* (Garrard, 1973, Grade 3 up). Give the children a closer look at what went on through the eyes of John Hancock, a kindly patriot, by reading aloud parts of *Will You Sign Here, John Hancock* (Coward, 1976, Grade 3 up) by Jean Fritz. Point out that the words *John Hancock* came to mean a signature with the words, "Put your John Hancock here." Have the children write a sentence to show what they would have put in the Constitution and to add their individual "John Hancock" signatures on a sheet of butcher paper for a mural display for the classroom.

Activity #131: "Fairness to All"

Discuss the idea that one valuable benefit from the American Revolution is not just that our ancestors got their freedom but also that the United States of America became a nation with ways to be fair to all. For instance, in our Constitution:

1. There is room for individualism as well as unity. There are words in the Constitution that indicate we have the freedom to be individuals, with an identity related to our roots, as well as to be unified with others, with an identity as Americans.

2. There is room for understanding freedom as well as authority, and room for understanding similarities as well as differences. Ask the children to give examples from their present experiences when (a) understanding and accepting authority was necessary and important to them, (b) accepting someone else's similarities or differences was necessary and important to them, and (c) they saw someone being fair to everyone in a particular situation.

Activity #132: "Citizens in Class"

America's constitutional law and rulings of the Supreme Court present a citizen's rights related to property loss and damage, legitimate educational purpose, health and safety, and disruption of the educational process. Some rulings are rights that children are guaranteed in their school and some represent the times when children can be deprived of those rights. To introduce the idea of guaranteed rights versus deprivation of rights in the classroom, invite children to discuss these topics and suggest guidelines that will help them fulfill their obligations as citizens in the classroom and at school. Write their suggestions on the board, such as:

How I Can Fulfill My Obligations as a Citizen

- I have the right to peaceably attend meetings, to petition, to receive fair treatment, and to privacy.
- I can put a problem on the agenda for a class meeting (e.g., to talk about damage or loss of my property, my educational purpose, my health and safety, any disruption of my educational learning, etc.).
- I can get a receipt for items confiscated when I have disrupted the educational process.
- I can go to arbitration and mentoring if I am involved in fighting or other disruptions, and then I can expect result or consequence (e.g., I can lose some privileges, make an apology, visit a school counseler, or control my actions/angry feelings that lead to disruptions).

America's Bill of Rights

Encourage the children to discuss some of the rights guaranteed under the United States Bill of Rights, the first 10 amendments written to support the concept of equality in the Declaration of Independence, and to emphasize the basic freedoms of citizens in the United States. Point out that some of the rights were controversial at the time, and arguments over the rights almost cost the unity of the colonists in this time period. Ask children to think why someone would argue for and against the following rights, and record their remarks on the board:

	For	*Against*
Freedom of religion	1.	1.
Freedom of speech	2.	2.
Freedom of press	3.	3.
Right to peaceful meetings	4.	4.
Petition the government	5.	5.

	For	*Against*
Right to arms	6.	6.
Right to fair treatment	7.	7.
Right to privacy	8.	8.
Right to bail	9.	9.
Right to public trial by jury	10.	10.
Freedom from cruel and unusual punishment if guilty	11.	11.

Activity #133: "Children's Bill of Rights"

Invite the children to suggest ideas for a Children's Bill of Rights for the classroom. Record their ideas in a graphic form on the board with headings similar to that shown in Figure 10–4. Ask the children to make brief speeches for each heading in the graphic, and ask their friends in class to vote on a proposed "right" they support. Ask them to design one-page broadsides (advertising posters) about the rights they advocate. Display the posters in the classroom just as the broadsides of Revolutionary Days were displayed. Have the children keep a record of the voting process and report their findings orally to other classrooms and in writing in a class newspaper.

America's Bald Eagle

Mention to the children that in 1784, Benjamin Franklin wrote a friend and acknowledged the bald eagle as America's national emblem. Elicit from the children some of the characteristics of the Bald Eagle and write the information they offer in a list on the board. Ask them to participate in two activities: (1) to suggest what meaning the eagle's characteristics have for them as Americans and to write brief

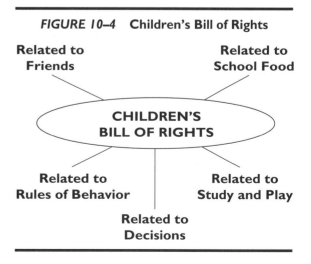

FIGURE 10–4 Children's Bill of Rights

informational paragraph(s) about the national emblem; and (2) to use what they learned to draw an illustration of the bald eagle. Collect the paragraphs and illustrations, and place them in a class book entitled America's National Emblem. Make it available for interested children to browse through and read.

Activity #134: "Selecting the Bald Eagle"

Ask the children to search for additional facts about the bald eagle that might influence someone to select the bird as the national emblem of the United States. Have them team up with partners for the search and then return to the whole group to report the facts they gathered. In the whole group, elicit the children' facts and ideas, and write their comments on the board in two columns with headings of Facts about the Bald Eagle and "Meaning for Us Today." Focus on the characteristics of the bald eagle that make it a fine candidate as our nation's emblem.

Facts about the Bald Eagle	*Meaning for Us Today*
	"I think the bald eagle is America's emblem because . . ."
1.	1.

If some children think that another bird would be a better choice as the country's emblem, invite them to do additional research and to read about the creature's characteristics. Have them focus on the traits they think would make the creature a better candidate for the emblem. Invite them to sketch a drawing of their selection(s), write the reasons for their choice(s), and present their choice to the whole group. If desired, invite the children to debate whether to vote for the bald eagle or a new choice. If a wider scale of debate is appropriate, have the children distribute information flyers with illustrations of their choice of a national bird, prepare ballots and ballot boxes, vote, tally the votes, and announce the results.

Revolutionary Era Songs

"All around the cobbler's bench, the monkey chased the weasel" are the words that introduce a song popular in the Revolutionary days found in *Pop! Goes the Weasel* (Lippincott, 1976, all grades) by Robert Quackenbush. Discuss the meaning of any words unfamiliar to the children (i.e., *weasel, cobbler*), and elicit the children's definitions of the words before

reading aloud the definitions from a dictionary. Show the illustrations that contrast how historical sites looked in 1776 and how they look today. Place the words of the song on a transparency, sing it aloud, then have children quickly sketch scenes on clear plastic baggies (sandwich size) that represent their feelings about the music. Project the words and scenes while the children sing the song several times. Have the children take the scenes home.

Activity #135: "'Yankee Doodle' to Summarize Event"

Initiate a two-minute Time to Remember period and ask, "What are some of the facts you remember about this event (or historical action, historical personality, place related to America's Revolutionary War days)?" As the children make suggestions, record the historical information they give on a chart, the board, or an overhead transparency. Refer to the information to write different words for the familiar tune "Yankee Doodle." Have the children sing the song to review the tune and to get reacquainted with the original words before they suggest any additional words they want to use to tell about an historical action or figure. For example, if the children have read or heard *Jack Jouett's Ride* (Viking, 1973, Grades 1–5) by Gail Haley, they can summarize the story of his late-night ride and the warning he gave to Jefferson and others about the marching British troops to the tune of "Yankee Doodle." One night, Jack sees Tarleton and his troops riding toward Charlottesville and Monticello, where Jefferson, Henry, and other revolutionaries are residing. Jack rides his horse, Sallie, to warn the leaders. As the leaders leave, Jack puts on a fresh red uniform to look like an officer and then borrows a swift horse to lead the British away in another direction. The children's words about this event might look like the following:

> *To the Tune of "Yankee Doodle"*
>
> Jack Jouett crept out to ride
> Fast on his mighty mare
> He rode and rode
> to Charlottesville
> to warn the leaders there.
>
> Tarleton's troops
> Are on their way
> Was Jack's warning cry
> to Patrick Henry, Jefferson
> and wounded General Stevens.

Refrain:

Jack Jouett just rode and rode
Across the countryside
The British soldiers marched and marched,
But Jack beat them with his try.

Johnny Appleseed Chapman: A.D. 1774–1845

"The maples, shedding their spinning seeds,/ Called to his appleseeds in the ground,/ . . . without a sound" describes Appleseed's observations of nature "In Praise of Johnny Appleseed" by Vachel Lindsay in *Story and Verse* (Macmillan, 1946) by Miriam Blanton Huber. After reading the poem aloud, select a biography about Johnny Appleseed, such as *Johnny Appleseed* (Morrow, 1988, all grades) by Steven Kellogg. Kellogg's book is a life story of John Chapman, the gentle healer, who carries apple seeds and is known to have a tame wolf as a companion. Sometimes, he dresses in ragged clothes and wears a cooking pot for a hat as he travels through Pennsylvania, Ohio, and Indiana. Since Kellogg's book is the story of a famous man's life who is now considered a folk legend, it can be an inspiring way to learn history about this time period.

Activity #136: "Appleseed Diagram"

After reading a biography about Johnny Appleseed to the children, engage them in contributing what they know about this famous figure. Write their ideas under headings on the board or chart in a character diagram similar to the one shown in Figure 10–5. Read excerpts from two stories about Appleseed aloud to the children, and select one or more of the following to engage the children further in activities:

1. As you read the first selected story, ask the children to draw their own character diagram with headings of birth, family, childhood, travels, interests, and friends, and write in the information they learned.
2. As you read aloud information from one book, engage the children in writing lists of facts under the headings of a character diagram.
3. As you read aloud information from the second story about Appleseed, ask the children to draw a *second* character diagram with the same headings of birth, family, childhood, travels, interests, and friends they used in the *first* character

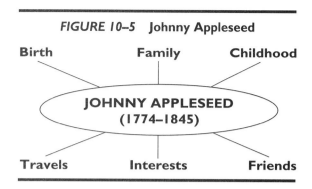

FIGURE 10–5   Johnny Appleseed

Birth   Family   Childhood

JOHNNY APPLESEED (1774–1845)

Travels   Interests   Friends

diagram. Have them write in the facts they recall from the second story.

4. Referring to both diagrams, ask the children to discuss the major points identified by the authors that the children heard as they listened to excerpts from the two books.
5. With the two character diagrams representing information from two books, ask the children to find similarities and differences in the two versions of Appleseed's life.

Activity #137: "Compare and Contrast"

Continue reading aloud different books about Appleseed to give different accounts of his life and ask the children to compare and contrast the ways this period is seen by the different authors. Since reading aloud a book about John "Appleseed" Chapman is a way to acquaint children with the story of a famous man's life, it can be an inspiring way for them to learn about lives in this time period. Books suitable for this are shown in Figure 10–6.

Appleseed and Apples

A study of the life of Johnny Appleseed can be a bridge to a study of the history about apples and to other types of literature about the topic of apples. For example, have the children study the types of apples, the fruit's life cycle, where apples grow, climate needed for growth, the jobs apples can provide, ways they were used by families in the 1700s and ways they are used today, or even ways apples are portrayed in stories. Prepare a display of books about apples and include *Apples* (Macmillan, 1972, Grades 2–3) by Nonny Hogrogian, an informational book, or a fanciful story such as *The Giant Apple* (Carolrhoda, 1990, Grades K–3) by Ursel Scheffler. Scheffler's story is a tale about the Appleville citizens who always lose to the Beet Valley people at

---

FIGURE 10–6   **Children's Books about Johnny Appleseed**

PERSPECTIVES

Aliki. *The Story of Johnny Appleseed*. Ill. by the author. Prentice, 1963. The text is a simple account of John Chapman and events in his life. Biography. Grades 2–3.

Kellogg, S. *Johnny Appleseed*. Ill. by the author. Morrow, 1988. This is a life story of John Chapman, who carries apple seeds through Pennsylvania, Ohio, and Indiana. Biography. All grades.

Hunt, M. L. *Better Known as Johnny Appleseed*. Ill. by J. Daughterty. Lippincott, 1950. Young John Chapman leaves western Pennsylvania, where he works as an orchardist, and enters Ohio country with a bag of appleseeds. He plants the seeds in the land so the pioneers will have apples when they arrive. Biography. Grades 1–5.

Lindbergh, R. *Johnny Appleseed*. Joy Street/Little, Brown, 1990. This text is suitable for a choral reading since it has poetic lines in rhyme that tell the story of John Chapman, naturalist and missionary. Biography. Grades 2–4.

Norman, G. *Johnny Appleseed*. Ill. by J. Caraway. Putnam's, 1960. This text tells the story of John Chapman from his childhood as a boy of 7 years old to his days as an elderly man in colonial America. He is given the name of Appleseed because he devotes his life to planting apple trees. Biography. Grades 1–2.

---

their annual Harvest Festival. They decide to concentrate on growing an enormous apple to win the contest for the "best and biggest." The giant apple furnishes them with applesauce, apple donuts, and apple fritters through the winter, but since they lack vegetables, they find out they have to buy what they need from the people in Beet Valley. Invite the children to browse or read through the books in the display and to tell the whole group what they learned about apples and their value.

Activity #138: "Peel, Pulp, and Pit"

Show the life cycle from flower to apple with the colorful illustrations in Charles Micucci's *The Life and Times of the Apple* (Orchard, 1992, Grades 1–3), and discuss what can be learned about the apple from the book—the grafting process, its cycle, and the related facts shown on time lines, charts, and diagrams. Invite the children to suggest additional ways they can learn more about apples. Write their ideas in a list on the board (e.g., visiting a nearby orchard; helping to harvest apples; talking to a grower about how apple trees are grafted; visiting a store to buy different types of apples to taste and compare; reading a cook book to discover recipes that use apples; copying unusual recipes that use apples to make apple cookies, apple

muffins, and apple sauce; drying apple slices; making apple juice; and constructing doll-figures from dried apples). If appropriate, relate the study of apples to other areas of the curriculum. Consider the following examples:

• *Related to Math:* Engage the children in counting apples, in cutting an apple in half to see the pattern of the seeds, in grouping apples according to attributes of color, size, type and weight, in weighing ("How many make a bushel?"), and in measuring the circumference of different types.

• *Related to Writing:* Invite the children to write fiction and nonfiction about apples and what they have learned.

• *Related to Science:* Ask the children to poll their class or family members to find out each one's favorite type of apple and then plant apple seeds from that favorite apple to start apple tree(s) for their family.

History Mysteries and Ghost Stories

To provide further background for the time period of the 1700s, introduce children to the goosebump

FIGURE 10–7   Children's Books about History Mysteries and Ghost Stories

PERSPECTIVES

Lars at Valley Forge: 1700s

Jensen, D. *The Riddle of Penncroft Farm*. Harcourt Brace Jovanovich, 1989. A ghost tells a boy what life was like during America's Revolutionary War. Historical fiction. Grades 3–6.

Charles Dickens in America: 1842

Curry, J. L. *What the Dickens!* McElderry, 1991. In a Harrisburg bookstore in Virginia, 11-year-old Cherry Dobbs overhears a plot to steal Dickens's manuscript in progress, *American Notes*. Cherry foils the scheme. Historical fiction. Grades 3–6.

A Mystery in the Arctic: 1845

Beattie, O., & J. Geiger. *Buried in Ice: The Mystery of a Lost Artic Expedition*. Scholastic, 1992. In spring, 1845, Sir John Franklin's expedition sets sail in two ships, the *Erebus* and the *Terror*, to look for a Northwest passage. Luke Smith, a stoker on board the *Terror*, tells the story of the harsh winter and a mysterious illness that affects the crew. In this expedition mystery, none of Franklin's party ever returned. Years later, in 1930, some explorers find the remains of two campsites, a few records, and skeletal remains of some party members. The author, an anthropologist, uses archaeological evidence to hypothesize about the fate of the Franklin expedition. Nonfiction. Grade 3 up.

A Mystery about a Keepsake: 1900s back to 1700s

Precek, K. W. *The Keepsake Chest*. Macmillan, 1992. In the attic of a house in Ohio, Meg Hamilton discovers an old cherry chest carved with the date 1774. Inside are quilts, old papers, baby clothes, and an old blue uniform coat. The chest helps her find clues to prove her family has a legal right to the land, and she stops a developer from building a housing development. Historical fiction. Grades 3–6.

idea of learning about history not from a "ghost of Christmas past" but from a ghost of Revolutionary Days. Read aloud *The Riddle of Penncroft Farm* (Harcourt Brace Jovanovich, 1989, Grade 3 up) by D. Jensen. In the story, Lars is contacted by a ghost who tells him about what life was like at Valley Forge during the Revolutionary War. After the children read or listen to this story, ask them to write their own responses about what they think life was like for soldiers and others at Valley Forge. Ask volunteers to read their responses aloud to the others.

Activity #139: "Interpretations"

Point out to the children that a history mystery or ghost story such as *The Riddle of Penncroft Farm* by D. Jensen is an *interpretation* of what happened and they can compare the story with other books that have factual information about the same event. To do this, have the children search for information about life at Valley Forge during America's Revolutionary Days and report their findings back to the group. For children interested in this studying history through mysteries and ghost stories, see Figure 10-7, and guide them to titles of additional stories that portray the 1700s as well as other time periods.

CHAPTER ELEVEN

A.D. 1800–1899

What was going on in the nineteenth century?

Multicultural Perspectives

For a study of this period, encourage the children to read about early champions of civil rights and the effects of slavery, rebellions against it, and ways people escaped from it. This period also offers opportunities to learn about some of our ancestors—the Native People, the Chinese workers in the gold camps in the West, the Latino/Hispanic people who rebelled against the rule of their governments, various peoples of color, as well as newcomers to the United States.

Some children may be interested in what life was like for slaves in the South, Abraham Lincoln, and the Civil War soldiers who lined up for mess, lived in crude shelters, and suffered severely from the cold during the winter months. Other children may want to inquire about those who were differently abled yet proved their abilities, the roles of women and religious groups, and the life stories of those who helped others or those who respected nature and the environment. Still other children may want to read folk literature that represents the heritage of different cultural groups or read tall tales that represent a type of story that is unique to America. For children interested in any of the following heritage perspectives on Figure 11–1, there are selections of children's literature about various people from different heritages and what they did during this period.

Lewis and Clark: A.D. 1804

The poem "Lewis and Clark" in *A Book of Americans* (Holt, 1986, all grades) by Rosemary and

Stephen Vincent Benet describes the trip of the two men up the Missouri River that takes one and a half years. To recognize this expedition that opened the western wilderness further through oral interpretation, ask the children to suggest ways to orally recite the verses (loud voices, soft voices, with motions, and so on) and have them read the poem aloud as a choral reading. Perhaps the children can add pantomime actions to the verses about Lewis (1774–1809) and Clark (1770–1838) suffering from the croup, being chased by a grizzly, and feeling that their teeth were "full of moss."

Activity #140: "John Colter"

Who'd Believe John Colter? (Macmillan, 1992, Grades 3–5) by M. B. Christian tells the fictionalized life story of John Colter, a member of Lewis and Clark's expeditionary force. Born in Virginia, Colter is a hunter-trapper and a teller of tall tales, and is believed to be the first European American to see the area now called Yellowstone National Park. Invite the children to listen to Colter's story to find out why, in one adventurous situation, Colter had to jump into some cold river water to save himself. With a map, have the children cross-check the information on page 56 of the book that says that the Platte River was the cold water into which Colter jumped. Since Colter at the time was in Montana near the headwaters of the Missouri, Madison, Galloti, and Jefferson Rivers, it seems that some people claim he jumped into the Jefferson Fork to save himself. Have the children look at a map of the area and determine from their points of view, which river—the Platte or the Jefferson Fork—was the

FIGURE 11–1   Children's Books about the 1800s

PERSPECTIVES

African Heritage

Adler, D. A. *A Picture Book of Sojourner Truth.* Holiday House, 1995. This story tells how Sojourner Truth became a passionate advocate against slavery. Biography. Grades K–3.

Aliki. *A Weed Is a Flower: The Life of George Washington Carver.* Ill. by the author. Simon and Schuster, 1988. This life story depicts the achievements and scientific efforts of George Washington Carver, especially his development of more than 300 uses for the peanut. Biography. Grades 2–3.

Barrett, T. *Nat Turner and the Slave Revolt.* Millbrook, 1993. Turner leads a rebellion against slave holders in Hampton County, Virginia, a revolt sometimes called the first war against slavery in the United States. Historical fiction. Grades 2–4.

Bennett, E. *Frederick Douglass and the War Against Slavery.* Millbrook, 1992. Douglass, born a slave, becomes a great writer and speaker in the abolitionist movement as well as an advisor to President Lincoln. Biography. Grades 2–4.

Blassingame, W. *Jim Beckwourth: Black Trapper and Indian Chief.* Garrard, 1973. This life story portrays the life of Beckwourth, a famous mountain man who was a war chief for the Crow people. Biography. Grade 3 up.

Bradby, M. *More than Anything Else.* Ill. by C. K. Soentpiet. Orchard, 1995. After emancipation, Booker T. Washington labors from early dawn to dusk in a West Virginia salt works. But more than anything, he has a desire to read and write. After a newspaper man in town explains the meaning of the alphabet letters, Booker learns how to write his name. Historical fiction. Grades Pre–3.

Brill, M. T. *Allen Jay and the Underground Railroad.* Ill. by J. L. Porter. Carolrhoda, 1993. Eleven-year-old Allen Jay helps a slave escape to freedom as early as 1842. Jay later becomes a well-known teacher and minister. Includes historical notes. Historical fiction. Grades 2–4.

Everett, G. *John Brown: One Man Against Slavery.* Ill. by J. Lawrence. Rizzoli, 1992. In 1859, 16-year-old Annie Brown stays awake at night worried over her father's decision to fight slavery through an armed attack on the arsenal at Harper's Ferry (in an area now West Virginia). The book includes paintings by Jacob Lawrence that show Brown's determination to end slavery, author's notes, and biographical information about the artist. Biography. Grades 3–6.

Ferris, J. *Go Free or Die: A Story about Harriet Tubman.* Carolrhoda, 1988. This is the life story of Harriet Tubman, born a slave, who escaped and courageously returned to the South to lead over 300 people out of slavery. It portrays her service as a scout and spy for the Union Army and her fight for human rights. Biography. Grade 3 up.

Johnson, D. *Now Let Me Fly: The Story of a Slave Family.* Macmillan, 1993. Through the story of Minna and her family and their life on a plantation, the text portrays an honest and painful view of the harsh lives endured by early American slave families. It does not have a happy ending. Historical fiction. Grade 3 up.

Johnson, D. *Seminole Diary: Remembrances of a Slave.* Macmillan, 1994. In a diary format, Libbie tells how her family escapes from slavery in 1834 and joins with Native Americans for safety and acceptance. Historical fiction. Grades 1–3.

Lester, J. *The Tale of Uncle Remus: The Adventure of Brer Rabbit.* Dial, 1987. This collection has more than 40 tales that are retold in contemporary southern black English. Folk literature. Grade 3 up.

continued

FIGURE 11–1   **Continued**

African Heritage

Lyons, M. E. *Master of Mahogany: Tom Day, Free Black Cabinetmaker*. Scribners, 1994. Set in the 1800s in Virginia and North Carolina, this traces Day's life as an apprentice, journeyman, and independent cabinetmaker who becomes known for his sculptured carvings. He becomes one of the largest furniture producers in North Carolina. Biography. Grades 3–5.

Merriwether, L. *The Freedom Ship of Robert Smalls*. Ill. by L. J. Morton. Prentice-Hall, 1971. This book presents the life of Robert Smalls (1839–1919), the captain of *The Planter*, who commandeered a Confederate gunboat and turned it into a freedom ship. Biography. Grades 2–4.

Miller, W. *Frederick Douglass: The Last Days of Slavery*. Ill. by C. Lucas. Lee & Low, 1995. A message of freedom is sent through Douglass and his actions, particularly his refusal to accept being a slave. Biography. Grades K–3.

Monjo, F. N. *The Drinking Gourd*. Ill. by F. Brenner. Harper, 1970. Young Tommy Fuller is sent home from church because of a prank and finds a runaway slave family in the barn. When a search party arrives, Tommy pretends that he is running away from home in the hay wagon. The marshal decides not to search the wagon. That night, his father explains that he knows he is breaking a law but that he must. Words to the code song to escape by following the North Star in the Big Dipper are included. Historical fiction. Grades 2–3.

Patterson, L. G. *Booker T. Washington*. Garrard, 1962. This life story relates Washington's life from a slave boy to college president at age 25. The text focuses on the positive aspect of his leadership for African Americans. Biography. Grades 2–4.

Pelz, R. *Black Heroes of the Wild West*. Open Yesterday and Today Hand Pub., 1990. Several brief life stories depict African Americans and their journeys to the frontier. Multiple biography. Grade 3 up.

Porter, C. *Meet Addy*. Pleasant Co., 1992. Addy Walker, an African American girl, grows up during the disturbing Civil War days in 1864. Historical fiction. Grade 3 up.

Winter, J. *Follow the Drinking Gourd*. Knopf, 1989. Peg Leg Joe, a one-legged sailor, teaches plantation slaves the way to freedom in the North. He sings a song with directions to the Underground Railroad. Following the lyrics, a family flees to freedom and travels north. Historical note and music are included. Historical Fiction. Grades 3–5.

Wright, C. C. *Wagon Train: A Family Goes West in 1865*. Ill. by G. Griffith. This life story portrays the hardships and endurance of an African American family who travels west. Historical fiction. Grades 1–4.

Asian Heritage

Coerr, E. *Chang's Paper Pony*. Ill. by D. K. Ray. Harper & Row, 1988. Working in the kitchen of a gold mining camp in California, Chang feels lonely and isolated. He wishes for a pony, something he knows his grandfather cannot afford. Chang finds gold nuggets in the floor boards of Big Pete's cabin, which he gives to Big Pete. For his honesty, Big Pete rewards him with a pony. Avoid displaying the illustrations of the Chinese men since they are shown in pigtails performing menial tasks. Historical fiction. Grades 2–3.

Ness, C. reteller. *The Ocean of Story: Fairy Tales from India*. Ill. by J. Mair. Lothrop, Lee & Shepard, 1996. This collection has 18 tales, including "Three Fussy Men" and "The Blacksmith's Daughter," from the oral tradition that were collected at the end of the nineteenth century. Includes source notes and bibliography. Folk literature. Grade 3 up.

FIGURE 11–1   Continued

European Heritage

Adler, D. A. *A Picture Book of Davy Crockett*. Ill. by J. and A. Wallner. Holiday, 1996. This brief life story introduces a remarkable frontiersman as a figure in real life and in folk legend. Crockett's life story begins with his birth in Tennessee and closes at the Alamo. Biography. Grades K–3.

Conrad, P. *Call Me Ahnighito*. Ill. by R. Egielski. HarperCollins, 1995. In 1894, a large metallic meteorite in Greenland is discovered by Robert E. Peary and other explorers. The meteorite narrates its own story as it is shipped it to New York City and finds a home at the American Museum of Natural Historical fiction. Historical fiction. Grades 1–2.

Conway, C. *Where Is Papa Now?* Ill. by author. Caroline House/Boyds Mills Press, 1994. In the mid-nineteenth century, the captain of a New England ship travels around the world. His daughter Eliza asks the question in the title as she waits for her father to return and sees the seasons go by. The illustrations show the different lands on her father's journey. Historical fiction. Grades 1–3.

D'Aulaire, I., & E. P. D'Aulaire. *Buffalo Bill*. Doubleday, 1952. This life story portrays events in Buffalo Bill's frontier life in the 1800s. Biography. Grade 3 up.

De Paola, T. *An Early American Christmas*. Ill. by author. Holiday House, 1987. This book shows how the spirit of the winter season is spread from a German family to a whole town. The customs are ones seen in a contemporary season today—singing carols, placing a tree inside, and putting bayberry candles in the windows. Historical fiction. All grades.

De Kay, O. *Meet Andrew Jackson*. Ill. by I. Barnett. Random House, 1967. This life story briefly depicts Jackson's effect as a military leader during the Civil War. Biography. Grades 2–4.

Henry, J. *A Clearing in the Forest: A Story about a Real Settler Boy*. Four Winds, 1992. This story portrays the activities of a well-to-do family in Indiana and shows how they cope with their crops and the weather. Historical fiction. Grades 3–5.

Kamen, G. *Fiorello: His Honor, the Little Flower*. Ill. by author. Atheneum, 1981. This life story portrays New York's well-liked mayor who becomes a national figure. Biography. Grades 3–5.

Lee, K. *Tracing Our Italian Roots*. John Muir Publications, 1993. This book describes life in southern Italy, particularly the economic hardships, and the people who emigrated to the United States. They face prejudice in their new land. The text discusses Geraldine Ferraro and other famous Italian Americans. Nonfiction. Grade 3 up.

Levinson, R. *Watch the Stars Come Out*. Dutton, 1985. This book is the story of immigrating to America by transatlantic crossing in the early 1890s is told from a child's point of view. Historical fiction. Grade 3–4.

MacLachlan, P. *Skylark*. HarperCollins, 1994. This is a sequel about the difficult life on the prairie for the Witting family—Anna, Caleb, Jacob, and Sarah of *Sarah, Plain and Tall* (HarperCollins, 1985, Grade 3 up). When people leave because of a long drought, Sarah and the children journey east to visit her family for the summer. When Jacob arrives, they all return to the farm, and Sarah announces they will have a baby in the spring. Jacob decides to stay on the prairie and says the family's names are "written" in this land and Sarah writes her name in the ground. Historical fiction. Grade 3 up.

Moscinski, S. *Tracing Our Irish Roots*. John Muir Publications, 1993. This book describes the conditions in Ireland, particularly the potato famine, that led people to emigrate as well as the prejudice they encountered in their working conditions in the United States. The book discusses John F. Kennedy and other famous Irish Americans. Nonfiction. Grade 3 up.

continued

FIGURE 11–1 **Continued**

European Heritage

Murphy, J. *Into the Deep Forest with Henry David Thoreau*. Ill. by K. Kisler. Clarion, 1995. This life story is based on Thoreau's journal entries about his 1857 trip into the Maine wilderness and his respect for nature. He travels with a friend and Native American guide, climbs Mount Katahdin, and observes the flora and fauna of the area. Biography. Grades 3–6.

Saunders, S. R. *The Floating House*. Ill. by H. Cogancherry. Macmillan, 1995. In 1815, the McClure family courageously face the dangers of journeying down the Ohio River on a loaded flatboat in search of new land in Indiana territory. Historical fiction. Grades K–3.

Shelby, A. *Homeplace*. Ill. by W. A. Halperin. Orchard, 1995. This story traces a family's history in the same house that a great-great-great-great grandfather built in 1810. Scenes move from the 1800s to the present and show the construction of an early log cabin as well as eating food at a fast-food drive-in of today. Historical fiction. Grades K–2.

Smiler, N. *Snowshoe Thompson*. Ill. by J. Sandin. HarperCollins, 1992. When John Thompson moves to California from Scandinavia in the early 1850s to make his fortune in the Gold Rush, he becomes a legend of the West. Thompson introduces skis to northern California and wears them to deliver mail over the mountains. This fictionalized story highlights his legendary career as a mailman. Historical fiction. Grades 1–3.

Sorensen, H. *New Hope*. Lothrop, Lee & Shepard, 1995. Grandfather tells Jimmy about Lars Jensen, his great-great-great grandfather, an immigrant from Denmark in 1885, who founded the town of New Hope. Traveling west on a wagon train, the family settles on a riverbank near a forest when a wheel axel breaks. Historical fiction. Grade 3 up.

Stanley, D. *The True Adventure of Daniel Hall*. Ill. by the author. Dial, 1996. This story is based on the 14-year-old's own account of his four-year journey on a whaling ship. Biography. Grades 1–4.

Stanley, D., & P. Vennema. *Charles Dickens: The Man Who Had Great Expectations*. Ill. by D. Stanley. Morrow, 1993. This life story traces major happenings in Dickens's life including his ill health as a child. This book includes partial listing of the novelist's works. Biography. Grades 3–6.

Wilson, J., & J. Hadley. *Justin Wilson's Cajun Fables*. Ill. by E. Troxclair. Pelican, 1986. In 1803, Napoleon sold Louisiana to the United States, a region inhabited by different groups of people, and among them were the Cajuns, the people of Acadian French descent (area once northeastern Canadian provinces). This is a collection of 24 nursery rhymes and fairy tales written with a South Louisiana Cajun setting and vocabulary. Folk literature. Grades 1–4.

Latino/Hispanic Heritage

Adler, D. A. *A Picture Book of Simon Bolivar*. Ill. by R. Casilia. Holiday, 1992. This brief life story portrays Bolivar's accomplishments and includes quotations. The illustrations show Bolivar both as a young child with his tutor and playing with other children as well as an older soldier wearing his ornamented uniform (c. 1800). Biography. Grades 2–4.

Anderson, J. *Spanish Pioneers of the Southwest*. Lodestar, 1989. This book highlights the courage of families who faced many hardships when they settled in the early southwest. Nonfiction. Grade 3 up.

de Varona, F. *Benito Juarez: President of Mexico*. Milbrook, 1992. Juarez, an Indian boy, overcomes prejudice to become the first president of Mexico. Biography. Grades 2–4.

de Varona, F. *Miquel Hidalgo y Costilla: Father of Mexican Independence*. Milbrook, 1992. Father Hidalgo, a Catholic priest, rings the church bell on September 16, 1810, to call his parishioners to a rebellion against Spain's colonial government. Biography. Grades 2–4.

FIGURE 11–1   **Continued**

Latino/Hispanic Heritage

de Varona, F. *Simon Bolivar: Latin American Liberator*. Milbrook, 1992. Bolivar, a military strategist, leads much of South and Central America to overthrow Spanish rule. Biography. Grades 2–4.

Howard, E. F. *Papa Tells Chita a Story*. Ill. by F. Cooper. Simon & Schuster, 1995. Chita wants to know what her father did in the war, he tells her about delivering a secret message during the Spanish-American war that began in 1989. Historical fiction. Grades K–2.

Palacios, A. *Viva Mexico!: A Story of Benito Juarez and Cinco de Mayo*. Ill. by H. Berelson. Steck-Vaughn, 1993. This depicts the life of Juarez up through his presidency in 1816 and discusses the Battle of Puebla, which is commemorated annually on May 5. Includes introductory and end notes. Biography. Grades 2–4.

Westridge Young Writers Workshop. *Kids Explore America's Hispanic Heritage*. John Muir Pub., 1992. This text tells of the Mexican soldiers fighting for their just cause at the Battle of the Alamo. Their view is presented in a way that balances the event for interested children. Nonfiction. Grades 3–6.

Native American Heritage

Banks, S. H. *Remember My Name*. Ill. by B. Saflund. Roberts Rinehart, 1993. Eleven-year-old Annie Rising Fawn prepares to leave her home on Star Mountain and go live with her uncle, William Blackfeather, a wealthy Cherokee land and slave owner. Before she leaves, she buries her favorite doll in a special place, a house of sunflowers that her father had made for her, and she also buries her Cherokee names, Agin' Agli. After Annie arrives in New Echota, the Cherokee capitol in Georgia, she is affected by the Native American Removal of 1838. Historical fiction. Grade 3 up.

Driving Hawk, V. *The Sioux*. Ill. by R. Himler. Holiday House, 1993. This book describes the history and the culture of the Sioux as well as what their lives are like today. Includes a map, a chart of Sioux people, and index. Nonfiction. Grades 1–3.

Freedman, R. *Indian Chiefs*. Holiday, 1987. This collection has brief biographical sketches of leaders of Native Americans. Multiple biography. Grade 3 up.

Jones, J. B. *Heetunka's Harvest: A Tale of the Plains Indians*. Ill. by S. Keegan. Roberts Rinehart, 1995. This Arikara legend of the Bean Mouse, recorded in 1810, emphasizes sharing and having respect for all living things. Folk literature. Grades K–4.

Keithahn, Ed. L. *Alaskan Igloo Tales*. Alaskan Northwest Books/GTE Discovery Publications, 1974. This is a collection of authentic tales from the Northern American Indian culture. Folk literature. Grade 3 up.

McLerran, A. *The Ghost Dance*. Ill. by P. Morin. Clarion, 1995. This book describes the results of white settlers moving westward and depleting resources needed by Native Americans. Tavibo, a Paiute visionary, and his son dreamed that if Native People danced, the white people would disappear and the wildlife would return. Nonfiction. Grade 3 up.

Roop, P., & C. Roop. *Ahyoka and the Talking Leaves*. Ill. by Y. Miyake. Lothrop, Lee & Shepard, 1992. When Sequoyah is ostracized from his Cherokee people and accused of magic, his daughter Ahyoka leaves with him. She realizes that letters relate to sounds (rather than just being pictures) and discovers the key to creating a syllabic alphabet. Together, they create a written language for their people. Biography. Grades 3–5.

continued

FIGURE 11–1   **Continued**

Middle Eastern/Mediterranean Heritage

Shepard, A. *The Enchanted Storks*. Ill. by A. Dianov. Clarion, 1995. This tale, written in the 1800s, is set in ancient Baghdad and tells about a good ruler and his assistant who are tricked by a magician. History of the tale included. Folk literature. Grades 3–6.

Differently Abled Heritage

Carrick C. *Stay Away from Simon!* Clarion, 1985. Simon, a developmentally different boy who is mentally retarded, proves his ability during a winter storm. Realistic fiction. Grades 1–3.

Echewa, T. O. *The Ancestor Tree*. Ill. by C. Hale. Lodestar, 1994. Nna-nna, an elderly blind man, tells the children in an African village that he is afraid there will be no tree for him in the Forest of the Ancestors. Realistic fiction. Grades 2–4.

Turner, B. *The Haunted Igloo*. Houghton Mifflin, 1991. Jean-Paul moves with his parents from Quebec to the Canadian Arctic. Jean-Paul is small, fearful, and has a limp caused by a birth defect—all of which make his adjustment to the move difficult. The native Inuit boys tease him and exclude him from their activities and Jean-Paul learns to deal with his physical limitations and his psychological ones—his fears. Through his ordeals, he learns the value of accepting himself for what he is, friendship, and loyalty. Realistic fiction. Grade 3 up.

Whelan, G. *Hannah*. Ill. by L. Bowman. Knopf, 1991. In the West in 1887, 9-year-old Hannah copes with her blindness and proves she can learn at school by listening and discovers she can read books in braille. At the closing, the children under the class bully's leadership earn money and buy her a Braille writer. Historical fiction. Grade 3 up.

Female Image Heritage

Blos, J. W. *Nellie Bly's Monkey*. Ill. by C. Stock. Morrow, 1996. In 1889, Nellie Bly, a journalist, travels around the world in 72 days. In Singapore, she purchases a monkey, names him McGinty, and brings him home to New York. Historical fiction. Grades 1–3.

Blumberg, R. *Bloomers!* Bradbury, 1993. In 1851, Libby arrives in Seneca Falls, New York, wearing trouserlike pants covered by a skirt that barely reaches her knees. This shocks the town but intrigues her cousin, Elizabeth Cady Stanton. Eventually, Susan B. Anthony and others wear the bloomers as the new uniform of the woman's movement. Historical fiction. Grades 1–2.

Fritz, J. *You Want Women to Vote, Lizzie Stanton?* Ill. by D. Disalvo-Ryan. Putnam, 1995. This life story depicts Stanton's work for women's rights. Biography. Grade 3 up.

Johnston, J. *Harriet and the Runaway Book: The Story of Harriet Beecher Stowe and Uncle Tom's Cabin*. Ill. by R. Himler. Harper, 1977. Born and educated in Connecticut, Harriet marries Calvin Stowe, a professor at the Lane Theological Seminary in Cincinnati, Ohio. Harriet sees many slaves escape to freedom across the Ohio River, which is the dividing line between the free states and slave states, and she becomes determined to write a book to show how terrible slavery was. Biography. Grades 3–5.

Jordan, D. *Susie King Taylor: Destined to be Free*. Ill. by H. Bond. Just Us Books, 1994. This is a brief life story of Taylor, born a slave, who grows up to be a heroine of the 1800s. She attends a secret school to learn to read and write, escapes slavery, and at age 14 becomes a teacher of black children and adults on St. Simon's Sea Island. She also becomes a nurse in the Union Army and writes *Reminiscences of My life in Camp*, a retelling of her army experiences. Biography. Grades 3–5.

FIGURE 11–1 Continued

le Image Heritage

ly, E. A. *The Bobbin Girl.* Ill. by the author. Dial, 1996. This story is based on the true account of arriet Hanson Robinson whose mother ran a mill boarding house in the nineteenth century in Low-l, Massachusetts. The house becomes the meeting place for the women to talk about their goals id working conditions during a mill walk-out in protest of a pay cut. Historical fiction. Grades 2–4.

, R. H. *The Story of Stagecoach Mary.* Ill. by C. Hanna. Silver Burdett Press, 1995. This life story escribes the accomplishment and nontraditional lifestyle of Mary Fields, the first African Amer-:an woman to carry the United States mail. She drives a stagecoach route from Cascade to St. 'eter's Mission, MT. Historical fiction. Grades K–3.

ael, E. & D. Bolognese. *Sacajawea: The Journey West.* Scholastic, 1994. This life story details a 'oung girl's journey west with the expedition of Lewis and Clark. Biography. Grades 1–3.

aport, D. *Trouble at the Mines.* Crowell, 1987. In 1899, in Amot, Pennsylvania, the coal miners go on strike and the troubled times are recounted by a miner's daughter, Rosie Wilson. In the community, Mary Harris, also known as Mother Jones, provides for the miners. Historical fiction. Grade 3 up.

Roop, P., & C. Roop. *Keep the Lights Burning, Abbie.* Ill. by P. Hanson. When Captain Burgess, a lighthouse keeper on the coast of Maine in 1856, goes after needed supplies for his family, he leaves young Abbie in charge of the lights while he is gone. A tremendous storm blows in and he is gone for four weeks. During this time, Abbie and her sisters care for their sick mother and Abbie keeps the lights burning. Based on a true story. Historical fiction. Grades 1–4.

San Souci, R. *Kate Shelley: Bound for Legend.* Ill. by M. Ginsburg. Dial, 1996. This story is based on a true account about a 15-year-old girl who gave warning that a train bridge was out and averted a major train wreck. Historical fiction. Grades K–4.

St. George, J. *By George, Bloomers!* Shoe Tree, 1989. This story is a fictionalized view of the topic of bloomers being worn as a symbol of the women's rights movement. Historical fiction. Grade 1–3.

Wettener, M. K. *Kate Shelley and the Midnight Express.* Ill. by K. Ritz. Carolthoda, 1990. In 1881 in Iowa, a 15-year-old girl overcomes her own fears and warns the railroad of a train bridge that is washed out in a flood. Her bravery during the storm saves hundreds of lives, and the state of Iowa, the railroad, and its workers recognize her bravery. Historical fiction. Grades 2–5.

Religious Heritage

Bial, R. *Shaker Home.* Houghton Mifflin, 1994. Information on homelife of the Shakers, individuals who live together in a community with discipline and kindness. Nonfiction. Grade 3 up.

Penn, M. *The Miracle of the Potato Latkes: A Hanukkah Story.* Ill. by G. Carmi. Holiday, 1994. During a potato famine, Tante Golda shares one potato with an old beggar who appears at her door, and the next day, two potatoes appear in the menorah. Each morning another potato appears and Tante Golda is able to invite guests for latkes. Folk literature. Grades K–2.

Smucker, B. *Selina and the Bear Paw Quilt.* Ill. by J. Wilson. Crown, 1996. Selina's Mennonite family flees to Canada to avoid persecution as the Civil War is about to break out. Her grandmother, too old to travel, gives Selina a bear-claw patterned quit she has been making from fabric remnants, including pieces from her wedding dress. Historic fiction. Grades 1–3.

Yoder, J. W. *Rosanna of the Amish.* Herald Press, 1996. This story is based on the true experience of an Irish orphan raised by the Amish in central Pennsylvania in the 1800s and the events that chronicle her lifespan—childhood years, youth, marriage, and raising her family. Historical fiction. Grade 3 up.

river into which Colter jumped. Christian's book also includes a map, sources of information, and suggests more books for further reading, which children can locate in the school library or in a branch of a nearby public library.

Activity #141: "Decision Making"

Discuss with the children the meaning of the word *expedition*. Ask them why they think Lewis and Clark decided to go on such a long journey, rather than refuse to travel so far. Ask them to join with partners and inquire into the lives of the leaders of this famous expedition. After the children's inquiries, have them make a brief presentation to the class to tell why Lewis and Clark decided to go on this expedition. In a general discussion, ask the children to suggest situations where they feel it would be better to be part of an expedition than to refuse to go, or vice versa. Have them give their reasons for their decisions. Write their reasons on the board:

Why I Would Be Part   *Reason*
of an Expedition
1.

Why I Would Refuse   *Reason*
to Be Part of an
Expedition
1.

Dolley Madison: 1768–1840

In *Dolley Madison, First Lady of the Land* (Children's, 1974, Grades 2–3) by Matthew G. Grant, children will learn about Dolley Madison's life as a young Quaker girl, her first marriage, and the epidemic of yellow fever that killed her first husband and one of her children. She is introduced to James Madison and they marry and move to Washington, D.C., where Dolley serves as hostess for President Thomas Jefferson. She later presides over the President's Palace for her husband when he is president (1809–1817). When the Palace is burned during the War of 1812, it is rebuilt and named the White House. After that, Dolley lives with Madison 20 years after his presidency. When he dies, she returns to Washington and becomes a social leader once more. After the story, ask the children to contribute words to describe Dolley as the First Lady during this time period. Write the children's contributions on a historical figure web on the board (see Figure 11–2) and ask the children to sketch scenes to represent the words.

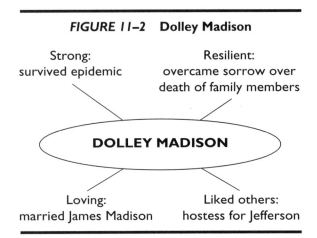

FIGURE 11–2   Dolley Madison

Strong: survived epidemic

Resilient: overcame sorrow over death of family members

DOLLEY MADISON

Loving: married James Madison

Liked others: hostess for Jefferson

Activity #142: "Presidential Wives"

The lives of the Madisons during the first years of America as a new nation are described by Robert Quackenbush in *James Madison & Dolley Madison and Their Times* (Pippin, 1992, Grades 2–5), a dual biography. Show the children that at the foot of each page is an illustration of contemporary children who are role-playing the actions of Dolley and James Madison and others. Ask the children to compare and contrast the role of Dolley Madison as the wife of the president with the role of the wife of the president today. Discuss any changes in the role as the children see them.

Dolley Madison   *Current Presidential Wife*
1.   1.

Ask the children to give reasons why they think the role of the wife of a president has changed over time. Engage them in illustrating any differences in the roles. Give all children a sheet of art paper and ask them to fold the sheet in half. On the left side, they should sketch Dolley Madison and her actions during an event, and on the other side, they should sketch the actions in a similar event with the wife of the current president. Similarly, have the children compare and contrast the role of a president's wife in another country today with the role of the president's wife in the United States. Discuss the differences they found. If appropriate, repeat the activity by asking the children to compare and contrast the role of James Madison and his actions as president during this time period with the role of the president today.

Activity #143: "Historical Story Props"

Invite the children to prepare a scarf, necktie, hat, or a neckerchief as a prop and write historical information on the prop about James Madison or about another historical figure of this period. In small groups, ask the children to meet and decide on what information about a historical figure they have read or heard about that they could write on the prop:

1. The main historical figure and the setting
2. A problem the figure faced and the solution
3. Two important events in the historical figure's life story

When this has been decided, have the children write the facts they selected about the historical figure on the scarfs, neckties, hat, and neckerchiefs, and then wear or show the props when retelling parts of the historical figure's life story. To make the props, children can:

1. Cut a 36″ square of inexpensive pellon into scarves (6″ × 36″) and into neckerchiefs (cut the 18″ square in half diagonally) or into neckties (3″ × 36″). Newspaper or butcher paper can be folded into three-corner hats.

2. Place newspapers on the tables or desks to prevent the colored markers from going through the props to stain the desks or tables.

3. Write on the props with permanent ink markers and let dry. Mention to the children that the ink can smear their work until it dries.

4. On the props, write the name of the historical figure, the setting, two exciting or important events that happened, and a problem and its resolution.

5. As an option, make similar props of butcher paper or cloth, and decorate with buttons and other materials around the border.

6. Have the children wear the props and refer to what they wrote while retelling their stories about historical figures. Display the items in the room.

7. Display the props in the school library or other display area on the school campus. Ask the children to write their names on index cards along with brief explanations about what they did to make the item. Place the index cards with the items in the display. Later, have the children take their items home and tell what they learned from this activity.

War of 1812

During the War of 1812, two sisters trick an invading British crew into thinking they were part of the Massachusetts Home Guard in *An American Army of Two* (Carolrhoda, 1992, Grades 1–3) by J. Greeson. This is historical fiction inspired by a true event: The crew members of menacing British ships invade the coastal town of Scituate, Massachusetts, for supplies, but they leave when they hear the fife and drum of the advancing Massachusetts Home Guard. The Bates sisters, Rebecca, 20, and Abigail, 16, play "Yankee Doodle" from the shore to trick the British into thinking the Home Guard is still there. Believing that the Home Guard had returned, the British crew members retreated. Additional details of the sisters' actions are told in *Abigail's Drum* (Pippin, 1995, Grade 3 up) written by J. A. Minahan and illustrated by Robert Quackenbush. Daughters of the lighthouse keeper on Cedar Point, the two sisters outwit the British sailors who come ashore, take their father hostage, and decide to burn the town.

Activity #144: "Yankee Doodle"

Engage the children in singing the song "Yankee Doodle" and ask them to contribute new words about Rebecca and Abigail's actions (explained in Activity #135) using the song "Yankee Doodle." Here is an example:

To the Tune of Yankee Doodle

British soldiers came to town
sailing up the coast
Sister Becky took a fife
and blew with her utmost
Yankee Doodle, Keep it up . . .

British soldiers left their ships
and rowed right up to shore
Sister Abby took a drum
and beat it more and more
Yankee Doodle, Keep it up . . .

America's National Anthem

"Then conquer we must,/ when our cause it is just,/ And this be our motto, 'In God is our Trust,'/ And the star-spangled banner in triumph shall wave/ O'er the land of the free and the home of the brave" are the final words of the last verse of the poem that Francis Scott Key wrote in his Baltimore hotel room the night of September 14, 1814, after he watched the English bombard Fort McHenry. Have children sing the words along with a recorded version of "The Star-Spangled Banner" by Francis Scott Key. Discuss some of the causes of the War of 1812 and why British and Americans were fighting at this time.

Read aloud one of several stories about Key watching the English attack star-shaped Fort McHenry: *Sunrise Over the Harbor: A Story about the Meaning of Independence Day* (Summit Group, 1993, Grades 1–3) by Louise Mandrell and Ace Collins, *By the Dawn's Early Light* (Atheneum, 1994, Grades 1–2) by Karen Ackerman, and from *By the Dawn's Early Light* (Scholastic, 1994, Grades 1–4) by Steven Kroll and illustrated by Dan Andreasen.

Activity #145: "Impressions"

Acquaint the children with the way our current version of the flag came to be by reading the included history of "Old Glory" in *Stars and Stripes: Our National Flag* (Holiday House, 1993, Grades 1–3) by L.E. Fisher and show the oversized illustrations in *The Star-Spangled Banner* (Doubleday, 1975, all grades) by Peter Spier on the opaque projector. After seeing the illustrations in both books, ask the children what meaning(s) the pictures and the words have for them today, and have them write their impressions of the flag during a time when they were impressed when they saw the flag waving overhead, just as Key wrote his impressions in his hotel room in 1814.

Daniel Boone: A.D. 1734–1820

Engage the children in telling what they know about the contributions made by Daniel Boone in settling the West, and write their ideas on the board. Introduce the children to the figure of Daniel Boone, a trailblazer who helped open paths in the wilderness, with the words, "Daniel Boone at twenty-one/ Came with his tomahawk, knife, and gun/ Home from the French and Indian War/ To North Carolina and the Yadkin shore/" from Arthur Guiterman's poem, "Daniel Boone" in *Story and Verse for Children* (Macmillan, 1965) by M. B. Huber. After hearing the poem, ask the children what they have learned about this man who helped settle the West and compare their new ideas with the former ones on the board.

Activity #146: "Trailblazer"

Write the word *trailblazer* on the board and ask the children what meaning the word has for them. Record their ideas on the board. To further the concept of a trailblazer, give the children information about the major facts in Boone's life from *Daniel Boone* (Putnam, 1965, Grades 2–4) by Patricia Miles Martin. Ask the children to look again at the illustrations with you and then talk about what they see in the illustrations and how they know or do not know

that Boone is a trailblazer from what they see in the illustrations. Encourage them to generalize about the concept of *trailblazer* by completing sentences beginning with, "A trailblazer is someone who . . ." Ask them which people in today's world could be considered a modern-day trailblazer. The large print and brief sentences makes Martin's story suitable for independent reading. For children in grade 3 and older, who are interested further in the life of Boone as a frontiersman, suggest Laurie Lawlor's *Daniel Boone* (Whitman, 1989, Grade 3 up) or *Daniel Boone: Frontier Hero* (Scholastic, 1996, Grades 3–5) by Elaine Raphael and Don Bolognese—both biographies of the American frontiersman. The latter book details the kidnapping of his daughter by the Indians, and has instructions for drawing pictures of Daniel Boone, his wife Rebecca, a log cabin, a Conestoga wagon, and a Native American.

Naturalists: A.D. 1820, 1834

Acquaint children with Audubon's 1820 journey to paint nature scenes of birds by reading aloud *On the Frontier with Mr. Audubon* (Coward, 1977, Grades 2–3) by Barbara Brenner and the travels of two naturalists, John Townsend and Thomas Nuttall, with Paul Fleischman's *Townsend's Warbler* (HarperCollins, 1992, Grades 3–7). Fleischman's story is set in 1834, when the two men journeyed west across America and made several wildlife discoveries. For example, Townsend was able to capture two specimens of the migrating birds that nested in the high trees in the Northwest forests, and in his honor, his colleague, Nuttall, named the bird Townsend's Warbler.

Activity #147: "Birdlife Gallery"

Invite the children to create their own birdlife gallery in the classroom, but first have them journey outside on a walking field trip with their note pads, pens, and crayons to "discover" birdlife in their area. Have them sketch the birds they see, just as Townsend and Nuttall did. Invite them to name the wildlife they sketch with original names or their own names (such as Carla's Bluebird) and display their sketches in a birdlife exhibit in the room.

Woman of Ghalas-hat: A.D. 1835

Read aloud the true story of a Native American woman from a tribe who lived on the island of San Nicholas off the coast of California in *Lone*

Woman of Ghalas-hat (R. C. Law, 1987, Grades 2–3) by Rice D. Oliver. In 1835, this young Native American woman, from the tribe called Ghalas-hat, is moved with her people off their home island. As the boat left the island, she discovers that her baby is missing. She dives into the water and swims back to the island but discovers that the baby is dead. The woman, later called Juana Maria, stays alone on the island for years, until she is discovered by a white man who has heard about her. With the children, discuss the ways this Native American woman faced difficult times alone, and ask the children what they learned about her strength as a person, what she valued in her life, and what survival skills she had to have to live along on the island. Record their comments in a graphic web with headings on the board (see Figure 11–3). Ask the children to meet with partners to select one of the headings and its related comments to use to write a brief paragraph to tell what they learned about the life of this Native American woman in the 1800s.

Activity #148: "To the Mainland"

When you reach the part in *Lone Woman of Ghalas-hat* where in later years, she is found by a white man and brought to the mainland, stop reading at this point and ask the children to discuss the ways they think Juana Maria will be as happy (or not as happy) as she was by herself on the island and to tell their reasons why they think the way they do.

The Alamo: A.D. 1836

With a large map of the United States, show the geographical location of the Alamo on the San Antonio River in Texas and tell what happened there. In 1836, Davy Crockett, James Bowie, and William Travis led 186 men in a hopeless battle during the war for the independence of Texas from Mexico. The Alamo (Spanish for cottonwood), was built in 1727 as a mission with a church and convent, and it stood alone in the battle surrounded only by 4,000 Mexican troops led by General Santa Ana. All of the defenders at the Alamo were killed; however, some members of the defenders' families survived. John Jakes's book, *Susanna of the Alamo* (Gulliver, 1986, Grade 3 up), relates the poignant story of Susanna Dickinsen, a young widow who survived along with her young daughter. Encourage interested children to inquire into the points of view of both sides of this war.

Activity #149: "Susanna of the Alamo"

To show the events of the battle at the Alamo, show the children the illustrations in Jakes's story with an opaque projector. After the battle, Susanna Dickinsen—a young wife, mother, and now widow—survives as a witness about what went on, and she also defies the powerful General Santa Anna when captured. When Santa Ana frees her, Dickensen meets Sam Houston, the Texas general, and his outnumbered band of Texans who use the cry "Remember the Alamo" as they fight back to defeat the Mexican soldiers in an subsequent battle. Show the children two or three pictures of the defenders of the Alamo and write the word *defenders* on the board. Have the children describe the pictures. Ask how they might know that the pictures are *really* showing the defenders of the Alamo. After each response, have children restate it in a sentence to make a generalization that begins with the words, "The Defenders of the Alamo were. . . ." If appropriate, introduce related information about the battle from other references.

Repeat the activity from the point of view of General Santa Ana and his soldiers and ask the children how they might know that the pictures also show the defenders of the land that belonged to Mexico. After each response to the illustration, invite the children to generalize in a sentence that begins with the words, "The Defenders of the land for Mexico were. . . ." If needed, introduce more related facts. Point out that the statements about "The Defenders of the land for Mexico were . . ." are also generalizations. Have the children tell their meaning of the concept *defenders* and write their comments on the board. Engage them in using the meanings on the board to develop a general definition of the word *defenders*. Ask them to show what the word *defenders* means to them in a drawing. Display the drawings in a class book.

FIGURE 11–3   Lone Woman of Ghalas-hat

Strength as a Person   What She Valued

LONE WOMAN OF
GHALAS-HAT, 1835

Survival Skills   Other

Andrew Jackson: A.D. 1767–1845

In the poem "Andrew Jackson" in *A Book of Americans* (Holt, 1986, all grades) by Rosemary and Stephen Vincent Benet, Andrew Jackson is called the pride of America's frontier with hair as white as "the hunter's moon" and eyes like a "forest-ranger's." Ask the children to listen to the poem to hear more about the way Jackson is described, and then review the words that help them imagine "Old Hickory." Discuss such phrases as "rough, free ways," "rifle, long and brown," and "has Tennessee opinions" and ask the children to tell the meaning the words have for them. Write their comments on the board.

Descriptive Words	*Meaning for Us*
1. Rough, free ways	1.
2. Has Tennessee opinions	2.
3. Pride of America's frontier	3.
4. White as the hunter's moon	4.
5. Eyes are the forest-ranger's	5.

Have the children use the information to sketch their own original portraits of "Old Hickory" and collect them for a class book. Additional information about "Old Hickory" can be found in O. De Kay's biography, *Meet Andrew Jackson* (Random House, 1967, Grades 2–4) illustrated by I. Barnett. De Kay's text portrays Jackson as a deeply religious man and a fighter who had various adversaries through his life that included other boys during his orphaned childhood, and later, the Native Americans, the Spanish, those against his candidacy for the presidency, and those against some of the laws he supported.

Activity #150: "How Jackson Coped"

Elicit the names of Jackson's adversaries from the children, and write them in a list on the board. Have the children recall ways Jackson coped with his adversaries, and write their comments in a second list:

Adversaries	*How Jackson Coped*
1. Boys during his orphaned childhood	
2. Native Americans	
3. Spanish	
4. Those against his presidency	
5. Those against laws he supported	

Ask the children to think of a time when they faced an adversary and to write about what they did to cope with the adversarial relationship. Ask vol-unteers, "In what ways did you do something that was similar to what Jackson did when he faced his adversaries?"

Santa Fe Trail: A.D. 1844–1845

Give the children a detailed picture of life on a wagon train to California and what happens when a fatherless family moves from the East to Arizona Territory by reading aloud M. Russell's *Along the Santa Fe Trail: Marion Russell's Own Story* (Whitman, 1993, Grades 2–3). Russell gives the points of view of a girl and her mother as they cope with the weather, the lack of water, and Native Americans—some friendly, others hostile. After their money and jewels are stolen, they are unable to pay for the rest of their trip and have to stay in Albuquerque instead of continuing on to California.

Activity #151: "Trail Impressions"

Give children long strips of paper (4-1/2″ by 11″) to pass on to another child after they write their impressions of traveling along the Santa Fe Trail. Have them pass their writing to the child on the right (or left) and ask the child who receives the paper to continue writing his or her impressions. Return the papers to the original writer. Have the children read the writing and sketch or draw an illustration to show the details mentioned in the writing.

Kit Carson: A.D. 1809–1868

Kit Carson joins a wagon train going to Santa Fe in M. E. Bell's biography, *Kit Carson, Mountain Man* (Morrow, 1952, Grades 3–5) illustrated by H. Daughtery. Born in Kentucky, Carson (1809–1868) spends his boyhood in Missouri, and at age 16, joins a wagon train going to Santa Fe, New Mexico. He becomes a horse driver, a daring beaver trapper, and a hunter in the Rockies. He traps beaver for clothing and hats. When men's silk hats become more stylish than beaver, Carson can not earn money trapping beaver and so becomes a hunter and guide in Colorado. Carson, with his horse, Apache, guides John Charles Fremont, a military explorer, on two trips across the Rocky Mountains. With a large map or globe, have the children trace the routes of some of the adventures in the lives of the two men.

Activity #152: "Walking Tour"

Related to a historical figure of this period, take the children on a historical walking tour in an area near them. Maps of historical areas usually are available from the state's bureau of tourism. Have the children follow the map around the historic site. After returning to the classroom, engage the children in making their own souvenir kit of surprises related to the tour. For example, some children in California who live near Carson City, Nevada, may be able to go on a field trip to this town that was named for Christopher "Kit" Carson. Following a map, the children can walk to see several historic sites, such as the historical home district, the Old Federal Building (1888) made of brick and sandstone, the Stewart Indian School Museum (a school organized in 1890 for children from many Western tribes}, the State Museum (which has an underground mine, Native American basketry, and is the site of a former U. S. Mint [1870–1893] and Federal Assay Office [1899–1933]). A kit of surprises related to a tour of the sites in Carson City can include:

- Sheriff's badge
- Trapper's cap
- Sample of dirt of this mining area
- Sketches of items seen in the Stewart Indian School Museum
- Examples of weaving to replicate Native American basketry
- Drawings of the U.S. Mint and Federal Assay activities
- List of contents in the kit of surprises

Activity #153: "Historical Show and Tell"

Invite the children to interview family members and friends about what they know of interesting historical sites and attractions in their region that date back to the 1800s. Have them report back to the whole group for a historical Show and Tell. For example, a child may report that one of the first towns in the region was a favorite hideout of desperadoes, that nearby lakes have been a migratory stop of waterfowl for over a century, or that a railroad depot and other buildings still show the architecture of the 1800s. Another child may contribute that a quaint farming community dates back to the 1800s and that some nearby towns have a Boot Hill cemetery, or a replica of the original courthouse, and or a historical museum with regional artifacts. Still others may mention that a once-thriving town is now a ghost town since the people left the town when the gold or silver (or other economic base) ran out. Have the children locate the places on a map of the community or state.

Activity #154: "Mystery History Places"

Introduce nearby historical sites and attractions as Mystery History Places and have the children look at a regional map and listen to the directions to the Mystery History Place. Have them look at the map as the directions to the site are read aloud and follow the directions as if they were traveling to the site. For example, to have children locate the site where Nevada's first newspaper was printed by Mark Twain, have children look at a map of Nevada and guide them with directions such as "Take Highway 80 and drive through Reno, Nevada, to this Mystery History Place where Nevada's first newspaper was printed by Mark Twain." Guide the children with additional directions to Virginia City, Nevada, without naming the actual site. Let the child who correctly guesses the Mystery History Place be the one to give other directions and descriptive words and phrases about a different Mystery History Place— perhaps the site the child reported about to the group Activity #153.

Activity #155: "History Brochures"

Ask the children to make suggestions about ways to respect the historic integrity of the sites when they visit. Suggestions can include such messages as "Please don't touch or remove anything," which will help remind people to preserve the part of history in their region. Write the children's suggestions on the board and ask each child to illustrate one of the suggestions. Ask the children to sign their artwork and put it in a History Brochure of the region. The children can add other pages of information and sketches to show topics of interest in their area such as buildings, bridges, and famous people. Encourage them also to select personalities related to the state in which they live. Collect the pages to make the brochure and place it on the reading shelf in the classroom.

Activity #156: "History in Alphabet Books"

Field trips to historical sites can be the stimulus for children to create their own original picture books about the outing. To show what can be done with different formats, show the children some examples of interesting ways that authors and artists have put together their books. Examples of easy-to-follow formats are available in alphabet books, from which the children can easily adapt one of the formats for their own picture books (see Figure 11–4).

FIGURE 11–4   **Children's Alphabet Books about History**

PERSPECTIVES

Alliteration Format

Brown, Marcia. *Peter Piper's Practical Principles of Plain and Perfect Pronunciation.* Scribner's, 1974. This book has examples of alliterative questions about Andrew Airpump, Billy Button, Captain Crackskull, and others. With this book as a model, interested children can present the information from their field trip in alliterative questions in their own books and use the alphabet as a sequence to introduce information about what they saw.

Free-Verse Format

Greenaway, Kate. *A Apple Pie: An Old Fashioned Alphabet.* Warne, n.d. This book, originally published in 1886, is an old-fashioned alphabet book with children skipping around a giant apple pie. The letter *I* is not included because this alphabet goes back to an early use when the letters *I* and *J* were used as one letter.

Rhyme Format

Provensen, Alice, and Martin Provensen. *A Peaceable Kingdom: The Shaker Abecedarius.* Viking, 1978. This book is an alphabet verse of the late 1800s. Taken from the Shaker Manifesto of 1881, the first line of 26 in this verse begins with an *A* word, the second line with a *B* word, and so on. Interested children could present the information from their field trip in a similar manner.

Full-Color Illustrations and List Format

Bannatyne-Cugnet, J. *A Prairie Alphabet.* Tundra, 1992. This text shows full-color paintings about life on the prairie with a list at the end of the book that identifies objects in the illustrations. After seeing this book, some children might be motivated to include a list at the back of their books that identifies the objects in their illustrations.

Object-Letter Format

Stroud, V. A. *The Path of the Quiet Elk: A Native American Alphabet Book.* Dial, 1996. This book by V. A. Stroud of Cherokee-Creek heritage, selects creatures in nature to introduce each letter as a way of looking at life which is the path of the quiet elk. For example, the letter *L* is introduced by Lizard, who protects people from harm by dragging his tail on the ground to erase footsteps. This format may inspire some children to present the information about the objects seen on their field trip in terms of what each does to help people in some way.

Object-Word Format

Mayers, Florence Cassen. *ABC, The Wild West Buffalo Bill Historical Center, Cody, Wyoming.* Abrams, 1990. This story presents large colorful illustrations of objects from the Buffalo Bill Historical Center. Objects include a stagecoach, dolls, feathers, gloves, jugs, and others. After seeing this format, some children may want to present the information about the objects seen on their field trip in large illustrations in self-prepared books.

Descriptive Text Format

Paul, Ann Whitford. *Eight Hands Round: A Patchwork Alphabet.* HarperCollins, 1991. This book has quilt patterns from *A* for *anvil* quilt to *Z* for a *zigzag* pattern. The origins of the designs are explained and relate to an activity or occupation people did in the past. Some children may want to present the information from their field trip as quilt patterns and include color illustrations of the patterns they design.

The Cumberland Road: A.D. 1850

Families also journeyed west on one of America's early roads—the dusty Cumberland Road that was first officially worked on in 1811. In *A Birthday for Blue* (Whitman, 1989, Grades K–2), Kerry Raines tells the story of Blue's family as they travel west from Cumberland, Maryland, to Pittsburgh, Pennsylvania. Blue's family and other travelers cross many creeks and rivers as they journey through the Allegheny mountains. At dusk on Blue's seventh birthday, his father takes him to the woods and plants seven seedlings in a special arrangement to celebrate his special day. After listening to the story, ask the children to point out examples of ways people tried to overcome the danger, deprivation, and drudgery of life on the trail in unfamiliar country. Then reread the parts where Blue walks beside the wagon, splashes in a stream while a broken wheel is mended, and meets another family along the way. Ask, "What would you have enjoyed the most and the least if you had traveled with Blue and his family?"

Activity #157: "Blue's Family"

Ask the children to draw their own sketches to show one of the events during the journey of Blue's family. Before sketching, have the children discuss what they think Blue will look like, what clothing Blue will wear, what locations their sketches will show, what weather is happening during the day, and what season of the year will be shown.

Activity #158: "Other Families"

Read aloud, over a period of days, several stories about other families who traveled west on the Cumberland Road and on other trails and what their lives were like during this time. With a map of the United States, mark the journeys and final destinations of families in the stories. For example, have the children listen to find out what happens to the Sheldon family in *Aurora Means Dawn* (Bradbury, 1989, Grades 1–4) by S. R. Sanders. The family journeys to Aurora, Ohio, and their final destination can be marked on the map. In this story based on facts from the 1800s, the Sheldons and their seven children believe they are traveling to a developed cabin community—a new homestead in Aurora. When the family is caught in a fierce thunderstorm, they take shelter under their wagon, and the next morning, they discover that their way is blocked by fallen trees. Mr. Sheldon goes for help in Aurora, finds no one there, and realizes the advertised "clustered cabin community" is a fraud. He walks on to get help and finally finds several men to help him clear the path and push the wagon out of the mud. That night in Aurora, the children huddle together in the hollow of a sycamore tree for shelter. As for other settlers who were supposed to be in Aurora, they did not come for three years. Ask the children, "In contrast to what the Sheldon family faced in a fraud situation, what recourse to fight back against fraud is available for citizens today?"

Introduce interested children to what the lives of other families were like as they traveled west with the stories in Figure 11–5.

Activity #159: "Cumberland Road Speaks"

Have the children use a map outline of the United States and mark the route of the Cumberland Road. Encourage them to talk further about experiences on the trail from the point of view of the inanimate Cumberland Road. To do this, ask the children to deliver brief speeches of warnings about the dangers and suggestions about safety as if they on the Cumberland Road and are speaking to Blue and the people who are traveling along. Have the children add some sketches to the map to show some of the dangers during an imagined journey with Blue and the others on the road.

Donner Pioneers: A.D. 1846

Elicit what the children know about the westward expansion during this period and make a list of their ideas on the board or on an overhead transparency. Show the children how to relate associated words, phrases, and ideas by regrouping the ideas from the list into an association web with the words *Westward Expansion* in the center (see Figure 11–6). With the new groupings at the end of lines from the center of the web, ask the children to choose one of the groups and locate, browse, and scan through books to gain further information about the topic. Back in the whole group, ask the children to report on what information they gathered related to America's westward expansion and add their facts to the groupings on the web.

Activity #160: "Patty Reed's Doll"

Read aloud selections of the historically accurate account of the Donner Party from R. K. Laurgaard's *Patty Reed's Doll: The Story of the Donner Party* (Tomato Enterprises, 1989, Grades 2–3) illustrated by E. Michaels. This is the story of 8-year-old Patty Reed, a true-life survivor of the Donner Party

FIGURE 11–5   Children's Books about Families Moving West

PERSPECTIVES

A Family Moves from Connecticut to Ohio

Warm as Wool (Bradbury, 1992, Grades 2–3) by S. R. Sanders is a story is based on an historically based account of the Ward family who journeys from Connecticut to the Ohio woods in 1803. Betsy Ward, the mother, buys sheep, shears the wool, spins the wool, and weaves it to provide warm and comfortable clothes for her family.

A Family Moves from Virginia to Michigan

To contrast with the fraud the Sheldons found at the end of their journey in *Aurora Means Dawn*, a friendship develops between a Native American girl and Libby Mitchell in *Next Spring an Oriole* (Random House, 1987, Grade 3 up) by Gloria Whelan. This is the story of Libby Mitchell and her parents who journey to Michigan from Virginia in 1837 to settle in the forest near Saginaw, where a Native American girl becomes Libby's new friend.

An African American Family Moves from Virginia to the West

After the Civil War, 9-year-old Ginny and her family leave a Virginia plantation and their former lives as slaves to travel the Oregon trail to California in *Wagon Train: A Family Goes West in 1865* (Holiday, 1995, Grades 2–4) written by C. C. Wright and illustrated by Gresham Griffith.

A Young Girl Travels West in 1845

Discuss the danger faced by Gretchen on the trail going west in the 1800s by reading excerpts from *The White Stallion* (Bantam, 1984, Grade 3 up) by E. Shub. Gretchen is saved by a mysterious stallion.

A Pioneer Family Moves West

Give children a detailed picture of life with a family on a claim stake in the prairie with Eve Bunting's *Dandelions* (Harcourt, 1995, Grades K–3). Zoe tells her story in a first person narrative and mentions the hard work that she and her sister Rebecca do to please their mother who is expecting a baby. On a trip to town for supplies, Zoe and her father find dandelions, which they plant on the roof of their sod home to bring cheer to the mother. Though the dandelions look dry and lifeless, a final page shows dandelions covering the fields of the farm in the future.

Two Families Move from Kentucky to Kansas

Two stories, *Wagon Wheels* and *Lottie's Dream*, give two different accounts of families who journey from Kentucky to Kansas. In *Lottie's Dream* (Simon & Schuster, 1992, Grades 1–3) by Bonnie Pryor, Lottie's mother has a picture of the sea pinned on the wall of their Kentucky home and it is the sea that young Lottie often dreams about. When the family travels west to Kansas in their covered wagon, Lottie hopes the sea would be there. It is only after Lottie grows up, marries, and has children that she has a birthday vacation by the sea. After years of being a wife, mother, and grandmother in Kansas, Lottie finally moves to live near the sea, which she feels is really her home.

Wagon Wheels (Harper & Row, 1978, Grades 1–3) by Barbara Brenner, is an account based on an actual incident in the 1870s in the lives of an African American family who travels from Kentucky to Kansas and recorded in the family's diaries. The story portrays life in late 1800s for the Middle family as they travel from Kentucky on the east coast to Kansas in a covered wagon. When their mother dies on the way, the three boys and their father make a home during the harsh Kansas winter and are confronted by the Native Americans in the region. They face a difficult winter in their dugout house and their father looks for a better life and leaves the motherless boys to look after one another. When he sends for them, the boys face the dangers of prejudice and prairie together.

FIGURE 11–5   Continued

A Newcomer Family Moves from Sweden to Minnesota

In Sweden, with their family's crops dying and no hope for the future, Klara and her parents decide to voyage to America and their story is told in J. Winter's *Klara's New World* (Knopf, 1992, Grades 1–4). They prepare their food for the difficult journey, lack fresh water to drink on the ship, and notice a bird that signals them that land is near. Journeying to Minnesota, they build a cabin and farm the land. In the winter, Klara's father writes a letter to their grandfather and Klara encloses a flower that grew from the seeds he had given her when she left Sweden.

tragedy, as seen through the eyes of her doll. The snowbound party of pioneers is led by George Donner of Illinois and they wait for help to complete their journey across the mountains; 45 of the original 81 pioneers lived to cross the mountains. Photocopy illustrations of artifacts used by the pioneers in this period and show them to the children. Have the children select any artifact or object that might have been carried by the Donner Party pioneers and ask them questions about it: "What would you use this for? What do you think the pioneers used it for?" Other questions can be similar to the following:

1. "If this belonged to you, how can you show others in our class a way you would use it? Demonstrate for us."
2. "In how many ways would you use it? When do you think the pioneers used it?"
3. "In what way would you have to be safe and careful in using it? Tell us why."
4. "What do you think it is? What would you name it? How can we find out what the pioneers named it?"

FIGURE 11–6   Westward Expansion

Heading by Children   Heading by Children

(WESTWARD EXPANSION)

Heading by Children   Heading by Children

Activity #161: "Field Trip"

Invite the children who are studying their local and regional history to write to offices of the state parks about available field trips. For girls and boys living near an historic state park, a field trip can be planned, organized, and scheduled during class meetings. For example, the children in northern California can visit the state's Donner Memorial State Park. After the trip, engage the children in preparing a field guide about the trip to donate to the rangers at the state park. Suggest that the rangers give the guide to other students who planned to visit the state park in the future.

Invite the children to suggest historical sites to visit as a group. With the children, plan a field trip and discuss various components of the trip. Consider these steps when you want to take the children to visit an historic site:

1. Think through the sequence of the trip so you can plan ways to make it educationally worthwhile. Before taking the trip, visit the site to determine its educational value and to learn the name of a contact person.
2. Anticipate any problem that might come up during the outing, and keep the safety of the children in mind.
3. Determine a purpose for the trip. (*Example:* to prepare a field guide for other classes who will be traveling to the historic site.)
4. Plan ways to create good public relations between the children and the citizens in the community.
5. Discuss the trip in a class meeting with the children and write their comments on the board (see History Master 15).

FIGURE 11–7   Community Resources

Airports and bus terminals	Fish hatcheries	Post offices
Aquariums	Flood plains and rivers	Railroad and light rail
Art galleries	Government buildings	stations
Assembly factories	Harbors	Refineries
Bakeries	Health care agencies	Schoolhouses
Broadcasting stations	Historical monuments and sites	Science centers
Canals	Hospitals	Shopping areas
Courthouses	Libraries	Telephone companies
Dams and deltas	Lighthouses	Transportation offices
Docks	Museums	Weather bureaus
Factories	Newspapers	Zoos
Farms	Parks and nature areas	Others as suggested by
Fire stations	Police stations	the children

There will be many historic places that you and the children can visit. Select those that will contribute to the children's understanding of historical study—including related geography, history, and current events. Some of the places that can make an educational contribution to a historical study are shown in Figure 11–7. Many of the places will have a history of development in the children's area and a contact person can share that history with the class.

America's First Stamp: A.D. 1847

Mention to the children that the picture of Benjamin Franklin first appeared on a five-cent stamp in 1847 and that, through the years, the post office has issued other stamps about other historic events. Invite a representative from the local post office to visit the class (or take a field trip to a branch office) to talk about some of the stamps that have historical events on them such as the stamps that commemorate Civil War battles. Mention that every year, a citizens' committee selects ideas for new stamps from people who have sent their suggestions to Washington, D.C. Ask, "If you were on the stamp committee, what scenes would you have selected related to history and why would you have selected them to put on stamps?" Record the children's suggestions on the board in a list and ask each to illustrate one of the suggestions in an enlarged stamp format. Display the stamp illustrations in the classroom.

Activity #162: "Design a Stamp"

Encourage interested children to write a business letter to the director of the United States Stamp Information Service (P.O. Box 764, Washington, D.C., 20044) to request a complimentary copy of the paperback *Stamp Selections, Who and Why*, a booklet that explains the stamp selection process. Discuss the purpose and format of a business letter with the group (see Figure 11–8). Help the children write their letters and mail them.

While the children are waiting for the material to arrive (it takes months), invite them to suggest designs for several different kinds of stamps of various topics from history to display in the room. Write their suggestions in a list on an overhead transparency. Ask them to give their reasons why they suggested what they did. When the booklets arrive, ask the children to read the booklets to find out what ideas for stamps have already been selected in the past and to see if any of the stamps in the booklet were ones they mentioned on their list on the transparency. Invite interested children to design other stamps for different topics. Encourage interested children to submit their designs to the United States Stamp Information Service for the citizens' committee review.

California's Gold Rush: A.D. 1849

The impact of the discovery of gold at Sutter's Fort, the hardships traveling to the diggings by ship, wagon, and hiking, and the different methods peo-

FIGURE 11–8   Business Letter

100 School Circle
Anywhere, U.S.A.
September 9, ___

Director
Unites States Stamp Information Service
P.O. Box 764
Washington, D.C. 20044

Dear Director:

My _____ grade class at _____ school is studying the stamp selection process. Please send me one free copy of the paperback book *Stamp Selections, Who and Why*. Thank you for sending me the material.

Sincerely,

_____ (name)
_____ (class)
_____ (school)

---

ple used to recover gold are detailed in *The Great American Gold Rush* (Bradbury, 1989, Grade 5 up) by Rhoda Blumberg, a book whose parts can be read aloud to the children. This informational book has drawings, sketches, notes, index, and a bibliography. Photocopy numerous illustrations of unfamiliar objects and artifacts related to the Gold Rush period from Blumberg's book, and ask the children to join in groups and give five or more illustrations to each group. Ask the children to tell one another their responses to the following "Top Ten" questions as a volunteer in each group shows one illustration after another to the children. Place a transparency of the Top Ten Questions about an Unfamiliar Object on the overhead projector so the children can keep track of the questions they discuss in their groups. Consider this example:

Top Ten Questions about an Unfamiliar Object

1. What do you think you would use this object for?
2. What do you think people of the Gold Rush period used it for?
3. In how many ways do you think you could use it?
4. When do you think the people in Gold Rush Days used it?
5. In what way would you have to be safe and careful in using it? Tell us why.
6. In what way would the people of Gold Rush Days have to be careful in using it?
7. What do you think it is?
8. What would you name it?
9. How can we find out what the people of Gold Rush Days named it?
10. If this belonged to you, how can you show others in our class a way you would use it? Demonstrate for us.

Activity #163: "Gold Rush Artifacts"

Related to the previous activity, have the children come back together as a whole group and ask a volunteer from each small group to give a report on their discussion of the illustrated objects as you show the illustrations one at a time.

Activity #164: "John Sutter: A.D. 1848–1849"

Elicit from the children their points of view about John Sutter and ask questions similar to the following:

1. If you had been John Sutter, what route would you have taken to Sacramento and why would you have gone that way? (Provide map of California that shows the rivers and delta areas.)

2. How might the history of California been different if John Sutter had found *exceptionally* hostile Indians near Sacramento instead of the friendly ones?

3. How has life in the Sacramento area (state of California, your state) changed since the days of John Sutter?

4. What is there about California today that relates directly to the discovery of gold started by John Sutter, James Marshall, and the others?

Activity #165: "References"

Display a biography about an historical figure of this period, such as John Sutter, and an encyclopedia that tells about the person. Lead the group in identifying ways the two books are different and alike. Ask a child to select a page from the biography and read excerpts from the page to the students. Then read a few sentences about the person from the encyclopedia. Lead the children in discussion about when and how they could use each book to look for information about the figure. If desired, contrast the two books with a picture dictionary and talk about when and how a dictionary could be used.

The Oregon Trail: A.D. 1851

"Squishing through the mudholes, drunken with the rain;/ Turn your face to heaven, boy—and punch those bulls again/" are words that reflect a part of the pioneers' lives described in Jim Marshall's poem "The Oregon Trail: 1851" in *Northwest Verse* by H. G. Merriam. Marshall writes descriptive phrases that can entice the children into further discussion about life on the trail from Independence to Oregon City (1843–1860)—for example, "whips cracking," "white sails of schooners," "keep y'r musket handy," "wagons bogged in prairie mud, teams stuck fast," and "trail's pinched out."

After listening to the poem, ask the children to imagine a flashback to 1843 and set a scene traveling on the Oregon Trail. To do this, ask them to visualize what is going on as you mark the trail on a map and read your own description of what is going on:

Imagine that you are with a thousand determined travelers—some are trappers after animal pelts—and are heading out in a wagon train from Independence, Missouri, to the green Willamette River Valley, over 2,000 miles away in Oregon country. You and the people on the wagon train will face hardships that test all your strength and endurance. The wagon train goes west across the Rocky Mountains from Independence,

Missouri. What will you do to help get the wagons across the mountains?

The train continues past Chimney Rock in Nebraska (one of the landmarks of the trail). The wagons make hip-deep ruts near Fairbury, Nebraska, and near Fort Laramie, south of Guernsey, Wyoming. At Fort Laramie, you find out what life was like for a soldier at the fort (see A Frontier Fort on the Oregon Trail *[Peter Bedrick, 1993] by Scott Steedman, an information book shows how Fort Laramie was constructed.)*

You stay on the wagon train for a 5- to 6-month journey, and sometimes you travel as slow as a few miles a day, and other days as fast as 20 miles. Your face is gritty and sometimes you're too hot or too cold, other times you are thirsty or hungry, and you hear that some of the wagoneers have gotten sick—they have cholera and scurvy. You are always on the lookout for cool springs so people can fill their water barrels. You see some accidents happen in the rugged mountains as the weary people try to climb up and over in the wagons. Other accidents happen when the wagoneers are stopped by a deep river that is very dangerous to cross. You are always afraid of the Native People in the region who are known to attack the wagon trains.

Invite the children to tell what wagon train scenes they imagined as you read the description and have them transform their thoughts into pictures. Show them a modern-day reenactment of a wagon trail with the photographs in the book *West by Covered Wagon: Retracing the Pioneer Trails* (Walker, 1995, Grade 3 up) written by D. H. Patent and illustrated by W. Munoz. Each year, a group called Westmong Wagoneers in western Montana makes a Memorial Day weekend journey using covered wagons, horses, and mules to retrace the trails of the early pioneers.

Activity #166: "Lost Pet"

In *Trouble for Lucy* (Clarion, 1979, Grades 1–3) by Carla Stevens, Lucy's terrier gets lost in a storm on the Oregon Trail and both are found by Pawnee Indians. After reading the story aloud, ask the children to think what it would be like caring for a pet traveling west on the Oregon Trail. Write their ideas on the board. Invite them to transform their ideas into short stories and write about what life would be like taking care a pet on the trail. Ask the children to read their stories to others in small group when finished.

Activity #167: "Pantomime Events"

Invite the children to act out motions in brief pantomime while a narrator reads some of the events faced by Lucy, Callie, and Native Americans in

Trouble for Lucy. Seat the narrator in front of the room to read occasional statements from an imagined diary of Lucy (or other pioneers of the 1850s). For example, Lucy might write, "The water here is very bad . . ." To prepare material for the narrator to read, ask the children to take the role of Lucy or a friend and write their own imagined entries on index cards and give the cards to the narrator. Have the narrator read some of the events while the children pantomime them. If appropriate, children can use some of the imagined situations listed on History Master 16.

Activity #168: "Lucy's Family"

Demonstrating the size of a covered wagon for the children, you can help them measure the dimensions for a typical "prairie schooner"—the kind Lucy and her pet terrier traveled in on the Oregon Trail. The schooner had a bed about 10 feet long and 4 feet wide. The canvas, waterproofed with paint or linseed oil, had about 5 feet of "head room." Ask the children to suggest what supplies, tools, and weapons they think a family like Lucy's would take in the wagon. List their ideas on a shape-chart resembling the outline of a schooner. Some items needed by a pioneer family might be a stove, medicines, lead for bullets, clothing, bedding, ax, hammer, shovel, and spare parts for the wagon (Ponte, 1993). Ask the children to give their reasons for their suggestions:

Tools, Supplies, and Weapons to Take	*Reason*
1.	1.

Display the chart in the room. The children can look in additional references to find illustrations of needed items and can sketch their own interpretations of the objects a family might have taken on such a journey. Have them paste the sketches to make a border for the chart.

Going West: A.D. 1860

To focus the children's interest on the restlessness of some people during this time period, read aloud excerpts from B. Harvey's *Cassie's Journey: Going West in the 1860s* (Holiday House, 1988, Grades 3–5), a book illustrated by D. K. Ray. In a point of view set in 1860, Cassie and her family travel the Immigrant Trail from Independence to Sacramento, Her life on the wagon train includes picking up buffalo chips and doing other chores. An included map helps place the geographic locations. Invite the children to describe the scenes that come to mind about Cassie and other children journeying on wagon trains. Write one or two of the descriptions on the board and have the children transform their descriptions into a choral reading and accompany the reading with the sounds of a great wagon train with excited families journeying across the land. Invite a child to imitate the sound of the leader's voice with a "Wagons, Ho!" while another child makes the sound of cracking oxen whips in the air. Several children can make the sound of lurching and creaking wagon wheels against the ground while another group can make the sound of bawling oxen, at first in low bawls that gradually become louder as the oxen get hungry and thirsty.

Activity #169: "Supplies"

Mention that an average pioneer family needed about half a bushel *each* of beans and corn meal, 200 pounds of flour, 75 pounds of bacon, 5 pounds of coffee, 10 pounds of salt, and 25 pounds of sugar. Use scales so children can get an idea of what a pound of flour, coffee, bacon, salt, sugar, and half a bushel of beans looks like and feels like when lifted. Ask the children to work with partners to estimate the amount of food supplies their own families would have to carry on a wagon train trip like this that would last six months—from May 22 until October 27—the time it usually took for the trip. If appropriate, distribute copies of calendars for the months of May through October so the children can count the days that food would be needed. Back together as a whole group, ask volunteers to tell their estimations and list them on the board.

Family	*Food Estimations*
John's family (3 people)	600 pounds of flour
	15 pounds of coffee
	30 pounds of salt
	75 pounds of sugar
	225 pounds of bacon
Carla's family (4 people)	

After the food estimation is listed for a child's family, ask the child to repeat what would be needed for his or her family by showing and lifting examples of the items and announcing each food item—"My family would need *15* pounds of coffee" (child lifts a 1-pound can of coffee to get a feeling for the weight of 1 pound); "My family would need *75* pounds of sugar," and so on.

Pony Express: A.D. 1860

To focus interest on the brave riders in America's historical mail service, read aloud excerpts from *Buffalo Bill and the Pony Express* (HarperCollins, 1995, Grades K–3) written by Eleanor Coerr and illustrated by Don Bologenese. In the fast-paced story, 16-year-old Bill goes to work for the Pony Express, where he is chased by thieves, stalked by wolves, caught in bad weather, and asked to ride additional miles when another rider is ill. He refuses to mention any of these harrowing times in his letters back home. Facts about this unique service are intertwined with Buffalo Bill's adventures in *The First Ride: Blazing the Trail for the Pony Express* (Ideal Children's Books, 1994, Grades 2–3) by Jacqueline Geis and *The Pony Express: Hoofbeats in the Wilderness* (Watts, 1989, all grades) by J. J. Dicerto. Geis's story describes the 10-day trip from St. Joseph, Missouri, to Sacramento, California, from the point of view of Billy Hamilton, one of the riders. Billy tells about the dangers of the trip and names some of the other riders and the places they picked up the mail for the mochila, the leather pouch in which the mail was carried. Dicerto's book explains how the Pony Express began service in 1860 and carried mail along the Oregon-California Trail in all kinds of weather between St. Joseph, Missouri, and Sacramento, California. In a cause-and-effect situation about which the children can inquire, the express ended a short time later in 1861 because the telegraph finally made connections from the East to the West Coast. To elicit several points of view about the Pony Express, ask the children such questions as:

1. "If you had been a rider for the Pony Express, what route would you have taken to Sacramento from St. Joseph and *why* would you have gone that way?" (Provide map).
2. "How might the history of California been different if there had been no telegraph and the Pony Express had continued to Sacramento instead of ending as it did?"
3. "How has life in St. Joseph (or Sacramento) changed since the days of the Pony Express?"
4. "What is there about California or Missouri (or your state) today that relates directly to the Pony Express?"

Activity #170: "How Mail Traveled"

Compare the Pony Express with how the mail traveled in Spanish California days from San Francisco to the king in Mexico City along El Camino Real (which meant "the King's Highway").

El Camino Real	Pony Express
1. Mail, orders, and reports sent with riders	1.
2. King's messengers rode on horseback	2.
3. Riders were slim, light men so the horses could carry them easily	3.
4. Riders were strong and rode daily with little rest	4.
5. Riders slept with mail sack under their heads	5.
6. Riders were brave and faced hostilities of the trail	6.
7. Riders had fresh horses along El Camino Real	7.

Activity #171: "Mail in the 1800s and Today"

To help children acquire additional facts about how the mail traveled on the pony express, read aloud selections from J. J. Dicerto's informational book, *The Pony Express: Hoofbeats in the Wilderness* or from *Pony Express!* (Scholastic, 1996, Grades 1–4) written by S. Kroll and illustrated by D. Andreason. Discuss the beginning of the express that carried mail at $5.00 a half ounce. Talk about the need for relay stations with fresh ponies to be set up every 10 to 15 miles along the route for the armed riders who could change horses in a few minutes time. Additionally, help children learn firsthand how the mail travels today through the postal system in the United States by visiting a post office. Back in the classroom, invite the children to design their own stamps, write letters to friends, sort the letters, and deliver them to their classmates.

Antislavery Movement: A.D. 1861

According to William J. Faulkner, an African American minister and folklore collector, the Brer Rabbit tales were comfort tales to show the people in bondage how to cope and triumph over the repressions of slavery. In the tales, Brer Rabbit is often a sly but charming critter. For example, in Faulkner's *Brer Tiger and the Big Wind* (Morrow, 1995, Grades K–4), Brer Rabbit organizes the animals into tricking the tiger into giving them food and water during a famine. Prepare a display of other Brer Rabbit stories for children's independent reading and browsing. Books suitable for this are *The Tales of Uncle Remus: The Adventures of Brer Rabbit* (Dial, 1987, Grades 2–3) retold by Julius Lester and illustrated by Jerry Pinkney and *More Tales of Uncle Remus: Further Adventures of Brer Rabbit, His Friends, Enemies, and Others* (Dial, 1988, Grades 2–3) also by Lester.

Activity #172: "Brer Rabbit Tales"

As children read or hear the tales of Brer Rabbit by Joel Chandler Harris in *Jump! The Adventures of Brer Rabbit* (Harcourt Brace Jovanovitch, 1986, all grades) and *Jump Again! More Adventures of Brer Rabbit* (Harcourt Brace Jovanovich, 1987) that have been adapted by Van Dyke Parks and illustrated by Malcolm Jones and Barry Moser, help them understand that the stories express a belief that no one can be wholly owned who does not wish it. Ask the children to discuss this main idea and ways that this idea is shown in the Brer Rabbit tales they read. Encourage them to recall ways that Brer Rabbit coped with what was going on. Record their ideas on the board.

Brer Rabbit Comfort Tales

Tale Title	*Brer Rabbit Copes*

Activity #173: "Frederick Douglass"

Ask the children to pantomime episodes after listening to D. A. Adler's *A Picture Book of Frederick Douglass* (Holiday House, 1992, Grades 2–5), a book illustrated by S. Byrd, or after hearing M. Davidson's *Frederick Douglass Fights for Freedom* (Scholastic, 1968, Grades 2–4). Adler's biography discusses Douglass's youth as a slave and how he learned to read and escaped to freedom. Douglass (1817–1895) assisted the Underground Railroad and wrote against slavery, and several of his quotes are included. Davidson's biography portrays Douglass as a child-slave, an escapee, and a conductor on the Underground Railroad which enables him to free over 400 slave. After the Emancipation, he becomes an advocate for the poor, women's rights, children, and animals. Pantomime related to the biographies can include the following:

1. Pass a book from one child to another. When each receives it, he or she should examine it and pantomime learning to read aloud. Through facial expressions, each can show the class how easy or difficult learning to read was at the time.
2. Each child in turn goes to a table and picks up a make-believe object owned by Douglass and mentioned in the biography and then shows by pantomime what it is by the way the child handles the "object." Other children can guess the object's name.
3. Say to the children, "Imagine this situation: In your Rochester home, the last station on the railroad before Canada, you (Douglass) are about to enter a room to greet some passengers on the Underground Railroad. Show by your actions what goes on in the room."

Activity #174: "Harriet Tubman"

Read aloud excerpts from David Adler's book, *A Picture Book of Harriet Tubman* (Holiday, 1992, Grades 2–3) or *Harriet Tubman* (Messner, 1989, Grades 2–3) written by K. B. Smith and illustrated by J. Seward. Adler's vignettes present Tubman's life (1821–1913) through selected events as a slave child, as a young woman who intervened between a slave owner and a runaway slave, as a conductor on the Underground Railroad, and as a nurse and spy during the Civil War. Smith's biography portrays Tubman as a young girl and field worker who escaped to the North. There, she decided to help others escape from slavery. She took trips into slave territory and led more than 300 slaves to freedom, thus earning her the name of "Moses." After the read-aloud, ask open-ended questions—ones that can elicit more than one point of view from the children. Here are some examples:

1. "If you had been Harriet Tubman, how would you have walked in the woods soundlessly? How could you pick a path through the woods without making a sound? What can you tell us that would help us move soundlessly?"
2. "How might the history of African Americans been different if Harriet Tubman had not been a conductor on the Underground Railroad?"
3. "How has life changed for African Americans since the days of Harriet Tubman?"
4. "What is there about your state today that relates directly to the contributions of Tubman?"
5. "What is there about Harriet Tubman's life that could also be played out in roles?"

Activity #175: "Escape Guide in the Sky"

Read aloud *The Drinking Gourd* (Harper, 1970, Grades 1–3) by F. N. Monjo, a story of a spirited boy who helps a slave family traveling to the North. Point out that the title is the name of the song that slaves in the South sang as a code for directions to escape. They followed the North Star and used the Big Dipper (the drinking gourd) as a guide in the sky. With the whole group, repeat the words to the song that are included in the back of the book and then sing the code words together. Also discuss the words in the song "Steal Away" another code song that told people when to leave to "catch" the underground "train." Have the children tell what the words *steal away* mean to them. Write their interpretations on a chart. Continue:

1. "Tell what kind of person(s) you think wrote the songs 'The Drinking Gourd' and 'Steal Away.' "
2. "Tell what you think others thought of the songs."
3. "Write a sentence or a brief paragraph describing your feelings about the songs."

Activity #176: "Escape Guide in a Quilt"

A young slave works as a seamstress and dreams of freedom in *Sweet Clara and the Freedom Quilt* (Knopf, 1993, Grades 1–3) by Deborah Hopkinson. Overhearing the talk of others escaping to the North gives her the directions to make a map of the area from quilt patches. When she uses the map and escapes to Canada, she leaves the quilt behind to guide others. Review several scenes from the story and discuss the feelings of the people in the illustrations (i.e., the back-breaking work in the cotton fields and the suffering of those who tried to run away). Ask the children what Clara's words mean to them when she reaches safety and says, "But not all are as lucky as we were, and most never can come." Ask the children to draw a map to get to a local area they know about and then turn the map into a class quilt made of paper squares and markers or real fabric and fabric paints.

Activity #177: "Quilts Have Meaning"

Just as Sweet Clara's quilt had a great deal of meaning for her and others, some book characters have quilts that are meaningful for them. In *The Boy and the Quilt* (Good Books, 1991, Grades 1–2) by Shirley Kurtz, a young boy sees that his sister and mother are going to make a quilt, and his mother tells him that he can work, too. The boy considers it

very important to him. He claims ownership of the work with the words, "It's my quilt," and the story ends with instructions about how to make a simple quilt with a child. Other quilts, with colorful patterns useful for students to use as models, have a great deal of meaning for their owners, too, and are found in Figure 11–9. Suggest several to interested children for independent reading.

Activity #178: "Quilts as Artifacts"

Show the children how artifacts such as quilts and other hand-me-downs reveal family history by reading aloud *From Me to You* (Orchard, 1988, Grade 2 up) by Paul Rogers. To celebrate quilting as art, engage the children in writing to artists to request their autographs for cotton squares for an author's quilt to be a display to recognize illustrators of historical fiction books. Children who are interested in the craft of quilting can read *My Grandmother's Patchwork Quilt* (Doubleday/Dell, 1994, all grades) by Janet Bolton and *Wearable Quilts* (Sterling, 1993, all grades) by Roselyn Gadia-Smitley, and look at Bolton's patchwork pieces and Gadia-Smitley's full-sized patterns and common quilting stitches. Further, they can read the step-by-step instructions for such wearable items as quilted vests and other garments. Additionally, *The Quilt-Block History of Pioneer Days: With Projects Kids Can Make* (Millbrook, 1995, Grades 2–6) by Mary Cobb will show children how to use any of 50 patterns, cut patterns from paper, and then paste items together to make such items as a bookmark, greeting card, and recipe folder. A bibliography, index, and U.S. map are included.

Civil War

To introduce Readers' Theater to reflect events in the Civil War period, engage the children in scripting scenes from C. Greene's *Robert E. Lee: Leader in War and Peace* (Children's, 1989, Grades 1–2) or from F. N. Monjo's *The Vicksburg Veteran* (Simon, 1971, Grades 2–5) illustrated by D. Gorsline. Greene's biography tells about Lee's family, early life, and education, with some background about slavery and the Civil War Years. Full-color and black-and-white illustrations show battlefield scenes, portraits, buildings, and events. In Monjo's book, General Grant's son participates in the Union victory that gains control of the Mississippi. Ask the children to read the script aloud and if there is an audience, remind the audience that their responsibility is to take notes and be able to tell what they learned after hearing the script about events in this period.

FIGURE 11–9   Children's Books about Family Quilt Stories

PERSPECTIVES

A Quilt in the Days of Covered Wagons

In Eleanor Coerr's *The Josefina Story Quilt* (Harper & Row, 1986, Grades K–2), a young girl, Faith, persuades her father to let her take Josefina, her pet hen, in the covered wagon, but her father sets up the condition that the hen would have to go if she caused trouble. Well, Josefina does cause trouble—a stampede and a river rescue—but Faith convinces her father each time that Josefina should stay. One night, Josefina cackles and warns of robbers and is hailed as the heroine of the night. When Josefina dies of old age, Faith creates a quilt that illustrates the story of Josefina.

A Quilt in the Days of Pioneers

The Quilt Story (Putnam, 1985, Grades K–2) written by Tony Johnson tells of a time when a small pioneer girl played with, slept in, imagined, and stayed warm on her mother's lap using a quilt made for her by her mother. On the quilt around her name—Abigail—were flowers, hearts, and shooting stars. Throughout her life, this quilt traveled with her across the prairie and was stored in the attic of her home. There, a mouse had her babies in it, a raccoon hid an apples in it, and a cat slept in it. Years later, in the 80s, another small girl looked for her kitten in the attic of the house and found the old quilt. Her mother added stuffing to it and fixed the falling stars. Repaired, the quilt comforted the little girl on her mother's lap just as it did for Abigail on her mother's lap many years earlier.

A Quilt in Frontier Days

Sewing Quilts (Macmillan, 1994, Grades K–3) written by Ann Turner and illustrated by Thomas B. Allen is a story of a frontier mother and her daughters sewing their quilts. They talk about their memories of animals in the woods, fireworks on Independence Day, and the mother says that their days (of life) are like a quilt because "sometimes you can't see the pattern . . . until it's all sewn up and laid upon the bed."

A Quilt in Civil War Days

Selina and the Bear Paw Quilt (Crown, 1996, Grades 1–3) written by B. Smucker and illustrated by J. Wilson portrays what happens when Selina's Mennonite family plans to flee to Canada to avoid persecution as the Civil War is about to break out. The Mennonites refuse to take sides in the conflict. Selina's elderly grandmother stays behind in Pennsylvania but gives Selina a bear-claw patterned quilt top she has been making. Grades 1–3.

A Quilt in the Late 19th Century

The Keeping Quilt (Simon & Schuster, 1988, Grades K–3) by Patricia Polacco is a true story about a quilt kept by the author's family. It begins with the time when the author's Great-Gramma Anna came to America from Russia during the last century as a Russian immigrant to start life anew in New York. Anna's mother makes a keeping quilt from Anna's dress and babushka, Uncle Vladmir's shirt, Aunt Havalah's nightdress, and Aunt Natasha's apron that later is handed down through four generations.

A Quilt in Early 20th Century

In *The Dream Quilt* (Tuttle, 1995, Grades 2–4) by Amy Zerner and Jessie Spicer Zerner, Alex, a small boy, visits his great-aunt Rachel and sleeps under the family quilt which inspires nightly dreams.

continued

FIGURE 11–9 **Continued**

A Quilt in the 20th Century

In *The Canada Geese Quilt* (Cobblehill/Dutton, 1989, Grade 3–4) by Natalie Kinsey-Warnock, a granddaughter's artistic sketches become part of the family's history. In Vermont, a granddaughter discovers her artistic abilities and sketches the geese flying overhead and the geese become a kindred link with her ailing grandmother and influence her grandmother's will to live.

A Quilt in Hawaii

Luka's Quilt (Greenwillow, 1994, Grades K–2) by Georgia Guback is a story of intergenerational love. Luka and her grandmother quarrel because the traditional plain Hawaiian quilt that her grandmother is making for her does not have the large beautiful flowers that Luka wants. On Lei Day, Luka's grandmother asks that they declare a truce so they can celebrate the festival together. Luka agrees and participates in making flower leis. In return, Luka's grandmother makes a colorful fabric lei to accent the plain quilt and this heals Luka's hurt feelings.

A Quilt in a Contemporary Setting

The Patchwork Quilt (Dial, 1985, Grades 2–3) by Valerie Flournoy, shows a loving family making a quilt together as they recall events related to the fabric remnants. As the caring family members help Grandmother sew, they come closer together, remember past experiences that are related to the quilt scraps, and are pleased with the finished quilt that displays so beautifully the memories of many events in their lives.

Activity #179: "North vs. South"

Another informational book, *If I Lived in the Civil War* (Scholastic, 1994, Grade 3 up) by Karen Kay Moore, shows scenes of what went on. In the comparative format of the book, a reader sees what went on in the North and can compare that with what went on in the South. Motivated by the scenes, ask interested children to meet with partners and have one child role-play a child in the North, and the other a child in the South. Ask the children to volunteer to role-play their events for the whole group. Remind the audience that their responsibility is to take notes and be able to tell what they learned from the role-playing.

Activity #180: "Jefferson Davis: A.D. 1808–1889"

Slavery becomes a divisive issue in the United States and the issue's heat attracts many personalities in the days before and during the Civil War period. For example, the president of the Confederate States of American during the Civil War is Jefferson Davis (1808–1889) and the military and political events of the war are presented along with Davis's

interesting quotes in *Jefferson Davis* (Children's, 1993, Grades 3–5) by Zachary Kent. Questions that arise from the book, and others, can be recorded on an overhead transparency for a class discussion:

1. "What is there about your state today that relates directly to the Civil War? How can you show this in a drawing, sketch or painting?"
2. "What rights did the Northern Yankees think were important? The Southern Confederates?"
3. "What was life like for people in the South during this time period? The North?"
4. "How does that life compare with ways you live today?"
5. "How has life changed for Americans since the days of the Civil War?"

Activity #181: "Charlie's Story"

Give the children a further sense of the times and the danger to all living things during war by reading aloud and showing the illustrations in the authentic retelling of a true story, *The Adventure of Charlie and His Wheat-Straw Hat: A Memory* (Dodd, 1986, Grades 1–3) by B. T. Hiser. Divide the whole group into three small groups and ask some of the children to listen to Charlie's story to find out how much Charlie loved his hat (group 1); other children to listen for the way that Charlie saved his squire's animals (group 2); and still others to listen so they can describe this event during the Civil war (group 3). In Appalachia, 7-year-old Charlie loves the hat that he and his grandmother made and he defends it from Confederate soldiers, which saves his squire's animals during the Civil War.

After each group reports on what it listened for in the story, ask each group to pantomime an incident from the story for the rest of the class to guess. The child who guesses correctly must document the guess by describing the event and can ask other children for any missing details. If appropriate, have the children inquire about other people in history who saved something or someone in times of danger or destruction, just as Charlie did. Ask them to report what they found back to the whole group.

Activity #182: "Cecil's Story"

Cecil, a young boy, worries if his father will be the same when he returns from the Civil War in *Cecil's Story* (Orchard/Watts, 1991, Grades 1–3) by George Lyon. At a neighbor's farm in 1864, Cecil waits for his mother to return with his wounded father. He spends the passing days by feeding the animals and doing other chores. When his father finally returns, Cecil's fears are unfounded when he realizes that his father is really the same even though he has one arm missing. Engage the children in relating the story to their own experiences by telling of a time when they had a fear or worried and waited for a member of their family or for someone they knew. Accept all responses and discuss some alternatives for resolving the fears.

Abraham Lincoln: A.D. 1809–1865

With an opaque projector, show the photographs in *Lincoln: A Photobiography* (Clarion, 1987, Grade 3 up) by Russell Freedman. The photographs are in chronological order and the text has quotations from newspapers, Lincoln's speeches, and other sources. The text tells of his early life, how the family moves to Indiana and Illinois, and the death of Lincoln's mother. Sarah Johnston Lincoln, his father's second wife, receives respect from the family and does much to make the Lincoln family close-knit. She encourages Lincoln's schooling. After Lincoln's election to the state legislature, he begins to study

law and shows an interest in the major issues of the times. His law practice grows and he meets Mary Todd when he works at the capitol. After a discussion of the Civil War years and his presidency (1861–1865), the book concludes with the funeral train trip to Springfield and Lincoln's final resting place. Some of the myths and legends about Lincoln can be discovered by the children as they learn that Lincoln never liked to be called Abe and objected to the name; that he was poor when he was young, but became wealthy when he was America's sixteenth president; that he saw slavery as a major issue of the times and detested it; and that he wanted to save the union of the states, but the horrible death and destruction of the war affected him deeply.

Activity #183: "Lincoln Study Groups"

Have the children divide into groups of four to read and study further about events in the life of Abraham Lincoln (or other historical figure of this period.) Assign responsibilities to each child in the group:

1. One child is a Pony Express rider who gets the book copies, the teacher's guiding questions, or other supplies and takes them back to the group.
2. One child is a reader who reads the story to the group or selects another group member to read aloud.
3. Another child is a recorder who first writes down three possible answers from the group to each of several guiding questions to allow the children to think of as many solutions as possible. Later, the group returns to each question to decide on which answer of the three they support.
4. Still another child is the speaker who gives the small group's answer for each question to the whole class.
5. In the whole group, elicit each group's answers and record them on chart paper. After the discussion, give children choices about completing an art project that further extends the answers to the questions.

Activity #184: "Gettysburg Address"

"The Gettysburg Address" is included in the book *Honest Abe* (Greenwillow, 1992, Grades 1–3) by Edith Kunhardt, a picture book biography. Discuss the brightly colored illustrations and several excerpts about writing the Gettysburg Address, as well as other important events in Lincoln's childhood and his many careers. Invite children to role-play with partners and take the role of Lincoln and an imaginary friend in situations such as working around a log cabin, attending school and studying at night, discussing his views about the slavery issue he faced as president, and writing the Gettysburg Address. Ask the children to trade roles and replay the scenes again. In the whole group, have them dictate what they learned from the role-playing. Write their dictations on a language experience chart for rereading.

Activity #185: "Lincoln's Personality"

"Lincoln was a long man,/ He liked out of doors/ He liked the wind blowing/And the talk in country stores" are words that begin the poem "Abraham Lincoln" in *A Book of Americans* (Holt, 1986, all grades) by Rosemary and Stephan Vincent Benet. The verses tell children that Lincoln (1809–1865) liked telling stories and jokes, carried his letters in his tall black hat, and wore a shawl around his shoulders to keep warm. After reading the verses aloud, select lines about Abraham Lincoln for the children to interpret orally. Use their suggestions of line-a-child, unison reading, low voices only, high voices only, and others to reread the lines for a choral reading.

Activity #186: "Lincoln in Drama"

After reading verses about Abraham Lincoln aloud, ask children for their ideas about ways to interpret what happened in the poem through creative drama. For instance, if the poem mentions that Lincoln talked to a friend in the country store (or any place), ask the children, "What would the two say to each other in a drama? How would they act toward one another? If the friend could ask a question of Lincoln, what might be asked? What might Lincoln reply?" Have the children pair up with partners and put their ideas into action. Poetry and prose to consider as springboards for classroom drama about Lincoln are in Figure 11–10.

FIGURE 11–10 Children's Books about Abraham Lincoln

PERSPECTIVES

Abe Lincoln (Harcourt, 1985, Grade 3 up) by Carl Sandburg relates the kind of life Lincoln had, his first experience seeing slavery, and acquiring his nickname, Honest Abe.

Abraham Lincoln: A Man for All the People (Holiday, 1993, Grades 1–3) by Myra Cohn Livingston is a folk ballad with rhythmic beginning words, "A man for all the people/ A man who stood up tall/ Abe Lincoln spoke of justice/ And liberty for all."

Abraham Lincoln, Friend of the People (Follett, 1950, Grades 2–3) by Clara Ingram Judson has a foreword that points out that conversations are the "talk" of a life story.

Abraham Lincoln: President of a Divided Country (Children's, 1989, Grades 1–2) by C. Greene tells of Lincoln's family, early life, and education with some background about slavery and the Civil War Years.

The Assassination of Abraham Lincoln (Millbrook, 1993, Grades 3–5) by R. E. Jakoubek presents Lincoln's activities, thoughts, and conversations on Friday, April 14, 1865. Not only are the events in the weeks that followed seen from Lincoln's perspective but they also are seen from the views of other witnesses—his family and cabinet members as well as John Wilkes Booth and his accomplices.

Just a Few Words, Mr. Lincoln: The Story of the Gettysburg Address (Grosset, 1993, Grades 2–3) by Jean Fritz details the challenge of writing his most famous speech, the Gettysburg Address. (The Address is found at the back of the book). The text includes anecdotes about Mr. Lincoln, his son, his work as president, and some of his remembered remarks.

"Lincoln" in *Story and Verse for Children* (Macmillan, 1966, all grades) by Miriam Blanton Huber. As a boy, Lincoln is wise in the woodspeople's ways, reads by firelight, and walks long miles to get a book on "which his heart was set."

Newcomers from Different Cultures

Ask the children to think about what it would be like to be a newcomer on a farm in America and to discuss the illustrations in Anne Pellowski's *First Farm in the Valley: Anna's Story* (Philomel, 1982, Grades 2–3). Read aloud the story about Anna, the daughter of a Polish immigrant, who is ready to start school and shows her "spunk. " She climbs the roof of the house to get a bag of nails and travels through a hail storm to bring home the sheep. As newcomers in Wisconsin, Anna and her family strive to keep the traditions of Poland alive in their new home. Just as Anna was a newcomer, ask the children to role-play the situation of a new child in the neighborhood with a partner being the welcoming neighbor. Have the children trade roles. Ask them to think of different ways to make a new neighbor feel welcome and have them role-play some of their ideas again. Related to this, invite a newcomer's family members or relatives into the classroom to talk about ways they keep the traditions of their native country alive in their new homes in America, just as Anna's family did.

Activity #187: "Newcomers on Farms"

After introducing the children to a personalized view of life on the farm through Anna's story, read aloud parts from *The Folks in the Valley: A Pennsylvania Dutch ABC* (HarperCollins, 1992, Grades Pre–3) by Jim Aylesworth, a book that gives children the bigger and more general picture about working and playing on a farm. In the first illustration, life in rural America is shown and the alphabetical text begins with a rhyme for the letter *A:* "Alarm clocks ring;/ It's almost dawn./ The folks in the valley/ stretch and yawn./" and for the last illustration, /"Z's the sound/ of their well-earned rest." Discuss what the children learned that related to life on a farm and engage in the following:

1. Have the children mime the actions of people working and playing on a farm and the idea that farm families were mainly self-sufficient as they built their own barns, raised their food, and entertained themselves.

2. Discuss the idea that the average modern family is not self-sufficient in the same way farm families were in this period and talk about ways things have changed through time. For example, help the children see that their families depend on several people— workers at the local power station; truck drivers who bring meat, produce, and medicines; workers who made the appliances used in the kitchen; mechanics who fix cars; and other workers—to survive in today's environment. Write the jobs of the people on the board.

3. After listing, engage them in thinking of ways they can help their families be more self-sufficient— planting a garden, baking bread, churning butter— and invite them to draw a picture to show one of the ways.

John Wesley Powell: A.D. 1869

In 1869, John Wesley Powell led an exciting but dangerous expedition down the Colorado River to explore the region that is now known as the Grand Canyon. At times, Powell's men questioned what their mission was, but the major kept the group together and tried to explore the river and the canyon as completely as possible. Tell the children you are going to read aloud Powell's story from the book *In Search of the Grand Canyon: Down the Colorado with John Wesley Powell* (Holt, 1995, Grades 3–5) by Mary Ann Fraser, and ask them to listen for the dangers that Powell faced. Fraser includes quotes about the expedition from the major's journal in the book. As you read aloud, ask the children to take notes (or sketch stick drawings) about the dangers (waterfalls, rapids) or any other factor (loss of supplies) that would make them accept or decline going on the expedition.

Activity #188: "Want to Go?"

Mention to the children that you want to know if they should go along on an imaginary expedition with Powell down the Colorado River. They need to find out if the trip has any dangers or situations that would make them choose to stay behind. Point out the significance of Powell's journal in the days when the telephone, computer, and fax were not even realistic dreams for humans. Mention that Powell's journal shows Powell's point of view, his calling, and what he thought about being part of this westward movement in history. In addition, Powell's journal adds an aspect greater than just Powell's "surface" life story. Powell's journal also shows his incidents, feelings, and attitudes and tells any critical incident that he chooses to tell.

Activity #189: "Powell's Journal"

Help the children understand that the writer of historical fiction and nonfiction who includes a journal must make choices about the material the writer includes in the journal. Write an example of one of Powell's journal entries on the board and discuss with the children:

- "What aspects of life in this time period could you include in this journal entry in Powell's story?"
- "What are some of the things that you can reveal about Powell's life in a journal entry of your own?"
- "What are some things that you can reveal to show what Powell stands for in a simulated journal entry?"

Have the children record the journal entry on paper and insert their own inclusions.

Activity #190: "Simulated Journal Entry"

Encourage the children to suggest what they would add if they put a simulated entry into Powell's journal. Discuss examples of what a journal entry can add to a story. As the children mention their examples, record them on the board or chart. Invite the children to meet with partners to create a journal entry written by Powell to add something further to his story. Here are some things journal entries can do:

1. A journal can tell a reader more about the actions of people or of a movement in history. "What told you something you didn't know previously about Powell's expedition *In Search of the Grand Canyon: Down the Colorado with John Wesley Powell?*"
2. A journal can tell more about an issue close to a writer's heart or tell about cultural changes going on. "In the book about John Wesley Powell, what did you discover about changes that were going on in this time period?"
3. A journal can personalize a character or a cause in history. "In what ways did the story about Powell make him more personable to you?"
4. A journal can give meaning to a person's faith and carry a personal touch—it can be a kind of "close thing." "What, if anything, made Powell's story 'a close thing' for you?"
5. A journal can add substance to a symbol or an idea. "What words in the story added something to your idea of what it means to go on a dangerous expedition?"
6. A journal can add facts and, in some cases, deliver life-altering messages. "What message did you get from Powell's story?"

7. A journal can mirror the personality of a common or uncommon person in history. It can represent hope, a longing for companionship, a need for love, or a request for knowledge of something faraway. "What did Powell's story tell you about his personality?"
8. A journal can add to a certain way of life (i.e., entries can record newspaper and magazine accounts of an event and bring a personality to life). "In what ways did the story make you think of Powell as a *real* person?"

Ask the children these additional questions:

1. "What journal entry in Powell's story would be most important to you? Why?"
2. "How do you think writing in a journal in the 1800s compares with the way you communicate today?"
3. "From your point of view, how did your journal entry add something to the story? Tell about it."

Activity #191: "Trip Journal Entry"

When a child mentions that he or she is going on a trip with others, give the child a copy of a Trip Journal Entry to take along on the journey. (See Figure 11–11 and History Master 17.) Trip Journal Entry, and the History Master 17 at the back of this book. Mention that when the child returns, the whole group can learn from the child's trip. Ask the child to write in some of the information requested on the journal sheet. If appropriate, someone else can help the child write in the information. A child can take as many journal entry sheets as the days the child plans to be away, and of course, add anything extra that the child thinks will be of interest to the group.

The Ingalls: A.D. 1870s

Introduce the children to life with the Ingalls family with Laura Ingalls Wilder's *Little House in the Big Woods* (Harper & Brothers, 1932, Grade 2 up) illustrated by H. Sewell & M. Boyle. The Ingalls family includes the oldest, Mary (who later becomes blind), Laura, and then baby Carrie. Grace eventually displaces Carrie as the baby. Ma is skilled in cooking meals out of limited resources. Sequels suitable for a display of books about Wilder in the classroom include the following:

- *Little House on the Prairie* (Harper & Brothers, 1935, Grade 3 up) tells about the Ingalls family on the Kansas prairie.

FIGURE 11–11 **Trip Journal Entry**

Trip Journal Entry for _____ (child's name)

Date _____

When you go on a trip, please take one of these trip journal entry sheets with you. Take as many sheets as the days you plan to be away. When you get back, we all will learn from your trip. If needed, have someone else fill in some of the information with you. Add anything extra that will be of interest to the group.

The way I traveled was:
The weather was:
I wore:
The best activity we did today was:
The most interesting thing I saw was:
The license numbers I read were:
My sketches of interesting things I saw are on the back of this sheet.

What I ate for breakfast:
Time I started breakfast: Time I finished breakfast:
Where I ate breakfast:
The town I was in:
Breakfast was: (good   fair   poor)

What I ate for lunch:
Time I started lunch: Time I finished lunch:
Where I ate lunch:
The town I was in:
Lunch was: (good   fair   poor)

What I ate for dinner:
Time I started dinner: Time I finished dinner:
Where I ate dinner:
The town I was in:
Dinner was: (good   fair   poor)

Where I slept at night:
Town/state:
Temperature when I went to bed:
Temperature when I got up:

Other:

- *On the Banks of Plum Creek* (Harper & Brothers, 1937, Grade 3 up) is about the family's two years in Minnesota.
- *By the Shores of Silver Lake* (Harper & Brothers, 1939, Grade 3 up) tells about the family's homestead in Dakota Territory in 1880.
- *Little Town on the Prairie* (Harper & Brothers, 1941, Grade 3 up) is about Pa working a claim for three years.
- *Farmer Boy* (Harper & Brothers, 1933, Grade 3 up) describes Alonzo Wilder's life as a farmer.
- *The Long Winter* (Harper & Brothers, 1940, Grade 3 up) begins in October 1881, when the first winter blizzards come to the Dakota Territory.
- *The First Four Years* (1971, Grade 3 up) is the story of 18-year-old Laura when she marries Alonzo in 1886.
- *These Happy Golden Years* (Harper & Brothers, 1943, Grade 3 up) portrays Laura's years of marriage in her own gray home in Almanzo's tree claim.
- *On the Way Home* (Harper, 1962, Grade 3 up) is a personal journal of the Wilders' move to Mansfield, Missouri, in 1894.
- *The Story of Laura Ingalls Wilder* (by M. Stine, Dell, 1992, Grades 2–5) discusses Wilder's early years and explains the genesis for writing her stories.
- *Little House on Rocky Ridge* (R. L. MacBride, HarperCollins, 1993, Grades 3–5) is a new volume written by Rose's adopted grandson. It continues the Little House books with a story of 7-year-old Rose, Laura's mischievous daughter. The family makes the long and difficult journey by wagon from South Dakota to a new farm at Mansfield, Missouri, in 1894.

Activity #192: "Survey of Laura's Family"

For a group survey, have the children ask their classmates to give them one word they would use to summarize what Laura's family was like. (Hardworking? Generous? Friendly?) Have the children record their answers on a sheet of paper.

Name of Classmate	*One Word to Describe Laura's Family*
1.	1.

   Back in the whole group, ask the children if any word appears more than once on their sheets. If so, record the words on the board. Have the children decide on one word that best gives a picture of Laura's

family. Invite the children to illustrate the one word with their original drawings of Laura's family.

Laura Wilder's 1800s

Organize a story lunch for the children. Four days a week during their lunch time, read aloud to those children whose parents or guardians have given permission for them to attend. Select stories that portray views of children and their families from different time periods in history. For example, kindergarten children can listen to *Going to Town* (HarperCollins, 1995, P–1) illustrated by Renee Grae, a picture book that retells Laura's first trip to town when she and Mary wear their best dresses, just one chapter from *Little House in the Big Woods*. First-graders can listen to *Little House in the Big Woods* by Laura Ingalls Wilder (Harper, 1953) and second-graders can hear Wilder's *On the Banks of Plum Creek* (Harper, 1953). If the children want to see the childhood homes and places in which Laura played, show the full-color photographs in *Searching for Laura Ingalls: A Reader's Journey* (MacMillan, 1993, Grades 2–6) by Kathryn Lasky. On a personal vacation, Lasky and her family visited the settings in most of the Little House books to try to bring the present and the past together. If the children want to sing some of the songs mentioned in the Little House series, sing the words from *My Little House Songbook* (HarperCollins, 1995, Grades 1–3) illustrated by Holly Jones. Songs include "America," "Yankee Doodle," "Pop! Goes the Weasel," and 11 others.

Activity #193: "Introducing Facts with Fiction"

Organize another story lunch for the children who are just as interested in the real world as they are in realistic fiction and fantasy and introduce them to the best information books related to an historical figure or event. For instance, you can read Kathy Jacobsen's *My New York* (Little, Brown, 1993, Grades 1–3) for a look at the Statue of Liberty, the Museum of Natural History, and Chinatown. Then show a contrast with the city at an earlier stage by reading Arnold Lobel's *On the Day Peter Stuyvesant Sailed into Town* (Harper, 1971, Grades 2–3).

Families in Dakota Territory: A.D. 1870

A. Turner's *Grasshopper Summer* (Macmillan, 1989, Grades 3–6) describes events in the Dakotas as farming families go west and settle on the land (c.

1870). In Kentucky, Sam's father dislikes the farm he tends with Sam's grandfather and takes the family to Dakota. Sam quarrels with his brother, finds friends, helps plant the first crop, and fights a plague of grasshoppers to save what he loves.

Activity #194: "Farming Family, Sioux Family"

Ask the children to reflect about the family life in the Dakotas for Sam's farming family and a Sioux family. Mention that you can tell a lot about what it took to survive in the Dakotas by studying the families. On a list, have the children write names of six family members (include Native Americans). Next to each name, ask them to write down what made that person successful in living in the Dakotas.

Names of Family Members	*Successful Because*
1. Sioux mother	1.

Red Hawk and Custer: A.D. 1876

An account of Custer's last battle is told by an Ogala Sioux, who was a 15-year-old in 1876, and Goble's retelling treats both sides fairly in *Red Hawk's Account of Custer's Last Battle* (Bradbury, 1971, Grade 3 up). Mention to children that Paul Goble, an author and illustrator who has always been interested in the Native Americans, was watching a TV account of Custer's last battle and was struck by how biased the story was (Stott, 1984). When he tried to find a book with the Native Americans' point of view, he couldn't, and so the idea for *Red Hawk's Account* came about. As excerpts from the story are read aloud, ask the children to listen for evidence that the native fighters had great respect for the bravery of their opponents and vice versa.

Activity #195: "Native Americans' POV"

Goble has written other books that will give children the Native Americans' point of view (POV). For example, Goble's *Brave Eagle's Account of the Fetterman Fight* (Bradbury, 1972, Grade 3 up) tells the events of a battle in 1866 in Wyoming. In another story, Cheyenne men derail a Union Pacific freight train in 1867 in *Death of the Iron Horse* (Bradbury, 1987, Grade 3 up). A fictionalized autobiography of a 14-year-old hero shows the connection between horses and the bravery of the rider who tries to prove himself a man in a raid of a Crow camp in *Lone Bull's Horse Raid* (Bradbury, 1973,

Grade 3 up). *Beyond the Ridge* (Bradbury, 1989, Grade 3 up) is the story of an elderly Native American woman who experiences death and goes to an afterlife.

Activity #196: "Mitakuye Oyasin— We Are All Related"

The Native Americans' belief about "ways we are all related" (a theme expressed by the Sioux from the Plains tribes as *mitakuye oyasin*) is portrayed in some of Paul Goble's retold legends: *The Girl Who Loved Wild Horses* (Bradbury, 1978), *The Gift of the Sacred Dog* (Bradbury, 1980), *Star Boy* (Bradbury, 1982), *The Friendly Wolf* (Bradbury, 1974), and others. *Mitakuye oyasin* is further explained by Goble in his notes in *Buffalo Woman* (Bradbury, 1984) where he states that the lives of both the buffalo and the people were closely interwoven, and the story (not for entertainment) teaches that buffalo and people were related. It was felt that retelling the story strengthened the people's bond with the herds, encouraged the herds to return so that the people could live, and had a power to bring about a change within each person. It was felt that in listening to the story, the people might all be a little more worthy of their buffalo relatives. This relationship is shown in the several legends of the Plains tribes that lend themselves to book talks found on History Master 18. Ask the children to reflect on what changes, if any, have happened to their thoughts because they heard a message in the story of Buffalo Woman and realize that everyone is related and we might all try to be a little more worthy of our relatives in the human family.

Multicultural Cowboys

"Open Range," a poem written by Kathryn and Byron Jackson in *The Arbuthnot Anthology of Children's Literature* (1976) can give the children a sense of the vastness of the West and its great open spaces where ranchers let their cattle roam freely. Give them a further picture of the Old West by reading excerpts from *Cowboy Country* (Clarion, 1993, Grades K–3) by Ann Herbert Scott, where an old-timer takes a boy on a overnight trek to Devil's Canyon and tells tales of the old west as he compares present-day ranching practices with those of the past. In *Cowboys: Roundup on an American Ranch* (Scholastic, 1996, Grades 3–5) written by J. Anderson and illustrated with photographs by G. Ancona, the harsh life of a ranch family in New Mexico is shown through the daily activities of a two-week round-up where the cattle are penned and branded.

Activity #197: "Cowboys in Our Class"

Prevail on two parents, classroom aides, university student teachers, relatives, managers of western stores, or others to dress in full cowboy regalia and visit the classroom. You and the two visitors can show off the practical purposes of the bandanas (blindfolding a frightened horse), 10-gallon hats (to carry water), vests (pockets), pants (pocketless for comfort in the saddle), boots (protection), spurs (to get the best work out of a horse), and rawhide chaps (protection against rope and brush burn) as you encourage the children to learn and write about the American cowboy. You can display western items, play recorded songs, recite poetry, and point out that cowboys came from every ethnic background. With your help, the visitors also can show students ways that cowboy poetry and songs, history, and multiculturism add to the study of this time period.

Some children can research such topics as the invention of barbed wire in the 1880s, the introduction of the ancestors of the longhorns by Spanish settlers, and the discovery that disease-carrying ticks caused Texas Fever—a disease that caused milk and beef cattle to die. Others can inquire about the major cattle trails in the 1800s (i.e., the Chisholm Trail from San Antonio to Abilene) and the *remuda* (herd) of different horses—a circle horse, a brush horse, a cutting horse, a roping horse, a river horse—available for different jobs. The children can learn to read the brands used on cattle, an idea that dates back to the early Egyptians who used brands on their livestock. They can sing cowboy songs they have found and learn to dance "The Gal from Arkansas" and other cowboy square dances that were popular in Dodge City and other bustling places (see Figure 11–12).

Activity #198: "Cowboy Clothes"

To direct the children's interest toward the historical west, show a picture of a cowboy dressed in his working clothes, and ask the students to name each article of clothing seen in the picture and discuss the hard work that the cowboy does related to each article. Explain why certain items of clothing were needed by the cowboys with *Why Cowboys Sleep with Their Boots On* (Pelican, 1995, Grades K–2) and *Cowboy Rodeo* (Pelican, 1992, Grades K–3) by James Rice. Write the children's suggestions on the board and invite them to use the information to dic-

tate a brief paragraph summarizing the life of a cowboy. Write their dictation on a chart as a language experience for rereading, and invite the children to sketch and color an article of cowboy clothing to add to the chart as a border.

Activity #199: "Cowboy Gathering"

With a map of cowboy country (Nevada and other states), invite the children to follow in the footsteps of cowboys in the wide open country and "travel" across the map with their fingers. As their fingers follow the Santa Fe trail and other well-known trails, ask them to mark the routes and imagine tawny hills, a variety of wildlife, wild horses running free, and game birds such as pheasant, chukar, quail, and sage hen. In this imaginary setting, invite them to participate in a Cowboy Poetry and Cowboy Music Gathering. To participate in the gathering, the children take the role of "dusty bards of the sagebrush" and recite some cowboy poetry (verses about the West), spin a tale such as *Cowboy Night Before Christmas* (Pelican, 1986, Grade 3 up) by James Rice, or sing some songs about life in the saddle and the wide open spaces of the range. Ask the children to make suggestions about which articles of clothing they could wear (such as simulated cowboy vests made from brown paper) for a Western Parade into other classroom to invite the other children to the gathering. Before the performance, engage the children in locating and practicing verses to recite, western tales to tell, and cowboy songs to sing.

Activity #200: "Cowboy Pa and Grandpa"

To see a cowboy's daily routine—dressing in their hats, chaps, and spurs, and mending fences, roping, branding, and herding, use the opaque projector and show the children the illustrations from *Just Like My Dad* (HarperCollins, 1993, Grades 1–2) by T. Gardella or read aloud *Grandpa Was a Cowboy* (Orchard, 1996, Grades K–4) written by S. Sullivan and illustrated by B. Dodson. Ask the children to discern what they can learn about the day of a cowboy from the projected accounts in the book. Ask them to imagine the book characters going about their daily activities. The daily activities of a cowboy can give the children an opportunity to write stories using personification. For example, the children can personify a cowboy's hat, a cowboy's boots, or the saddle or the bridle around the horse's neck. If appropriate, talk with the children about how an object feels—perhaps how the cowboy's hat feels being placed on top of the his head. Ask, "What

FIGURE 11–12   **Children's Books about Ethnic Cowboys**

PERSPECTIVES

African Heritage

Katz, W. L. *The Black West: A Documentary and Pictorial History.* Doubleday, 1973. This book helps children become aware of the history of the African Americans who were the cattle drivers in the nineteenth century and who gave today's children role models as cowboys who contributed to the settling of the west. Grade 3 up.

Miller, R. H. *The Story of Nat Love.* Silver Burdett, 1991. This life story provides information about an African American in the Old West. Born a slave in Tennessee, Nat became a skilled bronco buster at just 15 years old. He won a contest with his roping and shooting skills and contributed to the role of African Americans in the Old West. Grades 1–4.

McCafferty, J. *Holt and the Cowboys.* Ill. by F. S. Davis. Pelican, 1993. This book is a fictionalized account of Holt Collier circa 1850. Born a slave in Mississippi, Holt grew up hunting and riding. He fought with the Texas Brigade, worked on a ranch, and gained the respect of almost everyone he met. Collier meets some cowboys who don't believe he can ride or that he was a Confederate scout, and to show them, he rides a mare no one else can break. Grades 2–3.

Pinkney, A. D. *Bill Pickett: Rodeo-Ridin' Cowboy.* Ill. by B. Pinkney. New York: Harcourt, 1996. This is a true story of an energetic child-cowboy who invented bulldogging and became the most famous African American rodeo performer throughout the United States, even riding in Mexico, South America, and England. Historical notes of the Black West and a bibliography are included. Biographical fiction. Grades K–3.

Latino/Hispanic Heritage

Gordon, G. *Anthony Reynoso: Born to Rope.* Ill. by M. Cooper. Clarion, 1996. This is a picture book autobiography of Anthony, a dedicated 9-year-old rodeo *charro* (cowboy) who lives in a small town near Phoenix. He discusses his close Mexican-American family, his hours of roping practice, and the excitement of rodeo competition. Autobiography. Grades 2–4.

Whitman, S. "Vaqueros: The First Cowboys" in *Cobblestone,* 10, 4 (April 1989): 21–3. This is an brief overview of the history of the Mexicans who were the cow-herders (vaqueros) for Spanish settlers in the sixteenth century and who gave today's cowboys the names of *corral, rancho, la reata* (lariat), and *bronco.* Grade 3 up.

Native American Heritage

McCall, E. *Cowboys and Cattle Drives.* Children's, 1980. This book tells the life story of America's most famous cowboy, Will Rogers, the part-Cherokee Native American who entertained people with his humor and his roping abilities. Grade 3 up.

European Heritage

Lightfoot, D. J. *Trail Fever: The Story of a Texas Cowboy.* Lothrop, Lee & Shepard, 1992. This is the story of George Sanders, who grew up in a cowboy family. It seems he learned to ride before he could walk, helped to herd cattle by age 5, and helped run a cattle ranch as he grew up. In 1880, he goes on his first cattle drive. Becoming a Texas trail driver, he survives floods, droughts, freezing nights, and confronts raiders and bandits. Includes interviews with Saunders's grandchildren and has chapters entitled School Days, Stampede, and Up the Chizzum' Trail. Grades 2–3.

does the hat see? Feel? Touch? Where would the hat rather be, or is the hat satisfied with its position? Does the hat have any fears? Does the hat like the cowboy? The horse? What are some interesting happenings the hat might see?" After asking questions like these, engage the children in dictating or writing a story and personifying a cowboy's hat or another one of the cowboy's possessions.

Activity #201: "Cattle Drives"

After reading aloud excerpts from *Matthew the Cowboy* (Albert Whitman, 1994, Grades 1–3) by Ruth Hooker, *Cowboys of the Wild West* (Clarion, 1985, Grade 3 up) by Russell Freedman, or another favorite source about the work of cowboys, invite the children to dictate or list all of the facts they know about the topic and then tell the class the source where they got the information. Record pertinent facts about the discussion on the board:

What We Know	*Where We Got the Information*
1.	1.

After the discussion, engage the children in looking at other sources to see how the topic of cowboys/cowgirls is reported. With the whole group, review some of the sources that the children used and discuss the following:

1. "From all of the sources you saw, which book do you believe? Why?"
2. "In what way did the sources tell about the cowboys in the same way? In different ways?"
3. "In what ways can we find out which books give us facts closest to the truth?"

After the whole-group discussion, ask the children to work together with partners and write their own brief account of a day in a cowboy's life. Ask partners to join with two more children and read their accounts aloud to one another or tell about what they wrote about western life. Encourage them to elicit feedback about their writing and to consider what changes they might make.

How the West Was Fun

When Senator Roscoe McCorkle has an important meeting in Washington, D.C., with the president, he needs to travel from faraway Grass Valley by stagecoach and then by train in *Charlie Drives the Stage* (Holiday House, 1989, all grades) by Eric A. Kimmel. In the story, the senator is out of luck because there is no stage going anywhere because of several dangers—avalanches in the pass, bandits on the road, and Indians on the warpath. The senator is told that the river is rising, too, and the bridge may go out. Still insisting he leave right away, the senator makes a deal with Charlie Drummond to drive him to Washington. Charlie agrees but says, "Once we get going, we don't stop. And we don't turn back." The Senator agrees, and at the end of the story, faces a humorous surprise ending. After hearing the story, the students can locate their own books of humorous views of history about the West or select several books listed in Figure 11–13.

After the story, review objects in the illustrations (i.e., clothing, leather goods, hats) and ask students to determine what services, workers, and jobs were available in the stagecoach days (e.g., the workers who were needed to make the clothing, leather goods, hats, etc.). List them on the board. Review the list and ask the students how they could *really* know that these services, workers, and jobs were available in this time period. Invite them to search for more information in other data references about each one and report what they learned back to the whole group.

Activity #202: "Charley's Stagecoach"

Read aloud *Charley Drives the Stage*, the story of Senator McCorkle's fast-moving ride with Charlie, the determined stagecoach driver, as they outrun an avalanche, dodge falling boulders, and throw dynamite at bandits in Ambush Canyon. After they outdistance the arrows of Indians and chase the departed train so Senator McCorkle can get on it to travel to Washington, the senator thanks "Mister" Charles Drummond who says in return, "You got the name wrong." Let the students predict what might happen *before* showing and reading about the surprise ending, where "Mister Charlie" turns out to be "Miss Charlene."

Activity #203: "Participation Story"

Discuss the characters in the story and have the children suggest the sounds to make for each one in a participation story about Charlie's fast-driving stagecoach ride. Have the children also say the sounds for the horses and stagecoach and insert the sounds into the story as it is read aloud (use History Master 19).

FIGURE 11–13   Children's Books about How History Was Fun

PERSPECTIVES

Pirate Days

Scieszka, J. *The Not-So-Jolly Roger.* Ill. by L. Smith. Viking, 1991. Joe and his friends go back in time to have a laugh-out-loud adventure with Bluebeard. Historical fiction. Grades 3–5.

1700s: Davy Crockett

Kunstler, J. H. *Davy Crockett: The Legendary Frontiersman.* Ill. by St. Brodner. Simon & Schuster, 1995. This is a humorous account told in a tall-tale manner beginning with Crockett's birth in Tennessee, going on to his frontier life where he sweet-talks a bear, running for Congress, and ending with Davy's bragging lifting the spirits of the troops at the Alamo. Historical fiction. Grades 2–5.

Quackenbush, R. *Quit Pulling My Leg, Davy Crockett.* Prentice-Hall, 1987. This book portrays the life of Crockett as a frontiersman, and separates facts from fanciful stories. Biography. Grade 3 up.

1800s: Jigsaw Jackson, the Golly Sisters, Professor Potts, Nell Nugget, and Others

Birchman, D. F. *Jigsaw Jackson.* Ill. by D. San Souci. Lothrop, Lee & Shepard, 1996. J. J. Jackson, fast at putting things together, teams up with Sean McShaker, genius jigsaw-puzzle maker, to show off their skills and go on the road with Wild West Circus star "Bison Bob." Historical Fiction. Grades 2–5.

Byars, B. *The Golly Sisters Go West.* Harper & Row, 1986. Two energetic sisters, Rose and May-May, travel west in a covered wagon and sing and dance to entertain people. Their problems begin when May-May's magic word is the only thing that starts their horse on the journey; when they argue so long they lose their audience; when May-May loses her red hat; and when the returned hat is smashed after another argument. When their arguing frightens a prowler away one night, the two decide to argue only when they hear something outside their wagon from then on. Historical Fiction. Grades 1–3.

Byars, B. *The Golly Sisters Ride Again.* Ill. by S. Truesdell HarperCollins, 1994. May-May and Rose, the Golly sisters, travel the Wild West to entertain people in different towns. They face a goat in the audience, go to see a talking rock, and hide under the bed during a lightning and thunder storm. Historical Fiction. Grades 1–3.

Carrick, C. *Big Old Bones.* Ill. by D. Carrick. Clarion, 1989. Professor Potts and his family discover dinosaur bones in the West and reassemble them in his laboratory in the East in various ways and make some wrong conclusions about dinosaurs. Historical fiction. Grades 1–3.

Enderle, J. R., & S. G. Tessler. *Nell Nugget and the Cow Caper.* Ill. by P. Yalowitz. Simon & Schuster, 1996. Nell Nugget, singer and yodeler, discovers her favorite cow, Goldie, has been stolen and she searches with the help of her horse, Pay Dirt, and dog, Dust. She suspects Nasty Galoot and follows him with her piano. She causes great confusion and rescues Goldie after she sings campfire songs and calls the rest of the herd in to help. After bad man Galoot gets stuck in Muddy Mud Creek without his pants, Nell yodels her way back home. Historical fiction. Grades K–2.

Gerrard, R. *Rosie and the Rustlers.* Ill. by the author. Farrar, Straus & Giroux, 1989. A heroine takes on the bad guys in a frontier setting. Historical fiction. Grades 2–4.

continued

FIGURE 11–13 **Continued**

1800s: Jigsaw Jackson, the Golly Sisters, Professor Potts, Nell Nugget, and Others

Gerrard, R. *Wagons West!* Ill. by the author. Farrar, Straus & Giroux, 1996. With some humor, this is a story in verse about families on a wagon train who travel west with Buckskin Dan. A young girl helps save an Arapaho child, and in return, the families are rescued by the tribe when they run into cattle bandits. Historical fiction. Grades 2–4.

Isaacs, A. *Swamp Angel.* Ill. by P. O. Zelinsky. Dutton, 1994. In this tall tale set in Tennessee, Angelica Longrider (who built her first log cabin at age 2) earns her name by rescuing wagon trains stuck in Dejection Swamp. Historical fiction. Grades K–3.

Kimmel, E. A. *Charlie Drives the Stage.* Ill. by G. Rounds. Holiday House, 1989. In 1887, Charlie Drummond is the only stagecoach driver who has "a ghost of a chance of getting through" to take Senator Roscoe McCorkle to the train so the Senator can arrive in Washington for an important meeting with the president. Neither a mountain slide, ambushers, attacking Indians, nor a collapsing bridge can keep a young stagecoach driver from delivering Senator McCorkle to the train on time. The senator is bounced like a fly in a churn, picks glass out of his hat from exploding dynamite, and rides with so many arrows in the coach that it looks like "the main target at an archery contest." Humorous view. Historical fiction. Grades 2–5.

Lottridge, C. B. *The Wind Wagon.* Ill. by D. Clifford. New York: Silver Burdett, 1995. In 1860 in northern Kansas territory, Sam Peppard, a blacksmith, invents a wagon powered by wind and starts a journey of humorous events to Denver with three friends. Humorous historical fiction. Grades 2–4.

Quackenbush, R. *Don't You Dare Shoot That Bear!* Simon & Schuster, 1984. This book is a humorous introduction to the personality of Theodore Roosevelt (1858–1919). Fictionalized Biography. Grades 1–4.

Rounds, G. *Sod Houses on the Great Plains.* Ill. by the author. Holiday, 1995. This story provides facts in a humorous way about the sod houses build in areas now Kansas, Nebraska, and the Dakotas and shows frontier family life. Nonfiction. Grades 1–3.

Stanley, D. *Saving Sweetness.* Ill. by G. B. Karas. New York: Putnam, 1996. This is a humorous tale told by a kindly sheriff in his western twang. It is about Sweetness, an independent orphan at nasty Mrs. Sump's house, who runs away, and how the sheriff saves her from the dangers she faces. It is never Sweetness, however, who needs saving—it is the sheriff. Historical fiction. Grades K–3.

1900s: Cowboys, Model T Ford, and Amelia Earhart

Quackenbush, R. *Clear the Cow Pasture, I'm Coming in for a Landing! A Story of Amelia Earhart.* Simon & Schuster, 1990. This book portrays a humorous look at the life of the flyer. Historical fiction. Grades 1–3.

Rounds, G. *Cowboys.* Holiday House, 1991. Some humor is shown about the hard work in a cowboy's life. Nonfiction. Grades 1–3.

Spier, P. *Tin Lizzie.* Doubleday, 1990. This book tells about a Model T Ford through print and humorous pictures. Nonfiction. Grades 1–3.

Activity #204: "Lil' Annie"

To introduce Lil' Annie, the heroine, in this toe-tapping story-song in rhyme, read aloud *She'll Be Comin' Round the Mountain* (Lippincott, 1973, all grades) by Robert Quackenbush. In the story, Handsome Larry Lackawanna, the train's engineer and Lil' Annie's secret love, is taking Colorado Jack's Wild West show to Pugh Town. Three of the oneriest robbers who ever lived—Sneaky Pete, Rattlesnake Hank, and Crummy Joe—lie in wait and hold up the train. All surrender except Lil' Annie, the horsetender, who puts on a riding costume and leaps on horseback from the train. While all are busy, she snares the three robbers with a lasso and becomes Colorado Jack's new star in his Wild West Show. Write the word *heroine* on the board and ask the children what meaning the word has for them. List the actions the children consider heroic as they suggest them. If desired, sing the story together with the music on the filmstrip and cassette version (Weston Woods, Weston, CT). For the children interested in other stories about humor in settings of the Old West, suggest the ones in Figure 11–13.

America's Unique Tall Tales

America's tall tales of the West and other locales are highly exaggerated stories that always are evolving with new heroines, heroes, parodies, and fantastic situations. Invite the children to continue America's tradition of telling tall tales by listening to some tales and then retelling them to others. As an example of an original Paul Bunyan tale, read aloud *The Morning the Sun Refused to Rise* (Holiday, 1984, Grades 2–5) by Glen Rounds. This is a story of Bunyan and Babe, who discover that a blizzard had frozen the earth's axle to its bearings and caused the earth to stop turning. Bunyan and Babe work to set the world to moving again so the sun would rise. Before reading the ending in this tall tale (and others where the hero or heroine solves the problem), ask the children to suggest their own solutions.

Activity #205: "Geography with Tall Tale Heroes"

After you read aloud a tall tale, guide the children to the terms in the story that relate to geography. For example, *Pecos Bill* (Morrow, 1986, Grades 2–5) by Steven Kellogg has several terms that relate to geography: Bill's kin decide that *New England* is becoming entirely too crowded, so they get into covered wagons and go *West*. Ask the children to find the locations they would identify as *New England* and *West* on a map of the United States. With blank maps of America, have the children draw symbols or objects for other place names on the map as they listen again to the tall tale for places to locate—East Texas, Pecos River, and Hell's Gulch. Discuss the adventure where Bill chases Lightning, a wild stallion, to the Artic Circle and the Grand Canyon and back to Pinnacle Peak—and have the children find those places on the maps. Interested children can research the history of any of these locales with books that offer summaries.

Activity #206: "Geography with Tall Tale Heroines"

Sluefoot Sue, a tall tale heroine, and her mother came from the Chickasaw people, a tribe from a Woodland tribe in America's southeast, and Sue's adventures take place in the Washitaw Valley in Oklahoma and then in Texas in *The Legend of Pecos Bill* (Bantam, 1993) by Terry Small. Have the children locate additional geographical locations from the story. With their maps, ask children to mark these places on their maps and encourage children who are interested further in the topic to research the cultures of the Chickasaw people and other Plains tribes in America's southwest. Some children may be interested in the lives of other Native Americans—Eastern Apache, Comanche, Kiowa, Osage, Tonakawa, Waco, and Wichita.

Activity #207: "Maps for Tall Tale Heroes and Heroines"

Engage the children in working with partners and drawing maps of America's regions that are the locale(s) for the tall tale heroes and heroines being studied. For example, America's southwest region (which includes Oklahoma, Texas, and other states that are the setting for the adventures of Pecos Bill and Sluefoot Sue) can be drawn and sites labeled by children who are studying what changed in America's southwest over time by reading tall tales set in the Southwest. Additionally, children can sketch and color original small scenes of the tall tale hero/heroine and his or her adventures on their maps, just as Kellogg did for the endpapers of his book *Pecos Bill*. Repeat the activity with other tall tale heroes/heroines from other regions (see History Master 20). If appropriate, a large blank map of the United States can be used as the background for the children's sketches of heroes/heroines and labels of geographical sites.

Activity #208: "Lightning Larry"

Assign the children the roles of such characters as Crooked Curt, Devilish Dick, Dismal Dan, Evil-Eye McNeevil, and Moldy Mike from the humorous tall tale *The Legend of Lightning Larry* (Scribner's, 1993, Grades 2–5) by Alan Shepherd. Transform the tall tale into a Readers' Theater presentation. To do this, schedule time to practice the reading in sessions. Have the children suggest ways to begin and end the presentation—perhaps by holding up vaudeville-type placards to announce the presentation at the beginning and by serving cold glasses of lemonade for everyone at the end! Cheers for heroes and heroines and boos and catcalls for the bad guys might be suggested. For the children interested in more humor as a point of view, guide them to other children's books that reflect the West in a light-hearted way in Figure 11–13.

Activity #209: "Reversed Roles in Tall Tales"

"Back in the rugged pioneer days when Pecos Bill was a baby, his kinfolk decided that New England was becoming entirely too crowded, so they piled into covered wagons and headed west," writes Steven Kellogg to tell the tall tale of *Pecos Bill* (Morrow, 1986, Grades K–4). As children listen to or read *Pecos Bill* and other tall tales, encourage them to discuss what the actions in the tall tale would be like if the roles were reversed (e.g., the main character was a woman or girl rather than a man or boy, and vice versa). Whether intentionally or accidentally, women and girls have frequently been treated as inferior in children's literature and as unable to show their full range of human interests, traits and capabilities. The possible role of women and girls in tall tales, past and present, should not be overlooked, and, where appropriate, tall tales can show the actions and achievements of women and girls (as well as men and boys) as an important phenomenon in your class's literature that does not reflect or reinforce sexist bias. Several versions of tall tales are available for this exaggerated role reversal activity in the previously mentioned History Master 20.

Activity #210: "Reading Tall Tales"

As an example of the evolution of tall tales, read aloud *The Blizzard of 1896* (Carolrhoda, 1990, Grades 1–3) by E. J. Bird. A very heavy snowstorm with strong winds and cold temperatures arrives, and the people move slowly as they struggle to survive the very hard winter that they first called a *blizzard* in 1880 in America.

Three tales popular with the children relate to hunting and fishing. In the first, *Feliciana Feydra Le Roux: A Cajun Tall Tale* (Little, Brown, 1995, Grades 1–4), written by Tynia Thomassie and illustrated by C. B. Smith, Feliciana is not allowed to go alligator hunting in Cajun Louisiana with her brothers and Grandpa Baby. One night, Feliciana sneaks after them all alone in a pirogue, and her tall tale adventures begin. In the second tale, *The Baron on the Island of Cheese* (Philomel, 1986, Grades 2–3), by Adrian Mitchell, the author introduces a new tall tale character—the Baron—who, without a bullet for his gun, shoots a stag with a cherry pit and the stag sprouts a cherry tree 10 feet tall. In the third, *A Million Fish . . . More or Less* (Knopf, 1992, Pre–2) by Patricia C. McKissack, an African American boy, Hugh, makes up a tall tale of his own. Early one morning, after hearing tall tales told by bayou fishermen about giant turkeys, snakes, mysterious lamps, and strange happenings on the bayou, Hugh tells others he caught a million fish but he had to give some of his catch to an alligator, some to pirate raccoons, and some to trickster cats. He tells his tall tale to his family when he reaches home to explain why he has only three fish left.

Outrageous situations are found in *A Turkey Drive and Other Tales* (Greenwillow, 1992, Grades 1–3) by Barbara Ann Porte and *The Year of No More Corn* (Orchard, 1993, Grades K–3) by Helen Ketterman. In Porte's story, Abigail's good-natured father, a taxi driver, her mother, an artist, and the family dog each tell a tall tale with silly characters in outrageous situations. Ketterman's tale is a Hoosier tale set in 1928. Old Grandpa tells about the natural disasters that wiped out the corn three times—first, rain washed the state of Indiana into Ohio; second, wind blew the seed corn into the ocean; and third, the crop was popped by the heat and was eaten by a plague of crows.

Activity #211: "Recording Tall Tales"

Additional characters related to America's heritage can be selected from *The Diane Goode Book of American Folk Tales and Songs* (Dutton, 1989, Grade 3 up) collected by Ann Dorell and illustrated by Diane Goode. With Goode's book (or other tall tales) as a source, invite children to cut out their own original life-size outlines of tall tale characters. Make the characters puffy by stuffing newspapers between a front and a back body outline. Have children staple the outlines together to hold the paper inside. Display the characters and have the children attach a list of the tall tales they have read, as well as the names of America's regions where each tale takes place.

Activity #212: "Writing Tall Tales"

As an activity for the children after listening to this tall tale and others, tell the children they are going to work with partners and write a contemporary tall tale about a modern-day girl (boy) who does courageous and incredible things. Brainstorm what they think the character looks like, what the personality of the character should be, and other attributes, as well as some possible feats she (he) could perform. Write their ideas in an Idea Graphic on the board similar to Figure 11–14.

After the children have written their rough drafts with partners, ask them to read the tales aloud with a peer editor-partner. After incorporating the editor's suggestions, invite the children to rewrite and then read their tall tales to the rest of the class. The children can incorporate the stories into a class book for the reading area.

Activity #213: "My Family's Tall Tale"

Invite the children to interview family members and ask about some of the favorite stories about relatives. For instance, it might be about the day that Uncle Jerry put swimming goggles on the family dog before going on an outing to a nearby lake. Invite the children to select one of the stories and write it in a tall tale manner to save for a young child in the family to read when he or she gets older. Suggest story-openers such as "One winter, it snowed so hard that . . . ," "One rainy day, it was so wet that . . . ," or "One summer, it was so hot that. . . .

Activity #214: "Wild Bill Hickok"

Mention there are similarities between tall tale heroes and real life heroes, and read an example aloud with *Wild Bill Hickok* (Lothrop, Lee & Shepard, 1992, Grades 1–4) by Maryann Weidt, the story of this American legend known for his long, golden hair and his fancy clothes. In Weidt's version, James Butler Hickok learned to shoot a gun when he was 8 years old and this skill with pearl-handled pistols came in handy in adulthood as he helped keep law and order in the streets and saloons of the Old West. After the children hear or read about a favorite heroine or hero such as Wild Bill Hickok, engage them in listing on the board the attributes (characteristics) about the western frontier they found in the story.

Statue of Liberty: A.D. 1885

Acquaint the children with some of the history of the Statue of Liberty, a gift to America from France, through the text and finely detailed pictures in M. Shapiro's *How They Built the Statue of Liberty* (Random House, 1985, all grades) and from C. Stevens *Lily and Miss Liberty* (Scholastic, 1992, Grades 3–5). In Stevens's fictionalized account, Lily hears that Miss Liberty, designed by Frederic Bartholdi in 1884 as a symbol of friendship between France and America, is the largest statue ever made. It is arriving as a gift from the French people and she wants to make her own contribution to a fund, along with her class, to help build the statue's pedestal. She believes the statue is important because it will welcome new families into America for years to come. Her view is in contrast to the views of others who think that the money should be given to feed the poor. To earn money, Lily makes and sells crowns just like the one Miss Liberty wears. With help from her family and friends, Lilly makes a valuable contribution, an action based on a true incident. The book includes scenes of the statue, a proud woman, whose robe falls to the pedestal. Her right arm holds a torch and her left arms holds a tablet with the date of the Declaration of Independence. A crown with spikes, like sun rays, is on her head. At her feet is a broken chain, which stands for the bonds that chain people who struggle for their liberty. Discuss with the children what the symbolism of the statue means to them—to some it may

---

FIGURE 11–14   Our American Heritage

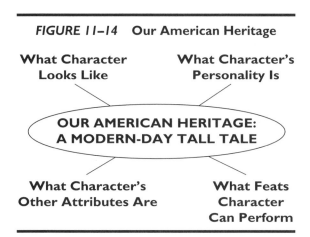

mean freedom for all, to others freedom of thought, and still others, freedom from oppression and a symbol of being part of the human family.

Activity #215: "A Personal Statue of Liberty"

Ask the children to reflect on the symbolism related to the Statue of Liberty and write their comments on the board.

Statue	*Symbol for*
Proud figure	Pride
Right arm holds a torch	Enlightenment
Left arm holds a tablet with the date of the Declaration of Independence	Freedom
Crown with spikes	Sun rays
Broken chain at her feet	Bonds broken that chain people who struggle for freedom
Statue's name	Freedom for all, freedom of thought, and freedom of oppression
Gift from France	Brotherhood, which the citizens of France and America share because of their democratic forms of government

Distribute sheets of art paper to the children and invite them to design their own personal Statue of Liberty.

Prairie Homesteaders: A.D. 1889

One way for the children to find out what family life was like on the prairie is to revisit the time vicariously while listening to *Beautiful Land: A Story of the Oklahoma Land Rush* (Viking, 1994, Grades 3–4) by Nancy Antle. In the story, Annie Mae's family and her uncle's family had waited at the Oklahoma border for the territory to open. The day had finally arrived—April 22, 1889. The family finds a plot of land, but later, Annie Mae's father is threatened by claim jumpers. Annie Mae and her bother go for help and succeed in thwarting the unscrupulous men. Additionally, a true account of the perils of home-

steading can be shared with B. Harvey's *My Prairie Year: Based on the Diary of Elenore Plaisted* (Holiday, 1986, Grades 3–4) illustrated by D. K. Ray. This fictionalized diary portrays the life of 9-year-old Elenore Plaisted, who moves from Lincoln, Maine, to the vast prairies of the Dakota Territory in 1889.

Activity #216: "Prairie Life"

Invite the children to try to write a two-voice verse poem that describes how both Elenore and Annie Mae felt about the perils and pleasures in their prairie lives. Have the voice of Elenore take the voice of pleasures, and Annie Mae, the voice of perils in her life.

Annie Mae's Voice	*Eleanor's Voice*
Threatened by claim jumpers . . .	

Battle of Wounded Knee: A.D. 1890

Black Elk tells his story in 1930 and begins with his birth in 1863 through the battle of Wounded Knee in 1890 in his autobiography *Black Elk: A Man with a Vision* (Children's, 1990, Grades 2–4) coauthored by C. Greene. Black Elk sees the decline of the Ogala Sioux Tribe in 1929 and the text ends with his death in 1950. Mention to the children that in the late nineteenth century, a Ghost Dance Revival was sweeping through several Indian tribes with the hopes of resisting the advance of other people into their lands. Practiced also by the Teton people, the people believe the dance will bring back the Native People who knew what the world was like before the Whites came. They think the ceremonies will restore their land and resources. Ghost-dance poems—really songs—report the visions of the Native People, including a vision that the white people would be driven from the land, are recorded in *Starting with Poetry* (Harcourt Brace Jovanovich, 1973, all ages) by A. C. Colley and J. K. Moore. Mentioned also are the eagle and the crow—both regarded as sacred birds. Have the children reflect on the Native American words that emphasize the return of their ancestors and the buffalo and focus on the Native Americans' dream of recovering their lost way of life: The whole world is coming./ A nation is coming, a nation is coming./ The Eagle has brought the message to the tribe./ The father says so, the father says so./ Over the whole earth, they are coming./ The buffalo are coming, the buffalo are coming./ The Crow has brought the message to the tribe./ The father says so, the father says so (p. 179).

Activity #217: "A Dream"

Invite the children to say the words "The Whole World Is Coming" in a choral reading to develop a perspective of the words and phrases sung by Native Americans as they dreamed of the return of a former way of life. Ask the children to divide into two groups to read alternate lines:

> Group 1: The whole world is coming.
>
> Group 2: A nation is coming, a nation is coming.
>
> Group 1: The Eagle has brought the message to the tribe.
>
> Group 2: The father says so, the father says so.
>
> Group 1: Over the whole earth, they are coming.
>
> Group 2: The buffalo are coming, the buffalo are coming.
>
> Group 1: The Crow has brought the message to the tribe.
>
> Group 2: The father says so, the father says so.

Repeat the choral reading with three different groups, with Group 1 reading the first line, Group 2 the second line. The entire group reads the refrain, "The father says so, the father says so."

William McKinley: A.D. 1897–1901

Give the children a point of view about what was going on during this period through the eyes of President McKinley (1843–1901), twenty-fifth President of the United States, as told by E. P. Hoyt in the biography *William McKinley* (Reilly, 1967, Grades 2–5). The book details McKinley's life, including his years as president from 1897–1901. Several important events happen in his administration:

- The people of the Hawaiian Islands were annexed to the United States.
- Blaming Spain for the destruction of the battleship, *Maine*, President McKinley sent a war message to the Spaniards in Cuba and ordered the troops to leave Cuba and to declare the Cubans free.
- America supported a civil government in the Philippines.
- Free trade was begun with Puerto Rico.
- An Open Door policy was initiated toward China.

Activity #218: "Seeing Both Sides"

Invite the children to dictate or write down several points about *both* sides of the events that happened in McKinley's administration. Encourage them to suggest sentences to support both sides of each event to try to "see" both sides of the event equally well. After the children suggest their sentence, have them revisit each event and determine which side they would have supported had they been living in McKinley's time period. Here is an example:

Both Sides of the Event

Event #1

- The people of the Hawaiian Islands were annexed to the United States.
- Not all the people of the Hawaiian Islands wanted to be annexed to the United States.

Princess Ka'iulai: A.D. 1897

Before you read aloud F. Stanley's biography *The Last Princess: The Story of Princess Ka'iulani of Hawai'i* (Four Winds, 1991, Grades 3–6) illustrated by D. Stanley, ask the children to listen for words that tell them something about the government of Hawaii and the government of the United States. Mention to the children that sometimes a person can tell a lot about a country by studying its government, or in the case of Hawaii, its royal family. In Stanley's biography, the Princess trains for her duties and responsibilities as a member of Hawaii's royal family until her mother's death in 1887. When the princess is sent to England to be educated, she discovers that her family's right to rule is threatened. Her aunt is forced to give up the throne in 1897, and the island kingdom is annexed to the United States. That year, the Princess returns to Hawaii, but dies in 1899 at the early age of 23. Notes on the Hawaiian language and bibliography for further reading are included. Ask the children to recall any parts of the story that told them something about the government of Hawaii and the government of the United States.

Activity #219: "Hawaii's Last Ruler"

As suggested in the previous activity, invite the children to dictate or write down several points about *both* sides of the event where the Hawaiian ruler was forced to give up the throne in 1897 and the island kingdom was annexed to the United States. Encourage the children to dictate or write sentences to support both sides of each event to try to "see" both sides of the event equally well.

The Chicago Fire: A.D. 1871

One story that can stimulate the children to feel and to think about past times is *The Story of the Chicago Fire* (Children's, 1982, Grades 3–6) by C. R. Stein. *The Story of the Chicago Fire* is a vivid portrayal of the heroes of the Great Fire of 1871, the looters, and the way spreading flames destroy miles of the city of Chicago. Additionally, Stein points out how the fire started—after a hot dry summer, the fire broke out on October 8, 1871, in Mrs. O'Leary's barn on DeKoven Street. Have the children relate the heroism—or looting—that took place during the Chicago Fire to a contemporary newspaper article about heroism or looting. Distribute newspapers to the children so they can search for articles. Read the articles aloud and display them in the room.

Activity #220: "Similar Stories"

Ask the children to relate the heroes of the Chicago Fire to the bravery of another individual—12-year-old Milton—told in *The Snow Walker* (Carolrhoda, 1986, Grades 1–3) written by M. K. and C. M. Wetterer and illustrated by M. O. Young. During the blizzard of 1888, Milton travels on his homemade snowshoes that he and his father make together. In spite of winds that blow at up to 80 miles an hour, determined Milton helps his neighbors and snow-walks errands for them in his Bronx neighborhood. Have the children relate the heroes of the Chicago Fire or Milton's heroic endurance to an event that has happened in their town or state. Distribute copies of a local newspaper and have the children work in groups to locate articles about recent events or heroes and heroines. Guide each group to finding information about any disastrous events or stories of bravery in the papers. Have the groups take notes. In the classroom, tell each group to make a chart of the collected facts, and then illustrate the chart. Ask each group to display its chart as a volunteer reads it to the whole group.

Casey at the Bat: A.D. 1888

"The outlook wasn't brilliant for the Mudville nine that day,/ The score stood four to two with but one inning more to play/" writes Ernest Lawrence Thayer in *Casey at the Bat: A Ballad of the Republic, Sung in the Year 1888* and Gerald Fitzgerald 's version (Atheneum, 1995, Grades K–3) brings the excitement of Casey's final "swing and miss" into the classroom. Share *Casey at the Bat* with children as an example of a humorous poem. The story of "Mighty Casey" who struck out in an important game can be just the way to introduce children to the popularity of baseball in America in the 1800s.

Activity #221: "Sound Poem"

Before reading the poem aloud to the children, point out that the poem-song was written in the post–Civil War Days and find out what knowledge the students have about this period and the people's lives at the time. Create a fact-web with the words *Post–Civil War Days* in the center. Ask the children what they know about the period, and write their ideas on the board. As the fact-web is created, group the ideas in categories to organize the students' thoughts. Provide additional background information about the way that people's interest in baseball helped pull the country together again after the Civil War—soldiers in blue and gray uniforms even played the game in prison camps during the war. The information on the fact-web will give students a better understanding of the context of the times in which the poem was written. Introduce the sequence of events in the poem and ask the children to suggest sounds they can make to accompany some of the events. Write the suggestions on the board after key words to identify the event.

Event	*Suggested Sound*
1. Lusty yell	
2. Casey responding to the cheers	
3. A sneer curled Casey's lip	
4. Other	

Decide together which sounds should be made when the poem is reread. Divide the children into small groups and ask each group to become responsible for one or more of the sounds and to make the sound(s) at the proper place in the poem when it is reread.

America, the Beautiful: A.D. 1895

To tell others what she saw when she viewed the Rockies, Katherine Bates wrote these familiar words: "O Beautiful for spacious skies./ For amber waves of grain./ . . . And crown thy good with brotherhood/ From sea to shining sea!," Provide an artist's interpretation of Bates's words by showing and discussing the illustrations in *America the Beautiful* (Atheneum, 1993, Grade 1 up) by Neil Waldman. Show Waldman's acrylic paintings of sites that represent "purple mountain majesty" and "fruited plain" and other phrases. There is an explanation of the sites at the back of the book to elaborate on the print and pictures.

Give the children some background information about Katharine Lee Bates, the 33-year-old Wellesley professor who traveled by mule train to Colorado's Pike's Peak about 100 years ago and was inspired to write a poem about the beauty of America. In 1913, Bates's poem was set to the tune "Materna" by Samuel Augustus Ward and became the song, "America, the Beautiful." Reading the lyrics aloud together, help the children get a feeling for the way Katherine Bates felt about the beauty of the United States and the way she later altered her poem to make it more direct:

What Bates Wrote First	What Bates Altered
1. O beautiful for halcyon skies	O beautiful for spacious skies
2. Above the enameled plain	Above the fruited plain
3. Till souls wax fair as earth and air and music hearted sea	And crown thy good with brotherhood from sea to shining sea

Ask the children to add a third column to the two columns above and to suggest ways *they* would alter these same lines today to make the words still more direct. Ask them to illustrate their suggestions with artwork and display their work in the classroom.

Activity #222: "My View of America"

With copies of Bates's first verse, sing the words together as a group and ask the children, "If Katherine Bates had been in our town and if you had been with Katherine Bates when she wrote those words, what beauty do you see in our area that she could have written about?" Tell the children to meet with a partner and write a list or draw sketches of some of the beautiful things that they have seen in their area, town, or city. After the children have finished their lists or drawn their sketches, ask them to return to a whole group setting and, working together, turn their ideas into a free-verse poem about America.

Activity #223: "Choral Reading"

Let the children sing the song "America, the Beautiful" along with a recording, and then distribute copies of Bates's *original* words to perform as a choral reading. Ask the children to divide into four groups with group 1 reading the first line, group 2 reading the second line, group 3 the third, and group 4 the fourth. The entire group can read the finale of the words. Here is an example:

Group 1: O Beautiful for *halcyon* skies
Group 2: For amber waves of grain
Group 3: For purple mountain majesties
Group 4: Above the *enameled* plain
All: America, America
God shed his grace on thee;
Till souls wax fair as earth and air and music hearted sea.

Invite the children to substitute other words for the italicized ones, and repeat the choral reading activity.

Artists Who Painted the 1880s

Collect examples of art that represent this historical period. For example, artworks—artifacts, sculpture, paintings—related to the latter part of the 1800s can be shown on an opaque projector with *ABC The Wild West Buffalo Bill Historical Center, Cody, Wyoming* (Abrams, 1990, all grades) by Florence Cassen Mayers. The paintings range from "The Buffalo Hunt" by Frederic Remington to "Madonna of the Prairie" by W. H. D. Koerner and are from the Buffalo Bill Center. To provide other choices, consider additional paintings such as *The Torn Hat* by Thomas Sully, *The Poor Man's Store* by John Frederick Peto, *Two Children* by Jefferson Gauntt, and *Umbrellas* by Maurice Prendergast shown in *ABC, Museum of Fine Arts, Boston* (Abrams, 1986, Grade 3 up) by Florence Cassen Mayers.

Activity #224: "Predictions from Paintings"

With a selected painting, ask the children to look at the clothing and possessions of the people in the picture. After observing articles of clothing, hairstyles, and other objects in the artworks, ask the children to predict (guess, determine) what workers and jobs were available at the time (e.g., the people who made clothing and the possessions) and list the workers and jobs on the board. For students pursuing the topic of artists and their art through historical time periods, guide them to some of the books on the previously mentioned History Master 8.

Photographs: 1800s

As a read-aloud book to foster younger children's interest in historical photographs, select Barbara Morrow's *Edward's Portrait* (Macmillan, 1991, Grades K–3), a story of Edward's family having their daguerreotype taken by Mr. Fitzpatrick, a photographer in a traveling wagon. Since having a picture taken during this time period, the mid-1800s, was a special occasion, Edward's father explains to him what the process does; however, Edward objects to placing his head in the headrest to keep him still for the many minutes it takes to make the picture. Finally, Edward stays still because of his interest in some of the stories told by Mr. Fitzpatrick about his travels. Invite the children to tell what stories would make them want to stay as still as Edward did while having their pictures taken (Moore, 1992b).

Activity #225: "Keeping Edward Still"

Invite some of the children to take the role of Mr. Fitzpatrick, the photographer who travels in a wagon, and think of a story to tell Edward and keep him still while he has his picture taken in the 1800s. Have them team up with partners and tell their stories to one another, and then to trade partners with someone and tell their stories again. Let them transform their stories from oral ones to written ones and illustrate them. Ask for volunteers to show their stories and drawings to the whole group and discuss what they did. Collect the writings and drawings to place in an original book in the class and invite some volunteers to design a book cover and suggest a title.

Activity #226: "Information"

Show a 1800s photograph of children (transferred to an overhead transparency) and ask them to look at the clothing and hairstyles of the children in the photograph. After observing articles of clothing, hairstyles, and other objects in the photograph, ask them to predict (guess, determine) what services, workers, and jobs were available at the time (e.g., the people who made clothing, ribbons, lace, shoemakers, leather factories, etc.) and list the services on the board. Review the list and ask the children to suggest pantomime actions related to the workers and to perform them for each of the words.

Activity #227: "Predictions from Photographs"

Show photographs of the time period to the children and ask them to predict reasons why they think each photograph was taken. To further extend some interaction with the photograph(s), ask the children to take roles pretending they are a "direct descendant" of the person in the photograph and let them write an original background for the person in the picture that connects the person with the student's family. While writing an imaginary background for the person, suggest that the children include a name, age, birthdate and place, family members, hobbies, work skills, interests, and perhaps family chores the person might have done.

Additionally, develop further appreciation for a family history, ancestors, and one's heritage and roots by taking children's photos with an instant camera. If an instant camera is available, invite the children to have their own pictures taken by a class "photographer" and show themselves as the "direct descendents" by displaying their own photographs with the "ancestor's" photograph, along with their written backgrounds.

For those interested further in the topic of photography, guide them to some of the books that can take them forward in history listed on Figure 11–15.

Homeless: Late 1800s

The feelings of homeless children in the 1800s are told in Eve Bunting's *Train to Somewhere* (Clarion, 1996, Grades 1–5), a story illustrated by Ronald Himler. Marianne and 14 other orphans in New York board a train that travels west. Each child hopes to find a family to love. Marianne, for instance, wants to find her mother who had promised to return for her. The text is based on the orphan trains between the 1850s and the 1920s that took over 100,000 children to families in America's midwest.

Activity #228: "Homeless Children"

Ask the children, "Would the solution used to find homes for homeless children in this time period work today? Why or why not?" After discussion, elicit the children's suggestions for assisting homeless children in their community. For example, some homeless and unnoticed children might go without books and reading and developing their literacy skills, and they can be helped. The group

FIGURE 11–15   Children's Books about Photographers

FIGURE 11–15   **Children's Books about Photographers**

PERSPECTIVES

1865

Hoobler, D. & Hoobler, T. *Photographing History: The Career of Matthew Brady*. Putnam's, 1977. This book portrays the life of the photographer who recorded scenes from America's Battle Between the States with his camera and film. Biography. Grade 3 up.

1902

Cech, J. *Jacques-Henri Lartigue: Boy With a Camera*. Ill. with photographs. Simon & Schuster, 1995. In 1902, Jacques-Henri was given a camera for his seventh birthday and he developed the skill of capturing the "right moment" on film to show his toys and family. Grades 1–4.

1912

Turk, M. *Gordon Parks*. Crowell, 1971. This text details Parks's boyhood of fishing and hunting, the death of his mother, and his life as an orphan. Parks's initial fame as a photographer (1912–   ) comes from his camera scenes in Harlem and his sensitiveness. Biography. Grades 2–3.

---

might want to take part in a book-making project to ensure that homeless children have access to books. Ask volunteers to write or telephone for information from people who are involved in homeless projects sponsored by the county office of education and the state department of education in the area.

Newcomers: Late 1800s

As a newcomer, 7-year-old Tilli travels from Europe to Missouri to rejoin her parents on a farm in *Tilli's New World* (Lodestar/Dutton, 1981, Grades 3–4) by L. Lehmann. In the story, Tilli dreams of an education and the family overcomes a great deal of sorrow with the loss of two infant sons and the near loss of a third child who almost drowns. As the children hear *Tilli's New World* and read other stories about newcomers, have them:

- Think about parts to read to their peers that would help them better understand the life of an immigrant, the idea of immigrants as a group, and the concept of immigration.
- Write down the sections and page numbers of the parts that they wanted to read aloud to others.

- Respond to "who, what, when, where and why" type questions and describe the living conditions of the immigrants, their problems and resolutions.
- Record any interesting facts and questions the children have after they read their sources.
- Engage in a role-play situation: Imagine that you have heard a lot of comments about solutions to the "problem" of some newcomers not speaking English. One such solution might involve starting special classes at school for those wishing to learn English. Role-play with your partner one or more of several people discussing a solution, and include the roles of one of the following: a dynamic English-speaking minority leader, the principal of the school, the parents of a non-English-speaking child, and a teacher. Remind the children that those in the audience have a responsibility to take notes so they can tell the whole group what feelings were shown in the role-play and what they learned from the situation after the role-play. Ask for the children's comments and write them on the board:

Feelings Shown	*What We Learned*
1.	1.

Activity #229: "Meeting Newcomers"

Related to the topic of newcomers, introduce drama situations for the children to play out with partners:

1. You are becoming friendly with an Asian (Latino/Hispanic, Native American, African American, European American) child (female or male). You are beginning to stay together, talk together, and do things after school. Your other friends begin to make fun of you and stay away from you. What do you decide to do in this situation?

2. You are interested in welcoming a new student who has come from Cambodia and does not speak much English. She is the only Cambodian child in your class and only one of few in the entire school. What do you decide to do in this situation?

After all of the drama situations by the partners, discuss with the whole group, the following:

- "How well did each partner-actor stay in her or his role?"
- "How did members of the partnerships feel about the issues related to newcomers?"
- "What feelings were shown by the players?"
- "What did you learn from the role-play situation?"

Activity #230: "Newcomers' Courage"

As a whole group, point out to the children that early immigrants—the Pilgrims and others—as well as later newcomers have often suffered and prevailed only through great courage. To demonstrate this, read aloud excerpts from *It's Only Goodbye* (Puffin, 1992, Grades 2–6) by V. T. Gross, a story of a young boy's courage. A young boy, Umberto, and his father, Pietro, traveled by boat from France to New York City in 1892. On ship, Piero was arrested for assaulting a passenger who insulted him and was thrown into the ship's brig. This meant that Umberto had to work off payment for their trip by working for the ship's captain. Ask the students to relate the story to their own experiences and tell of a time when they had to "work off" a payment of some kind and the feelings they had about the "fairness" and "justice" of the situation.

Activity #231: "Was Your Family a Newcomer Family?"

Invite the children to consider one or more of the following activities related to the topic of *newcomers:*

1. If you are part of a newcomer family, interview your parents/grandparents/others to find out some of the stories about your family roots when your family was a newcomer family in the United States. Write the story for others to read.

2. If you are new to America, write a brief story about an experience you have had.

3. If you are part of an Original Native American family, write a brief story about something from your family's experience.

4. Interview relatives, read old diaries and letters, and look at family photo albums to get information about your family's roots. Make a booklet about your family and write brief stories about two or more of your ancestors.

5. Write a brief story about the most famous member of your family.

6. Write a brief story about an interesting ancestor in your family that you would like to emulate (be like).

Activity #232: "Discrimination of Newcomers"

With selected books, engage children in reading stories about some of the various families of ethnic and cultural groups that have come to the United States and the discrimination that members of each family have faced. Talk about terms or names that are used to respect members of ethnic groups. Refer to the harmful effects on newcomers of denigration and discuss the resiliency needed by newcomers. A resource for this topic is *Developing Resiliency through Children' s Literature: A Guide for Teachers and Librarians, K–8* (MacFarland, 1992) by Nancy Lee Cecil and Patricia L. Roberts. If needed, the children can create a chart or diagram on the writing board about ways to show respect to others. Use it as the center for a discussion about the positive effects of respect as well as the harmful effects of discrimination.

Ways to Show Respect to Others
1.
2.

Invite the children to talk about the implications of name calling and why the use of certain terms is denigrating and discuss the various feelings that name calling evokes—especially in newcomers.

Activity #233: "Newcomers' Feelings"

Before role-playing some of the vignettes about newcomers from selected children's books, discuss the idea that children in all time periods of history who were newcomers have had difficulties in feeling "different," in being excluded, in being laughed at for having a language "accent," and in facing name calling, negative labeling, and other prejudicial acts. Newcomers today also face these difficulties: (1) family stress related to such things as fears of drug addiction, deportation, family separation, gang activity, unemployment, and unwanted pregnancies; (2) fear, tension, and hostilities between ethnic and racial groups; and (3) stresses from being caught between two cultures and two worlds. As examples of children who are caught between two cultures, English Second Language children may be Limited English Proficient and have Native languages of Spanish, Vietnamese, Cantonese, Mandarin and other Chinese, Cambodian, Filipino/Tagalog, Hmong, Korean, Lao, and Japanese. If desired, select a story about newcomers, read it aloud, and invite children to work in partnerships to role-play some of the incidents. The partners can take turns expressing the feelings of being the *newcomer* and the *native-born child*.

School: Late 1800s

Have the children suggest details of the lives of some children in a photograph of children in an early schoolhouse. Have each child select a name and assume the role of that child for a school day in the late 1800s. Elicit the children's decisions about what food they will bring for lunch (wrapped in cloth or rags). Show slides, book illustrations, or transparencies made from old photographs and have children select hairstyles and clothing to wear.

For the school day in 1888, have the children play appropriate games, engage in activities, and perform routines, including a lesson from the *McGuffey Readers* (American Book Company). Read from textbooks about the times and give lessons about geography and mathematics. In their characters' roles as children of the 1800s, they can complete academic exercises (McGuffey suggests *both* the word method and the phonic method) and seatwork, write on slates, do choral reading, and then participate in calisthenics and games on the playground. In the afternoon of the school day, give the children directions for making ink and pens, and ask them to write poems and essays to extend the role-playing as students in a school of the 1800s in the classroom.

Activity #234: "McGuffey's *First Eclectic Reader*"

Invite the children to react to the remarks in the text of the last lesson in McGuffey's *First Eclectic Reader*, which asks children if they have taken good care of their books and kept the books neat and clean. What are the messages that the following words from the *First Eclectic Reader* send to the children?

> *Are you not glad to be ready for a new book?*
>
> *Your parents are very kind to send you to school. If you are good and if you try to learn, your teacher will love you, and you will please your parents.*
>
> *Be kind to all, and do not waste your time in school.*
>
> *When you go home, you may ask your parents to get you a Second Reader. (pp. 93–94)*

CHAPTER TWELVE

A.D. 1900–Present

What was going on in the twentieth century?

Multicultural Perspectives

Learning about this time period means the children can have an out-of-the-decade experience through the stories they read. They may be interested in the history of the conflict of different cultures such as that faced by Native Americans and others in various ethnic and cultural groups. When interested in any of the heritage perspectives in Figure 12–1, guide the children to several examples of children's literature about the people and the way their lives are reflected for this time period.

1900–1909

Earthquake: A.D. 1906

To portray the concerns of a child during the frightening earthquake in San Francisco in 1906, read aloud *Francis, the Earthquake Dog* (Chronicle, 1996, Grades K–2) a story based on fact written by J. R. Enderle and S. G. Tessler and illustrated by B. Scudder. A young boy, Edward, saves a stray terrier from being hit by a vegetable cart and takes him to his father, a chef at the St. Francis Hotel. At the time, Edward's father is busy preparing food for a party for Enrico Caruso, and the terrier eventually goes unnoticed. The terrier wanders away, rides down an elevator with Caruso, and can't be found. The earthquake starts that night and Edward worries about the lost dog, even while he and his father seek shelter in the tent city at Golden Gate Park. When the two return to the hotel, they hear barking from under the ruins and discover the lost terrier.

Activity #235: "Effects on People"

Elicit the children's comments about the effect of an earthquake on people, animal companions, and buildings. Write their comments on the board. Reread aloud excerpts from the story that relate to the children's comments. Invite the children to sketch their ideas of the story's descriptions of what was going on during this natural disaster. Discuss with them the idea of whether the solution of a tent city in Golden Gate Park used for the earthquake homeless in 1906 would work today, and what assistance, if any, is provided for animal companions today.

Help the children get involved in a project to ensure that they know what to do during an earthquake and how to be prepared to survive independently for several days without government help after a major quake. What food, clothing, and first-aid materials could be made available for their families? Preparations for animal companions? Engage the children in writing or telephoning for information and talking to people about earthquake preparedness programs that are sponsored by city, county, and state agencies in the area.

Teddy Roosevelt: A.D. 1858–1919

Acquaint the children with Teddy Roosevelt's busy life in the White House (1901–1909) by reading aloud F. Monjo's *The One Bad Thing about Father* (Harper, 1970, Grades 2–3), a story illustrated by R. Negri. Roosevelt is a man of energy—he hates inactivity and practices the strenuous life. In the White House, his second wife, Edith Carow, takes care of five children and carries on a busy life of her own. She makes the White House a home for the

FIGURE 12–1   Children's Books about the 1900s

PERSPECTIVES

African Heritage

Bertol, R. *Charles Drew*. Crowell, 1970. This is the life story of a distinguished African American doctor who became the first director of the Red Cross Blood Bank. Biography. Grades 3–4.

Blue, R., & C. Naden. *Colin Powell: Straight to the Top*. Millbrook, 1991. This life story describes Colin Powell as a warm and dedicated person who prepared for his military career. The text focuses on his leadership abilities. Maps, photographs, and index included. Biography. Grades 2–4.

Cavan, S. *Thurgood Marshall and Equal Rights*. Millbrook, 1992. Marshall, the first black justice on the U.S. Supreme Court, is the NAACP lawyer who successfully argues *Brown* v. *Board of Education*. Nonfiction. Grades 2–4.

Cavan, S. *W. E. B. Du Bois and Racial Relations*. Millbrook, 1992. Du Bois, one of the founders of the NAACP, dedicates his life to improving race relations in the United States and writes influential reports, articles, and books. Nonfiction. Grades 2–4.

Coles, R. *The Story of Ruby Bridges*. Ill. by G. Ford. Scholastic, 1995. Ruby, a courageous 6-year-old, enters a whites-only school in New Orleans in 1960. Biography. Grades K–4.

Cwiklik, R. *A. Phillip Randolph and the Labor Movement*. Millbrook, 1992. Randolph crusades for the rights of sleeping car porters, blacks in the armed forces, and blacks in labor unions. Nonfiction. Grades 2–4.

Gutman, B. *Hank Aaron*. Grosset, 1973. This is the life story of a superstar in baseball. Biography. Grade 3 up.

Howard, E. F. *Chita's Christmas Tree*. Bradbury, 1989. In the early twentieth century, the daughter of one of Baltimore's first African American doctors tells the story of their Christmas. Historical fiction. Grades 2–3.

Lawrence, J. *The Great Migration: An American Story*. HarperCollins, 1993. Lawrence offers a pictorial essay—a sequence of paintings with captions—to show the 1916–1919 migration of African Americans from the South. A poem by Walter Dean Myers concludes the presentation. Nonfiction. Grade 3 up.

Pinkney, A. D. *Alvin Ailey*. Ill. by B. Pinkney. Hyperion, 1993. This life story portrays Ailey's childhood in Texas, his life in Los Angeles where he begins to dance, and his success in New York when he forms his own dance troupe. Biography. Grades 1–3.

Ritter, L. S. *Leagues Apart: The Men and Times of the Negro Baseball Leagues*. Ill. by R. Merkin. Morrow, 1995. This books is an overview of the brief history of the Negro League and introduces some of their star performers. Nonfiction. Grades 2–4.

Rosen, M. J. *A School for Pompey Walker*. Ill. by A. B. L. Robinson. Harcourt, 1995. This book was inspired by a true story of a free slave in Ohio who sold himself into the bitter life of slavery over 30 times to raise money for a school for children. Historical fiction. Grades 2–5.

Rudeen, K. *Wilt Chamberlain*. Ill. by F. Mullins. Crowell, 1970. This life story describes events in the development of one of America's basketball superstars. Biography. Grades 2–4.

Smith, K. B. *Martin Luther King, Jr*. Messner, 1987. This life story uses authentic illustrations from the Smithsonian Institution and the National Portrait Gallery. Biography. Grade 3 up.

continued

FIGURE 12–1 **Continued**

African Heritage

Walker, A. *Langston Hughes, American Poet*. Ill. by D. Miller. Crowell, 1974. This life story portrays Hughes as an important writer (1902–1967) who publishes his first poem, "The Negro Speaks of Rivers," at age 19. Born in 1902, Hughes writes during the Harlem Renaissance of the 20s and 30s and publishes poems, short stories, and anthologies. He produces plays and operas and continues to write until his death in 1967. Biography. Grades 2–4.

Young, M. B. *The Picture Life of Ralph J. Bunche*. Watts, 1968. This life story conveys the dignity of Bunche and his contributions as a great American. Biography. Grades 1–3.

Asian Heritage

Brown, T. *Konnichiwa! I Am a Japanese American Girl*. Photographs by Kazuyoshi Arai. Holt, 1995. This book is a description of a young girl's life in San Francisco with her extended family. Her activities include attending public school where she learns Japanese and participating in Japanese American cultural activities such as the Cherry Blossom Festival. Glossary of Japanese words and reading list included. Nonfiction. Grades 3–5.

Cha, D. *Dia's Story Cloth: The Hmong People's Journey of Freedom*. Ill by C. Cha and N. T. Cha. Lee & Low, 1996. A Hmong story cloth is folk art that was created in refugee camps and the author's story cloth was designed by her aunt and uncle. It tells of how Laos was divided by war in the 1960s and her father, a farmer, joined the Loyalists while the rest of her family fled from the fighting. After living in a refugee camp in Thailand, the family emigrated to America. Autobiography. Grades 3–6.

Garland, S. *The Lotus Seed*. Ill. by T. Kiuchi. Harcourt Brace Jovanovich, 1993. In Vietnam, a young girl takes a seed from a lotus in the emperor's garden as a momento to remember the dethroned emperor. Through her life, the seed sustains the girl as she marries, escapes from the bombs of war, and arrives in America. When her grandson plants the seed, it grows and blooms producing a pod full of new seeds to give to her family members so they might remember her. Historical fiction. Grades 1–3.

Graff, N. *Where the River Runs: A Portrait of a Refugee Family*. Ill. by R. Howard. Little, Brown, 1993. This story depicts the struggles of the Prek family who escape the civil war in Cambodia and journey to the United States. Sohka Prek, her mother, and three young sons learn to adjust to a new language and culture while trying to keep their own heritage. Historical fiction. Grade 3 up.

McMahon, P. *Chi-Hoon: A Korean Girl*. Ill. by M. O'Brien. Caroline House/Boyds Mills, 1993. With diary entries, the story accounts for a week in the life of 8-year-old Chi-Hoon, who lives in a changing world of old-versus-new culture in Seoul. Each week's award to a meritorious student inspires Chi-Hoon to have outstanding behavior at school. Contemporary realism. Grades 3–4.

Rattigan, J. K. *Dumpling Soup*. Ill. by L. Hsu-Flanders. Little, Brown, 1993. Seven-year-old Marisa explains how her aunts and uncles and cousins from all over Oahu gather to celebrate New Year's Eve. Her grandma calls the family "chop suey," which means all mixed up in "pidgin," because most of them are Korean but some are Japanese, Chinese, Hawaiian, and *haole* (Hawaiian for white people). At this year's party, Marisa gets to help make the dumplings for the soup, a two-day project. Contemporary realism. Grades 1–3.

Schmidt, J., & T. Wood. *Two Lands, One Heart: An American Boy's Journey to His Mother's Vietnam*. Ill. by T. Wood. Walker, 1995. Heather, an escapee from earlier war-torn Vietnam, takes her oldest son, 7-year-old TJ, home to meet his relatives. Contemporary realism. Grades 3–5.

Tran-Khanh-Tuyet. *The Little Weaver of Thai-Yen Village*. San Francisco: Children's, 1987. This is the story of a war orphan from Vietnam who arrives in America. The story has words in both English and Vietnamese. Contemporary realism. Grade 3 up.

FIGURE 12–1 **Continued**

European Heritage

Baker, S. A. *Grandpa Is a Flyer*. Ill. by B. Farnsworth. Albert Whitman, 1995. A grandfather share his passion for flying with his granddaughter and tells her how, as a 9-year-old boy, he saved his money to pay for his first flight in an open-cockpit biplane with a visiting barnstormer. Historical fiction. Grades 1–3.

Beirne, B. *Siobhand's Journey: A Belfast Girl Visits the United States*. Ill. First Avenue Ed., 1992. This book is a photo essay of a 10-year-old girl, Siobhan McNulty, who spends a summer with an American family sponsored by Project Children, which helps children in Northern Ireland involved in religious/political conflict. Contemporary realism. Grades K–4.

Dooherty, B. *Snowy*. Ill. by K. Bowen. Dial, 1992. Rachel lives in a canal community where the family's horse Snowy pulls the *Barge BeetleJuice* up and down the bank of the canal. Historical fiction. Grades 1–2.

Graham, S. *Dear Old Donegal*. Ill by J. O'Brien. Clarion, 1996. This is a picture book version of a song written by Graham in the 1840s about young Patrick McGuigan's successful return to Ireland. His mother reintroduces him to many friends and relatives with a rhyming collection of Irish names. Piano notes and songs history included. Historical fiction. Grades K–4.

Harvey, B. *Immigrant Girl: Becky of Eldridge Street*. Holiday House, 1987. This is the story of Russian immigrants who live in New York City in 1910. It is based on the diary of a young girl. Historical fiction. Grade 3 up.

Joosse, B. M. *The Morning Chair*. Ill. by M. Sewall. Clarion, 1995. Bram and his parents leave Holland for New York City and Bram is comforted by family rituals, especially the one of sitting in the morning chair in which he and his mother drink tea with milk. Historical fiction. Grades K–3.

Schertle, A. *Maisie*. Ill. by L. Dabovich. Lothrop, Lee & Shepard, 1995. Born on a farm at the beginning of the 1900s, Maisie reveals highlights of her life up to her 90th birthday. Historical fiction. Grades K–3.

Schwartz, D. M. *Supergrandpa*. Ill. by B. Dodson. Lothrop, Lee & Shepard, 1991. In 1951, 63-year-old Gustav Hakansson decides to enter the Tour of Sweden, a 1,000-mile bicycle race, but the judges will not let him enter the race because of his age. But Gustav enters the race and shows his courage and determination. Based on a true story. Historical fiction. Grades 2–3.

Wyman, Andrea. *Red Sky at Morning*. New York: Holiday House, 1991. In 1909, Callie Common, 12 years old, experiences many hardships endured by her family on their farm in Indiana. After her mother dies, her father goes to Oregon and her sister leaves the farm to take a job. Callie and her grandfather are the only ones left to work the farm and find themselves caught in a diphtheria epidemic. Historical fiction. Grade 3 up.

Middle Eastern/Mediterranean Heritage

Heide, F. P., & J. H. Gilliland. *Sami and the Time of the Troubles*. Ill. by T. Lewin. Clarion, 1992. In Beirut, 10-year-old Sami stays with his family in a basement because of the danger and noises of bombings and gunfire. Only where there is a stop in the fighting during the day does Sami go out to play, and then, Sami is back in the dark, listening as the "noises of the night" begin. Historical fiction. Grade 3 up.

Hennessy, B. G. *Olympics!* Ill. by M. Chesworth. Viking, 1996. Useful as a comparison with the early Olympics, this is an overview of what it takes to prepare and participate in the Olympics today. Nonfiction. Grades 1–3.

continued

FIGURE 12–1 **Continued**

Middle Eastern/Mediterranean Heritage

Matthews, M. *Magid Fasts for Ramadan*. Ill. by E. B. Lewis. Clarion, 1996. Eight-year-old Magid wants to fast for his Egyptian Muslim family's celebration of Ramadan, an Islamic practice usually reserved for children age 12 and older. Contemporary Realism. Grades 2–4.

Segal, Sheila F. *Joshua's Dream: A Journey to the Land of Israel*. Ill. by J. Iskowitz. Roberts Rhinehart, 1994. After listening to stories of his great-aunt Rivka, a pioneer who goes to Palestine in 1906 to help make the desert "bloom," Joshua wants to help build the land, too. He goes with his family to Israel and plants a tree in the Negev Desert. Historical fiction. Grades 1–4.

Native American Heritage

Ancona, G. *Powwow*. Photos by the author. Harcourt Brace Jovanovich, 1993. This book portrays the Crow Fair in Montana and Native American music, customs, and crafts. Nonfiction. Grade 3 up.

Chandonnet, A. *Chief Stephen's Parky*. Roberts Rinehart, 1993. Eighteen-year-old Olga, wife of Chief Stephen, gathers various materials to sew her husband a parka, and its functionality makes possible the chief's success as a trapper, hunter, and leader of the village. Historical fiction. Grade 3 up.

Cossi, O. *Fire Mate*. Roberts Rhinehart, 1994. On a California reservation, a young Native American girl searches for her "Fire Mate," a person or thing that is needed to light her "Soul Fire," a historical tradition and concept that is a part of her people's folklore. Contemporary realism. Grade 3 up.

George, J. C. *Everglades*. Ill. by W. Minor. HarperCollins, 1995. In a dugout touring through the Everglades, a Native American storyteller tells five children about ways people affected the original species and predicts a future the children can control. Contemporary realism. Grades 2–5.

Gilliland, H. *Flint's Rock*. Roberts Rinehart, 1994. Flint Red Coyote, a young Cheyenne, finds the right stones to make his arrowheads, part of his people's values and traditions that his grandfather has taught him. He is totally devastated when he learns that he must live with his sister in the city and leave his beloved grandfather, his dog, O'Kolome, and his village. Contemporary realism. Grade 3 up.

Griese, A. *Anna's Athabaskan Summer*. Ill. by C. Ragins. Caroline House/Boyds Mills Press, 1995. Set near an interior Alaskan river, the text portrays the fish camp activity of an Athabaskan Indian girl and her mother and grandmother. Activities include telling stories, showing respect for animals and the land, and continuing family traditions. Contemporary realism. Grades 2–6.

Hoyt-Goldsmith, D. *Arctic Hunter*. Holiday House, 1992. This is the story of Reggie and his family, who live in an Alaskan town north of the Arctic Circle in the winter. In the summer, they travel to a camp to do the fishing and hunting that will sustain them through the long cold Alaskan days. They do daily chores and play games and include both ancient and modern ways in their family life. Contemporary realism. Grades 1–3.

Rand, J. T. *Wilma Mankiller*. Ill. by W. Anthony. Steck-Vaughn, 1993. This book portrays the life of the first female Principal Chief of the Oklahoma Cherokees, born in 1945. Biography. Grade 3 up.

Sneve, V. D. H. *The Cherokees*. Ill. by R. Himler. Holiday, 1996. This is a picture book history that details what has happened to the Oklahoma and North Carolina bands in the last 200 years since they were removed from their land. Nonfiction. Grades 2–4.

FIGURE 12–1 **Continued**

Native American Heritage

Von Ahnen, K. *Charlie Young Bear*. Ill. by P. Livers Lambert. Council for Indian Education Series/ Roberts Rinehart, 1994. In Iowa in 1955, Charlie dreams of buying a red and silver bicycle with government funds to be awarded his Mesquakie people for past treaty violations. Historical fiction. Grades 2–3.

Whitehorse, B. *Sunpainters: Eclipse of the Navajo Sun*. Northland, 1994. Kit, a contemporary Native American, listens to his grandfather's story about the Na' ach' aahii, the little Painters who repaint the world during an eclipse. Folk literature. Grades K–3.

Latino/Hispanic Heritage

Ancona, G. *Pablo Remembers: The Fiesta of the Day of the Dead*. Lothrop, Lee & Shepard, 1993. In Oaxaca, 12-year-old Pablo Montano Ruiz prepares for the Hispanic holiday of the Day of the Dead, a time of remembering those who have died, and goes shopping for special items (candles, sugar skulls, and foods, to prepare special dishes—tomatoes, radishes, and sugar cane). Contemporary realism. Grades 2–4.

Cedeno, M. E. *Cesar Chavez: Labor Leader*. Millbrook, 1993. Chavez, a union leader, leads the struggle to improve working conditions for fellow migrant workers. Biography. Grades 2–4.

Gonzalez, F. *Gloria Estefan: Cuban-American Singing Star*. Millbrook, 1992. Gloria Estefan immigrates to the United States as a Cuban exile and becomes a star in the international music world. Biography. Grades 2–4.

Hawxhurst, J. C. *Antonia Novello: U.S. Surgeon General*. Millbrook, 1993. Novello, a Puerto Rican girl, overcomes health problems to become a pediatrician and then Surgeon General of the United States when George Bush is president. Biography. Grades 2–4.

Lasky, K. *Days of the Dead*. Photographs by C. G. Knight. Hyperion, 1994. This book portrays a contemporary rural family's preparation for a traditional Mexican celebration and observances of customs. Author's notes included. Nonfiction. Grades 3–6.

Reed, L. R. *Pedro, His Perro, and the Alphabet Sombrero*. Ill. by the author. Hyperion, 1995. For his birthday, Pedro receives a perro (dog) and a sombrero, which he decorates with objects from *A* (avion/airplane) to *Z* (zorillo/skunk). Pronunciation guide and endnote about the letters *W, RR, X,* and *K* are included. Nonfiction. Grades K–3.

Roberts, N. *Henry Cisneros*. Children's, 1988. This life story recounts the achievements of Cisneros, a noted San Antonio mayor. The text is accompanied with black-and-white photographs. Biography. Grade 2 up.

Thomas, J. R. *Lights on the River*. Ill. by M. Dooling. Hyperion, 1994. Teresa and her family, now migrant workers, remember Christmas in Mexico with her grandmother. Teresa thinks of her favorite activities—putting river candles on the water and singing. Her mother takes a river candle that Teresa's grandmother has given them and lights it to give the family hope and to keep the thoughts of the village alive in their hearts. Contemporary realism. Grades K–3.

West, A. *Roberto Clemente: Baseball Legend*. Millbrook, 1992. Clemente, a Puerto Rican boy, becomes the Pittsburgh Pirates rightfielder and a humanitarian who shows compassion for the disadvantaged throughout his life. Biography. Grades 2–4.

Williams, V. B. *A Chair for My Mother*. Greenwillow, 1984. This is the story of a young girl and her mother who are saving money to buy a new chair after they had a fire in their apartment. Contemporary realism. Grade 2 up.

continued

FIGURE 12–1 **Continued**

Differently Abled Heritage

Alexander, S. H. *Mom's Best Friend*. Ill. by G. Ancona. Macmillan, 1992. This story portrays a family who returns to the Seeing Eye Agency to obtain a new guide dog, Ursula, who does important work for Sally's blind mother. Contemporary realism. Grades 1–3.

Blue, R. *Me & Einstein: Breaking Through the Reading Barrier*. Human Sciences, 1979. Nine-year-old Bobby hides the fact that he can't read until he goes to a special school where he begins to know success. Contemporary realism. Grades 1–3.

Goldin, Barbara Diamond. *Cakes and Miracles: A Purim Tale*. Ill. by E. Weihs. New York: Viking, 1991. In Eastern Europe in the early 1900s, Hershel, blinded by illness, is bored and misbehaves at school. At home, Herschel likes to mold riverbank mud into shapes and landscapes. After dreaming that an angel tells him to make what he sees in his imagination, Herschel uses his mother's dough to sculpt unusual cookies in shapes of the images he sees in his mind and helps his mother sell them for Purim. Includes recipe for *hamantashen*, the three-cornered pastries. Historical fiction. Grades K–3.

Heide, F. P. *Sounds of Sunshine, Sound of Rain*. Parents Magazine Press, 1970. This story portrays a day in the life of a young blind African American boy whose sister feels the hurt of rejection and is told that there is "no best color, that colors are just the same." Contemporary realism. Grades 1–3.

Lasker, J. *He's My Brother*. Whitman, 1974. This story is about a young boy's brother, Jamie, who has problems at school and play but is supported by a warm family. Contemporary realism. Grades 1–3.

Robinson, V. *David in Silence*. Lippincott, 1966. Thirteen-year-old Michael meets newcomer David, who is deaf, and the two communicate with signs, mime, and writing messages. Contemporary realism. Grades 2–4.

Rosenburg, M. B. *My Friend Leslie: The Story of a Handicapped Child*. Ill. by G. Ancona. Lothrop, Lee & Shepard, 1983. Leslie, a kindergarten child, has auditory and visual disabilities. With her understanding teacher, a best friend, and her encouraging class mates, Leslie does as well as she can. Contemporary realism. Contemporary realism. Grades 1–3.

Female Image Heritage

Brown, D. *Ruth Law Thrills a Nation*. Ticknor & Fields, 1994. In 1916 in Chicago, Ruth Law, aviatrix, attempts to fly to New York City in one day—a remarkable flying accomplishment. Historical fiction. Grades K–3.

Cooney, B. *Hattie and the Wild Waves: A Story from Brooklyn*. Viking, 1990. At the turn of the century, Hattie, who dreams of being an artist, and her immigrant family face the keeping of their family traditions and face the expanding horizons of their new life on Brunswick Avenue in Brooklyn. Based on author's childhood. Historical fiction. Grades 1–5.

Giblin, J. C. *Edith Wilson: The Woman Who Ran the United States*. Viking, 1992. This life story details the years Edith was the wife of President Wilson as she supports her husband during the U.S. entry into World War I in 1917. When Wilson becomes ill, Edith takes on more and more and makes valuable contributions to America. Line drawings included. Biography. Grades 2–3.

Hays, W. P. *Little Yellow Fur*. Coward, 1973. In 1913 in South Dakota, Suzanna and her family homestead near the Rosebud Indian Reservation on land that once belonged to the Indians. Based on the author's childhood experiences in North Dakota. Historical Fiction. Grades 2–4.

Igus, T., editor. *Great Women in the Struggle*. Just Us Books, 1991. This collection has brief profiles of over 80 African American women with photographs and quotes from the subject or other sources. Includes a bibliography and chronology of dates in African American history. Multiple biography. Grade 3 up.

FIGURE 12–1 **Continued**

Female Image Heritage

Kerby, M. *Amelia Earhart: Courage in the Sky*. Ill. by E. McKeating. Puffin, 1990. Amelia Earhart is the first person in the world to cross the Atlantic twice and continues to make her life an adventure with flying. However, in 1937, she disappears on an around-the-world flight. Biography. Grades 3–5.

Ransom, C. F. *Listening to the Crickets: A Story about Rachel Carson*. Carolrhoda, 1993. This life story focuses on Carson's love of nature and her difficulties in being a female marine biologist. Biography. Grade 3 up.

Rappaport, D. *Living Dangerously: American Women Who Risked Their Lives for Adventure*. Harper-Collins, 1991. This collection presents the lives of adventurous women in a collective arrangement. In 1901, Bessie Coleman becomes the world's first black licensed pilot and Annie Edison Taylor, age 63, goes over Niagara Falls in a barrel and survives. Other women include mountain climber Annie Smith Peck, taxidermist Delia Akeley, diver Eugenie Clark, and Thecla Mitchell who overcomes handicaps to train for and compete in the New York City Marathon. Multiple biography. Grade 3 up.

Veglahn, N. *The Mysterious Rays: Marie Curie's World*. Ill. by V. Juhasz. Coward, 1977. This life story recounts the research life of Marie Curie (1867–1934), born in Poland, who becomes a French chemist. It also details the long years of research that leads Curie to the tracing and isolation of radium. Biography. Grades 3–5.

Weaver, L. *Close to Home: A Story of the Polio Epidemic*. Ill. by A. Arrington. Viking, 1993. Some scientists, like Betsy's mother, are working hard to perfect a vaccine against polio. Betsy and her friends fear polio and they wonder about how someone catches it—from swimming or from getting chilled. Contemporary realism. Grades 2–5.

West, T. *Fire in the Valley*. Silver Moon Press, 1993. In 1905, word comes to the farmers in the valley that Los Angeles wants to "take" water from the valley for the city's needs. Eleven-year-old Sarah Jefferson and her farming family protest along with the other valley farmers. When a mob member's lamp sets their barn on fire, her brother Sam tries to save the animals and is hurt by a falling beam. Sarah rides through the night to find the doctor. Historical fiction. Grades 3–5.

Religious Heritage

Bruchac, J. *Between Earth & Sky: Legends of Native American Sacred Places*. Ill. by T. Locker. Harcourt, Brace, 1996. Old Bear discusses 11 legends from specific Native People about the sacred places all around them with his nephew, Little Turtle. Looking at the Earth in a spiritual way, Old Bear mentions that the sacred places are found in seven directions—east, north, south, west, above, below, and within. Pronunciation guide and map. Folk literature. Grades 3–6.

De Angeli, M. *Yonie Wondernose*. Doubleday, 1989. This is a reprint of a 1940 story that portrays the life of an Amish boy. Historical fiction. Grade 3–4.

Foster, S. *Where Time Stands Still*. Putnam, 1987. This book has black-and-white photographs that show the lives of Amish children of today. Nonfiction. Grades 1–3.

Good, M. *Nicole Visits on Amish Farm*. Walker, 1982. This is a story of how Nicole, a child from the city, spends her summer on an Amish farm. She does some of the chores and learns about the traditions of the Amish. Contemporary realism. Grades 2–3.

Good, M. *Reuben and the Blizzard*. Ill. by P. B. Moss. Good Books, 1995. This is a story of what happens when Reuben and his Old Order Amish family are affected by a heavy snowstorm. Contemporary realism. Grades K–3.

continued

FIGURE 12–1 **Continued**

Religious Heritage

Kalman, B. *We Celebrate Hanukkah*. Crabtree, 1992. This book describe the origin of the holiday with stories, games, recipes, and activities. Nonfiction. Grades 2–3.

Lehrman, Robert. *The Store That Mama Built*. Macmillan, 1992. Set at the turn of the century in a small Pennsylvania town, this is the story of Mrs. Fried, a strong Jewish immigrant woman and widow who operated a family store even though she didn't know conventional business ways or American ways. Her adherence to her faith often interfered with the store's operation and the odds against success seemed too great until the family joined together. Historical fiction. Grade 3 up.

Livingston, M. C. *Festivals*. Ill. by L. E. Fisher. Holiday, 1996. Fourteen poems celebrate festivals from different cultures: Chinese New Year, Hindu *Diwali*, Iranian *Now-Ruz*, Jewish Purim, Kwanzaa, Mexican Day of the Dead, Muslim Ramadan and *Id-Ul-Fitr*, and Vietnamese *Tet Nguyen-Dan*. Nonfiction. Grades K–4.

Mitchell, B. *Down Buttermilk Lane*. Ill. by J. Sandford. Lothrop, Lee and Shepard, 1993. This book presents a picture of the friendly relationships of members of an Amish family during one day. Nonfiction. Grades 1–3.

Oberman, S. *The Always Prayer Shawl*. Ill. by T. Lewin. Caroline House/Boyds Mills, 1994. Having grown up in Russia under a Czar, Adam, a young boy, emigrates to the United States with his family. His grandfather gives him a prayer shawl used in worship that his grandfather had given to him long ago. Adam passes the shawl on to his own grandson and the young boy promises to carry on the tradition of naming a son Adam and passing the family treasure on to him. Historical fiction. Grades 1–3.

Portnoy, M. A. *Matzah Ball: A Passover Story*. Ill. by K. J. Kahn. Kar-Ben, 1994. Going to see the Baltimore Orioles, Aaron is reminded by his mother that it is Passover and he cannot eat crackerjacks, ice cream, or pretzels. Aaron's non-Jewish friends eat the snacks and Aaron is unhappy being different. An elderly man sits beside him and gives Aaron a special piece of matzah and Aaron catches a home-run ball hit into the bleachers. Contemporary realism. Grades 1–3.

Saint James, S. *The Gifts of Kwaanzaa*. Albert Whitman, 1994. A child describes her family's preparation for the African American Harvest Festival. Nonfiction. Grades K–1.

Schur, M. R. *Day of Delight: A Jewish Sabbath in Ethiopia*. Ill. by B. Pinkney. Dial, 1994. This story is about the Amharic-speaking people of the Ethiopian highlands as told through Menelik, a 10-year-old boy. He narrates his family's activities before a Sabbath and during a Sabbath. Contemporary realism. Grades 2–3.

Schur, M. R. *When I Left My Village*. Ill. by B. Pinkney. Dial, 1996. Menelik, now age 12, and his family, Ethiopian Jews, escape drought and persecution by walking at night in the desert to a Sudanese refugee camp where they are airlifted to Israel. Contemporary realism. Grades 3–6.

Silverman, M. *The Glass Menorah and Other Stories for Jewish Holidays*. Ill. by M. Levine. Four Winds, 1992. This book portrays the Berg family and the children, Abby, Ben and Molly, as they celebrate different Jewish holidays. Contemporary realism. Grades 1–3.

children, and they race through the halls of the mansion, ride their ponies in the capital's parks, and even take them up to their rooms in the elevators.

Activity #236: "Lifespan Mini-Booklets"

Encourage the children to make mini-booklets to show the fun activities they have had in their lives, as the Roosevelt children did. Have children accordion-fold a strip of adding machine tape to make eight folds. The folds form the pages of a mini-booklet. On the first page, have the children sketch or draw a scene to show what was going on in their lives as a baby, on page two, as a 1-year-old, on page three, as a 2-year-old, and so on up to their last birthday celebration. Have them include, if anything, clothing articles and other objects they know about that are available now that was *not* available when they were born.

Mary McLeod Bethune:
A.D. 1875–1955

Read aloud the life story of *Mary McCleod Bethune: A Great Teacher* (Enslow, 1991, Grades K-2) by P. and F. McKissack or *Mary McCleod Bethune* (Watts, 1992, Grades 3–5) by R. E. Wolfe. Wolfe tells the story of the life of Bethune, a renowned teacher who overcame struggles in education and civil rights. There is a description of her personal conflicts, problems, and deep convictions. There is an appendix, a list for further reading, and bronze-tone photographs. The biography by the McKissacks describes Bethune's childhood, education, work, and leadership in government and civic affairs. As an example, Bethune, educator and founder of the National Council of Negro Women in 1935, opens a school for black girls in 1904 in Florida with limited funds and resources.

Activity #237: "Contributions and Convictions"

Have the children suggest the contributions Bethune made to others during her life and write their comments on a profile web on the board (see Figure 12–2). Ask the children to contribute their thoughts about the convictions that Bethune displayed. Write their comments on the board in a list. Ask the children to point out any similarities between Bethune's convictions and their own.

Convictions Bethune Had	*My Convictions*
1.	1.

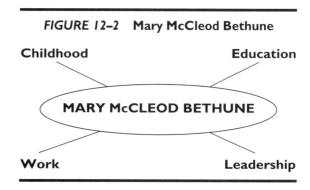

FIGURE 12–2   Mary McCleod Bethune

James Weldon Johnson: Lift Every Voice

"Lift every voice and sing/ 'till earth and heaven ring-/ Ring with the harmonies of liberty" are the opening words of the Negro National Anthem, written by James Weldon Johnson (1877–1938). His life story begins in the late 1800s and is told in *James Weldon Johnson* (Crowell, 1974, Grades 2–5) by O. S. Egypt. The biography also details Johnson's service as a diplomat and consul in Venezuela and Nicaragua.

Activity #238: "Lift Every Voice"

Have the children read or sing the words of Johnson's "Lift Every Voice and Sing," the national anthem of African Americans in story form with the music included in the book *Lift Every Voice and Sing* (Hawthorn Books, 1970, all grades) by J. W. Johnson and J. R. Johnson. Ask the children:

1. "How does the song tell you something about the actions of the people or about a movement in history?"
2. "How does the song tell you something about the issue close to Johnson's heart, or about cultural changes going on?"
3. "How does the song make Johnson's cause more personal to you?"
4. "How does the song give meaning to Johnson's faith? In what ways is the song 'a close thing?' "
5. "How does the song add substance to Johnson's idea?"
6. "What does the song tell you about Johnson's personality? In what ways does the song represent hope, companionship, and love?"

Native Americans

Discuss with the children some examples of change that happened in the lives of Native Americans in the 1900s. As an example, read aloud L. Larrabee's reflection *Grandmother's Five Baskets* (Harbinger, 1993, Grades 2–3), a story illustrated by L. Sawyer. A Native American woman reflects back to the time when she was 12 years old when an elder taught her how to make a traditional basket. The basket had the ritual designs according to the history of the Poarch Creek people who have lived in Alabama almost 150 years.

Activity #239: "Lessons from an Elder"

Ask the children to reflect back to a time when an older family member or friend taught them something. Write their reflections on the board in a list. Show the children how to group items on the list into categories or groups. For instance, if a child states that she learned to knit a scarf from her grandmother, the item could be placed in a category with the heading Making Clothing, or Clothing. Write the headings of the different groups on the board.

Distribute sheets of art paper to the children and ask them to make a drawing of what they learned from the elder person. When the drawings are finished, have the children categorize them in groups similar to categories shown in the board.

1910–1919

World War I

Two stories satisfy a child's interest in a family's life during World War I: *Rufus M.* (Harcourt, Brace, 1943, Grades 3–5) written by E. Estes and illustrated by L. Slobodkin, and Z. Oneal's *A Long Way to Go* (Viking, 1990, Grade 3 up). In Estes's book, the Moffat children live with their widowed mother, who is a seamstress in Cranbury, Connecticut. Rufus assists the war effort as he and his classmates knit washcloths for the soldiers. He grows a crop of beans in his Victory garden, starts a popcorn business with Janey, and sees World War I end on Armistice Day. In Oneal's book, some background for World War I is given as many American families assist war efforts in every way they can. Everyday life in the United States during the war is shown through the eyes of an 8-year-old girl as she learns about what is going on— particularly the women's suffrage movement.

Activity #240: "Families in World War I"

Read aloud one of the previously mentioned stories and ask the children to listen for statements that they believe are facts. Write the facts in a list on the board, a chart, or overhead transparency. Ask the

children, "In what ways can you check to see if the facts are really facts?" Show the children how to look through various references to cross-check some of the facts from the story. Have them underline a fact that has been cross-checked with a colored chalk or marker. Then have them use the facts to write or dictate a factual paragraph about U.S. families and their lives during World War I. Display the writing or dictation.

1920–1929

Depression Days

Focus the children's attention on how the lives of children were contrasted in different parts of the United States during the Depression, and locate the state of Kansas on a map as the setting for the story of *Boys Here—Girls There* (Lodestar Books, 1992, Grades 1–3) by R. Levinson. Read Levinson's story aloud about the tough times of Jennie's loving family during the Depression. Jennie starts school and the year becomes one full of changes. Pap loses his job, Mama goes to work, and Jennie becomes the big sister when Mama has a baby.

In contrast to the tough times in Levinson's book, beauty and peace during the Depression are emphasized in N. Kinsey's book *The Wild Horses of Sweetbriar* (Lodestar Books, 1992, Grades 1–3), a story illustrated by Ted Rand. On a map, have the children locate the islands off the coast of Massachusetts. Read aloud Kinsey's narrative that is told by a young woman who remembers what it was like to live for a year with her mother and a herd of wild horses on an island off the coast of Massachusetts (c. 1920).

Activity #241: "Big Sister, Big Brother"

Discuss Jennie's activities as big sister in *Boys Here—Girls There*. Ask the children, "Is there a typical big brother or big sister?" Ask them to give you one word that would tell what a big brother or big sister is like. Record their answers in a list on the board:

Big Sister   *Big Brother*
1.   1.

Review each list and ask if certain words appear more than once. Ask the children if their big sister or big brother "fits" any of the words. Have the children decide on one word that best gives a picture of a big sister and a big brother. Ask the children to sketch an illustration of what they think a big sister or brother should be like and how they helped in hard times as Jennie helped during the depression days. Display the illustrations in a class booklet for the children to review during an independent reading time.

1930–1939

The Rainbow People and *Tongues of Jade*

To focus the children's interest on historical storytelling, discuss the evenings of storytelling after a hard work day enjoyed by the Chinese elderly who picked fruit in the orchards near Sacramento, California, and other cities in the 1930s. In *Tongues of Jade* (HarperCollins, 1991, Grades 3–7) by Laurence Yep, short stories and folktales are given that were told by the Chinese working on a Works Progress Administration (WPA) project. The stories are based on the oral Chinese American tradition with sections such as Roots and Family Ties. Yep's mini-essays introduce the sections.

Activity #242: "Storytelling for Chinese Elderly"

After reading aloud excerpts from *Tongues of Jade* and *The Rainbow People* (Harper & Row, 1989, Grades 3–7) by Laurence Yep, discuss with the children the various characters in the tales—tricksters and fools—as well as the virtues and love reflected in the lives of Chinese Americans shown in the tales. Point out that the promise of a "good life" and a "golden mountain" in the United States attracted immigrants from China. Ask the children what their idea of a "good life" might be. Write their comments on the board in a list with the heading A Good Life. Invite the children to work with partners and write their descriptions for a good life on a sheet of paper. Have them read their writing to one another. Repeat the activity by having two partners meet with another two partners to read their writing aloud.

Blue Willow

Stories of the Great Depression and migration of the people from the Dust Bowl farms and the depressed cities can be unfamiliar stories for some children, familiar for others. Farming in the Dust Bowl put special demands on families that are not known by most of today's children. For instance, when their

Dust Bowl farm fails to produce, the Larkin family members become migrant workers and follow the crops in *Blue Willow* (Viking, 1940. Grade 3 up) by Doris Gates. In September, the family reaches the San Joaquin valley in California and moves into an abandoned shack so Mr. Larkin can work and pick cotton. A Blue Willow plate is their only beautiful possession and is a symbol for the permanent home that they long for in the valley. The plate has a story in the design of willow trees, a pagoda, and doves, and Janey Larkin tells it to her new neighbor, Lupe:

> *Once upon a time over in China there was a rich man who had a beautiful daughter. . . . Well, this rich old man had promised another rich man to let him marry the beautiful daughter. But the daughter was already in love with a poor man who was very handsome. And when the father found it out, he shut his daughter up in a tower. But the handsome man stole her away, and they ran across the bridge to an island and there they lived for quite a while. But the father found out about it and went to the island to kill them. . . . And he would have done it, too, but just as he got to their house, something changed the lovers into two white birds, and so they escaped and lived happily ever after.*

Activity #243: "Story of the Blue Willow Pattern"

Give the children more detailed information about the pattern that was invented in the 1800s in Great Britain in *The Willow Pattern Story* (North-South Books, 1992, Grades 1–3) by Allan Drummond. In Drummond's explanation of the Blue Willow pattern, two lovers lose their lives to the woman's vengeful father and are reborn as the doves that are seen in the blue-and-white painted landscape. Distribute photocopies or duplicates of the Blue Willow pattern to the children and ask them to meet with partners to think of another story that would match the pattern. Have them join in a group with two other partners and tell their stories to one another. Collect the stories for a class book entitled Our Stories of the Blue Willow Pattern.

Eleanor Roosevelt: A.D. 1884–1962

Introduce the children to Eleanor's kindness and strength with *Eleanor Roosevelt: A Life of Discovery* (Clarion, 1993, Grade 3 up) by Russell Freedman. This is the life story of a sensitive woman, wife of President Franklin Delano Roosevelt, who feels she is inadequate but who is very successful in all that she does. She creates her own identity and uses her positive relationships with others as a way to be productive. She is smart and lives her life to the fullest. She always has time for her family of five children and her grandchildren. Ask the children to reflect upon the qualities of Eleanor Roosevelt and write their comments on the board in a list. Here is an example:

Eleanor Roosevelt

1. Kind
2. Strong
3. Interested in human rights

Invite the children to make a collage of pictures from magazines and newspapers to show the qualities exhibited by Eleanor Roosevelt. Display the collages in the room.

Activity #244: "Achievements"

To focus children's interest on the woman who was called the First Lady of the World, discuss some of the achievements in Eleanor's life taken from another biography, *Eleanor Roosevelt* (Crowell, 1970, Grade 3 up) by Jane Goodsell. Point out her contributions and, if appropriate, ask the children in what ways Roosevelt's actions might inspire them in the future. Record their suggestions on the board and then ask them to sketch some of their own achievements they wish for in their own futures.

What Roosevelt Did	***What I Am Interested in Doing***
1.	1.

1940–1949

Leaving for America as War Comes

Give the children a sense of what Jewish life in eastern Europe was like in pre–World War II days by reading aloud selections from R. Bresnick-Perry's book *Leaving for America* (Children's, 1992, Grades 1–3) with illustrations by M. Resiberg. In the story, a 7-year-old girl in America thinks about her friendship with her cousin Zisl, who later dies in the Holocaust, and remembers other events in her life in the small Jewish town in Russia where she was born.

Activity #245: "Friendship"

Ask the children to reflect about a time when they had a special friendship with a relative and to recall the events they did together that were part of the friendship. Have the children make accordion-pleated booklets by folding a strip of adding machine tape (12″ long) over and over to make small pages. Ask them to sketch scenes of their friendship on the pages and to take the booklets home to discuss the drawings with a relative or a friend.

World War II: A.D. 1939–1945

Show one point of view about what life was like for an American family during World War II by reading aloud *Waiting for the Evening Star* (Dial, Grades 1–3) by Rosemary Wells. Berty, a young boy, senses a mystery about his older brother's interest in leaving the family and their safe, secluded life on a farm in rural Vermont to fight in the war in Europe. Young Berty tells of his childhood when "time went by like a slow song" and he had to do chores with each season—there was ice to cut on the lake, maple syrup to tap from the trees, and seeds to start in Grandma's pots on the windowsill. There was butter to make, and trading for a lamb they needed, and caring for elderly neighbors. Berty recalls the end of each day when everyone in the family took time to be together and enjoy one another as a family.

Another point of view can be shown with *The Farm Summer 1942* (Dial, 1994, Grades K–3) by Donald Hall and illustrated by Barry Moser. In the story, 9-year-old Peter spends the summer on his grandparents' farm while his father is serving on a destroyer in the South Pacific and his mother works on a government project. Peter listens to the news of the war on the radio and helps his loving grandparents on the farm.

After the children hear the stories about Berty and Peter, ask them to express their ideas of the feelings the two children might have had during their experience, such as:

> Berty's feelings when "time went by like a slow song"
>
> Berty's feelings when he was with his family at the end of each day
>
> Peter's feelings when he hears reports about the war on the radio
>
> Peter's feelings as he helps his loving grandparents

Activity #246: "Fear"

After reading both the stories aloud, discuss inner fears that Berty and Peter might have. With the children who feel comfortable doing so, have them tell an inner fear they have had. Talk about how one's imagination can magnify fears. Ask each child to write or tell about something where imagination has increased a fear. Ask each to tell about something that has helped him or her overcome a fear.

Activity #247: "War's On"

J. Stevenson's autobiography *Don't You Know There's a War On?* (Greenwillow, 1992, Grades K–4) tells what it was like when he was young during World War II as he misses his father and older brother. It is a time where spies are everywhere, and he lives with victory gardens, ration books, Spam (canned ham substitute), and air raid drills. While *Don't You Know There's a War On?* gives children a personalized picture of the war days, another book, *The Victory Garden Alphabet Book* (Charlesbridge, 1992, Grades K–3) by Jerry Pallotta and Bob Thomson, presents a specialized feature of during this time period—the interest in victory gardens that many families had. The text explains that the name *victory garden* was the name given to gardens that families grew to help feed themselves and others. Commercially grown vegetables were being shipped overseas to the troops, and families were encouraged to grow their own vegetables in home gardens.

Activity #248: "Victory Garden"

Ask the children, "What ways could a victory garden still be helpful to others in today's setting?" List their suggestions on the board. Have the children review the list and tell the suggestions they would support, along with their reasons why they would support the ideas. Use the heading Ways a Victory Garden Can Help Today.

If appropriate, have the children suggest what is needed to plant a garden and plant the seeds of a vegetable (such as cucumbers and green peppers) in a garden area on the school ground. As the plants mature, send the children home with the produce to give to a family member or friend. As an option, have the children grow bean seeds in water in paper cups, and when the seeds have sprouted, send the sprouts home with the children to give to someone who has a garden.

Activity #249: "War Jobs"

The book *When Mama Retires* (Knopf, 1992, Grades 1–3) by Karen Ackerman is suitable for children who are becoming aware of World War II and

its effect on families in the United States. Ackerman's story is a glimpse into one U.S. family's life during the war, and it sends a gender-positive message that any person can do almost any job. The story, set in the days of World War II, is about a mother who is thinking about "retiring from housework" and becoming a needed riveter in a wartime airplane plant. She knows that her new job means changes at home, so she introduces her boys to housework. The boys learn to wash clothes in the wringer washtub and hang them on the line to dry. They set the table for lunch, dust the house, and take turns pushing the carpet sweeper. They learn that housework doesn't mean all work and no play. Listening to a Big Band radio station, Mama and the boys sing along with "Mairzy doats and dozey doats and little lambs ki-divy—a kiddle-lee-ivy too, wouldn't you?" They also listen to "Boogie Woogie Bugle Boy" and jitterbug across the kitchen floor to the rhythmic tune. To involve the children further in a story such as this one, Bromley (1991) suggests that a story web be drawn. Encourage the children to contribute information for some of the literary elements—characters, setting, point of view, and themes. They can dictate or write their thoughts for a web similar to the one shown in Figure 12–3.

After the children read the story, engage them in discussing each of the categories listed on the web, the conflicts among the characters, and the reasons for the conflicts they discern from the story. In addition, interested children can create a web for

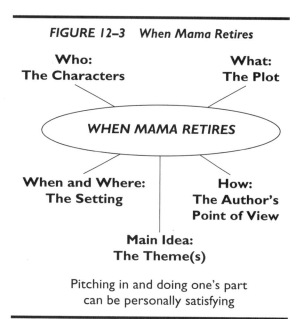

FIGURE 12–3 *When Mama Retires*

Who:
The Characters

What:
The Plot

WHEN MAMA RETIRES

When and Where:
The Setting

How:
The Author's
Point of View

Main Idea:
The Theme(s)

Pitching in and doing one's part
can be personally satisfying

other stories set in this time period that introduce children to the effects of World War II on American families:

All Those Secrets of the World (Little, Brown, 1991, Grades 2–4) by Jane Yolen. Yolen's book discusses the good-byes and the welcome-homes that take place during World War II. It has a poetic text that establishes the mood for the time period of World War II.

But No Candy (Philomel, 1992, Grades 2–4) written by G. Houston and illustrated by L. Bloom. A young girl first feels the effects of war when sugar and candy become scarce.

Hang Out the Flag (Macmillan, 1992, Grades 3–6) by K. M. Marko. Everything changes for Leslie Jamieson during World War II—there are rationing cards, blackouts, air-raid drills, and her father's absence. Her sixth-grade teacher asks the class to decide on a gift for the Americans going off to war, and Leslie decides her gift will be the biggest flag in town. She finds a way to give it to her father before he leaves.

My Daddy Was a Soldier (Holiday House, 1990, Grade 3 up) by Deborah Kogan Ray. Ray's story is a personal one told through the eyes of Jeanie, who tells what her life was like in the United States during World War II.

The Holocaust

There is value in reading an author's personal truths about war in quality books that look at war through a child's perspective. Such books can help a child face questions about war, the Holocaust, and the importance of freedom. Books about war as it has been experienced by the children and adults can help today's children examine their questions about war. Such a book is *Child of the Warsaw Ghetto* (Holiday, 1995, Grades 2–4) written by David A. Adler and illustrated by Karen Ritz. Adler portrays 20 years in the life of Froim Baum, a teenager in the Ghetto who manages to look enough like a Polish boy to escape the walls and find food to feed his family. He is later captured with his family but survives imprisonment in concentration camps. He lives to emigrate to Israel and then to Canada.

Activity #250: "The Frank Family"

Introduce the children to Anne Frank as an historical figure by reading *A Picture Book of Anne Frank* (Holiday, 1992, Grades 2–4) by David Adler, a book that shows the experiences of the Frank family members who meet tragedy during the Holocaust. Adler tells about Anne and her lively spirit, her family, and what was going on in the time period. He clearly explains why Anne's family had to go into hiding, details what their life was like in the attic annex, and tells about the others who had to share their hiding place. Detailed drawings are included to show the children what Anne's living quarters were like, and later, what life in the concentration camp was like.

Ask the children to write a list of all the things they do all day, and for each item, to write all the things for which a person needs to be outside to do. Ask the children to meet in small groups and discuss how they would do things differently if they had to be hidden as Anne Frank was. Back in the whole group, discuss ways the group talk changed their ideas, opinions, and feelings, as well as their ways of thinking about families who lived in Europe during World War II. Additionally, children in grade 3 and older can:

1. Listen to *Terrible Things* (Harper & Row, 1989) by Eve Bunting.
2. Invite speakers who have some knowledge of the Holocaust. Perhaps there are survivors (or relatives of survivors) in the community who can speak to the class about the Holocaust.

Activity #251: "Grandma and Grandpa"

"Why didn't the Jews fight back?" is the question that a grandchild asks of her grandparents in *The Grey Striped Shirt: How Grandma and Grandpa Survived the Holocaust* (Alef Design Group, Grades 3–4) written by Jacqueline Jules and illustrated by Mike Cressy. In the story, Frannie discovers an old striped shirt and asks her grandmother why she saved it. This starts a narrative over several years as Frannie grows older and her grandparents tell her of their experiences during World War II—there is even the answer to Frannie's question: "We fought the Nazis by staying alive." Help the children see the story as a celebration of life and elicit from them ways that people they know celebrate life and "stay alive" such as showing love for family and friends, offering charity and kindness, and tending to a beautiful yard or garden. Write their offerings on the board or a chart entitled Celebrating Life.

Effects of War in the United States

Read aloud a story of two best friends living in pre–Pearl Harbor days in California and what happens after that with *American Dreams* (Silver Moon,

1993, Grades 2–3) by Lisa Banim. Jennie, and Amy, who is Japanese American, are best friends until the attack on Pearl Harbor, which changes the lives of all the members of Amy's family when they are forced to relocate to an internment camp. The girls discover how war creates irrationality, bigotry, and causes civil rights of some people to be violated. The book also includes an afterword about the reasons for the war with Japan, America's policies at the time, and the Redress Bill of 1988, which attempted to compensate survivors of internment.

Activity #252: "Effects of Fighting"

Ask the children to think of a time they know about from their experience when fighting caused irrationality, bigotry, and perhaps even caused the civil rights of some people to be violated. Encourage the children to form a Friendship Court with a judge, attorneys, jury, and audience to hear a serious case that is a "nonfriendship" situation that they know about from a story they've read. If the verdict for the book character is guilty of being a "nonfriend," have the children offer suggestions for a change in attitude and behavior for the character, which includes a recommendation of doing a certain number of friendship services for others.

Effects of War in England

In England, Anna's mother promises Anna that she will have a new coat when the war is over. This story is based on a true account and is told in H. Ziefert's *A New Coat for Anna* (Knopf, 1986, Grades K–2). When the war ends, the shops remain empty because materials and money are scarce. Anna's mother decides to use her prized possessions and barters to get the coat made. She trades a gold watch, a lamp, a garnet necklace, and a teapot to a farmer, spinner, weaver, and tailor. They all help make the new coat for Anna. On Christmas Eve, Anna's mother invites to her home all those who played a part in creating the coat, and on Christmas Day, Anna visits the sheep to show them the results of the shearing last spring.

Activity #253: "Anna's Coat"

Mention to the children that after World War II, materials and supplies were scarce for people in the cities. People had to rely on others in different ways because things changed. Ask the children to recall the people Anna's mother relied on to make a coat for Anna. Write their thoughts on the board in a cause-and-effect sentence:

Anna's mother wanted a coat for Anna—which means she needed sheep's wool.

She got the wool—which means she needed the wool spun.

She got the wool spun—which means she needed the wool woven into cloth.

She got the wool woven—which means she needed the wool cloth tailored into a coat.

Ask the children to show the steps in making Anna's coat by folding a strip of adding machine tape (15″ long) into five sections and sketching scenes to represent the actions needed to produce the coat.

Activity #254: "I Could Do without . . ."

Ask the children to reflect about the scarcity of supplies during World War II. Have them meet with partners to make a list for their families of things they would not "have to have" to survive. Back in the whole group, ask for volunteers to read their lists and tell their reasons why they put the items on their lists.

Effects of War in Europe

Read aloud excerpts from C. H. Bishop's *Twenty and Ten* (Viking, 1964, Grades 2–5) to show the children what life was like in a boarding school in France as it became a refuge for Jewish children. Select R. D. Ballard's informational book *Exploring the Bismarck* (Scholastic, 1991, Grades 3–8) to show the danger on the seas during World War II. In May 1941, the German battleship *Bismarck* ventures into the North Atlantic and sinks the British battleship *Hood*. After a long chase, the British navy finally sinks the *Bismarck* in retaliation. Diagrams, drawings, and historical and contemporary photographs are included.

Activity #255: "Battleship Rules"

Mention to the children that there are many developments, such as the development of ships, that can be used for harmful purposes as well as beneficial ones. On one hand, a ship can be used for useful purposes—transportation of people and goods, observing sea life, rescue, research on the seas, and so on. A battleship, on the other hand, is most often used for war and attack and defense. Ask the children to reflect on the use of ships and if they think rules are needed for controlling the use of ships (especially for harmful purposes.) If appropriate, have the children suggest rules for controlling the use of ships. Write the children's suggestions on the board under the heading of Rules for Ships.

Review the list with the children and ask for their reasons why they made the suggestions they did. Invite them to select two suggestions from the list and illustrate the ideas with their own drawings. Distribute art paper and have the children fold the sheet in half so they can make a drawing on the left and right sides of the sheet. Collect the drawings and place them in a class book for independent reviewing. Repeat the activity with other modern items that could be used in harmful as well as helpful ways, and invite the children to make rules for the items that would benefit people.

Effects of War in Asia

The aftermath of the detonation of the world's first atomic bomb is shown through pictures and print in T. Maruki's *Hiroshima No Pika* (Lothrop, Lee & Shepard, 1982, Grades 3–5). A more personalized view of the aftermath is told through *Sadako* (Putnam, 1993, Grades 2–6) written by E. Coerr and illustrated by E. Young. This is the story of Sadako's fight against leukemia, the atom bomb disease, and is similar to Coerr's *Sadako and the Thousand Paper Cranes* (Putnam, 1977, Grades 2–6).

Activity #256: "Remembrance"

Invite the children to create their own remembrance mobile of paper-folded birds to acknowledge their reading of *Sadako and the Thousand Paper Cranes*. If appropriate, introduce the children to the art of paper folding to replicate bird-like shapes to add to hanging mobiles in the classroom. One source for this activity is *The ABCs of Origami: Paper Folding for Children* by Claude Sarasas (Tuttle, 1986, all grades). There are easy-to-follow directions to make an albatross, crow, flamingo, gull, peacock, and robin and trilingual captions in English, French, and Japanese. The paper shapes can be tied with yarn to coat hangers to finish the mobiles.

Baseball in Internment Camps

"A is for at bat./ You step up to the plate./ The pitch is a fastball,/ Which makes you swing late"/ opens a baseball primer titled *A is for At Bat* (Culpepper Press, 1988, Grades K–6) by Ken LaZebnik and Steve Lehman. It has rhyming verses that can lead to a discussion of the children's experiences with baseball—the same sport that was played in America's internment camps during World War II. Ask the children to talk about their feelings of being too small or not good enough to play a game of baseball and relate their experiences to *Baseball Saved Us* (Lee & Low, 1993, Grades 1–4) by Ken Mochizuki, a story of a Japanese American child's experience with baseball while he was interred in a camp—an often overlooked chapter in America's history. To do this, read aloud excerpts from Mochizuki's story of the young boy who was too small to play baseball as well as his friends did. In the camp, his father wisely added variety to the children's boredom by building a baseball diamond; the idea caught on and everyone helped. The team's uniforms were made from mattress covers. On the field, the boy developed his skills as he played with children his own size. After their release at the end of the war, the boy and his family faced the inevitable racial taunts and experienced loneliness, but the boy's baseball skills paid off when he earned the respect of others at school for his skills. Some of the children may be interested further in the postwar era of baseball and will want to read Robert Rosenblum's *Brooklyn Dodger Days* (Atheneum, 1991, Grades 1–3). Set in 1947 in postwar Brooklyn, the city celebrates the end of the war and the return of the Brooklyn "bums."

Activity #257: "Baseball Saved Us"

Discuss with the children the boy's feelings when he was considered too small to play baseball and encourage the children to work with their partners to cut out pictures from magazines of children with various expressions that they think the small boy could have had in his experiences in *Baseball Saved Us*. Have the children write a sentence or two about the feelings shown by the expressions in the picture(s). Together in the whole group, ask them to read to others what they wrote. Ask them to identify the feelings shown by the expressions and to talk about the ones that they think the small boy would have had. Discuss the way that the Japanese children's boredom in camp was changed to interest through baseball. What other suggestions do the children have that could have improved the lives of the Japanese American children? Suggest that the children begin their participation in the conversation with "If I had been the small boy, I would. . . ."

With large chart paper, encourage the class to write a class letter to the small boy who played baseball. To do this, ask for ideas from the children and write their suggestions for the letter on the chart. When the letter is completed, invite them to add their names to it. Fold the paper, put it into a large manila envelope, and display it on the bulletin board or in a history center for children to reread.

1950–1959

Rosa Parks

To acquaint the children with a famous event in America's civil rights movement of the 1960s, read aloud excerpts from the biography *Rosa Parks* (Crowell, 1973, Grade 3 up) written by E. Greenfield and illustrated by E. Marlowe. This is the life story of Rosa Parks, the woman who, on December 1, 1955, refused to give up her seat to a white man on a segregated bus, and who sparked the bus boycott in Montgomery, Alabama.

Activity #258: "Courage"

Ask the children what the word *courage* means to them. Write their definitions on the board as a center for a word web about Rosa Parks. Ask them to reflect on the story of Rosa Parks and ask them to identify some of her characteristics as a person who showed courage. Write their reflections on the board around the center of the word web. Ask the children to identify other people who they believe are courageous and to tell their reasons why they believe them to be courageous. Add the names to the web. Ask the children to tell of instances of courage they know about from their experience and to compare how courage has been shown in various cultural and ethnic groups.

1960–1969

Vietnam War Action

Heroes (Lee & Low, Grades 1–3) by Ken Mochiruki is a Vietnam-era story about Donnie, a Japanese American boy whose father and uncle have told him "real heroes don't brag." In a neighborhood game, Donnie always has to play the "bad guy" (because he looks like the enemy) while the other children hunt him down. The game gets out of hand and the others chase a sobbing Donnie into his father's gas station. The next day, his father and uncle

pick up Donnie at school wearing their military uniforms that show their medals for fighting in the U.S. Army during World War II in Italy and France and in Korea.

Activity #259: "Vietnam Memorial Wall"

For young children, write the word *memorial* on the board and ask them what meaning the word has for them. Tell them that they are going to hear a story about a boy who visits the Vietnam Memorial Wall in Washington, D.C. He has never known his grandfather and wishes he were with him when he sees a boy and *his* grandfather at the memorial. Read aloud the story of how the boy and his father search for his grandfather's name in *The Wall* (Clarion, 1992, Grades 1–4) by Eve Bunting with illustrations by R. Himler.

Mention that the drive for a Vietnam Memorial wall was led by a Vietnam veteran, Jan C. Scruggs, and its design was by Maya Ying Lin. Background information about the wall is given in B. Ashabranner's *Always to Remember: The Story of the Vietnam Veterans Memorial* (Dodd, Mead/Putnam's, 1988, Grade 3 up) illustrated by J. Ashabranner. The life story of the wall's designer is told in *Maya Lin: Honoring Our Forgotten Heroes* (ABCO, 1993, Grade 3 up) by Bob Italia, a biography that will interest children who want to know more about the award-winning Asian American designer.

Activity #260: "Memorials"

With a map of Washington, D.C., point out that the Vietnam Memorial is only a short distance away from the Lincoln Memorial and the Washington Memorial and that the closeness of the three memorials can symbolize a message for the children who have the insight to recognize all three monuments and what they signify about the three wars that affected Americans. Encourage children to talk about the idea that the war action in Vietnam and two other wars—America's Revolutionary War and the Civil War—have *divided* people of the United States in different ways.

Ask the children to meet in small groups to list events or times that can be called memorials in their experience and to talk about how they could contribute to memorials that are respected by their families. Back in a whole-group situation, encourage the children to mention ways their group discussion changed their ideas about the meaning of the word *memorial*.

Activity #261: "Classroom Memorial Mural"

With interested children, start a drive for a recognition mural in the classroom to reflect the recognition of students and their service to others at school. For example, have the children record the names of the outstandingly friendly students in the school on the mural. Names can be added weekly or daily.

Martin Luther King, Jr.: A.D. 1929–1968

Introduce to the children the problem of accuracy that a writer has in investigating the life of a historical figure, and ask them to listen or read two or more biographies of Dr. King's life. An easy biography, *The Picture Life of Martin Luther King, Jr.* (1968, Grades 2–3) by Margaret B. Young, covers the tumultuous years of the bus boycott in Montgomery, Alabama, in one sentence: *After a year the laws were changed.* More difficult books such as *Meet Martin Luther King, Jr.* (Messner, 1982, Grade 3 up) by Doris and Harold Faber, J. T. DeKay's *Meet Martin Luther King, Jr.* (Random House, 1989, Grades 3–4), and D. Macmillan's *Martin Luther King, Jr.* (Enslow, 1992, Grades 2–4) have additional details about the violence during the boycott and raise questions about a writer's accuracy that interested children can explore further. As an example, ask the children to consider which of the author's descriptions mention what happened during the bombing attempt on King's house, and, if mentioned, which description might be the most accurate from their point of view. Read the descriptions aloud to the children to draw the children's attention to the idea that few biographies are *totally* accurate because writers have to simplify facts for readers, and sometimes, they do not have all the research they need for the life story.

Activity #262: "I Have a Dream"

Speaking out for freedom and justice on August 28, 1963, Dr. King delivered goosebump words in his "I Have a Dream" speech that still sends an emotional message to those who hear it. Elicit the children's interest in discovering that their speaking voices can be as effective as King's with a choral speaking activity using excerpts from Dr. King's speech. Demonstrate a line arrangement for the words the children select from the speech. To do this, ask a student or a small group to read the first line, another to read the second line, and so on through the lines. If desired, introduce this activity with History Master 21 or with a pattern similar to the following:

All:	So let freedom ring . . .
First student or group:	In the process of gaining our rightful place, we must not be guilty of wrongful deeds.
Second student or group:	Let us not seek to satisfy our thirst for freedom by drinking from the cup of bitterness and hatred.
Third student or group:	We must forever conduct our struggle on the high plain of dignity and discipline.

Discuss Dr. King's words about his dream that included a vision that children would live one day in an America where they would "not be judged by the color of their skin but judged by the content of their character." Ask the students what these words mean to them today and invite them to draw or sketch their dreams about America today.

1970–1979

Black History Week and Women's History Week

Help the children understand the achievements of women and black Americans when they are related to the content of history being studied. Note the contributions during the year, not just during National Women's History Week or Black History Week. Of course, National Women's History Week and Black History Week give children an opportunity to review the contributions of women and Black Americans. In the classroom, display posters from the National Women's History Project (P.O. Box 3716, Santa Rosa, CA 95402) to feature the photographs and brief biographies of women who are part of the wide spectrum of our country's history. Women who have been commemorated in the past years include Chien-Shiung Wu, Mary McLeod Bethune, Sarah Winnemucca, and Elizabeth Cady Stanton. Interested teachers and students may write the National Women's History Project for additional information and a current price list.

Activity #263: "Eliminating Stereotyping"

With the children, consider alternative ways to confront stereotyping in the classroom by the following:

1. Teach the children to "see" stereotyping and to question stereotyped portrayals of anyone. Two useful sources of ideas for the classroom are *African American Black History Map Rap* (Chip Taylor Communications, Grade 3 up) with raps about famous and noteworthy African Americans, including Harriet Tubman, George Washington Carver, Muhammad Ali, and Michael Jordan; and *Gender Positive! A Teachers' and Librarians' Guide to Nonstereotyped Children's Literature, K–8* (MacFarland, 1993) by Patricia L. Roberts, Nancy Lee Cecil, and Sharon Alexander, a resource of children's books and activities.

2. Read aloud books that acknowledge the achievements of women and girls and that show them as strong and lively females engaged in interesting activities.

3. Read aloud books that acknowledge the achievements of black Americans and that show them as active contributing people engaged in interesting activities.

4. Teach children to examine and discuss their own attitudes, beliefs, and behaviors toward others in and out of the classroom. For example, classroom meetings on this subject have been useful vehicles that take children into in-depth examinations of stereotyping.

1980–1989

Sally Ride and Guion Bluford

On July 20, 1969, two American astronauts landed on the moon, and space travel has continued since that event. Many children's books document not only what has happened because of this achievement but also predict what could happen in the future (Roberts, 1991). Read aloud excerpts about life on the space shuttle from *To Space and Back* and *Space Challenger: The Story of Guion Bluford*. Sally Ride, a Stanford physicist and the first American female astronaut, tells her story of the space shuttle fight from lift-off to landing in 1983 in *To Space and Back* (Lothrop, Lee & Shepard, 1986, Grade 3 up) written by Sally Ride and Susan Okie. NASA photographs, glossary, and index are included. The story of Guion Bluford, the first black American in space (1984) is told in *Space Challenger: The Story of Guion Bluford* (Carolrhoda, 1984, Grade 3 up) by Jim Haskins and Kathleen Benson. The book has short chapters, quotes, and photographs. The stories of these two astronauts have implications for the future. Elicit the children's points of view about any or all of the following:

1. "Who should own the moon and its resources (other planets)?"
2. "If you were a planner and could start all over on a space station, the moon, or another planet, what kind of place would you like to live in? What would the buildings (homes, schools, offices) be like? What jobs would people do for work? Play? How would people get from one place to another? What services would be needed? Laws?"
3. "Related to space travel, can you imagine three jobs in the future that do not exist today? What amazing jobs can you think of?"

Activity #264: "Is There a Typical Astronaut?"

Discuss with the children what it would be like to be an astronaut and fly on a shuttle into outer space, live in zero gravity, and wear a space suit. Talk about what could happen as a person eats, sleeps, and works in space. Have the children survey their classmates to give them one word they would use to sum up what an astronaut is from their point of view. Have the children record the words. In a whole-group situation, elicit the words from the children and determine if certain words keep appearing on the children's lists. In what ways do the astronauts Sally Ride and Guion Bluford represent any of the reappearing words? If no single word reappears on the children's lists, have them decide on one word that best gives a picture of an astronaut to them.

Differently Abled Americans

Help promote understanding of other children who are different in a special way—children who are developmentally different because they are blind, deaf, or mentally retarded. Read aloud books that deal with developmental differences and help the children understand and accept those who appear different. As examples, several books are listed in the first figure at the front of each chapter in this book under the entry heading Differently Abled Heritage. The books have believable heroines and heroes and demonstrate children's growth toward success as they face their difficulties and deal with them.

Activity #265: "Understanding"

Introduce the children to stories portraying sensitive understanding of the differently abled to foster empathy for a differently abled person. *Developing Resiliency through Children's Literature* (MacFarland, 1993) by N. L. Cecil and P. L. Roberts has activities for extending stories such as *Our Teacher's in a Wheelchair* (Whitman, 1986, Grades 1–3) by Mary Ellen Powers. Here is an example of an activity for Powers's book:

1. Invite the children to make a list of what they do from morning until evening. For each item on the list, the children should write all the things for which a person needs to be able to *move about* to do them, and then all the walking a person needs to do.
2. Ask the children to meet in groups and discuss how they would spend the time doing those things during the day if they had the movement limitation that the teacher in a wheelchair had.
3. Together in a total group, have children mention ways their discussion changed their way of thinking about a differently abled person.

1990–PRESENT

Gulf War: A.D. 1991

When the Gulf War begins in January in 1991, 5 children—Alice, Jessica, Karl, Michael, and Sara—write to their former student teacher, Miss Loria, in *The War Began at Supper: Letters to Miss Loria* (Dell, 1991, Grades 3–5) written by P. Giff and illustrated by B. Lewin. In their letters, each child tells how he or she is affected by the war and how he or she copes with what is going on.

Activity #266: "How One Copes"

Just as the children wrote to Miss Loria about how each was affected by the war and how they coped with what was going on at the time, invite the children to write a letter to an anonymous friend to tell how they have been affected by a war, fighting, or something similar in their experience or in the experience of someone they know. Ask them to include ways they coped with what was going on. Writing a letter such as this can help a child examine questions

about war, especially if he or she was affec experience of the Gulf War is a member of a family. Some of the concerns of children brought about by war are separation, fear or tion, and a change in people's values (i.e., som civil liberties erode, communities can polarize, the innocent can suffer through no fault of t' own). Additionally, there are the emotions of turning service people and their families th be recognized and appreciated.

Poetry to Review History

Invite the children to select poems to rehearse portray different historical time periods for an tivity, An Hour's Worth of Poetry. Place the ch dren into small groups and provide each group wit books of poetry, and ask them to find a poem representing a particular time period. Encourage the children to perform one or two poems and to think of dramatic techniques for each poetry presentation. For example, a poem can be augmented with a simple percussion instrument, with a musical chorus, or with a single student musician, duet, or trio who will embellish the piece. The children can use different choral arrangements, divide a poem into segments for each student, or for dyads, and sometimes they can recite as one voice. After a poem's presentation, ask the children such questions as "How does the poem make you feel about this historical time period? How you ever acted (felt) in a way similar to the one the poem describes?" Interested children can add their favorite poetic selections to the ones listed on Figure 12–4.

Songs to Review History

Give the children a context of the big picture of history and related time periods by inviting them to sing about events in America's history through songs related to different time period in an activity, Singing Songs to Review History. Distribute a variety of story songs and/or song books to children in small groups and ask each group to select and learn a song from a particular time period. One book, *From Sea to Shining Sea: A Treasury of American Folklore and Folk Songs* (Scholastic, 1993, Grade 1 up) compiled by Amy L. Cohn, has songs related to different time periods and people, including "In the Beginning," "O Pioneers," and "In Our Time." The book also has poetry, chants, speeches, and excerpts from books to accompany the songs. If desired, the chil-

FIGURE 12–4   Children's Books about Poetry to Review History

PERSPECTIVES

Dinosaur Days

Dinosaurs (Harcourt, 1987, Grade 2 up) by Lee Bennett Hopkins has 18 reading choices about the intellectual giants of the times.

Prehistoric Times

"Orion" in *One at a Time* (Little, Brown, 1980, all grades) by David McCord is a "giant in stellar space" who walks steadfast and alone.

Early Times

"Eskimo Chant" in *The New Wind Has Wings: Poems from Canada* (Oxford University Press, 1984, all grades) by Mary Alice Downie and Barbara Robertson is collection of poetic words from North American Native people.

Hiawatha (Putnam, 1988) and (Dutton, 1983) and *Hiawatha's Childhood* (Farrar, 1984) by Henry Wadsworth Longfellow focus on the peacemaker's boyhood.

In the Trail of the Wind: American Indian Poems and Ritual Orations (Farrar, 1987) by John Bierhorst presents thoughts of Native Americans from a time before White settlers arrived. Grade 5 up.

Shadow (Scribner's, 1982, Grade 3 up) by Blaise Cendrars and illustrated by Marcia Brown is a description of shadows and how they act during the day and in night's darkness.

Middle Ages Period

Fly with the Wind, Flow with the Water (Scribner's, 1979) and *Haiku: The Mood of Earth* (Scribner's, 1971, Grade 3 up) both by Ann Atwood are collections of Haiku thoughts about actions in nature.

"Robin Hood and Alan a Dale" in *The Golden Treasury of Poetry* (Golden/Western, 1959, Grades 1–6) by Louis Untermeyer.

Sir Cedric (Farrar, 1984, Grade 3 up) by Roy Garrard recounts heroic deeds.

Exploration Period

"The Discovery" by J. C. Squire in *O Frabjous Day: Poetry for Holidays and Special Occasions* (Macmillan, 1977, all grades) edited by Myra Cohn Livingston.

Mojave (Crowell, 1988, Grades 1–2) by Diane Siebert is a lyrical poem about the desert, its roaming animals, and its history.

Where the Buffalo Roam (Ideals, 1992, Grades 2–5) by J. Geis.

Colonial Period

Hot Cross Buns and Other Old Street Cries (Atheneum, 1978, Grade 1 up) by John Langstaff is a collection of old English street cries, the first commercials of the times, often called out by fruit sellers, knife grinders, and others who sold their goods.

Revolutionary War

A Book of Americans (Holt, Rinehart and Winston, reissue, 1988, Grades 1–6) by Rosemary and Stephen Vincent Benet portrays historical figures through verses.

Beat the Drum: Independence Day Has Come (Harcourt, 1976, Grades 2–4) by Lee Bennett Hopkins has verses related to freedom.

continued

FIGURE 12–4   **Continued**

America's Civil War

Pass It On: African-American Poetry for Children (Scholastic, 1993, Grade 3 up), a collection about the Black experience selected by Wade Hudson. With the children, also read aloud the words about "Harriet Tubman" by Eloise Greenfield or the thoughts of Nikki Giovanni or other selections by such poets as Gwendolyn Brooks, Lucille Clifton, or Langston Hughes. Information about the writers in endnotes.

Singing Soldiers: A History of the Civil War in Song (Grosset & Dunlap, 1969, Grade 3 up) by Paul Glass has poetic lyrics of songs from the time period.

Post–Civil War

The Voyage of the Ludgate Hill: Travels with Robert Louis Stevenson (Harcourt, 1987, Grade 3 up) retold by Nancy Willard, relates Stevenson's adventures on a cargo ship.

Newcomers

Doctor Knickerbocker and Other Rhymes (Ticknor & Fields, 1993, Grades 2–6) by David Booth has rhymes grouped by topics under categories of "Echoes from Long Ago: A Century of Schoolyard Rhymes," "Mamma Said It and I Say It, Too: Schoolyard Rhymes Said Yesterday and Still Heard Today," and "Out Loud Right Now."

Bronzeville Boys and Girls (Harper & Row, 1956, Grade 3 up) by Gwendolyn Brooks explores the feelings of children.

If I Had a Paka: Poems in Eleven Languages (Greenwillow, 1982, Grade 3 up) by Charlotte Pomerantz has a variety of verses.

Civil Rights Movement

Let Freedom Ring: A Ballad of Martin Luther King, Jr. (Holiday House, 1992, Grades Pre–3) by Mya Cohn Livingston includes quotes from Dr. King's speeches and sermons and the refrain, "From every mountain, let freedom ring," and recalls his famous "I Have a Dream" speech on the steps of the Lincoln Memorial in 1963.

Multicultural: 2000 and Beyond

And the Green Grass Grew All Around (HarperCollins, 1992, Grade 3 up) collected by Alvin Schwartz is a collection of children's folk poetry, including "On Top of Spaghetti" and "Mine Eyes Have Seen the Glory (of the Closing of the School)."

At the Crack of the Bat: Baseball Poems (Hyperion, 1992, Grade 3 up) compiled by Lillian Morrison offers "The New Kid," where a girl saves the game for a little league team, and other poems about the sport.

Grandmother's Nursery Rhymes/Las Nanas de Abuelita (Holt, 1994, Grades K–2) by Nelly Palacio Jaramillo and illustrated by Elivia is a collection of South American lullabies, tongue twisters, and riddles told in Spanish and English.

Honey I Love and Other Poems (Crowell, 1978, Grade 1 up) by Eloise Greenfield is a collection of brief poems from the heritage of African Americans.

My Song Is Beautiful: Poems and Pictures in Many Voices (Little, Brown, 1994, Grades 2–5), selected by Mary Ann Hoberman, is a collection of verses that recognize what is special about each individual.

FIGURE 12–4   **Continued**

Multicultural: 2000 and Beyond

Spin a Soft Black Song (Farrar, 1985, Grade 1 up) by Nikki Giovanni has poems about the childhood days of young African Americans as seen through their eyes.

Talking Like the Rain: A First Book of Poems (Little, 1992, Grades K–4) selected by Dorothy and X. J. Kennedy features poets and their work over time periods—Stevenson, Milne, Lear, Ciardi, Livingston, and Yolen.

Who Shrank My Grandmother's House: Poems of Discovery (HarperCollins, 1992, Grades 2–5) poems collected by Barbara Juster Esbensen are written in the first person and narrated by various ethnic voices.

dren can create their own songs to sing. Write the time periods and the song titles on the board when they are selected. After the songs are selected, rehearse the songs with the whole group, letting a small group be the song leaders. Then, if appropriate, rehearse a singing presentation with a narrator who briefly describes the event, historical figure, or place related to each song before it is sung.

Know the Story of Our Country: We Go On

It is hoped that this book will help you in gaining additional firsthand experience with children's books related to history that lead to enrichment activities in your classroom and that the experience will be a rewarding one for you and the children. Historian James E. O'Neill (1993) referred to a rewarding experience such as this during an Annual National Archives Lecture in Washington, D.C., when he said, "The legendary trunk in the attic exists and I would like people to feel the depth and color and adventure and tragedy and the stirring story of our culture—we don't know anything until we feel it." O'Neill emphasized, "Know the story of your country. We go on." Encourage the children to draw posters to show an adventurous person, place, or event that made them "feel" something about our country's history. Display the posters in appropriate places at school to promote knowing the story of America.

REFERENCES

Abel, S., & A. Street (1992). "Stars: Stories, Authors, Research." *The California Reader 25*, 3 (Spring): 14–16.

Adamson, L. G. (1994). *Recreating the Past: A Guide to American and World Historical Fiction for Children and Young Adults*. Westport, CT: Greenwood.

Ammon, R., & D. Weigard (1993). "A Look at Other Trade Book Topics and Genres." In *The Story of Ourselves*, ed. by M. O. Tunnell & R. Ammon. Portsmouth, NH: Heinemann, pp. 93–113.

Anderson, B. S., & J. P. Zinsser (1988). *A History of Their Own: Vols. 1 and 2*. New York: Harper & Row.

Ark, C. E. (1984). "Building a Famous Personality File." *School Library Journal* (May): 44.

Ayala, A. (1989). "K. E. E. P. H. R. A." Unpublished paper that explains features to study in concept of culture. Sacramento, CA: California State University.

Barfield, K. (1993). "Go from Drab to Dramatic with Vinegar Painting." *The Sacramento Bee*, January 2, p. C4.

Benet, R., & S. V. Benet (1961). *A Book of Americans*. New York: Holt.

Bromley, K. D. (1991). *Webbing with Literature*. Boston: Allyn and Bacon.

Brown, M. W., editor (1988). *Homes in the Wilderness: A Pilgrim's Journal of Plymouth Plantation in 1620 by William Bradford et al*. Repr. 1939. New Haven, CT: Linnet.

Caldwell-Wood, N. (1992). "Native American Images in Children's Books." *School Library Journal* (May): 47–48.

Camarata, C. (1991). "Making Connections: Introducing Multicultural Books." *School Library Journal 37*, 9 (September): 190–192.

Carr, J. (1981). "What Do We Do about Bad Biographies?" *School Library Journal* (May): 19–20.

Cecil, N. L., & P. L. Roberts (1992). *Developing Resiliency through Children's Literature: A Guide for Teachers and Librarians, K–8*. Jefferson, NC: MacFarland.

Chamberland, F. (1991). "Connecting Threads: The Quilt Project." *School Library Journal 37*, 5 (May): 51.

Coe, M., et al. (1986). *Atlas of Ancient America*. New York: Facts on File.

Cohen, C. L. (1985). "The Quest in Children's Literature." *School Library Journal 31*, 10 (August): 28–29.

Collier, C. (1982). "Criteria for Historical Fiction." *School Library Journal* (August): 32–33.

Columbus, C., & R. H. Major (1961). *Four Voyages to the New World*. New York: Corinth Books.

Committee on Geographic Education (1983). *Guidelines for Geographic Education: Elementary and Secondary Schools*. Washington, D.C.: National Council for Geographic Education and the Association of American Geographers.

Crystal, J. (1972). "Role-Playing in a Troubled Class." In *The Challenge of Teaching Social Studies in the Elementary School: Readings*, ed. by Dorothy J. Skeel. Pacific Palisades, CA: Goodyear, 195–206.

Cummings, M. (1987). "Literature Based Reading." *Focus: A Potpourri of Practical Ideas 13*, 2 (Winter): 23–27.

Davis, J. R. (1989). "Genealogy: Making Us a Part of History." *Teaching K–8* (October): 60–61.

de Filippo, K. B. (1984). "Little Girls and Picture Books: Problem and Solution." *Jump Over the Moon*. New York: Holt, Rinehart and Winston, pp. 261–266.

de Gerez, T. (1981). *My Song Is a Piece of Jade*. Ill. by W. Stark. Organizacion Editorial Novaro, S. A./Little, Brown.

De La Habra, L. (1976). "The Shelters and the City: Four Ancient Societies." In *Clues to America's Past*, ed. by Charles E. Stuart. Washington, D.C.: National Geographic Special Publications Department.

De la Vega, G. (1961). *The Incas*. New York: Orion Press.

Diaz, B. (1963). *The Conquest of New Spain*. New York: Penguin Books.

Dobrez, C. K. (1987). "Sharing and Preserving Family Stories. *School Library Journal 33*, 6 (February): 40.

Downey, M. T., & Levstik, L. S. (1988). "Teaching and Learning History: The Research Base." *Social Education* (September): 336–342.

Downs, A. (1993). "Breathing Life into the Past: The Creation of History Units Using Trade Books." In *The Story of Ourselves*, ed. by M. Tunnell & R. Ammon. Portsmouth, NH: Heinemann, pp. 137–145.

Drury, M. (1993). "Why She Wrote America's Favorite Song." *Reader's Digest* (July): 90–93.

DuBois, E. C., & V. Ruiz (1990). *Unequal Sisters: A Multicultural Reader in U.S. Women's History*. New York: Routledge, Chapman and Hall.

Eagle, D. H. Jr. (1986). *The Earth Is Our Mother: A Guide to the Indians of California, Their Locales and Historic Sites*. San Francisco: Trees Company Press.

Erasmus, C. C. (1989). "Ways with Stories: Listening to the Stories Aboriginal People Tell." *Language Arts 66*, 1 (March): 267–275.

Fisher, A. B. (1957). *Stories California Indians Told*. Emeryville, CA: Parnassus Press.

Fisher, L. E. (1993). "Historical Nonfiction for Young Readers: An Artist's Perspective." In *The Story of Ourselves*, ed. by M. Tunnell & R. Ammon. Portsmouth, NH: Heinemann, pp. 19–26.

Fredericks, A. D. (1991). *Social Studies through Children's Literature: An Integrated Approach*. Englewood, CO: Teacher's Idea Press/Libraries Unlimited, Inc.

Gallagher, A. F. (1993). "Readers' Theater and Children's Literature." *CBC Features: The Children's Book Council 46*, 1 (Winter/Spring): 6–7.

Giddings, P. (1984). *When and Where I Enter: The Impact of Black Women on Race and Sex in America*. New York: Bantam.

Heizer, R. F., & M. A. Whippie (1967). *The California Indians: A Source Book*. Los Angeles: University of California Press.

Helbig, A. K., & A. R. Perkins. (1994). *This Land Is Our Land: A Guide to Multicultural Literature for Children*. Westport, CT: Greenwood.

Helper, S. (1990). "Fooling with Folktales: Updates, Spin-Offs, and Roundups." *School Library Journal 36*, 3 (March): 153–154.

Hepler, S. (1979). "A Visit to the Seventeenth Century: History as Language Experience." *Language Arts 56*, 2 (February): 126–131.

Holternman, J. (1970). "Seven Blackfeet Stories." *Indian Historian 3*: 39–43.

Hopkins, N. (1992). "Whether Good or Bad, Columbus's Impact Can't Be Ignored." *CTA Action* (October): 16–19.

Hurst, C. O., & R. Otis (1992). "Whole Language and History." *Teaching K–8*. (August/September): 86–87.

Jakes, J. (1990). *California Gold*. New York: Random House.

Johnson, E., E. Sickels, & F. Sayers (1970). *Anthology of Children's Literature*. Boston: Houghton, Mifflin.

Jones, J. (1993). "Perform Your Poetry." *Writer's Digest* (June): 66.

Kalisa, B. G. (1990). "Africa in Picture Books: Portrait or Preconception." *School Library Journal 36*, 2 (February): 36–37.

Kellough, R., & P. L. Roberts (1997). *A Guide to Elementary School Teaching: Planning for Competence* (4th ed.). New York: Macmillan.

Kirberg, M. (1992). "Student Archaeologists." *Learning 92* (October): 15.

Kuipers, B. J. (1991). *American Indian Reference Books for Children and Young Adults*. Englewood, CO: Libraries Unlimited.

Laughlin, M. K., & P. P. Kardaleff (1991). *Literature-Based Social Studies: Children's Books & Activities to Enrich the K–5 Curriculum*. Phoenix, AZ: Oryx Press.

Li, M. H., & P. Li (1990). *Understanding Asian Americans: A Curriculum Resource Guide*. New York: Neal-Schuman.

Lyngheim, L. (1986). "Build a State and Local History Collection." *School Library Journal 33*, 1 (September): 51.

McCunn, R. L. (1988). "Chinese Americans: A Personal View." *School Library Journal 35*, 9 (June/July): 50–55.

McFarlane, M. "On to Oregon." *Odyssey* (Summer): 37–39.

Macon, J. (1993). "The Rough-Faced Girl." *The California Reader 27*, 2 (Fall): 33.

Macon, J. (1993). "Teach Story Structure with Shirts and Shawls." *The California Reader 26*, 3 (Spring): 24–25.

Makino, Y., compiler (1985). *Japan through Children's Literature: An Annotated Bibliography*. Westport, CT: Greenwood.

Mandell, P. L. (1992). "Native Americans." *School Library Journal* (May): 63–69.

Maness, M. (1976). "War Is Glorious; War Is Hell; War Is Absurd." *Language Arts 53*, 5 (May): 560–563.

Manning, P. (1989). "History Outside the 900s: A Non-Dewey Approach." *School Library Journal 35*, 9 (May): 47–48.

Manning, P. (1992). "The World of 1492: In Company with Columbus." *School Library Journal 38*, 2 (February): 26–30.

Marchart, N. C. (1979). "Doing Oral History in the Elementary Grades." *Social Education 43* (October): 479–480.

Miles, R. (1989). *Women's History of the World*. New York: Harper and Row.

Millhofer, D. J. (1993). "The American Frontier—

Tall Tales." *Voyages: Teaching History through Literature 3*, 2 (Spring): 3.

Miller, S. (1993). "Writing to Authors." *School Library Journal 39*, 6 (June): 8.

Misheff, S. (1991). "The Jewish Experience in America." *The Dragon Lode 9*, 2 (Spring): 3.

Moore, A. W. (1985). "A Question of Accuracy: Errors in Children's Biographies." *School Library Journal 31*, 6 (February): 34–35.

Moore, K. (1992). "The Book Bonanza." *Voyages: Teaching History through Literature IRA SIG 2*, 1 (Fall, 1992): 2.

Moore, K. (1992). "Teaching Idea: Primary: A Snapshot of Time." *Voyages: Teaching History through Literature IRA SIG 2*, 2 (Spring): 5.

Moore, K. (1992). "Teaching Idea: Intermediate/Junior High: The ABCs of History. *Voyages: Teaching History through Literature SIG 2*, 2 (Spring): 6.

Moore, K. (1993). "Joan Lowery Nixon: Journeys of the Past." *Voyages: Teaching History through Literature IRA SIG 3*, 2 (Spring), 5.

Moore, K. (1993). "Literature Companions: History from Many Voices." *Voyages: Teaching History through Literature 4*,1 (Fall, 1993): 3.

Morgan, N., & J. Saxton (1988). "Enriching Language through Drama." *Language Arts 65*, 1 (January): 34–40.

Morrissey, J. (1991). "Pilgrim's Primer." *The Sacramento Bee*. Scene p. 1, November 28.

Nelson, P. A. (1988). "Drama, Doorway to the Past." *Language Arts 65*, 1 (January): 20–25.

O'Neill, J. E.(1993). "Know the Story of Your Country." Presentation at the Annual National Archives Lecture, Washington, D.C., Monday, July 5.

Peters, D. (1992). *The Incas: A Magical Epic about a Lost World*. New York: Random House.

Peters, D. (1986). *The Luck of Huemac: A Novel about the Aztecs*. New York: Random House.

Polese, C. (1991). "War through Children's Eyes." *School Library Journal 37*, 4 (April): 43–44.

Polkingham, A. (1983). "Brown Bag Book Exchange." *School Library Journal 30*, 1 (September): 50.

Poma, H. (1978). *Letter to a King*. London: George Allen & Unwin.

Ponte, L. (1993). "The Trail That Won the West." *Reader's Digest* (August): 100–105.

Ramsay, D. (1992). "Putting History in Perspective." *Learning 92* (October): 77–79.

Ravitch, D. (1985). "The Precarious State of History." *American Education 9*, 4 (Spring): 11–17.

Rinehart, J. (1980). "Heritage & Concept Boxes." *School Library Journal* (March): 108.

Roberts, P. L. (1994). *Alphabet: A Handbook of ABC Books and Activities for the Elementary Classroom, 2nd Edit*. Metuchen, NJ: Scarecrow.

Roberts, P. L. (1992). "History through Story Songs in Picture Books." *Voyages: Teaching History through Literature 3*, 3 (Fall): 3.

Roberts, P. L. (1991). "Let's Take Off: Revisiting People and Places with Books about Flight." *The Dragon Lode 9*, 2 (Spring): 1–2.

Roberts, P. L. (1988). *Alphabet Books as a Key to Language Patterns*. Hamden, CT: Library Professional Publications.

Roberts, P. L. (1977, January). "Sugar and Spice and Almost Always Nice: A Study of the Caldecotts." *Resources in Education*. ED127556.

Roberts, P. L. (1976). *The Female Image in the Caldecott Medal Books*. Monograph N 2 Laboratory of Educational Research, University of the Pacific, Stockton, CA. ERIC ED181467.

Roberts, P. L. (1976) "Getting the Message Via Content Analysis." *Resources in Education*, October.

Roberts, P. L. (1976, November). *Have a Star-Spangled Bicentennial with Children's Literature*. Pamphlet published by the Sacramento Public Library, Sacramento, CA.

Roberts, P. L., & N. Cecil (1993). *Developing Multicultural Awareness through Children's Literature: A Guide for Teachers and Librarians, Grades K–8*. Jefferson, N.C.: McFarland.

Roberts, P. L., N. Cecil, & S. Alexander (1993). *Gender Positive! A Teachers and Librarians' Guide, K–8*. Jefferson, NC: MacFarland.

Rossabi, M. (1988). *Khublai Khan: His Life and Times*. Berkeley/Los Angeles: University of California Press.

Rovenger, J. (1988). "Children's Literature As a Moral Compass." *School Library Journal 34*, 11 (August): 45–51.

Rubin, N. (1991). *Isabella of Castile*. New York: St. Martin's Press.

Sales, K. (1990). *The Conquest of Paradise: Christopher Columbus and the Columbian Legacy*. New York: A. A. Knopf.

San Jose, C. (1988). "Story Drama in the Content Areas." *Language Arts 65*, 1 (January): 26–33.

Scarre, C., ed. *Timeline of the Ancient World: A Visual Chronology from the Origins of Life to Ad 1500*. Smithsonian/Metropolitan Museum of Art, 255 Gracie Station, New York, NY 10028-9998.

Schiissel, L. (1989). *Women's Diaries of the Westward Journey: 1840–1870*. New York: Random House.

Schon, I. (1978). *A Bicultural Heritage: Themes for the Exploration of Mexican and Mexican-American Cultures in Books for Children and Adolescents*. Metuchen, NJ: Scarecrow.

Schon, I. (1990). "Recent Good and Bad Books about Hispanics." *The Reading Teacher 34*, 1 (September): 76–77.

Searle, B. P. (1984). "Add Some Facts to Your Fiction." *School Library Journal* (August): 35.

Slapin, B. & D. Seale (1992). *Through Indian Eyes: The Native Experience in Books for Children*. New York: New Society Pub.

Smith, J. A. (1992). "Literature Study Groups: Combining History and Literary Response." *2 Voyages: Teaching History through Literature SIG* (Spring): 4–5.

Sorin, T. (1993). "One More River." *The Web 26*, 3 (Spring/Summer): 13–14.

Soustelle, J. (1961). *The Daily Life of the Aztecs*. London: Weidenfeld & Nicholson.

Spender, D. (1988). *Women of Ideas and What Men Have Done to Them*. New York: Pandora Press.

Sperling, J. (1993). "Dear Brother." *The Web 26*, 3 (Spring/Summer): 2–3.

Stark, L. S. (1986). "Understanding Learning Disabilities through Fiction." *School Library Journal 32*, 5 (January): 31.

Stott, J. C. (1984). "Profile: Paul Goble." *Language Arts 61*, 8 (December): 867–873.

Stotter, R. (1993). "Storytelling as a Cooperative Learning Experience." *The California Reader 27*, 2 (Fall): 2–6.

Stuart, G. C. (1976). *Clues to America's Past*. Washington, D.C.: National Geographic, Special Publications Division.

Stuart, G. E. (1993). "New Light on the Olmec." *National Geographic* (November): 88–115.

Thuente, M. H. (1985). "Beyond Historical Fiction: Speare's the Witch of Blackbird Pond." *English Journal 74*, 5 (October): 50–55.

Touscany, M., & T. C. McDermott (1993). "Geography through Literature: Strategies for Successful Traveling." *The California Reader 26* (Summer): 30–31.

Trease, G. (1972). "The Historical Novelist at Work." *Children's Literature in Education* (March): 12.

Tunnell, G., & J. Ammon (1991). "Teaching the Holocaust through Trade Books." In *The Story of Ourselves*, ed. by M. O. Tunnell and R. Ammon. Portsmouth, NH: Heinemann, pp. 115–134.

Van Kirk, E. (1993). "Imagining the Past through Historical Novels." *School Library Journal 39*, 8 (August): 50–51.

Vugrenes, D. E. (1981). "North American Indian Myths and Legends for Classroom Use." *Journal of Reading 24*, 6 (March): 494–496.

Wagner, S. R. (1988). *A Time of Protest: Suffragists Challenge the Republic: 1870–1887*. New York: Sky Carrier Press.

The Web. (1993). "African Americans," *27*, 2 (Winter): 18–21.

Wilford, J. N. (1992). *The Mysterious History of Columbus*. New York: Knopf.

Wolfson, E. (1988). *From Abenaki to Zuni: A Dictionary of Native American Tribes*. New York: Walker.

Wooster, J. (1993). "Approaches for Using Children's Literature to Teach Social Studies." In *The Story of Ourselves*, ed. by M. O. Tunnell & R. Ammon. Portsmouth, NH: Heinemann, pp. 105–113.

Wright, R. (1991). *Stolen Continents*. Boston: Houghton Mifflin.

Zarnowski, M. (1990). *Learning about Biographies: A Reading and Writing Approach*. National Council for the Social Studies and National Council for Teachers of English, joint publication.

Zarnowski, M. (1988). "Learning about Fictionalized Biographies: A Reading and Writing Approach." *The Reading Teacher 42*, 2 (November): 136–142.

Zvi, Dor-Ner (1991). *Columbus and the Age of Discovery*. New York: William Morrow.

Zwick, L. Y. (1989). "Recordings in Spanish for Children." *School Library Journal 35*, 6 (February 1989): 23–25.

RESOURCES

Barr Films, 12801 Schabarum Ave., Box 7878, Irwindale, CA 91706. *Indians of the Southeast* (1991) presents Cherokee activities, customs, and tribal organization. Grades 3–6. *Queen Victoria and the Indians* (1985) is an account of Ojibwa Indians who danced at the opening of the Indian Gallery (London, 1840) and had an audience with Queen Victoria. Grades 3–6.

Bullfrog Films, Oley, PA 19547. *The Taos Pueblo* (1986) portrays traditional activities at the 1000-year-old pueblo in Taos, New Mexico. Grades 2–6.

Catalog of Western History. Jefferson National Expansion Historical Association, 11 North Front St., Saint Louis, MO 63102. For free catalog, call 1-800-537-7962.

Chip Taylor Communications, 15 Spollett Dr., Berry, NH 03038. *African American Black History Map Rap* celebrates Black History Month with raps about famous and noteworthy African Americans, including Harriet Tubman, George Washington Carver, Muhammad Ali, and Michael Jordan. Grade 3 up.

Cobblestone Publishing, Inc. Peterborough, NH. *The Cobblestone American History CD-ROM 1980–1994*. Database from 15 years of *Cobblestone* magazines useful for research, report writing and activities. Grade 2 up.

Encounter Video, 2580 N.W. Upshur, Portland, OR 97210. *Kids Explore Alaska* (1990) shows pen-pal correspondence, a way for children to learn about the culture and history of Alaska, the Gold Rush Days, and the life of Native people. Grades 3–5.

Finley-Holiday Film Corp., Box 619, Whittier, CA 90601. *Monument Valley: Navajo Homeland* (1991) shows tribal lands, customs, and crafts. Grades 3–6. *Ancient Indian Cultures of Northern Arizona* (1985) portrays ancient civilizations of the Sinugua and Anasazi developed and shows national monuments of Montezuma Castle, Wupatki, Tuzigoot, Walnut Canyon, and Sunset Crater. Grades 3–6. *Mesa Verde* (Finley-Holiday Film Corp., 1989) portrays ancient and early history of Mesa Verde, Colorado, and its cliff dwellings, ancient pottery, and exhibits of other artifacts. Grades 3–6.

Hearth Song, PO Box B, Sebastopol, CA 95473-0601. Senet is an ancient game modeled after ancient Egyptian games found in archeological ruins.

Magazine Market Place, Inc., Peoria, IL 61644. Inquire about complimentary and reduced fee copies of magazines for a class display related to historical subjects and time periods: *Archaeology, Wild Bird*, and *Natural History* (all time periods); *Quilting* (1600s–1700s) *Civil War* (1860s); *Wild West* (1800s); *The Information Please Almanac, American Artist*, and *The Artist's Digest* (1990s).

Montana Council for Indian Education, 3311 1/2 4th Avenue North, Billings, MT 59101. Has extensive list of books about Native People, which includes Kathleen Meyer's Tul-tok-A-Na, the legend of El Capitan; Olga Cossi's Fire Mate, the struggle of a modern California Indian girl; and Allan Shields's The Tragedy of Tenaya, a true account of Tenaya, the leader of the Indians in Yosemite Valley.

Random House. 400 Hahn Rd., New York, NY. Filmstrip: *A Medieval Feast*; cassette: *Hiawatha's Childhood*. Grades 1–4.

Readings for the Christopher Columbus Quincentenary, Kindergarten through Grade Twelve: An Annotated List. Sacramento, California Department of Education, 1992.

Wireless Productions, Minnesota Public Radio, P.O. Box 64422, St. Paul, MN 55164-0422. "The Story of Flight Wall Chart," videos of Laurel and Hardy films, tapes of radio shows such as "The Whistler," "Suspense," "The Shadow,," and "Fibber McGee and Molly." All grades.

Yellow Moon Press, Box 1316, Cambridge, MA 02238. Has Iktomi tales and other Native American stories on an audio cassette, *Wopila: A Giveaway, Lakota Stories*. Grade 3 up.

Multicultural Legends and Myths

African

Aardema, V. *Bringing the Rain to Kaiti Plain*. Dial, 1981. This is a Kenyan tale with an accumulating style about animals during a long drought. Folk literature. Grade 3 up.

Anderson, D. A. *The Origin of Life on Earth: An African Creation Myth*. Sights Productions, 1993. Tells of humankind's respect for determination, effort, generosity, and the sacredness of life. Folk literature. Grade 3 up.

Asian

Carpenter, F. *Tales of a Korean Grandmother*. C. E. Tuttle, 1972. This is a collection of folktales illustrated with Korean paintings. Folk literature. Grades 1–3.

Heyer, M. *The Weaving of a Dream: A Chinese Folktale*. Viking, 1986. In this tale, a poor widow weaves her dreams into a beautiful brocaded fabric. When some fairies steal it, it seems the widow will die of grief if her three sons cannot recover her treasured dreams. Folk literature. Grades 1–3.

European

Bible. *The Story of the Creation: Words from Genesis*. Ill. by Jane Ray. Dutton, 1993. This version has a brief King James text that culminates with Eve and Adam in Eden. Folk literature. Grades 1–3.

Latino/Hispanic

Alexander, E. *Llama and the Great Flood: A Folktale of Peru*. Crowell, 1989. This tale from the Andes is about a llama who leads the people to safety and saves them from a flood. Folk literature. Grades 2–3.

Beals, C. *Stories Told by the Aztecs: Before the Spaniards Came*. Abelard, 1970. These are myths about the Plumed Serpent, Toltec leaders, and the Aztec war god, Mexitli. Folk literature. Grade 3 up.

Heuer, M. *El Zapato y el Pez*. Mexico City: Trillas, 1983. This is the story of the shoe and the fish, a Spanish language story. Folk literature. Grades 2–3.

Lewis, R. *All of You Was Singing*. Atheneum, 1991. This is a lyrical version of an Aztec myth. Folk literature. All grades.

Mediterranean

Al-Saleh, K. *Fables, Cities, Princes and Jinn from Arabic Myths and Legends*. Schocken, 1985. These tales for storytelling are from Arabian and Persian cultures. Folk literature. Grade 3 up.

dePaola, T. *The Legend of the Persian Carpet*. Ill. by C. Ewart. Putnam, 1992. This is a Persian legend about wise, kindly King Balash, whose problem (the theft of a large diamond that gave light to his palace) is solved by a resourceful boy, Payam, an apprentice weaver. Payam and others create a beautiful carpet that brings light to the King's palace. Folk literature. Grades 1–2.

Native American

Goble, P., & D. Goble. *The Friendly Wolf*. Bradbury, 1974. Two Indian children of the plains are befriended by a wolf. Folk literature. Grades 2–3.

Van Laan, N. *Buffalo Dance: A Blackfoot Legend*. Little, Brown, 1993. This is a story of the interdependence of humans and animals. Folk literature. Grades 1–4.

Others Selected by Children:

Topics and Children's Books about Ancient Egypt

Achievements

Giblin, J. C. *The Riddle of the Rosetta Stone: Key to Ancient Egypt.* Crowell, 1990. This is the story of the discovery of the stone, how its message was deciphered, and the ways the message affected our knowledge of Egyptian people and their civilization. Nonfiction. Grades 2–3.

Architecture

Courtalon, C. *On the Banks of the Pharaoh's Nile.* Young Discovery Library, 1988. This book introduces children to the culture by illustrations through a text that should be read aloud by an adult. Nonfiction. Grades 1–3.

Art

Stolz, M. *Zekmet, the Stone Carver: A Tale of Ancient Egypt.* Ill. by D. N. Lattimore. Harcourt Brace Jovanovich, 1988. Egyptian King Kharfe orders a monument and the vizier, Ho-tep, meets with Zekmet, a skilled stone carver, whose ideas result in the Great Sphinx. Contributions of the stone carver are portrayed. Fiction. Grades 2–4.

Walsh, J. P. *Pepi and the Secret Names.* Ill. by F. French. Lothrop, Lee & Shepard, 1995. To assist his artist-father in decorating a royal tomb, Pepi makes friends with real animals, guesses their secret names, and gets them to pose for his father. Hierglyphics and key included. Fiction. Grades 2–5.

Mayers, F. C. *ABC Egyptian Art from the Brooklyn Museum.* Abrams, 1988. Full-color illustrations show such items as amulets, rings, necklaces, statues in the form of animals, and paddle dolls. Nonfiction. Grade 2 up.

Sibbett, E., Jr. *Egyptian Design Coloring Book.* Dover, 1980. This book shows designs from the eighteenth to the twentieth Egyptian dynasties. Nonfiction. All grades.

Gods in Ancient Egyptian Myths

Clements, A. *Temple Cat.* Ill. by K. Kiesler. Clarion, 1996. An Egyptian temple cat, worshipped as a god with servants to wait on him, sneaks away to be a "cat." He reaches a fisher-family's hut by the sea and enjoys playing with the children, being scratched behind the ears, and eating a hearty supper. Historical fiction. Grades K–3.

Netherworld of Egypt

Lattimore, Deborah Nourse. *The Winged Cat: A Tale of Ancient Egypt.* Harper & Row, 1990. In a story of honesty and deception, Merit and her cat are betrayed by an unscrupulous high priest. The priest kills the sacred cat but the spirit of the cat lives on to guide Merit through the netherworld. Includes translations of heiroglyphics so readers can decode messages. Historical fiction. Grades 3–6.

Mummies

Reeves, N. *Into the Mummy's Tomb: The Real-Life Discovery of Tutankhamun's Treasures.* Scholastic, 1992. In Highclere Castle in 1988, the author finds artifacts hidden since their discovery in the 1900s in King Tut's tomb by Howard Carter and his sponsor, Lord Carnarvon. Reviews mysteries about Tut's reign and his untimely death. Nonfiction. Grades 3–6.

Pharaohs

Mike, J. M. *Gift of the Nile: An Ancient Egyptian Legend.* Ill. by C. Reasoner. Troll, 1992. This is the story of wise and talented Mutem Wia, who is given by her father to Pharaoh Senefru as a gift. When she becomes homesick, Senefru imprisons her but finally gives her freedom. Folk literature. Grade 3 up.

Sabuda, R. *Tutankhamen's Gift.* Atheneum, 1944. Discusses the tools, utensils, and weapons early people needed to build the tomb of the pharaoh. Nonfiction. Grades 1–3.

Stanley, D. & P. Vennema. *Cleopatra.* Ill. by D. Stanley. Morrow, 1994. This is a portrayal of Cleopatra (69–30 B.C.) as an astute and politically active ruler. Includes, notes, map, epilogue, pronunciation guide, and bibliography. Biography. Grades 3–6.

Writing

Der Manualian, P. *Hieroglyphs from A to Z: A Rhyming Book with Ancient Egyptian Stencils for Kids.* Museum of Fine Arts, Boston, 1991. This introduces letters of the English alphabet from *A* to *Z* along with a colored hieroglyph that shows a picture of a word that begins with the letter. It discusses the way that the Egyptians combined one hieroglyph with another to create new words and has a closing of ancient Egyptian stories: "Its beginning has come to its end, as it was found in writing"—a phrase that means "the end." Includes stencil. Nonfiction. All grades.

Gerrard, R. *Croco'Nile.* Farrar, 1995. This book has a key to decode one of the 10 messages in the story. A stencil of hieroglyphs is inserted. Fiction. Grades K–3.

Rossini, S. *Egyptian Hieroglyphics: How to Read and Write Them.* Dover, 1989. Includes easy-to-follow instructions for writing messages in hieroglyphs. Nonfiction. All grades.

Sibbett, E., Jr. *Egyptian Design Coloring Book.* Dover, 1980. This book has several re-creations of some of the designs from the eighteenth to the twentieth dynasties suitable for children to use in their own art projects. Nonfiction. All grades.

Others Selected by Children:

Values of People

Unselfishness

African: Aardema, V. *Bringing the Rain to Kapiti Plain: A Nandi Tale.* Ill. by B. Vidal. Dial, 1981. This cumulative tale from Kenya portrays a man's unselfishness and his contribution to his people. Folk literature. Grades 3–6.

Asian: Ishii, M. *The Tongue-Cut Sparrow.* Trans. by Katherine Paterson. Ill. by S. Akaba. Dutton, 1987. Different rewards are given to a selfish greedy wife and a kind husband. Folk literature. Grades 3–5.

European: Watts, B. *The Elves and the Shoemaker.* North-South Books/Holt, 1986. This is a version of the Grimm Brothers' recorded tale. Folk literature. Grades 1–2.

Latino/Hispanic: Almedla, F. L. de. *La Margarita Friolenta.* Caracas: Coledccion Ponte-Poronte, n.d. This is the story of a child who discovers that her plant needs love. A Spanish language book. Fiction. Grades 1–2.

Native American: de Paola, T. *The Legend of the Bluebonnet.* Putnam, 1983. The unselfish actions of a young girl are rewarded in this Comanche tale. Folk literature. Grades 1–4.

Others:

Compassion

African: Anderson, D. A. *The Origin of Life on Earth: An African Creation Myth.* Sights Productions, 1993. This myth tells of humankind's respect for the sacredness of life and generosity. Folk literature. Grade 3 up.

Asian: Shute, L. *Momotaro, the Peach Boy.* Lothrop, 1986. This tale portrays the boy's courage through acts of compassion and kindness. Folk literature. Grades 1–2.

European: Stevens, J. *Androcles and the Lion.* Holiday, 1989. This is a classic Aesop story. Folk literature. Grades 1–2.

Latino/Hispanic: Carreno, M. *The Travels of the Youth Matsua/El Viaje del Joven Matsu.* Ill. by G. Suzaan. Mexico City: Trillas, 1987. Matsua rescues a boy from the Tarahumara people. Folk literature. Grades 1–3.

Native American: Cohen, C. L. *The Mud Pony.* Ill. by S. Begay. Scholastic, 1988. A poor boy is comforted by a mud pony that comes to life as a gift from Mother Earth. Folk literature. Grades 1–3.

Others:

Cinderella Tales

COUNTRY AND BOOK

Africa

Onyefulu, O. *Chinye: A West African Folk Tale*. Ill. by E. Safarewicz. New York: Viking, 1994. Grades K–3.

Korea

Climo, S. *The Korean Cinderella*. Ill. by R. Heller. HarperCollins, 1992. Grades 1–3.

France

Perrault, C. *Cinderella*. Ill. by M. Brown. Scribner's, 1954. Grades 1–3.

Perrault, C. *The Glass Slipper: Charles Perrault's Tales of Time Past*. Trans. J. Bierhorst. Ill. M. Miller. Four Winds, 1981. Grades 2–3.

Perrault, C., & A. Ehrlich, reteller. *Cinderella*. Ill. by S. Jeffers. Dial, 1985. Grades 1–3.

Germany

Grimm, J. & W. *Cinderella*. Ill. by P. Galdone. McGraw-Hill, 1978. Grades 1–3.

Grimm, J. & W. *Cinderella*. Retold by B. Karlin. Ill. by J. Marshall. Little, Brown, 1989. Grades 1–3.

Grimm, J. & W. *Cinderella*. Ill. by E. LeCain. Puffin Books, 1976. Grades 1–3.

Grimm, J. & W. "Aschenputtel." In *Household Stories*. Dover, 1963. Grades 2–3.

Huck, C., reteller. *Princess Furball*. Ill. by A. Lobel. Greenwillow, 1989. Grades 1–3.

Ireland

Nimmo, J. *The Starlight Cloak*. Ill. by J. Todd. Dial, 1993. Grades K–4.

Italy

Hamilton, V. "Cenerentola." In *Favorite Fairy Tales Told in Italy*. Little, Brown, 1965. Grades 2–3.

Russia

Cole, J. *Bony-Legs*. Four Winds, 1983. Grades 1–3.

United States

Compton, J. *Ashpet: An Appalachian Tale*. Ill. by K. Compton. Holiday, 1994. Grades 1–3.

Kroll, S. *Queen of the May*. Holiday, 1992. Grades 1–2.

Martin, R. *The Rough-Faced Girl*. Ill. by D. Shannon. Putnam. 1992. Grades 2–5.

Perlman, J. *Cinderella Penguin or The Little Glass Flipper*. Viking, 1993. Grades 1–2.

San Souci, R. D. *The Talking Eggs*. Ill. by the author. Dial Books, 1989. Grade 3 up.

Others Selected by Children:

Heroines and Heroes

COUNTRY	HERO, REAL OR IMAGINED
Partnership #1　　China	**Bawshou and Others**

Lee, J. *Legend of the Li River: An Ancient Chinese Tale*. Holt, 1983. This is an account of the beginnings of magical hills along the Li river. Grades 2–3.

Yeh, Chun-Chan. *Bawshou Rescues the Sun*. Ill. Michelle Powell. Scholastic, 1992. The hero rescues the sun and causes death of the King of the devils. Grades 1–3.

Partnership #2　　Greece	**Hercules and Others**

Bendall-Brunello, J. *The Seven-and-One-Half Labors of Hercules*. Ill. by the author. Dutton, 1992. Here is a humorous view of Hercules doing seven chores his parents want done. Grades 2–3.

Fisher, L. E. *The Olympians: Great Gods and Goddesses of Ancient Greece*. Holiday, 1984. Biographical sketches are given. Grades 1–3.

Partnership #3　　Eire/Ireland	**Fin M'Coul**

DePaola, T. *Fin M'Coul: The Giant of Knockmany Hill*. Holiday, 1981. This is a picture book account of a Fenian tale. Grades 2–3.

Partnership #4　　England	**Robin Hood**

Heyer, C. *Robin Hood*. Ideals, 1993. There is a retold version of the contest in which Robin receives the golden apple and escapes from the Sheriff of Nottingham. Grades 2–3.

Partnership #5　　Hawaii	**Maui**

Williams, J. *The Surprising Things Maui Did*. Four Winds, 1979. The deeds of a deity from Polynesia are told. Grades 2–3.

Partnership #6　　Japan	**Various Folk Heroes**

Carlson, D. *Warlord of the Gengi*. Atheneum, 1970. Heroic acts of folk heroes in Japan are told. Grades 2–3.

Partnership #7　　**Area Now America**	**Appleseed and Others**

Kellogg, S. *Johnny Appleseed*. Ill. by the author. Morrow, 1988. This story is about the role of a nature advocate as legend. Grades 2–3.

Kellogg, S. *Paul Bunyan*. Ill. by the author. Morrow, 1984. The role of a lumberjack in exaggerated in this tall tale. Grades 2–3.

Partnership #8　　**Area Now South America**	**Lucia Zenteno**

The Women Who Outshone the Sun: The Legend of Lucia Zenteno. Ill. F. Olivera. Children's, 1991. Lucia, of great beauty and harmonious with nature, is driven out of her village, causing the people to realize they need her to return. Grades 1–3.

Partnership #9   **Area Now Hapsburg**   **William Tell**

Fisher, L. E. *William Tell*. Ill. by the author. Farrar, Strous & Giroux, 1996. In 1307 in Altdorf, Tell and his son refuse to kneel before Governor Hermann Gessler's hat in the town square. Gessler challenges Tell to shoot an arrow through an apple placed on his son's head. Grades 1–3.

Others Selected by Children:

Castles

Book	Feature
Aliki. *A Medieval Feast.* Harper & Row, 1983.	Feast for a king
Black, I. *Castle, Abbey and Town.* Holiday House, 1963.	Roles of people
Boardman, F. W. *Castles.* Walck, 1957.	History of famous structures
Bulla, C. R. *The Sword in the Tree.* Crowell, 1956.	Reclaiming a family castle
Corbin, C. *Knights.* Watts, 1989.	Training
Cunningham, J. *The Treasure Is the Rose.* Pantheon, 1973	Woman defends a castle
De Angeli, M. *The Door in the Wall.* Doubleday, 1949.	Historical fiction
Gee, R. *Castle Times.* EDC Pub, 1982.	Background knowledge
Glubok, S. *Knights in Armor.* Harper & Row, 1969.	Knights, training, and weapons
Gray, E. *Adam of the Road.* Viking, 1942.	Historical fiction
Hastings, S. *Sir Gawain and the Loathly Lady.* Mulberry, 1987.	Arthurian legend
Holland, J. *Christopher Goes to the Castle.* Scribner's, 1957.	Knights, training, and tournaments
Macaulay, D. *Castle.* Houghton Mifflin, 1977.	Castle construction
MacDonald, F., ed. *The Middle Ages.* Silver Burdett, 1984.	Art appreciation
Brouchard, P. *Castles of the Middle Ages.* Silver Burdett, 1980.	Art appreciation
Oakes, C. *The Middle Ages.* Harcourt Brace Jovanovich, 1989.	Background; daily life
Prego de Oliver, V. *Castles: A Read and Build Book.* Wayland, 1975.	Castle construction
Ruis, M. *A Journey through History: The Middle Ages.* Barron's, 1988.	Background knowledge
Smith, B. *Castles.* Wayland, 1988.	Ghost stories
Steele, P. *Castles.* Kingfisher, 1995.	Castle construction, inhabitants, celebrations

Book	Feature
Unstead, R. J. *Living in a Medieval City*. A & C Black, 1971.	People, clothing, work, schooling, and amusements
Unstead, R. J. *Living in a Medieval Village*. A & C Black, 1971.	Serfs, villagers, and manor lords

Others Selected by Children:

Be a Member of the Book Selection Committee

• If you enjoy reading books, you can be a member of the book selection committee.

• You can read as many as you like and select the best books to add to a reading list to give to other students in another classroom.

• When you have read a book that you would suggest to others, write information about the book below and then place the page in a class book, *The Best Books We've Read*.

- cut -

_____   _____

Author   Title

_____   _____

Illustrator   City Where Published and Publisher

_____

Publishing date

Remarks about the Book:

Artists and Their Art

Leonardo da Vinci in Italy: 1400s

Noble, I. *Leonardo da Vinci: The Universal Genius*. Norton, 1965. The life of the painter is depicted. Biography. Grade 3 up.

Hieronymus Bosch in The Netherlands: 1500s

Willard, N. *Pish, Posh, Said Hieronymus Bosch*. Ill. by L. & D. Dillon. Harcourt Brace Jovanovich, 1991. Bosch (1450–1516) is an unconventional but creative Dutch artist who creates scenes of worlds filled with fantastic creatures. Dissatisfied, his housekeeper complains about the three-legged thistles and other creatures that keep her from her duties and says, "I'm quitting your service, I've had quite enough of your three-legged thistles asleep in my wash." When she leaves, she is followed by winged fish and other creatures who want her attention. She returns, resigned to a life with Bosch's creatures (based on Bosch's painting *Heaven and Hell*, now in the Vienna Academy.) Fiction. Grade 3 up.

Velaquez and Rembrandt: 1600s

Johnson, J. *The Princess and the Painter*. Ill. by the author. Farrar, 1994. Portrays the structure life in a Spanish court and discusses each character in Velazquez's seventeenth-century painting *Las Meninas*, a painting of the Infanta Margarita in a Spanish palace. Historical fiction. Grades 1–3.

Pesci, C. *Rembrandt and Dutch Painting of the 17th Century*. Peter Bedrick Books, 1994, all ages. Pesci discusses paintings by Rembrandt (1606–1669), Includes reproductions. Grade 3 up.

Benjamin West in America and England: 1700s

Henry, M., & W. Dennis. *Benjamin West and His Cat Grimalkin*. Ill. by W. Dennis. Bobbs, 1947. Portrays the life of one of America's first artists (1738–1820) who was widely recognized in England for his historical paintings of figures wearing regular clothing, not long classical gowns or robes. Born in Springfield, Pennsylvania, West studied art in Philadelphia and then in London where George III was his mentor. West submitted plans for England's Royal Academy and also mentored Robert Fulton and others. Biography. Grades 3–6.

John James Audubon: 1800s

Brenner, B. *On the Frontier with Mr. Audubon*. Coward, 1977. John James Audubon journeys down the Ohio and Mississippi Rivers to paint portraits of birds in 1820. This book is a fictionalized account of his "assistant's journal" of the trip. Based on the journal of John James Audubon. Biographical fiction. Grades 3–5.

Whistler in London: 1856

Merrill, L., & S. Ridley. *The Princess and the Peacocks*. Ill. by T. Dixon. Hyperion, 1992. Told from the point of view of a princess in a painting, this describes the manner in which James Abbott McNeill Whislter created the Peacock Room (now in Washington's Freer Gallery) with his painting *The Princess from the Land of Porcelain* as the centerpiece. Fictionalized biography. Grades 3–6.

continued

R. C. Gorman: 1900s

Hermann, S. *R. C. Gorman, Navajo Artist.* Enslow, 1995. This highlights the important events in Gorman's life, beginning with his school years and his interest in art, then as a young man who sculpted and drew, his service in the navy, and finally, his one-man art show at Taos, New Mexico, where he opened his art gallery. Biography. Grades 3–6.

Gordon Parks: 1900s

Price, A. *Haunted by a Paintbrush.* Children's, 1968. Gordon Parks, a famous African American artist and illustrator, tells of his sharecropping, poverty visits to a psychiatrist, and how drawing became very important to him. Biography. Grades 3–4.

Others Selected by Children:

Selected Inventors, Inventions, and Discoveries

1400s

Yue, C., & D. Yue. *Christopher Columbus: How He Did It.* Houghton Mifflin, 1992. This book details the instruments and calculations used by Columbus, the course he sailed, and his life at sea. Nonfiction. Grades 3–6.

1700s

Daugherty, C. M. *Benjamin Franklin: Scientist-Diplomat.* Ill. by J. Falter. Macmillan, 1965. This life story highlights Franklin's scientific and political achievements. Biography. Grades 3–6.

Fritz, J. *What's the Big Idea, Ben Franklin?* Ill. by M. Tomes. Coward, 1976. Franklin follows his ideas and invents many useful objects. Biography. Grades 3–6.

Pinkney, A. D. *Dear Benjamin Banneker.* Ill. by B. Pinkney. New York: Gulliver/Harcourt, 1994. This life story discusses Banneker, the eighteenth-century African American scientist, and his achievements. It begins with Banneker's youth and goes on to portray his years as a tobacco farmer, his passion for learning and interest in astronomy, as well as his accomplishment in writing an almanac in 1791. Biography. Grades 1–3.

1800–1900s

Aliki. *A Weed Is a Flower: The Life of George Washington Carver.* Ill. by the author. Prentice, 1965. Carver (1864–1943) discovers many uses for the peanut and the sweet potato. Portrays his humble beginning, poor health, diligent work, and his contributions to science. Biography. Grades 1–4.

Reef, C. *Albert Einstein, Scientist of the 20th Century.* Ill. by L. & D. Dillon. Macmillan, 1991. This is a life story of Einstein (1879–1955), the German scientist who lives in the United States and makes important discoveries in modern physics. The text emphasizes the importance of his discoveries including his theories on time, light, and the nature of energy and matter. Biography. Grades 3–6.

Towle, W. *The Real McCoy, The Life of an American Inventor.* Ill. by W. Clay. Scholastic, 1993. Elijah McCoy (1844–1929) is born in Canada of former slaves and educated in Scotland as a mechanical engineer. In spite of obstacles facing him, McCoy patents more than 50 inventions, and the most famous is the automatic oil cup for locomotives and related heavy machinery that became known as "the real McCoy." Biography. Grades 1–4.

Veglahn, N. *The Mysterious Rays: Marie Curie's World.* Ill. by V. Juhasz. Coward, 1977. This life story depicts the years of research accomplished by Marie Curie to trace and isolate radium. Biography. Grades 3–5.

Others Selected by Children:

Christopher Columbus

1492 A.D. and Later

Adler, D. *A Picture Book of Christopher Columbus*. Ill. by J. Wallner & A. Wallner. Holiday House, 1991. This life story focuses on the contributions of Columbus. Biography. Grades 2–3.

Anderson, J. *Christopher Columbus: From Vision to Voyage*. Ill. by G. Ancona. Dial, 1991. The text goes back to 1459, his childhood in Genoa and his early life as agent in his father's weaving business. He learns navigation and languages and dreams of sailing to India. The chapters have fictionalized conversations and include his 1492 voyage. Members of Spanish National Opera are dressed in period clothing for the illustrations. A map of four voyages and a list of important people and places are included. Biography. Grades 3–5.

Ceserani, G. P. *Christopher Columbus*. Ill. by P. Ventura. Random House, 1979. This life story highlights the first voyage of Columbus to the Americas. Biography. Grades 1–3.

D'Aulaire, I., & P. D'Aulaire. *Columbus*. Ill. by the authors. G. P. Putnam's, 1980. This life story portrays not only his childhood but also the voyages to the new lands. Biography. Grades 3–6.

Levinson, N. S. *Christopher Columbus: Voyage to the Unknown*. Lodestar, 1991. This life story emphasizes where Columbus *really* landed and where he thought he was, and it provides details about the four voyages (1493, 1498, 1502–1504) as well as his relationship with his men and with the original Native Americans. Includes bibliography, chronology, list of crew members, letters authorizing his voyages, early maps, and index. Biography. Grades 3–5.

Los Casos, B. *The Log of Christopher Columbus' First Voyage to America in the Year 1492*. Repr. 1938/84. Linnet Press, 1989. This is an account of Columbus's journal and how he falsified daily distance records so the men would not be terrified about how far they had gone. The text mentions the false hope, daily tedium, and the twigs and birds that signaled landfall before landing at Guanahani where Native people were met. Nonfiction. Grade 3 up.

Roop, P., & C. Roop. *I, Columbus: My Journal*. Walker, 1991. This life story has excerpts from the journal of Columbus about his first voyage to the New World. Primary source material is given about his navigational choices, the politics, the mood aboard ship, and some of the encounters with the original Native Americans. Endpapers show maps of voyage to the New World and his return home. Nonfiction. Grades 3–5.

Sis, P. *Follow the Dream: The Story of Christopher Columbus*. Ill. by the author. Knopf, 1991. This life story provides details of the life of Columbus in Genoa, his early childhood, and includes maps of the times. Biography. Grades 2–4.

Weil, L. *Christopher Columbus*. Atheneum, 1981. This life story emphasizes the idea that Columbus thought the Americas were actually the Far East and the ways he exploited friendly Native People. Biography. Grades 1–3.

Others Selected by Children:

Maya, Aztec, and Inca

Baquedano, E. *Aztec, Inca & Maya*. Knopf, 1993. This book introduces three major civilizations of the Americas in a compare-and-contrast approach through photographs of the Mexican National Archeological Museum's recreations of ancient activities such as trading, paying tribute, and healing. Nonfiction. Grade 3 up.

Gaudiano, A. Azteca: *The Story of a Jaguar Warrior*. Roberts Rinehart/Denver Museum of Natural History, 1992. This is the story of an Aztec warrior and how his beliefs in the power of the jaguar influenced his life. Folk literature. Grade 3 up.

Gerson, S., & S. Goldsmit. *Las culturas prehispanicas: Olmecas, Zapotecos, Mixtecos, Teotihaucanos, Toltecas (Prehispanic Cultures)*. Ill. by B. Lopez. Mexico City: Trillas, 1987. A mythical narrator gives details about the early civilizations of Mexican tribes from the third to ninth centuries and explains customs, calendars, and ways of life. Historical fiction. Grades 3–5.

Greger, C. S. *The Fifth and Final Sun: An Ancient Aztec Myth of the Sun's Origin*. Houghton Mifflin, 1994. When the first four suns are destroyed by jealous gods, humans live in the Age of the Fifth Sun. Folk literature. Grades 1–4.

Grifalconi, A. *The Bravest Flute: A Story of Courage in the Mayan Tradition*. Ill. by the author. Little, 1994. To honor his family during a ceremony of the New Year, a young boy must carry a drum on his back and play a flute in the long procession. Nearly exhausted at the end of the long ceremony, he feels his strength return when the widow of a master flutist replaces his flute with her husband's. He receives a generous reward from the elders of the village so that he can support his family. Fiction. Grades 1–3.

Hicks, P. *The Aztecs*. Thomson Learning, 1993. This text has basic information along with photographs of artifacts and ancient buildings. Pronunciation guide included. Nonfiction. Grades 3–5.

James, S. *The Aztecs*. Viking, 1992. Clear acetate pages are sequenced throughout the book and can be lifted to show the inner workings of illustrated Aztec structures. Also shows social life and customs in the empire. Nonfiction. Grades 3–5.

Kurtz, J. *Miro in the Kingdom of the Sun*. Ill. by D. Frampton. Houghton Mifflin, 1996. In this Incan folktale, Miro runs swiftly and understands the language of the birds. Her abilities help free her imprisoned brothers when she finds a magic lake and a cure for the ailing son of the Incan king. Folk literature. Grades K–4.

Meltzer, M. *Gold: The True Story of Why People Search for It, Mine It, Trade It, Steal It, Mint It, Hoard It, Shape It, Wear It, Fight and Kill for It*. HarperCollins, 1993. This is an overview of the history of gold and what people do because of it. Nonfiction. Grade 3 up.

Rohmer, H. *The Legend of Food Mountain/La Montana del Alimento*. Ill. by G. Carillo. Children's, 1982. In both English and Spanish, this is the tale of how the earth was created by the god Quetzalcoatl. Folk literature. Grades 2–3.

Others Selected by Children:

Civilization: Explore a Concept

Concept	Maya	Aztec	Inca	Time Period
Architecture				
Family pattern				
Work done				
Schooling				
Government				
Jewelry				
Recreation				
Religion				
Authority				
Health care				

Others Selected by Children:

Role of Women and Girls

Prehistory

Bernhard, E., reteller. *The Girl Who Wanted to Hunt: A Siberian Tale*. Holiday House, 1994. Anga, a young girl, wants to be a hunter like her father. Folk literature. Grades 1–4.

Four Million Years Ago

Maddern, E. *Rainbow Bird: An Aboriginal Folktale from Northern Australia*. Ill. by A. Kennaway. Little, Brown, 1993. Bird Woman snatches fire from the open jaws of tough Crocodile Man, puts fire into the heart of every tree and people can make flames from dry wood. Folk literature. Grades K–3.

19,000 Years Ago

Kimmel, E. *Rimonah of the Flashing Sword: A North African Tale*. Ill. by O. Rayyan. Holiday, 1995. Princess Rimonah escapes her jealous stepmother and queen and joins a band of thieves. Folk literature. Grades K–4.

1200 B.C.

Yep, Lawrence. *The Shell Woman and the King*. Dial, 1990. In China, a young girl outsmarts a selfish king. Folk literature. Grades K–3.

500 B.C.–1 A.D.

Jiang, W. *La Heroina Hua Mulan/The Legend of Mu Lan*. Ill. by the author and Xing Gen. Monterey: Victory Press/T. R. Books, 1992. Set in ancient China, Mu Lan disguises herself as a boy to fight for her country. Folk literature. Grades 2–3.

Lee, J. M. *The Song of Mu Lan*. Ill. by the author. Front Street, 1995. Set around 400 B.C., this Chinese poem is the story of courageous Mu Lan who takes her ailing father's place in battle. Folk literature. Grades K–5.

A.D. 1–1399

San Souci, R. D. *Young Guinevere*. Ill. by J. Henterly. Doubleday, 1992. This is a life story account of Guinevere (c. 1100) as a young girl who journeys to King Arthur's court to request assistance during the seige of her father's castle. Biography. Grades 3–5.

1400–1499

Fisher, A. *Jeanne d'Arc*. Ill. by A. Fortenberg. Crowell, 1970. A 19-year-old girl (1412–1431) wears white armor and leads the French army. Biography to be read aloud to young children. Grade 5 up.

Garden, N. *Dove and Sword: A Novel of Joan of Arc*. Ill. by the author. Farrar, Straus & Giroux, 1995. Gabrielle, a young girl, joins the Maid's call to the battlefield and to war. Historical fiction to be read aloud to young children. Grade 5 up.

continued

1500–1599

Brighton, C. *Five Secrets in a Box.* Dutton, 1987. Virginia, the daughter of Galileo (1564–1642), uses her famous father's instruments. Historical fiction. Grade 2 up.

McCully, E. A. *The Pirate Queen.* Ill. by the author. Putnam, 1995. Grania O'Malley is courageous in raids in the Mediterranean. Historical fiction. Grades 2–5.

Stanley, D., & P. Vennema. *Good Queen Bess: The Story of Elizabeth I of England.* Ill. by D. Stanley. Four Winds, 1991. This life story emphasizes the queen's (1533–1603) influence on sixteenth-century people and events. Biography. Grades 3–5.

1600–1699

Accorsi, W. *My Name Is Pocahontas.* Ill. by the author. Holiday House, 1992. An Indian princess (1595–1617), daughter of Indian leader, Powhatan, becomes friends with John Smith and journeys to England as the wife of John Rolfe. Biography. Grades K–2.

Christian, M. B. *Goody Sherman's Pig.* Macmillan, 1990. This story is based on historical facts and is the account of Goody Sherman in 1636 who takes up a legal battle over her runaway pig with church elders and the courts. Historical fiction. Grade 3 up.

Fradin, D. B. *Anne Hutchinson.* Enslow, 1990. This is the life story of Hutchinson (1591–1643) who preaches that true religion is the following of God's guidance through an "Inner Light." Biography. Grades 3–5.

Fritz, E. I. *Anne Hutchinson.* Chelsea, 1991. The text describes Anne's early life, her education, and her banishment from the colony. Biography. Grades 3–5.

Moskin, M. *Lysbet and the Fire Kittens.* Coward, 1974. Eight-year-old Lysbet builds the fire in their home too high and starts a fire on their roof. Historical fiction. Grades 2–4.

Raphael, E., & D. Bolognese. *Pocahontas: Princess of the River Tribes.* Ill. by the authors. Scholastic, 1993. This is a brief narrative with lists of facts about selected events in the life of Pocahontas (d. 1617). Biography. Grades 1–3.

Van Woerkom, D. *Becky and the Bear.* Ill. by M. Tomes. Putnam's, 1975. Becky, a young girl, confronts a bear, feeds it, and, with the help of her grandmother, ties it to a tree. Historical fiction. Grades 1–3.

1700–1799

Dalgliesh, A. *The Courage of Sarah Noble.* Macmillan, 1987. In 1707, an 8-year-old girl goes with her father to the wilderness. True story based on actual incident. Historical fiction. Grades 3–4.

Griffith, J. D. *Phoebe the Spy.* Scholastic, 1977. A tavern keeper's daughter spies for General Washington. Historical fiction. Grades 3–4.

McGovern, A. *Secret Soldier: The Story of Deborah Sampson.* Scholastic, 1875. A young woman disguises herself as a boy in the army during America's War of Independence. Biography. Grades 3–4.

Stevens, B. *Deborah Sampson Goes to War.* Ill. by F. Hill. Carolrhoda, 1984. This life story describes Sampson's experiences during America's Revolutionary War. Biography. Grades 2–6.

1800–1899

Blumberg, R. *Bloomers!* Bradbury, 1993. Eventually, Elizabeth Cady Stanton, Susan B. Anthony, and others wear bloomers as the new uniform of the woman's movement. Biography. Grades 1–2.

Johnston, J. *Harriet and the Runaway Book: The Story of Harriet Beecher Stowe and Uncle Tom's Cabin.* Ill. by R. Himler. Harper, 1977. Harriet sees many slaves escape to freedom and becomes determined to write a book to show how terrible slavery is. Biography. Grades 3–5.

1800–1899

Jordan, D. *Susie King Taylor: Destined to be Free*. Ill. by H. Bond. Just Us Books, 1994. This is a brief life story of Taylor, born a slave, who escapes and grows up to be a heroine of the 1800s. Biography. Grades 3–5.

McCully, E. A. *The Ballot Box Battle*. Ill. by the author. New York: Knopf, 1996. On Election Day in 1880, Elizabeth Cady Stanton, an advocate for women's rights, takes young Cordelia, her neighbor, to the polls in their town of Tenafly, New Jersey, where her attempt to vote is denied. Except for the fictional character of Cordelia, this is a true story based on the memoirs of Mrs. Stanton. Historical fiction. Grades 2 up.

Miller, R. H. *The Story of Stagecoach Mary*. Ill. by C. Hanna. Silver Burdett Press, 1995. Mary Fields was the first African American woman to carry the United States mail. Historical fiction. Grades K–3.

Raphael, E., & D. Bolognese. *Sacajawea: The Journey West*. Scholastic, 1994. This life story records a young Native American girl's journey west with the expedition of Lewis and Clark. Biography. Grades 1–3.

Rappaport, D. *Trouble at the Mines*. Crowell, 1987. The troubled times of a coal miners' strike are recounted by a miner's daughter. Historical fiction. Grade 3 up.

Roop, P., & C. Roop. *Keep the Lights Burning, Abbie*. Ill. by P. Hanson. Young Abbie is left in charge of the lights in the lighthouse while her father is gone. Based on a true story. Historical fiction. Grades 1–4.

St. George, J. *By George, Bloomers!* Shoe Tree, 1989. This story is a fictionalized view of the topic of bloomers being worn as a symbol of the women's rights movement. Historical fiction. Grades 1–3.

Wettener, M. K. *Kate Shelley and the Midnight Express*. Ill. by K. Ritz. Carolthoda, 1990. A 15-year-old girl warns the railroad of a train bridge that is washed out in a flood. Historical fiction. Grades 2–5.

1900–Present

Brown, D. *Ruth Law Thrills a Nation*. Ticknor & Fields, 1994. Ruth Law, aviatrix, attempts to fly to New York City in one day. Historical fiction. Grades K–3.

Cooney, B. *Hattie and the Wild Waves: A Story from Brooklyn*. Viking, 1990. Hattie and her immigrant family keep their family traditions in their new life in Brooklyn. Based on author's childhood. Historical fiction. Grades 1–5.

Giblin, J. C. *Edith Wilson: The Woman Who Ran the United States*. Viking, 1992. Edith was the wife of President Wilson and supported her husband during American's entry into World War I in 1917. Biography. Grades 2–3.

Hays, W. P. *Little Yellow Fur*. Coward, 1973. Suzanna and her family homestead near the Rosebud Indian Reservation on land that once belonged to the Indians. Based on the author's childhood experiences in North Dakota. Historical fiction. Grades 2–4.

Igus, T., ed. *Great Women in the Struggle*. Just Us Books, 1991. This collection contains profiles of over 80 African American women with photographs and quotes from the subject or other sources. It includes a bibliography and chronology of dates in African American history. Multiple biography. Grade 3 up.

Kerby, M. *Amelia Earhart: Courage in the Sky*. Ill. by E. McKeating. Puffin, 1990. Amelia Earhart is the first person in the world to cross the Atlantic twice. Biography. Grades 3–5.

Lindbergh, R. *Nobody Owns the Sky: The Story of "Brave Bessie" Coleman*. Ill. by P. Paparone. Candlewick, 1996. This is a life story in a picture book format with a narrative poem that portrays Coleman's dream of flying and her first courageous flights. Grades 1–3.

continued

1900–Present

Purdy, C. *Least of All*. Ill. by T. Arnold. Macmillan, 1987. Seven-year-old Raven Hannah is the youngest of six children on her family's Vermont farm. Historical fiction. Grades K–2.

Ransom, C. F. *Listening to the Crickets: A Story about Rachel Carson*. Carolrhoda, 1993. This life story emphasizes Carson's love of nature and her difficulties in being a female marine biologist. Biography. Grade 3 up.

Rappaport, D. *Living Dangerously: American Women Who Risked Their Lives for Adventure*. Harper-Collins, 1991. This collection depicts lives of adventurous women such as Bessie Coleman, Annie Edison Taylor, Annie Smith Peck, Delia Akeley, Eugenie Clark, and Thecla Mitchell. Multiple biography. Grade 3 up.

Veglahn, N. *The Mysterious Rays: Marie Curie's World*. Ill. by V. Juhasz. Coward, 1977. This life story portrays the research life of Marie Curie (1867–1934), born in Poland, who becomes a French research chemist. Biography. Grades 3–5.

Weaver, L. *Close to Home: A Story of the Polio Epidemic*. Ill. by A. Arrington. Viking, 1993. Betsy's mother and other scientists work hard to perfect a vaccine against polio. Contemporary realism. Grades 2–5.

West, T. *Fire in the Valley*. Silver Moon Press, 1993. The city of Los Angeles wants to "take" water from the valley for the city's needs, and 11-year-old Sarah Jefferson and her farming family protest along with the other valley farmers. Historical fiction. Grades 3–5.

Others Suggested by Children:

People Risked Their Lives

REVOLUTIONARY AMERICA

1772

Fritz, J. *Why Don't You Get a Horse, Sam Adams?* Ill. by T. S. Hyman. Coward, 1974. A graduate of Harvard, Adams is elected to the Massachusetts legislature and helps form the Committees of Correspondence in the Colonies. He believes people should be free from Great Britain and supports the Colonies' independence. Biography. Grades 3–5.

Sabin, L. *Patrick Henry, Voice of the American Revolution.* Ill. by B. Ternay. Troll, 1982. This book describes Henry's childhood in the colony of Virginia and focuses on some of the skills and traits he had: his love of music and ability to play the violin, sense of humor, sense of fairness, love of freedom, and ability to debate with persuasive oratory. Biography. Grades 3–6.

1775

Fritz, J. *Will You Sign Here, John Hancock?* Ill. by T. S. Hyman. Coward, 1976. This is the life story of Hancock, who is educated at Harvard and is a leader of the Patriot Party. He is seen as a dangerous revolutionary by the British and General Gage marches on Lexington and Concord in 1775 to capture him. His act as the first signer of the Declaration of Independence and president of the Continental Congress leads to the expression "John Hancock" to mean a signature. Biography. Grades 2–5.

1776

Rappaport, D. *The Boston Coffee Party.* Ill. by E. A. McCully. Harper & Row, 1988. Based on historical records, two sisters, Sarah and Emma, become involved with their mother and the other women of Boston who are angry about the high prices of sugar and coffee during America's revolutionary days. Fiction. Grades 2–4.

Turner, A. *Katie's Trunk.* Ill. by R. Himler. Macmillan, 1992. The colonists dump tea into the Boston Harbor, and Katie's family, loyal to England, are disliked by former friends and neighbors. Warned that the rebel colonists are coming, the family hides in the woods but Katie returns to defend the family's home. Hearing the rebels' voices, she hides in her mother's wedding trunk and is saved by one of her brother's friends. Historical fiction. Grades Pre–3.

1777

Adler, D. A. *A Picture Book of George Washington.* Ill by J. & A. Wallner. Holiday, 1989. This brief life story describes Washington's traits, family members, and life events. Biography. Grades 1–3.

Bulla, Clyde. *Washington's Birthday.* Ill. by D. Bolognese. Crowell, 1967. This life story focuses on Washington's early life as the Colonies struggle to become a nation and his part in the later events. As America's first president in colonial times, he receives Henry Lee's tribute at his death of "First in war, first in peace, first in the hearts of his countrymen." Biography. Grades 2–3.

Fleming, A. *George Washington Wasn't Always Old.* Simon & Schuster, 1991. This life story highlights Washington's years before age 21 and his relationships with his family—mother, father, and half-brother. Biography. Grade 3 up.

Griffin, J. D. *Phoebe the Spy.* Scholastic, 1977. This is the story of a tavern keeper's daughter, Phoebe Frances. She spies for General Washington and the colonists. Historical fiction. Grades 3–4.

continued

1777

McGovern, A. *Secret Soldier: The Story of Deborah Sampson*. Scholastic, 1975. This is the story of a young woman who disguised herself as a boy and joined the army to serve in America's War of Independence. Biography. Grades 3–4.

Roop, P., & C. Roop. *Buttons for General Washington*. Carolrhoda, 1986. In British-occupied Philadelphia in 1777, 14-year-old John Darragh takes coded messages his mother sews into his coat buttons to his brother at George Washington's fall camp. Historical fiction. Grade 3 up.

Stevens, B. *Deborah Sampson Goes to War*. Ill. by F. Hill. Carolrhoda, 1984. This life story describes Sampson's early life and her experiences, including injuries and illnesses as a soldier in America's Revolutionary War. Her true identity is discovered near the end of the war. Biography. Grades 2–6.

1781

Haley, Gail E. *Jack Jouett's Ride*. Ill. by the author. Viking, 1973. Most children will know about Paul Revere's ride but may not know the ride of Jack Jouett in 1781. Jouett rides his horse, Sallie, 40 miles at night through wooded terrain to Monticello and Charlottesville to warn Virginia's legislators that "Bloody Tarleton" and the British troops were marching in their direction. Historical fiction. Grade 3 up.

Others Selected by Children:

Field Trip

Purpose: To prepare a field guide for other classes who will be traveling to the historic site.

1. What written permission do we need?

2. What do we want to know?

3. What transportation do we need?

4. What will we need on the trip? (lunches, water fountain locations, first-aid supplies, restroom locations)

5. What time should we arrive and depart? Eat lunch?

6. What adults will be going?

7. What should we see on the trip?

8. How should we act on the trip? (conduct of safety and courtesy)

9. What pre-trip study should we do?

10. What notes and sketches should we make?

11. How can we arrange the notes and sketches into a field trip guide book for others?

Diaries of Pioneers in the 1850s

Imagined Diary Entries

Write or sketch the following:

1. Reasons why you would leave your home in a canvas-topped wooden wagon to journey to a new home.
2. Waving good-bye to your friends or grandparents as the wagon train leaves.
3. The first time you heard these sounds:
   A whip crack by a drover
   The jolting and creaking of your wagon
   The bawling of the oxen
4. What you did and how you felt the first time you:
   Forged a stream
   Climbed a rock
   Had to take care of a baby
   Helped cook the evening meal
   Milked a cow
5. Milking the cows in the morning and hanging the milk in lidded pails from the wagon back. Show how surprised you were to learn that the rocking motion of the wagon churned the liquid into butter and buttermilk.
6. Your ideas about why some people called the wooden wagons *prairie schooners*.
7. Your actions and feelings the first time you had to help get a wagon down a steep hill.
8. Ways some families lock their wagon wheels to make them slide down the steep hill; ways other families hook the oxen behind the wagons to pull backward and slow the descent; ways families held their wagons back with ropes to keep the wagons from speeding out of control and breaking apart.
9. Your actions when your wagon train finally rests at a camping place at the foot of a large sandstone cliff after traveling from Fort Laramie. While camping, you and your friends scratch your names and dates into the soft sandstone rock, which will become known as Register Cliff. What will your scratched name and date in the cliff look like?
10. The actions you have at Three Island Crossing on the Snake River. This is where your family finds that the river—your nearest water source—has turned into the most treacherous river crossing of the entire journey. It takes days to get all the livestock, wagons, and people across the swirling Snake River, and not everyone makes it.
11. The actions of the discouraged families as everyone tries to survive the difficult crossings in the mountains known as the Blues. Your family members discover there is no firewood and no available water in the mountains. One day, you have to stop and make camp because of an early snowstorm.
12. The actions of the grateful families on your wagon train when they made it to Flagstaff Hill where they stop, camp, rest, and look down on Lone Pine Valley, a lush green area.

13. The actions of the families on the wagon train at the riverfront town of The Dalles, a gateway to the Columbia River Gorge. At the town, your family has to choose between two dangerous ways to continue: whether to lash your wagon to rafts and try to float down the unpredictable river for 60 miles or take the overland trail across the steep, forested ridges of Mt. Hood. Which path will your family choose? Why?

14. The actions of the families of your friends who camped near the Columbia Gorge as they prepared their wagons and rafts for the journey plunging down the rushing Columbia rapids under the soaring rock cliffs of the deep gorge.

15. The actions of the other families of your friends who camped near the Columbia Gorge and wanted to avoid the rapids. They were busy getting ready to forge a trail (the Barlow Road) through the dense forest area across the Cascade Mountains.

16. The actions of the families who took the mountain trail when they had to abandon their wagons in the deep mud and walk on foot toward Oregon City and to finish their journey.

17. The actions of the weary but grateful families who, either by river or by the overland trail, finally reached Oregon City on the Willamette River.

Journal Trip Entry

Trip Journal Entry for _____ (child's name)

Date _____

When you go on a trip, please take one of these trip journal entry sheets with you. Take as many sheets as the days you plan to be away. When you get back, we all will learn from your trip. If needed, have someone else fill in some of the information with you. Add anything extra that will be of interest to the group.

The way I traveled:
What the weather was like:
What I wore:
The best activity we did today was:
The most interesting thing I saw was:
The license numbers I read were:
My sketches of interesting things I saw are below:

What I ate for breakfast:
Time I started breakfast: Time I finished breakfast:
Where I ate breakfast:
The town I was in:
Breakfast was (good   fair   poor)

What I ate for lunch:
Time I started lunch: Time I finished lunch:
Where I ate lunch:
The town I was in:
Lunch was (good   fair   poor)

What I ate for dinner:
Time I started dinner: Time I finished dinner:
Where I ate dinner:
The town I was in:
Dinner was (good   fair   poor)

Where I slept at night:
Town/state:
Temperature when I went to bed:
Temperature when I got up:

Mitakuye Oyasin:
We Are All Related

Tales That Show the Idea That We Are All Related

Anderson, D. A. *The Origin of Life on Earth: An African Creation Myth.* Sights Productions, 1993. This myth emphasizes humankind's respect for determination, effort, generosity, and the sacredness of life. Folk literature. Grade 3 up.

Aroner, M. *The Kingdom of Singing Birds.* Kar-Ben, 1993. This is a classic Hasidic tale about making one's own choices. Rabbi Zusya tells the king that if he truly wants to hear the songs of the birds, he must set them free. Folk literature. Grades 1–3.

Goble, P. *The Friendly Wolf.* Ill. by the author. Bradbury, 1974. Wandering about from a berry-picking expedition, two small children become lost in the hills and are protected by a wolf who leads them back to the tribe.

Goble, P. *The Girl Who Loved Wild Horses.* Ill. by the author. Bradbury, 1978. In this tale, a girl feels close to the horses and is eventually transformed into one, becoming the wife to the leader of a wild herd.

Goble, P. *Buffalo Woman.* Ill. by the author. Bradbury, 1984. In this tale, a buffalo turns herself into a woman and marries a young man and says, "You have always had good feelings for our people. . . . My people wish for the love we have for each other will be an example for both our peoples to follow."

Goble, P. *The Gift of the Sacred Dog.* Ill. by the author. Bradbury, 1980. Native Americans hope they can acquire some of the powers of the horse. A boy climbs a mountain seeking a vision that will help his starving people.

Goble, P. *Star Boy.* Ill. by the author. Bradbury, 1982. A boy journeys to the sun and brings back the secrets of the Sun Dance Lodge, which becomes the sacred center of annual festivals for the people. Just as the scarfaced boy was renewed through his journey to the sun, so too were the people physically and spiritually renewed by observing their rituals.

Greene, E. *The Legend of the Cranberry: A Paleo-Indian Legend.* Simon & Schuster, 1993. This is a Delaware legend about the friendship between the mastodons and the People. At the mastodons' demise, cranberries, a gift from the Great Sprit that symbolizes peace, appear wherever the giant animals fall. Folk literature. Grades 2–3.

Hodges, M. *The Golden Deer.* Ill. by D. San Souci. Scribner's, 1992. This is one of the *Jataka Tales* that reflects Buddhist origins in which the king realizes that all living creatures should be protected. Folk literature. Grades 2–3.

Kurtz, J. *Miro in the Kingdom of the Sun.* Ill. by D. Frampton. Houghton Mifflin, 1996. This is an Incan folktale about Miro, who runs swiftly and understands the language of the birds. Her abilities help free her imprisoned brothers. Folk literature. Grades K–4.

Maddern, E. *The Fire Children: A West African Creation Tale.* Ill. by F. Lessac. Dial, 1993. This is a "Why tale" that explains why people come in so many different skin tones. Folk literature. Grades 1–3.

Maddern, E. *Rainbow Bird: An Aboriginal Folktale from Northern Australia.* Ill. by A. Kennaway. Little, Brown, 1993. Bird Woman snatches fire from the open jaws of tough Crocodile Man and puts fire into every tree. From that time, people can make flames from dry wood. Folk literature. Grades K–3.

continued

Moroney, L. *The Boy Who Loved Bears: A Pawnee Tale*. Ill. by C. W. Chapmen. Children's, 1994. A man saves the life of a bear cub and names his son Little Bear. Little Bear develops a bond with the bears and when killed by tribal enemies, he is returned to life as a healer by the grizzlies. Folk literature. Grades K–3.

Others Suggested by Children:

Participation Story

As the story is read aloud, make sounds for characters, objects, events, and period punctuation at the end of sentences. Examples:

1. Dangers—boo—ugh
2. Senator McCorkle—whistle
3. Charlie Drummond—clap or yea
4. Stagecoach and horses—neigh or clap knee
5. Train—train whistle
6. Period for punctuation—make tongue click

Once upon a time in the 1800s, Senator Roscoe McCorkle **(whistle)** had an important meeting in Washington with the president and he wanted to travel from faraway Grass Valley by stagecoach **(neigh and clap knees for horses)** and then by train **(train whistle)**. *Period.* The senator **(whistle)** is out of luck because there is no stagecoach **(neigh and clap knees for horses)** going anywhere because of the dangers—avalanches in the pass **(boo-ugh)** and bandits on the road **(boo-ugh)**. *Period.* The senator **(whistle)** is told that there is danger because the river is rising **(boo-ugh)**, too, and the bridge may go out **(boo-ugh)**. *Period.*

Still insisting he leave right away, the Senator **(whistle)** makes a deal with Charlie Drummond **(clap-yea)** to drive him through. Charlie **(clap-yea)** agrees but says, "Once the stagecoach **(neigh and clap knees for horses)** gets going, the stagecoach **(neigh and clap knees for horses)** doesn't stop. *Period.* And the stagecoach **(neigh and clap knees for horses)** doesn't turn back." *Period.*

The Senator **(whistle)** and Charlie **(clap-yea)**, the determined driver, go on a fast-moving ride as they outrun an avalanche **(boo-ugh)**, dodge falling boulders **(boo-ugh)**, and throw dynamite at bandits waiting in Ambush Canyon **(boo-ugh)**. *Period.* At the station, they chase the departed train **(train whistle)** so the Senator **(whistle)** can get on it to travel to Washington. *Period.* The Senator **(whistle)** thanks "Mister" Charles Drummond **(clap-yea)** who says in return, "You got my name wrong." *Period.* Charlie removes the driver's hat. *Period.*

Guess Who the Senator Saw?

"Mister Charlie" **(clap-yea)** turns out to be "Miss Charlene." **(clap-yea)** *Period.*

Tall Tales

Baseball Player

Sachs, M. *Fleet-Footed Florence*. Doubleday, 1981. Two sports rivals marry and live happily ever after in a nonsexist baseball story.

Cowboy

Felton, H. W. *Bowleg Bill: Seagoing Cowpuncher*. Prentice, 1957. This is tall-tale nonsense about a cowboy who solves his problems in a unique manner.

Kellogg, S. *Pecos Bill*. Mulberry Books, 1992. This tells how Bill invented cattle drives, lassos, and rodeos.

Keelboat Worker

Kellogg, S. *Mike Fink: A Tall Tale Retold*. Morrow, 1992. This tells the story of the King of the Keelboatmen who floated cargo downriver to New Orleans and his adventures of facing former king Jack Carpenter in a wrestling match and H. P. Blathersby and his powerful steamboat.

Lumber Worker

Kellogg, S. *Paul Bunyan*. Morrow, 1984. This offers many details in double-page spreads as it retells Bunyans adventures with Babe the blue ox.

Rounds, G. *The Morning the Sun Refused to Rise*. Holiday, 1984. This is a story of Bunyan and Babe, who discovered that a blizzard had frozen the Earth's axle to its bearings and caused the Earth to stop turning.

Rounds, G. *Ol' Paul, the Mighty Logger*. Holiday, 1949. This is a hearty retelling of Paul Bunyan and his blue ox.

Prairie People

Kellogg, S. *Sally Ann Thunder Ann Whirlwind Crockett*. Morrow, 1995. Sally is busy with several fast-moving events. As one example, Sally screams the feathers off the eagles when she rescues Davy Crockett and claims she invented bald eagles.

Purdy, C. *Iva Dunnit and the Big Wind*. Dial, 1985. This is the story of Iva and her six children. They live alone on the prairie and confront a big wind that comes up. They use their wits to save the house and the hens.

Rounds, G. *Mr. Yowder and the Train Robbers*. Holiday, 1981. This is about the self-proclaimed "World's Bestest and Fastest Sign Painter" and his run-in with robbers and rattlers.

Sailor

Day, E. C. *John Tabor's Ride*. Knopf, 1989. This is an account from a 1846 book of whaling adventures kept as a seaman's journal, about a Tabor's self-told story to a young seaman. Tabor was young and on his first whaling voyage. He complained about everything, wanted to go home, and annoyed his mates. One night, Tabor gets the ride of his life on the back of a huge whale. They go down the Mississippi, through the oceans, and then back to the ship. Afterward, John was known to stare out at the ocean at night as if something fearful were out there.

Felton, H. W. *Tall Tales of Stormalong: Sailor of the Seven Seas*. Prentice-Hall, 1968. Exaggerations of a sailor's life aboard ship and his adventures.

Sailor

Lent, B. *John Tabor's Ride*. Atlantic, 1966. This is a tall tale based on a New England legend about a shipwrecked sailor with exaggeration, fantastic situations, and salty marine terms.

Metaxas, E. *Stormalong: The Legendary Sea Captain*. Ill. by D. Vanderbeek. Simon & Schuster, 1995. Born in a hurricane of 1826, Stormy grows fast and loves the sea. At age 16, he sails on a clipper ship and ties a sea serpent in knots. When he leaves the sea and decides to farm, he becomes homesick and cries until the Great Salt Lake is formed. Grades 1–4.

Sign Painter

Rounds, R. *Mr. Yowder and the Train Robbers*. Holiday, 1981. This story is about the self-proclaimed "World's Bestest and Fastest Sign Painter" and his run-in with robbers and rattlers.

Steel Driver

Keats, E. J. *John Henry: An American Legend*. Pantheon, 1965. This retells the familiar tale of the steel-driving man.

Others Suggested by Children:

"I Have a Dream" Speech by Dr. Martin Luther King, Jr.

All:	So let freedom ring . . .
First Student or Group:	In the process of gaining our rightful place, we must not be guilty of wrongful deeds.
Second Student or Group:	Let us not seek to satisfy our thirst for freedom by drinking from the cup of bitterness and hatred.
Third Student or Group:	We must forever conduct our struggle on the high plain of dignity and discipline.
Fourth Student or Group:	We must not allow our creative protest to degenerate into physical violence.
All:	So let freedom ring . . .
All:	And when we allow freedom to ring, when we let it ring from every village and every hamlet, from every state and every city, we will be able to speed up that day when all God's children . . .
Fifth Student or Group:	black men and white men . . . ,
Sixth Student or Group:	Jews and Gentiles . . . ,
Seventh Student or Group:	Protestants and Catholics . . . ,
Eighth Student or Group:	Will be able to join hands
Ninth Student or Group	And sing in the words of the old Negro spiritual:
All:	Free at last,
All:	Free at last,
All:	Thank God almighty, we are free at last.

INDEX OF CHILDREN'S BOOKS, AUTHORS, AND ILLUSTRATORS

SUBJECT INDEX